Research In Developmental Psychology: Concepts, Strategies, Methods

Thomas M. Achenbach

THE FREE PRESS
A Division of Macmillan Publishing Co., Inc.
NEW YORK

Collier Macmillan Publishers
LONDON

To my parents, Hans and Mary Achenbach

The Free Press
A Division of Macmillan Publishing Co., Inc.
866 Third Avenue, New York, N.Y. 10022

Collier Macmillan Canada, Ltd.

Library of Congress Catalog Card Number: 77–81429

Printed in the United States of America

printing number
2   3   4   5   6   7   8   9   10

BF
713
.A25

Library of Congress Cataloging in Publication Data

Achenbach, Thomas M
   Research in developmental psychology: concepts, strategies, methods.

   Bibliography: p.
   Includes index.
   1. Developmental psychology.   2. Psychological research.   I. Title.
BF713.A25   155   77–81429
ISBN 0–02–900180–3

    This book was written by Dr. Achenbach in his private capacity; no official support or endorsement by the Public Health Service is intended nor should be inferred.

Contents

iii

Preface

IN TEACHING undergraduate and graduate courses on a variety of developmental topics and in pursuing various kinds of developmental research myself, I have often felt handicapped by the lack of integration among approaches to the study of development. Like most behavioral sciences, developmental psychology can call upon a rich array of theories, each of which translates behavior into its own conceptual language. Yet much developmental research is topical, in that it is designed to answer questions about a particular developmental period—such as infancy—or phenomenon—such as language acquisition—in ways that cut across theoretical boundaries. Moreover, important social questions revolving around such issues as education for the disadvantaged, day care, and the effects of television on children demand practical answers that are unlikely to emerge from a single theoretical viewpoint.

If progress is to be made in answering the questions of greatest interest to developmentalists and in grappling with social issues that cry out for systematic study, developmental researchers must be prepared to integrate concepts, strategies, and methods from diverse sources. I have therefore tried to bring together the diverse tools of developmental research—conceptual as well as methodological—in ways that I hope will help students and professionals alike to integrate their work around a common core of developmental questions. Chapter 1 illustrates various issues for developmental research in the context of "case history" examples of contrasting types of research. Chapters 2 and 3 are intended to provide an overview of the most prominent theoretical paradigms and their convergences and divergences within specific studies. Because most textbooks on statistics and design ignore the special problems of developmental research, chapters 4 through 7 focus upon research strategies, designs, statistics, data-collection methods, and sources of error having particular relevance to developmental research. The need for taking account of changes in the nature of variables as subjects age and for analyzing qualitative differences is especially stressed. These chapters are supplemented with an appendix containing instructions and tables for statistical techniques that are helpful for analyzing developmental data, are easy to use, and are not readily available in general statistics texts. Chapter 8, on mission-oriented research, presents applications of developmental research to important social questions, while chapter 9 delineates new directions in which developmental research is expanding beyond the paradigms presented in chapters 2 and 3. These new directions are important not only because they reflect topics of current interest to developmentalists, but also because they have inspired amalgamations of existing paradigms, efforts to forge new paradigms, and the creation of new methods for answering developmental questions. The final chapter deals with ethical issues raised by developmental research, including the ethical implications of drawing socially significant conclusions from theory and data, as well as ways of safeguarding the rights and well-being of subjects.

In writing this book, I have aimed to assist students who have had an introduction to child development but who wish to learn more about translating developmental questions and concepts into new knowledge through research. The book is especially intended for research methods courses in child development, developmental psychology, life-span developmental psychology, and education at the undergraduate and graduate levels. It should be most useful to students who have had an introduction to statistics that includes the chi square, t test, Pearson correlation, and simple analysis of variance. However, as most of the book does not presuppose any prior mastery of statistics, it could be used in introductory developmental courses designed to sensitize students to research. For students and professionals with more advanced backgrounds, the research designs, nonparametric tests and tables, scalogram approaches, and multivariate methods including path analysis comprise a collection of tools from scattered sources that have not been brought together in any other book, as far as I know.

Since my primary goal is to facilitate the growth of students into mature thinkers who will advance developmental research beyond its current level, I have been extremely fortunate to have the continuing advice of Michael E. Lamb and John R. Weisz, students who were maturing into first-class professional researchers while I was working on the book. I am also grateful to Harold W. Stevenson and Roger Brown for their editorial assistance. My deepest thanks go to my wife, Susan, who not only read and commented on successive drafts, but gave me the encouragement to continue when it would have been far easier to quit.

Acknowledgments

We wish to thank the following publishers and authors for materials used in this book that are not otherwise credited:

THE AMERICAN PSYCHOLOGICAL ASSOCIATION: for figure 2–3, from Ciaccio's A test of Erickson's theory of ego epigenesis in *Developmental Psychology*, 1971, vol. 4; for figure 3–2, from Noblin, Timmons, and Kael's Differential effects of positive and negative reinforcement on psychoanalytic character types in *The Journal of Personality and Social Psychology*, 1966, vol. 4; for figure 5–2, from Bart and Airasian's Determination of the ordering among seven Piagetian tasks by an ordering-theoretic method in *The Journal of Educational Psychology*, 1974, vol. 66; for figure 8–3, from Eron, Huesmann, Lefkowitz, and Walder's Does television violence cause aggression? in *The American Psychologist*, 1972, vol. 27; and for figure 9–3, Perry and Garrow's The "social deprivation-satiation effect": An outcome of frequency or perceived contingency? in *Developmental Psychology*, 1975, vol. 11.

THE SOCIETY FOR RESEARCH IN CHILD DEVELOPMENT, INC.: for table 1–1, from Schwartz and Scholnick's Scalogram analysis of logical and perceptual components of conservation of discontinuous quantity in *Child Development*, 1970, vol. 41; for figure 4–3, from Clarke-Stewart's Interactions between mothers and their young children: Characteristics and consequences in *Monographs of the Society for Research in Child Development*, 1973, vol. 38, serial no. 153; and for figure 9–1, from Schachter et al.'s Everyday preschool interpersonal speech usage: Methodological, developmental, and sociolinguistic studies in *Monographs of the Society for Research in Child Development*, 1974, vol. 39, serial no. 156.

DR. ELLIN K. SCHOLNICK AND DR. MARILYN M. SCHWARTZ: for table 1–1, from their Scalogram analysis of logical and perceptual components of conservation of discontinuous quantity in *Child Development*, 1970, vol. 41.

THE UNIVERSITY OF MINNESOTA PRESS, MINNEAPOLIS: for figure 2–2, from Harris's *The concept of development*, 1957.

DR. N. V. CIACCIO: for figure 2–3, from his A test of Erickson's theory of ego epigenesis in *Developmental Psychology*, 1971, vol. 4.

DR. W. C. MCGREW AND ACADEMIC PRESS: for figure 2–4, from McGrew's *An ethological study of children's behavior*, 1972.

HARVARD UNIVERSITY PRESS AND ROUTLEDGE AND KEGAN PAUL, LTD.: for figure 3–1, from Inhelder, Sinclair, and Bovet's *Learning and the development of cognition*, 1974.

DR. CHARLES D. NOBLIN: for figure 3–2, from Noblin, Timmons, and Kael's Differential effects of positive and negative verbal reinforcement on psychoanalytic character types in *The Journal of Personality and Social Psychology*, 1966, vol. 4.

DR. K. ALISON CLARKE-STEWART: for figure 4–3, from her Interactions between mothers and their young children: Characteristics and consequences in *Monographs of the Society for Research in Child Development*, 1973, vol. 38, serial no. 153.

DR. WILLIAM M. BART: for figure 5–2, from Bart and Airasian's Determination of the ordering among seven Piagetian tasks by an ordering-theoretic method in *The Journal of Educational Psychology*, 1974, vol. 66.

S. KARGER AG, BASEL: for table 6–3, from Braun's Finding optimal age groups for investigating age-related variables in *Human development*, 1973, vol. 16.

JOHN WILEY AND SONS: for figure 8–1, from Love and Kaswan's *Troubled children: Their families, schools, and treatments*, 1974; and for figure 8–2, from Love and Kaswan's *Troubled children: Their families, schools, and treatments*, 1974.

DR. LEONARD D. ERON: for figure 8–3, from Eron, Huesmann, Lefkowitz, and Walder's Does television violence cause aggression? in *The American Psychologist*, 1972, vol. 27.

DR. FRANCES FUCHS SCHACHTER: for figure 9–1, from Schachter et al.'s Everyday preschool interpersonal speech usage: Methodological, developmental, and sociolinguistic studies in *Monographs of the Society for Research in Child Development*, 1974, vol. 39, serial no. 156.

DR. ROSS G. PARKE: for figure 9–2, from his Rationale effectiveness as a function of age of the child, an unpublished research report for the Fels Institute, 1972.

DR. DAVID G. PERRY: for figure 9–3, from Perry and Garrow's The "social deprivation effect": An outcome of frequency or perceived contingency? in *Developmental Psychology*, 1975, vol. 11.

THE HARVARD EDUCATIONAL REVIEW: for quotes from Brazziel's A letter from the South in *The Harvard Educational Review*, 1969, vol. 39; and for quotes from Jensen's Reducing the heredity-environment uncertainty in *The Harvard Educational Review*, vol. 39, 1969, copyright © 1969 by President and Fellows of Harvard College.

BIOMETRIKA TRUST: for table A–3, from Finney's *Biometrika tables for statisticians*, vol. 1, 3rd ed., 1966; and for table A–12, from Glasser and Winter's Critical values of the coefficient of rank correlation for testing the hypothesis of independence in *Biometrika*, 1961, vol. 48.

MCGRAW-HILL BOOK CO.: for table A–4, from Dixon and Massey's *Introduction to statistical analysis*, 1957; and for table A–7, from Dixon and Massey's *Introduction to statistical analysis*, 1957.

ADDISON-WESLEY PUBLISHING COMPANY, INC., READING, MASS.: for table A–6, from Mosteller and Rourke's *Sturdy statistics*, 1973.

INSTITUTE OF MATHEMATICAL STATISTICS, CALIFORNIA STATE UNIVERSITY AT HAYWARD: for table A–8, from Massey's Distribution table for the deviation between two sample cumulatives in *The Annals of Mathematical Statistics*, 1952, vol. 23; and for table A–13, from Friedman's A comparison of alternative tests of significance for the problem of *m* rankings in *The Annals of Mathematical Statistics*, 1940, vol. 11.

AMERICAN STATISTICAL ASSOCIATION: for table A–9, from Kruskal and Wallis's Use of ranks in one-criterion variance analysis in *The Journal of the American Statistical Association*, 1952, vol. 47; and table A–11, from Friedman's The use of ranks to avoid the assumption of normality implicit in the analysis of variance in *The Journal of the American Statistical Association*, 1937, vol. 32.

DR. MARJORIE P. HONZIK: for quotes from Honzik and Macfarlane's Personality development and intellectual functioning from 21 months to 40 years, a paper presented at the American Psychological Association meetings in Miami, 1970.

1 The Nature of Developmental Research

THE FIELD traditionally known as "child development" or "child psychology" is becoming increasingly known as "developmental psychology." This shift reflects a greater emphasis on the processes whereby organisms change as they grow older. It also reflects a broadening of interest to include the study of developmental processes in adults and nonhuman organisms. As a consequence of this shift, research on individuals at any given age is being conceived less in terms of characteristics limited to those individuals than in terms of the way such characteristics fit into a developmental sequence. The broadening conception of developmental psychology means that findings on individuals defined as "children" or "children of age X" are important not only as statements about a particular class of subjects, but as new pieces to be fitted into the puzzle of how and why organisms change as they grow older and how certain characteristics may nevertheless remain stable.

While there is great diversity in the interests, objectives, and theoretical orientations of people who study development, there is also an expanding core of concepts, strategies, and methods common to developmental researchers. The goal of this book is to bring together basic approaches to developmental research and to demonstrate ways in which these approaches, together with the standard tools of behavioral research, can be applied to questions that are of special concern to students of development. To illustrate some of the special methodo-

1

logical and conceptual problems encountered in the study of development, three kinds of developmental research are presented here in case-history form. One is a longitudinal study, the second is an attempt to enhance development, and the third is a laboratory test of some developmental hypotheses. These are by no means the only types of developmental research, but they raise issues encountered in many other types as well.

A Longitudinal Study

An obvious way to study development is to observe the same individuals repeatedly as they grow older, i.e., to study them *longitudinally*. One of the lengthiest and most comprehensive longitudinal studies ever attempted was begun in 1929 at the Fels Institute in Yellow Springs, Ohio. Like other longitudinal studies begun during that period, the Fels study was inspired by the hope that massive data on the same individuals from birth through maturity would reveal how adult behavior is molded from childhood characteristics and experiences. To obtain comprehensive records of development, trained observers wrote narrative descriptions and made ratings of the behavior of children observed in their homes, schools, and a special summer camp. IQ and personality tests were also administered and the children's parents were observed and interviewed. After 30 years of data collection, teams of researchers attempted to piece together patterns and relationships that would expose the nature of behavioral development. What did they find and how did they find it?

Advances in methodology, changes in the focus of research interest, and the advancing age of the subjects produced many variations in the type of data available over the course of the study. As a result, a detective-like approach was required, whereby evidence for causes had to be reconstructed from diverse sources of varying reliability. Unlike detectives, however, to whom the outcome of a crime is already known and only the causes need to be discovered, the Fels investigators had to sift the evidence to find outcomes that were reliably measurable and meaningful enough to make their antecedents worth discovering. What follows is an account of a foray into the Fels data to identify antecedents of one of the few variables that was not only measurable with reasonably high reliability, and meaningful in the sense of correlating with other important behavior, but was also measurable in a uniform way over a wide age range. This variable was IQ.

Stability and Change in IQ

When IQ scores were analyzed, it was found that the relationship between IQ at early ages and IQ at age 12 increased steadily from a correlation of .46 between IQs at ages 3 and 12, to .90 between ages 11 and 12 (Sontag, Baker, and Nelson, 1958). Further analysis showed that, when major IQ changes did occur, they consisted not of erratic fluctuations from year to year, but of cumulative increases or decreases over several years. This suggested that the IQ changes were due not to short-term irregularities in test-taking behavior, but to systematic, long-term changes in the children. Were these changes reflected in anything else that had been observed about the children?

In hope of finding personality correlates of the IQ changes, Sontag and his colleagues turned to the mass of behavioral observations made on the Fels children. Since many of the increases and decreases in IQ began or ended at about the ages of 6 and 10, separate analyses were made for children whose IQs increased or decreased steadily from either the age of $4\frac{1}{2}$ to 6 or from the age of 6 to 10. For children whose IQs changed greatly during either the preschool or elementary school period, raters who were ignorant of the IQ scores read the observational material in the children's records up until the age of 6 and made ratings on personality traits hypothesized to relate to the IQ changes. For children whose IQs changed between the ages of 6 and 10, the raters then read all the material gathered from the age of 6 to 10 and made a second set of ratings.

Ratings on each personality trait were divided at the median and the proportion of IQ *ascenders* having scores above the median on a trait was compared to the proportion of IQ *descenders* having scores above the median on that trait. It was found that significantly more IQ ascenders than descenders were above the medians on independence, aggressiveness, self-initiated behavior, problem solving, orientation toward future reward, competitiveness, sibling rivalry, scholastic competition, and self-motivation in scholastic achievement.

Prediction and causality.   Did the personality differences between IQ ascenders and descenders *cause* the differences in IQ changes? To answer this question, it was necessary to ascertain whether the personality differences *preceded* the IQ changes. This was done by comparing personality ratings *prior to age 6* on children whose IQs increased between 6 and 10 with those on children whose IQs decreased. It was found that significantly more of the IQ ascenders had been rated above the medians on aggressiveness, self-initiation, and competitiveness prior to age 6. Since many of the children who were high on these traits before age 6 and then increased in IQ between the ages of 6 and 10 had not been increasing in IQ during the preschool years, it was concluded that these traits played a *causal* role in the IQ changes, because they *preceded* the changes. Furthermore, since ratings on these traits correlated significantly with one another, Sontag et al. inferred that they represented a unitary trait of achievement motivation. High achievement motivation during the preschool years thus appeared to increase IQ during the elementary school years.

Detection of causal relations between early and later characteristics of individuals is a major goal of developmental research. The Fels researchers attempted to move from *patterns* of changes in IQ scores, to *correlations* between these changes and other characteristics, to *predictive* relations between earlier and later characteristics, to *causal* inferences based on the predictive relations. But how certain can we be that achievement motivation indeed caused the IQ differences? Other possibilities need to be considered as well. One such possibility is that an environmental variable affected both early achievement motivation and later test behavior. For example, parental pressure for intellectual achievement might have stimulated achievement motivation at the early period and might have maximized IQ test performance later, when the children recognized the IQ test as an achievement situation like that in which their parents expected high performance.

Parent behavior. To determine whether parent behavior was responsible for the IQ changes, a second team of researchers drew profiles portraying the IQs obtained by the Fels children from ages 2 to 17 (McCall, Appelbaum, and Hogarty, 1973). They then analyzed the relations between these profiles and parental characteristics rated by the original Fels observers. It was found that parents of children whose IQs increased during the preschool and elementary school years had striven to train their children in mental and motor skills. Perhaps parental training was thus the crucial variable causing both high achievement motivation during the preschool period and IQ increases during elementary school.

However, the upward trend in the scores obtained by IQ ascenders reached a peak at about the age of 10 and their scores declined thereafter. By the age of 17, they had dropped to their preschool levels. The mean IQ of these children was still high, but the extraordinary increases that had apparently been facilitated by parental behavior were reversed when the highest stages of mental functioning were reached. To explain this reversal in IQ changes, McCall and his co-workers suggested that parents may have been successful in accelerating intellectual development only as long as they had firm control over their children, but that the parental pressures were resisted after the children passed the age of 10. However, another possibility is that the type of development occurring until age 10 is much more susceptible to acceleration by parental training than is the type of development occurring after age 10. The inflection points noted for increases and decreases in IQ at the ages of about 6 and 10 coincide roughly with the onsets of the concrete and formal operational periods of intellectual development hypothesized by Piaget (1970). Perhaps factors intrinsic to the nature of intellectual development make it responsive to parental pressures during the concrete operational period but not during the formal operational period.

Implications for Developmental Research

From the questions raised as well as from the answers given by the Fels findings, a number of important implications can be drawn. One is that group correlations obtained across ages on a variable such as IQ can create an impression of stability that masks individual patterns of change. A second is that an apparent causal relationship between variables at two ages—such as that between personality and IQ—may result from the influence of a third variable—such as parent behavior—on both the earlier and later variables. Another implication of the Fels findings is that trends and relationships occurring within a particular segment of development may change and even be reversed during other segments, as exemplified in the reversal of IQ trends from ages 6 to 10 and 10 to 17. One reason for such changes is that the effects of environmental inputs may vary with the child's developmental level: The Fels children may have responded favorably to parental pressure during the preschool period but negatively to the same pressures later.

The Fels study points up both the power of longitudinal research for obtaining a comprehensive picture of what happens as individuals age and the pitfalls encountered in making causal interpretations of the findings. Recognition of the pitfalls has recently inspired attempts to formulate more powerful strategies for designing and analyzing longitudinal research in order to separate the effects of aging per se from the effects of specific environmental inputs. These new strategies will be presented in chapter 4.

An Attempt to Enhance Development

In contrast to the relatively passive observation of development typified by the Fels study, much developmental research is designed to enhance development. As will be discussed in chapter 8, the new social programs and the social activism of the 1960s spurred a dramatic increase in "mission-oriented" research designed to benefit children.

One of the chief aims of mission-oriented research has been to aid children variously labeled as "underprivileged," "culturally deprived," "disadvantaged," "economically disadvantaged," "poverty stricken," and just plain "poor." The variety of euphemisms is symptomatic of the confusion over what should be done to help them. However, there is little confusion over who they are. The most conspicuous concentrations of these children are among the Chicanos of the West, whites of the rural South and Appalachia, blacks in many urban and rural areas, Puerto Rican immigrants, and Indians of the West and Midwest.

When the first eight-week Head Start programs were introduced in 1965, great claims were made for their success. Great claims, but no evidence. Could a brief preschool program really give poor children an educational headstart that would eventually rescue them from the welfare rolls, as President Johnson proudly proclaimed? There was no way to know without long-term comparisons of children who did and did not have preschool experience. Such a comparison had, in fact, been undertaken in a small Southern city in 1962.

Known as the "Early Training Project for Disadvantaged Children" (Klaus and Gray, 1968), the research began with the random assignment of 61 disadvantaged black children to one of two treatment groups or a control group. One of the treatment groups was to attend a ten-week preschool program each summer for three years. A home visitor was also to meet weekly with the parents of each child throughout these years. A second treatment group was to receive two summers of preschool plus two years of meetings with the home visitors. The third group, a *proximal* (near) control group, was to receive no special program but was to be tested at the same times as the other children. However, since this control group might be affected by contacts with experimental children living in the same neighborhood, a *distal* (far) control group was also selected from children living in a similar city 60 miles away.

The preschool programs met four hours daily, five days per week. Programs were individually tailored as much as possible to the level and needs of each child. Reinforcement principles were employed to reward desirable new behavior, and attempts were made to move children from the need for immediate concrete reinforcement to more abstract, internalized, and delayed reinforcement.

Each home visitor was a mature black woman who served as a liaison between the school and home during the ten-week summer sessions. The home visitor arranged for parents to visit the school, introduced them to staff, and explained the objectives of the program. She also suggested ways in which the parents could encourage and reinforce their children's school activities, followed up absences from school, made arrangements for special needs such as clothing, and helped teachers obtain information about the children. From September through May, she made weekly home visits to encourage the parents in educational efforts with their children, to help them take advantage of opportunities for themselves and their children, and to provide children's books and adult magazines such as *Ebony*.

When the children reached first grade in public school (there was no public kindergarten), the home visitor spent several hours a week in the children's classrooms and continued to serve as a liaison between the school and parents by consulting with the parents and teachers about the children's progress. An unanticipated confounding factor was that most of the three-year experimental group ended up with a first-grade teacher who proved to be uncooperative, while most of the proximal control children had an exceptionally cooperative teacher.

Effects of the Program

How could any benefits of the program be detected? Because aptitudes and attitudes toward achievement were both expected to influence ultimate school success, several measures of each were employed. As a direct measure of school success, achievement test scores were also obtained after the children entered elementary school.

Effects on aptitude. The aptitude measures included tests of perceptual development, concept formation, and language development. However, because these measures were found to have low reliability, it was necessary to fall back on the Stanford–Binet IQ score as the most reliable index of academic aptitude. As can be seen from Figure 1-1, the mean IQs of both experimental groups were slightly superior to those of the control groups before the project began. The IQs of the three-year group then jumped dramatically from a mean of 87.6 to 102.0 at the end of their first summer of preschool! Evidently, a single summer program *could* have a major impact. Thereafter, however, the three-year group declined in IQ while the two-year group caught up and surpassed it, retaining its advantage through the end of the study. The effect of an extra year of the project apparently did not outweigh preexisting differences reflected in the two-year group's initial advantage in IQ.

Several other features of the IQ curves should be noted. One is that the greatest overall differences between the two experimental and two control groups occurred at the testings following the summer programs, in August 1963 and 1964. The fact that the curves of the two experimental groups were so close to one another, while the curves of the two control groups were also so similar suggests that the large differences between the experimental and control groups at these points were not just chance fluctuations. Thus, the preschool programs appear to have had genuine effects on IQ test performance. By the end of the study, however, the differences in IQ between the two experimental groups and the proximal control group were actually less than they had been at the beginning, although the distal control group had declined sharply in IQ.

Since the distal control group lived in another community and attended a different school, perhaps its marked decline was due to local conditions. Or perhaps a similar decline was prevented in the proximal control group by "diffusion" effects of the project. Such diffusion effects could occur through contacts among the experimental and control children and their parents, and through effects the home visitor may have had on the quality of first grade schooling.

In attempting to distinguish between the effects of diffusion and of differences in the schools attended by the children, Klaus and Gray (1968) discovered that achievement test scores in the school attended by the distal control group had generally been lower in previous years than the scores in the school attended by the other three groups of children.

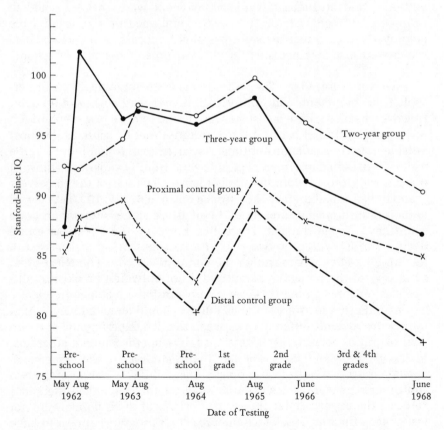

Figure 1-1. Average Stanford-Binet IQ at each testing. (Data from Klaus and Gray, 1970.)

This suggested that local school conditions contributed to the gap between the distal and proximal control groups.

On the other hand, there was considerable anecdotal evidence for the spread of effects from the experimental groups to the proximal control group. Mothers of control children, for example, often asked mothers of experimental children what was being provided by the home visitor. Local merchants also reported a run on the kinds of children's magazines being provided to the experimental group mothers.

Another point to be noted from Figure 1-1 is that *all four* groups showed increases in IQ at the August 1965 testing, following their first year in school. Similar findings have been reported in other studies of preschool interventions, where control groups receiving no preschool programs often caught up to experimental groups during the first year of school. Nevertheless, all of Klaus and Gray's groups declined in IQ during their later years in school. The overall pattern suggests that both the preschool and public school experiences caused jumps in test performance. However, the increased scores tended to be maintained among the experimental children as long as they were receiving the special preschool program, whereas the regular public school program did not maintain the increases shown in Grade 1.

Effects on attitude. Among the measures of attitude and motivation, the only clear-cut finding was that the experimental children were significantly more reflective and made fewer errors than the control children on the Matching Familiar Figures test, a test of impulsive versus reflective cognitive styles (Kagan, Rosman, Day, Albert, and Phillips, 1964). However, it has since been found that differences in impulsivity–reflectivity can be accounted for by differences in ability, as measured by the Stanford–Binet (Achenbach and Weisz, 1975b). Thus, the differences on the Matching Familiar Figures test may simply have reflected the same differences in aptitude manifest in the IQ scores.

Effects on achievement. Whether or not the measures of aptitude and attitude were greatly affected, did the project accomplish its ultimate goal of improving school achievement? Figure 1-2 portrays the average achievement test scores obtained by each group in first, second and fourth grades. As can be seen from the figure, the superiority of the two-year group and the inferiority of the distal control group found for IQ were also apparent in their achievement scores. The differences between the three-year group and the proximal control group were minimal, but favored the control group at all points. Gray and Klaus (1970) reported that the combined experimental groups were significantly superior to the combined control groups on some comparisons of subtest scores. However, this was primarily due to the

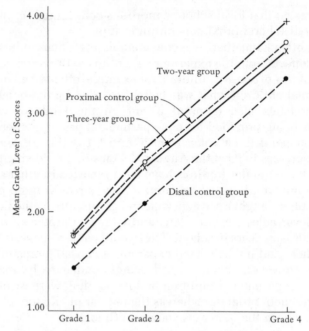

Figure 1-2. Average scores of four achievement subtests given in first, second, and fourth grades. (Data from Gray and Klaus, 1970.)

superior performance of the two-year experimental group and the inferior performance of the distal control group, because the proximal control group was superior to the three-year group in most comparisons.

Implications for Developmental Research

While many innovative preschool programs have come and gone since Klaus and Gray launched the Early Training Project, few have been followed up over so long a period. Among the issues raised by their study, several have particular importance for developmental research. One is the problem of uncontrolled variables in "real-life" attempts to influence development. Even though social and political conditions made the study much more feasible than it might have been in other times and places, three potentially powerful factors could not be controlled. These were (a) the diffusion of interest to mothers of the proximal control children; (b) the placement of most of the experimental children with an uncooperative first grade teacher; and (c) the traditionally lower achievement scores in the distal control school than in the school attended by the other three groups. Certain unanticipated factors, such as the diffusion effect, may cast an entirely new light on a problem.

The diffusion effect indicated, for example, that parents of disadvantaged children were highly motivated to educate their children and that taking advantage of this motivation might provide one of the most effective ways to help such children. As will be discussed in chapter 8, parent involvement has since become an important facet of preschool enrichment programs.

The Klaus and Gray findings, like the Fels study, also underscore the importance of studying relationships over extended periods of development. If the study had ended with the August 1964 or even the August 1965 testing, the differences between the experimental and control groups would have been so dramatic as to raise unjustified hopes of miracles to be wrought through preschool training programs, just as such hopes were raised when great claims were made for the first eight-week Head Start programs. The final testing indicated, however, that the initial gains were not maintained very far into elementary school (Gray and Klaus, 1970). Yet the marked decline in the IQs of the distal control group and the divergence of this group from the proximal control group suggest that something in their schools or general environments was differentially affecting their development.

The superiority of the two-year group at the beginning and again from the time it received the preschool program until the end of the study points up the importance of children's existing abilities prior to an experimental input. Even though the three-year group received 50 per cent more input, and the input had its biggest effect at the youngest age, when only the three-year group was receiving it, the effects of the input evidently depended upon the initial capabilities of the children in determining their final rank ordering. The effects of intervention programs are thus likely to depend as much on individual differences in capabilities and developmental levels as on the design of specific curricula.

A Laboratory Test of Two Developmental Hypotheses

The Early Training Project and the Fels study were both designed to assess behavior under conditions of naturally occurring complexity. Even though the Early Training Project subjected children to a special educational program, and structured testing conditions were imposed to measure certain aspects of behavior in both studies, the primary focus was upon behavior occurring in environments over which the researchers had little control, such as the school and home. Research in situations representative of the subjects' usual environment, uncontrolled by the researcher, is known as "field" research, in contrast to "laboratory" research in which the investigator exercises precise control over environmental inputs to his subjects. As in the Fels and Early Training studies, much developmental research combines control over some aspects of the environment with observations under field conditions. However, other developmental research, like that to be described next, employs controlled conditions to assess behavior that may not be observable at all under naturally occurring conditions.

The experimental tasks devised by the Swiss psychologist, Jean Piaget, are designed to reveal children's thinking about physical and logical principles. Probably more famous than anything else originating with Piaget are his studies of children's understanding of *conservation* of quantity. Piaget has reported that, before the age of about 7, children believe that transferring something from a container of one shape to a container of a different shape changes its quantity. However, Piaget's findings initially met with skepticism. Could children as old as 5 or 6 really believe that, when a quantity of beads in Glass A equals a quantity of beads in Glass B, and the quantity in Glass B is poured into a narrower container, the quantity no longer equals that in Glass A? As a result of this skepticism, American attempts to follow up on Piaget's work were at first aimed mainly at eliminating possible methodological artifacts that might account for children's failure to conserve and at determining what skills were required for conservation.

In analyzing the achievement of conservation, Schwartz and Scholnick (1970) hypothesized that it requires a series of progressively more complex logical judgments and that the ability to make each of the judgments emerges in a developmentally uniform order. First, the child must be able to judge whether two quantities are equal. Second, the child must be able to judge that transferring beads from Glass B to a narrower container does not change the amount—the *quantitative identity*—of the beads. Third, the child must be able to reason that, if the quantity of beads is not changed by transferring it to a narrower container, then it must still equal that in Glass A, even though the level of the beads is higher in the narrower container.

The ability to make logical judgments may not be the only prerequisite for conservation, however. Because the quantity of beads *looks* greater when it rises to a higher level in a narrow container, the child must be willing to favor logic over appearances. Since overcoming conflicts between perception and logic may thus be another step in the achievement of conservation, Schwartz and Scholnick hypothesized that children would be able to make correct logical judgments where perceptual cues were *congruent* with logic before they could make such judgments where the perceptual cues *contradicted* the logic.

Testing the Hypotheses

To test their hypotheses, Schwartz and Scholnick carried out a study of young children's ability to make each type of judgment when the perceptual cues were congruent with the logic and when the perceptual cues contradicted the logic. Theirs was a "laboratory" study in the sense that it was designed to rigorously control all inputs expected to affect the behavior of interest.

The subjects were 40 nursery and kindergarten children. The children were first tested for conservation with a task like Piaget's glasses of beads, except that the glasses were filled with M&M candies to heighten the children's interest. To enable them to respond in a manner requiring little verbal skill, they were then trained to indicate their judgments of quantity by pointing to either a happy face or a sad face. When presented with two quantities of candy, they were to point to the happy face if one of the quantities, designated as belonging to a boy named Billy, was at least as great as the quantity belonging to the experimenter. If they thought Billy had less candy than the experimenter, they were to point to the sad face. After being trained to indicate their judgments of quantity by pointing to the appropriate face, the children were presented with tasks designed to test their abilities to make each type of judgment hypothesized to be necessary for conservation. These included (a) tasks requiring direct *comparisons* of amounts in two containers; (b) tasks requiring judgments of the *identity* of a quantity before and after it was transferred from one glass to another; and (c) tasks requiring judgments of the *equivalence* of an initial quantity and a similar quantity that had been transferred to another container.

The congruence between the perceptual cues and the quantitative relationships was varied by repeating each type of task using glasses of the *same* diameter and glasses *differing* in diameter. Thus, in some of the tasks involving direct *comparisons* of candy in two glasses, both glasses were of the same diameter, while in other comparisons the glasses differed in diameter. In the comparisons involving glasses of different diameters, the glasses were filled to the same height, so that the narrower glass contained less candy and the perceptual cues of equal height were incongruent with the difference in quantities.

In the tasks requiring judgments of *identity*, candies were poured either into a glass of the same diameter as the original or into a glass of different diameter. In the tasks requiring judgments of *equivalence*, two similar glasses were presented which held equal amounts of candy. The contents of one glass were then poured either into a third glass of the same diameter as the first two or into a glass of different diameter. The latter was like Piaget's conservation task except that the child's response was merely to choose Billy's happy or sad face, indicating whether the quantity in the new glass was equal to the quantity in the other glass.

Identifying an Ordered Sequence of Abilities

How could the hypothesized sequence of abilities be detected? Schwartz and Scholnick tabulated each child's pattern of successes and failures in order to determine whether there was a consistent order in the tasks passed and failed. As Table 1-1 reveals, there was indeed considerable consistency in the ordering of successes and failures: Only 6 of the 40 children passed a task that was difficult for the group as a whole while failing an easier task. A technique for evaluating the consistency of ordering, known as *scalogram analysis* (to be discussed further in chapter 5), showed that the ordering was consistent enough to be considered reliable.

It can be seen from Table 1-1 that all the tasks involving conflicts between the perceptual cues and the actual relations between quantities were more difficult than the tasks in which the perceptual cues were congruent with the quantitative relations. This indicates that the perceptual cues definitely influenced the judgments. Table 1-1 also shows

TABLE 1-1. Patterns of Correct and Incorrect Quantitative Judgments.

			Tasks[a]				No. of Subjects Showing Each Pattern
E–D	*VC*	*C–D*	*I–D*	*I–S*	*E–S*	*C–S*	
+	+	+	+	+	+	+	3
+	+	–	+	+	+	+	1[b]
+	–	+	+	+	+	+	2[b]
–	+	+	+	+	+	+	1
–	–	+	+	+	+	+	5
–	–	–	+	+	+	+	7
–	+	–	–	+	+	+	2[b]
–	–	+	–	+	+	+	1[b]
–	–	–	–	+	+	+	11
–	–	–	–	–	+	+	2
–	–	–	–	–	–	+	3
–	–	–	–	–	–	–	2

Adapted from Schwartz and Scholnick (1970).
[a]Type of task: C = comparison; E = equivalence; I = identity; VC = verbal conservation. Diameters of glasses: D = different (i.e., conflict between perception and logic); S = same (i.e., congruence between perception and logic).
[b]Subjects deviating from consistent order.

that the ordering of task difficulty supported the authors' hypothesis about the sequence of abilities: *Comparison* of quantities in glasses of the same diameter was easiest; *conservation of the identity* of a quantity when it was transferred to a glass of another diameter was more difficult; and *conservation of the equivalence* between a transferred quantity and a quantity remaining in its original glass was the most difficult.

These findings have an important bearing on Piaget's theory. As Piaget (1968) describes it, the concept of conservation applies to the quantitative *identity* of a single stimulus as it undergoes perceptual changes. However, Piaget's conservation tasks require judgments about the continued quantitative *equivalence* of two stimuli as one undergoes perceptual changes. Since the data show the judgment of equivalence to be more difficult than the judgment of identity, either the tests of the theory should be revised to focus on identity judgments, or the theory should be modified to take account of the additional step required to advance from correct identity judgments to correct equivalence judgments.

Implications for Developmental Research

The Schwartz–Scholnick study exemplifies laboratory research designed to test specific developmental hypotheses. While much behavioral research is designed to test hypotheses about differences between groups or between experimental conditions, such differences are often of less interest in developmental research than are *sequential* patterns of behavior. Methods such as the scalogram analysis employed by Schwartz and Scholnick may in some cases permit effective tests of sequential hypotheses without the need for longitudinal studies.

Although the Schwartz–Scholnick study was carried out in schools, it was a "laboratory" study in that it was designed to measure the effects of specific inputs (type of question regarding quantity, type of perceptual cues) on specific behaviors (conservation responses), with extraneous variables controlled as precisely as possible. Because the subjects for most developmental research must be studied outside formal laboratory settings, the nature of laboratory research on development inheres more in its procedures and goals than in its location. Since the settings for laboratory research are often not very different from those of field research, there is much interplay between field and laboratory approaches. Experience in each can contribute to work in the other in terms of the kinds of procedures that motivate children and are intelligible and harmless to them.

While most laboratory studies are designed to test theoretical concepts, research oriented toward the solution of specific practical problems also requires a firm grounding in knowledge and methods developed through laboratory research. Both the Fels study and the Early Training Project were handicapped by a lack of clearly defined and measurable variables whose relationships to other variables had previously been established. It has repeatedly been found that developmental research on practical problems cannot advance without progress in basic theory and measures (e.g., Anderson, Messick, and Hartshorne, 1972).

Structure of the Book

Diversity of theory, method, and goals will be evident in the research presented throughout the book. Amidst the diversity, however, a common core of conceptual problems confronts the various approaches to knowledge about development. Because attempts to solve these problems are inevitably shaped by theoretical assumptions, it is important to examine the major theoretical frameworks that guide developmental research. This is done in chapter 2, where the differing assumptions and foci of the four major developmental paradigms are presented. While the various paradigms are of interest in themselves as sources of concepts and explanations for development, it is their application to research that is most pertinent to our purposes. Consequently, in chapter 3, the convergence and divergence of the major paradigms are assessed in the context of specific studies.

Against the theoretical background provided by chapters 2 and 3, chapter 4 presents strategies for designing research to answer developmental questions. Because developmental questions often require statistical approaches not emphasized in ordinary statistics courses, chapters 5 and 6 present statistical methods and issues of special relevance to developmental research. These chapters are supplemented by a statistical appendix that contains instructions and tables for methods that are easy to use but are not available in many general statistics texts. Having proceeded from developmental theory to strategies of developmental research design and statistical analysis, we move in chapter 7 to a survey of methods for obtaining developmental data and an appraisal of sources of bias in the various methods.

Of great concern to researchers and students alike is the role of research in finding solutions to social problems. The relevance of developmental research to such problems as improving education for disadvantaged children was evident in the Early Training Project, but chapter 8 provides more detailed analyses of a variety of mission-oriented research designed to solve practical, here-and-now social problems.

Despite the influence of the major theoretical paradigms presented in chapter 2, much developmental research reflects themes and theories that extend beyond the major paradigms. Some of these new directions in developmental research—to be detailed in chapter 9—have spawned new paradigms, whereas others represent hybrid syntheses of existing paradigms.

Left to chapter 10 because a full appreciation of them presupposes a thorough knowledge of developmental research, ethical issues are of increasing concern to all researchers, but especially to those who work with children. Not only the potential risks to the subjects of research, but the ethical implications of drawing socially significant conclusions from inadequate data and other aspects of the sociopolitical context of research will be discussed.

Summary

The purpose of this book is to bring together basic tools for developmental research. Accounts of a longitudinal study, a study designed to enhance the development of disadvantaged children, and a laboratory test of developmental hypotheses illustrated the diversity as well as some of the common issues in developmental research. The Fels study pointed up both the power of the longitudinal approach for obtaining a comprehensive picture of changes with age and the pitfalls encountered in drawing causal inferences from age changes. It also demonstrated that correlations between measurements of a variable at various ages can create an impression of stability that masks individual patterns of change, and that relationships found in one developmental period may be reversed during other periods.

The Early Training Project illustrated issues raised by attempts to enhance development. These include the difficulty in attaining adequate control over important variables in field settings, the necessity for studying the effects of interventions over extended periods of development, and the importance of tracking variations in environment and behavior that cannot be controlled by the researcher.

In contrast to the Fels study and the Early Training Project, Schwartz and Scholnick's study exemplified laboratory research designed to test theoretical hypotheses about relationships between specific environmental inputs and specific responses by the subjects. The study also illustrated how patterns of successes and failures on tasks can be analyzed to identify sequences of development. The need for a continuing interplay between laboratory and nonlaboratory approaches to research will be repeatedly evident as we move from discussion of the major theoretical paradigms, research designs, statistical techniques, and methods of data collection, to mission-oriented research, new directions in developmental research, and ethical issues in carrying out and interpreting research.

2 Theoretical Foundations of Developmental Research

THEORETICAL CONCEPTS and assumptions guide the goals, choice of variables, procedures, methods of analysis, and conclusions of all research. Whether a researcher divides the subject matter of development into stimuli and responses, instinctual drives and defenses, cognitive structures, or fixed action patterns, he is imposing categories that will dictate his choice of data, the questions he asks of his data, and the types of answers he can obtain. In short, any study of development begins with a set of assumptions on the part of the researcher.

The social and behavioral sciences have produced a multitude of conceptual systems. These include broad theories that attempt to explain nearly all behavior, such as Skinnerian theory and psychoanalytic theory; less broad theories that concentrate on only a few large aspects of behavior, such as Piagetian theory; "miniature" theories for relatively limited situations, such as Bandura's modeling theory; and theoretical approaches, such as ethology, that imply ambitious programs for explaining behavior but that have not yet been worked out in detail for very many aspects of human behavior. Since no theory of development provides a complete account of developmental change, they might all be better regarded as theoretical frames-of-reference or points-of-view, in recognition of their tentativeness. Nevertheless, the various theoretical viewpoints play important roles in generating the questions and tentative answers around which developmental research is organized. The purpose of this chapter is to present the major conceptual paradigms in which prominent developmental theories are grounded. As will become evident in later chapters, the paradigms and theories to be presented here are by no means the only ones shaping developmental research, but they form much of the foundation on which developmental research has been built.

The Nature and Function of Conceptual Paradigms

A *paradigm* is a schematic model for representing phenomena and the relations among them. It provides terms and categories into which complex "real world" phenomena are translated in order to make them easier to grasp and study. In psychology, the stimulus–response (S–R) paradigm represents behavior in terms of mechanical, one-to-one relationships between environmental inputs (stimuli) and behavioral outputs (responses). The psychodynamic paradigm portrays behavior as resulting from the distribution of energy that can be blocked and rechanneled in various ways. A third paradigm, the organismic–developmental paradigm, portrays behavior in terms of organic growth and reorganization. And a fourth paradigm, that of ethology, portrays behavior as one aspect of a species' phylogenetically determined adaptive equipment.

A paradigm is typically a more general conceptual system than a theory, in that a theory is designed to provide specific explanations, whereas a paradigm consists of terms and concepts shared by workers who do not necessarily agree on particular theoretical explanations. Two or more theories may exist within the same general paradigm, but differ in their *hypothetical constructs*—concepts invented to explain observations and to suggest new, testable statements about reality. Examples of constructs proposed to explain behavioral change include *drive*—a motivating state of the organism hypothesized by certain learning theorists; *libido*—sexual energy hypothesized by Freud; and *cognitive developmental stages*—hypothesized by Piaget. The theories that spawned these constructs each originated in a different paradigm for studying behavior, but not everyone who accepts one of the paradigms necessarily accepts all of the constructs associated with it.

The Rise and Fall of Paradigms

Kuhn (1970) has proposed that the history of various sciences can be divided into phases according to whether the science was progressing as a "puzzle-solving" operation guided by a dominant paradigm or whether it was in a "crisis" period when an old paradigm had lost credibility, but had not yet been supplanted by a new paradigm. During periods of the first type, described by Kuhn as *normal science*, the way in which an accepted paradigm defines the questions in the field and the procedures it provides for answering them make science seem like a process of fitting together the pieces of a puzzle. However, an accumulation of unexpected discoveries or disconfirmations of predictions derived from an accepted paradigm may undermine confidence in the paradigm to the point where new ways of looking at the problems are proposed and eventually give birth to a new paradigm.

In psychology, periods of normal science have been few, short-lived, and circumscribed in scope. However, from the early 1930s until the late 1950s, S–R behaviorism dominated much of American psychology in a manner reminiscent of Kuhn's examples of normal science in astronomy, physics, and chemistry. Although diverse variants of S–R behaviorism flourished, they shared basic assumptions about the subject matter of psychology (observable behavior); the primary variables (stimuli and responses); the mechanism of behavior change (learning); and the eventual applicability of the same principles of learning to all behavior, no matter how complex. Gestalt theory and psychoanalysis dominated some areas of psychology during this period, but S–R theorists actively translated Gestalt and psychoanalytic concepts into their own paradigm.

By the late 1950s, however, there was a flowering of interests and theories outside the strict S–R paradigm. In developmental psychology, it was the rediscovery of Piaget's work (a cause or effect of the change?) and new looks at language development, spurred by Chomsky's (1959) attack on S–R explanations of language, that most clearly heralded the change. Outside developmental psychology, a similar interest in cognition blossomed during the 1960s, and cognitive approaches have since become popular in virtually all areas of psychology. This is not to say that the S–R paradigm has withered and died. On the contrary, the widespread application of the S–R paradigm to psychopathology and teaching during the 1970s demonstrates that it is still very much alive. However, much current S–R work is designed to study questions posed by cognitive approaches and to integrate cognitive and behavioral concepts. This is especially true in developmental psychology, behavior modification, and instructional methods. Thus, the current scene is not so much one in which a dying S–R paradigm is being replaced by a sparkling new paradigm, but one that offers a variety of interesting paradigms, including S–R approaches that have been stimulated by challenges from cognitive approaches. Since the various paradigms are in many ways complementary, we may be at the threshold of a new synthesis of them, or we may continue to be challenged by diverse views of development.

As Kuhn's analysis has shown, paradigms have both advantages and disadvantages. A widely shared paradigm fosters clear communication, coordinated efforts, and cumulative progress in a science. On the other hand, the categories and methods of a paradigm may confine the researcher's thinking to the phenomena highlighted by his paradigm and may blind him to other interesting phenomena. Nevertheless, because paradigms—implicit or explicit—are inescapable, it is essential that the researcher recognize the assumptions and biases in his paradigm's version of reality by making them as explicit as possible. In a field like psychology, where many paradigms coexist and their lives are often short, the ability to assimilate and synthesize ideas from various paradigms is especially important. In the following accounts of the major paradigms and theories emerging from them, the emphasis is upon the theoretical assumptions that shape various approaches to developmental research. Chapter 3 will portray ways in which different paradigms converge and diverge when brought to bear on the same research problem.

The S–R Paradigm

It is important to distinguish between the theoretical and methodological aspects of the S–R paradigm. The *theoretical* view that the environment is the primary determinant of thought and behavior predates by thousands of years the advent of S–R methodology. Aristotle proposed that the child begins life as a *tabula rasa* or unmarked tablet. Development then consists of a process whereby sensory impressions write their messages on the tablet. In more recent times, the view that sensory experience is the primary source of thought and behavior received theoretical refinement in the work of a long line of British "empiricist" philosophers, beginning with John Locke (1632–1704), and including David Hume (1711–76), James Mill (1773–1836), and his son, John Stuart Mill (1806–73). The basic process hypothesized by these philosophers to account for mental development was *association*—the linking together of sensory impressions by means of associative bonds among them, with complex ideas being no more than associative combinations of sensory inputs.

The "empiricism" of the British associationist philosophers refers to their assumption that experience is the source of all knowledge, rather than to empirical methodology for gathering data. Their methodology was, in fact, no more empirical than that of nativist philosophers like Immanual Kant, who maintained that important aspects of mental functioning are inborn rather than deriving from experience. Both the empiricist and nativist philosophers relied upon the same nonempirical methods of introspection, logical analysis, and speculation.

The *methodological* aspect of S–R psychology originated in the laboratory study of animal learning around the turn of this century. Pavlov and Bekhterev in Russia and Thorndike in the United States showed that it was superfluous to credit animals with thought processes, since so much of their behavior seemed explicable by stimulus and reward contingencies. Although he was not the first to extrapolate the findings on animal learning to human behavior, it was John B. Watson (1913) who popularized the doctrine of *methodological* behaviorism that was to spread far beyond the S–R *explanations* for behavior. While Watson shared the traditional empiricist–associationist theory that thought and behavior were determined by environmental inputs, his methodological message was that the subject matter of psychology should be restricted exclusively to the environmental inputs and observable responses of organisms, human as well as nonhuman. Whether or not they actually existed, consciousness and thought were not legitimate subjects for psychology because they were eternally private and not observable by the scientist. Thus, while retaining the environmentalist faith of his empiricist forebears, Watson rejected their introspectionist methods.

Despite his dismissal of subjective experience as a datum for psychology, Watson did not rule out speech and other observable correlates of subjective experience. Self-reports and even movements of the vocal cords occurring when a person talks to himself were acceptable data as long as it was recognized that these observable responses—and not the subject's unobservable private experience—were the object of study. Not all of American psychology was won over to Watson's S–R *explanations* for behavioral development, but it gradually did accept his *methodological* credo. Introspectionist methods for describing and analyzing subjective experience gave way to the study of behavior in virtually all areas of psychology.

Under the dominance of the S–R paradigm from the 1930s through the 1950s, American psychology was preoccupied with relations between physically defined stimuli and responses. However, the upsurge of research on language and cognition in the 1960s demonstrated that S–R theories are not the only ones that can utilize methodological behaviorism. Computer models of thinking, nativistic theories of grammar, concepts of cognitive structure, and behavior genetics represent but a few of the nonS–R approaches in which research on behavior provides the ultimate test. All of the research discussed in this book is "behavioristic" in the broad sense of employing behavioral measures. But what the various versions of the S–R paradigm have in common, over and above methodological behaviorism, is a commitment to explaining change in terms of observable conditions in the environment, i.e., of "learning" from "experience." Applications of this paradigm to the study of development are presented in the following sections.

Operant Conditioning

The most ambitious version of the S–R paradigm, in terms of how much behavior it seeks to explain, is the "operant" or "instrumental" conditioning approach. The fundamental principle of operant conditioning was stated by Thorndike (1913) as the *Law of Effect*: Responses producing a satisfying state of affairs for an organism tend to be repeated, whereas those producing an annoying state of affairs tend not to be repeated. In other words, the probability that a certain response will be emitted depends upon the *effect* the response has previously had.

Under Skinner's leadership, operant conditioners have attempted to explain behavioral change primarily in terms of the effects *operants*—responses that operate on the environment—produce for the organism. Dispensing with inferences about the state of the organism, operant conditioners have restated the law of effect as the *Empirical Law of Effect*. This does away with Thorndike's reference to the satisfying or annoying implications of response-produced events and holds that the effects of an operant-produced event should be inferred exclusively from the subsequent course of the operant under the same stimulus conditions. Thus, if an operant is followed by a particular event, and the operant subsequently *increases* in frequency or intensity under the same stimulus conditions, then the event is defined as a *reinforcer* of the operant. On the other hand, if an operant is followed by an event and the operant subsequently *decreases* in frequency or intensity, then the event is defined as a *punishment*, without any inferences about whether it produces an annoying state of affairs for the organism.

The operant view of development. The operant approach makes two basic assumptions about behavioral development. One is that the principles of behavioral change are the same in all organisms. The second is that complex behavior is merely a chaining of responses governed by the same principles as simple behavior. Bar-pressing responses by rats have therefore been studied to identify principles that have then been extrapolated to complex human behavior such as speech. While it is acknowledged that gross physical characteristics of an organism limit the behavior it can acquire (e.g., humans cannot fly), there is a firm belief that reinforcement contingencies are the primary determinants of the behavior that actually occurs. It is likewise assumed that scientific control of reinforcement contingencies can be used to elicit any behavior the organism is capable of.

In addition to minimizing differences between species and between types of behavior, operant conditioners reject developmental differences as explanations for behavioral change. Donald Baer (1970, 1973) has argued the operant view that developmental psychology should not be concerned with cataloging behavior by age, but with the processes whereby learning brings about behavioral change. To contrast the operant approach with what he regards as the traditional age-cataloging approach, Baer cites numerous studies in which young or handicapped children were conditioned to make developmentally more advanced responses than they had previously made. He concludes from these studies that waiting for developmental changes to occur is unnecessary, because many of them can be brought about quickly by environmental programming. Since Baer considers the sequence of programming to be a critical determinant of behavioral change, he ascribes the slowness of many behavioral changes to the haphazardness of stimuli and reinforcements in the natural environment. He also maintains that changes in environmental contingencies, rather than changes in the organism, are the primary cause of behavioral change over the course of development.

Operant technology. Besides offering a theory of behavioral change, operant conditioning provides techniques used by many who do not share the operant assumption that important developmental changes are caused primarily by environmental contingencies. In fact, operant techniques are sometimes used to determine the age at which organisms become biologically capable of particular behaviors. This is especially true in studies of infant behavior where operant techniques are used to determine when infants become capable of discriminating among various classes of stimuli, even though the capabilities are not assumed to have resulted from environmental programming. For example, in order to determine whether there is a biologically determined tendency to discriminate speech sounds according to discrete categories, Eimas, Siqueland, Jusczyk, and Vigorito (1971) studied the reinforcing effects of changes in speech sounds on sucking responses by month-old infants. Using an apparatus that enabled the infants to increase the volume of a recorded sound by sucking faster on a special nipple, it was found that they sucked faster to hear a sound from a different category of adult speech than the sound they had previously been hearing. Since the sounds were similar in all respects except those that enable adult hearers to distinguish them as conveying differences in meaning (/ba/vs./pa/), the change in sucking rate indicated that, with little experience in hearing speech and none in producing it, infants discriminate sounds according to categories like those employed by adults. In short, the differential reinforcing effects of the different sounds on the operant response of sucking suggested that perception of speech sounds according to discrete categories is biologically determined.

Mediation Theory

In contrast to the tendency of operant conditioners to focus exclusively on observable Ss and Rs, a second major approach within the S–R paradigm has spawned interest in unobserved intermediary or *mediating* variables within the organism that might aid in explaining relationships between observed Ss and Rs. The second approach originated largely in the Pavlovian model of "classical" or "respondent" conditioning. Unlike operant conditioning, in which the power of a stimulus to elicit a response results from the reinforcement contingent on the response, respondent conditioning results from the repeated pairing of a stimulus (e.g., a bell) with another stimulus (e.g., food) that already elicits a particular response (e.g., salivation). The power that the conditioned stimulus (bell) acquires to elicit the response (salivation) without the unconditioned stimulus (food) led Russian psychologists to study the ways in which conditioned stimuli come to function as if they were signals for the unconditioned stimuli. Because so much of human learning involves words, Pavlov proposed that language serves as a *second signal system* whereby words, including words uttered to the self, come to stand for other stimuli and can be responded to as if they were the stimuli they stand for. Accordingly, an important objective of Russian developmental psychology has been to identify changes in conditioning that occur as language is acquired.

In the United States, the primary source of S–R mediation theory has been Hull's (1952) learning theory. Unlike Skinner, Hull employed hypothetical constructs to aid in explaining the relations between stimuli, responses, and reinforcements. Hull's primary constructs concerned the condition of the organism in terms of its motivational or *drive* state (e.g., length of food deprivation) and its history of reinforcement for making a particular response in a particular stimulus situation. According to Hull's drive-reduction theory, an event is reinforcing only if it reduces tension arising from a drive, or if it has become a "secondary" reinforcer through having been repeatedly paired with events that reduce drives.

Hull also hypothesized that an observable physical stimulus can elicit covert responses in the organism, such as the focusing of attention on critical aspects of the stimulus situation. Representing them with small rs, Hull depicted these covert responses as serving as stimuli (represented by small ss) for other covert rs. A behavioral sequence could be portrayed as a chain, S–r_1–s_1–r_2–s_2–R, wherein an external stimulus (S) elicits a covert response (e.g., an attentional response, r_1), which serves as a stimulus (s_1) for another covert response (e.g., a verbal label r_2). The verbal label (r_2) then serves as a stimulus (s_2) for an overt response (R) that has been conditioned to that particular verbal label.

Kuenne's study.   One of the most fundamental links between Hullian mediation theory and developmental research was forged by Margaret Kuenne (1946), who hypothesized that children's learning patterns would change as they began to employ verbal mediators. Kuenne tested her hypothesis with a discrimination learning task in which children were presented with two squares of different sizes and were consistently reinforced for choosing one of the sizes. It had previously been found that, if an animal was reinforced for choosing the larger of two stimuli and was then presented with that stimulus, plus a still larger one, the animal would choose the new stimulus rather than the previously reinforced one. The transfer of a response to a new stimulus situation according to the *relative* rather than the absolute values of the stimuli is called *transposition*. Nonmediational S–R theory had explained transposition by assuming that the initial training reinforces excitatory tendencies toward the positive stimulus and inhibitory tendencies toward the negative (unreinforced) stimulus, but that the excitatory tendencies toward the positive stimulus are stronger than the inhibitory tendencies toward the negative stimulus (Spence, 1937). When the generalization gradients of the excitatory and inhibitory tendencies were drawn according to these assumptions, they revealed the relationships portrayed in Figure 2-1.

As can be seen from Figure 2-1, the *difference* between the hypothetical generalization gradients for the excitatory and inhibitory tendencies is 72.1 units (of an arbitrary scale) for a 256-centimeter stimulus, but only 51.7 units for the originally reinforced 160-centimeter stimulus. Consequently, transposition should occur when the new stimulus is not too different in size from the pair of stimuli on which the animal was trained. However, a second look at Figure 2-1 shows that, if the 256-centimeter and 409-centimeter stimuli were presented together, the net excitatory tendency of 72.1 units toward the 256-centimeter stimulus would be greater than the net excitatory tendency of 52.1 toward the 409-centimeter stimulus. As a result, the animal would choose the smaller, 256-centimeter stimulus rather than continuing to respond to

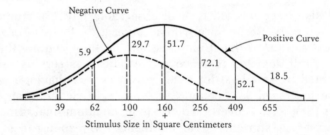

Figure 2-1. Relations between the positive and negative generalization curves hypothesized by Spence when the 160 cm. stimulus had been reinforced and the 100 cm. stimulus had not been reinforced during training. (Adapted from Kuenne, 1946.)

the relationship "bigger than." Thus, nonmediational S–R theory predicted—and it was found—that animals would transpose on stimuli near the size of the originally reinforced stimuli but not on stimuli far from the original stimuli in size.

Kuenne applied this model to children's learning with one important difference: She predicted that *young* children would behave like animals who conformed to the nonmediational model, but that *older* children would spontaneously make verbal responses, such as "pick the bigger one," which would cause them to transpose on stimuli far from the original stimuli in size, as well as on "near" stimuli. In terms of the Hullian S–r–s–r–s–R sequence, Kuenne theorized that one of the little rs was a verbal label, e.g., "bigger." This label, based on *relations* between the stimuli, would become a stimulus for the child's overt response R, and would cause him to transpose regardless of the sizes of the stimuli.

Using children at four mental-age levels, Kuenne found that all groups transposed on the near test, but that transposition on the far test increased from chance levels at the mental age of 3 years to 100 percent at the mental age of 6 years. Thus, the nonmediational model, according to which responses become conditioned to absolute values of stimuli, proved to be inappropriate for children old enough to use language in their thinking. However, Kuenne's hypothesis that covert verbal responses serve to mediate between external Ss and Rs preserved the structure and parsimony of the S–R paradigm while taking account of the differences in learning by animals and young humans, on the one hand, and older humans on the other. Other S–R research has also demonstrated changes in learning like that which the advent of verbal mediation has been invoked to explain (e.g., Kendler and Kendler, 1970).

Modeling Theory

Albert Bandura (1972) has been the primary exponent of another S–R mediation approach called *modeling theory*. *Modeling* refers to a person's use of behavior he has witnessed to guide his own behavior. Although imitation has long been of interest to developmental psychologists, Bandura distinguishes modeling from imitation on the grounds that modeling involves "much broader psychological effects than the simple response mimicry implied by the term 'imitation'" (Bandura, 1972 p. 37). For example, subjects witnessing a model in various situations may respond to new situations in a manner consistent with the model's behavior even though they have never observed the model responding to those situations.

In effect abandoning the S–R ideal of explaining behavior as a chain of one-to-one links between stimulus input, response output, and reinforcement contingencies, Bandura analyzes modeling into four components: *attentional processes, retention processes, motor reproduction processes,* and *motivational–reinforcement processes.* Incentive conditions, observer characteristics, and the salience of the model are all assumed to determine whether an observer's attention will become focused enough to instigate the discriminative observation necessary for learning. If the observer does attend closely enough to a model, then overt and covert rehearsal of the model's behavior and symbolic coding of the modeling stimuli determine whether the stimuli are retained. Bandura's research has been particularly concerned with the role of images and words in the encoding and organization of stimuli into easily remembered schemes. He has shown, for example, that inducing subjects to visualize, to verbally describe, and to adopt summary verbal labels for observed behaviors all enhance later performance of the behaviors (cf. Bandura, 1972).

The third component of modeling—*motor representation*—is the overt reproduction of modeled behavior according to representations the person has retained. This depends upon the availability of the appropriate motor responses, as well as upon accurate symbolic representation of behavior.

The remaining determinants of modeling—*motivational–reinforcement processes*—include incentives for attending to a model's behavior in the first place and for translating observations into actions. Unlike S–R approaches that focus on the control of behavior through externally administered consequences, Bandura stresses that vicarious reinforcement and self-reinforcement can influence behavior. For example, a model who is rewarded for his behavior is more likely to be imitated than a model who is punished, and an individual may control his own behavior by rewarding or punishing it according to self-imposed standards. Behavioral development can thus be affected by the reward and punishment contingencies a child observes and imposes on himself, as well as by those imposed on him by others (Bandura, 1974).

Cumulative–Hierarchical Learning

The fourth contemporary version of the S–R view has not crystalized into a theoretical model as unitary as the other three. Instead, it consists of a variety of attempts to utilize S–R concepts in constructing models for complex intellectual achievements, primarily to provide guides for teaching. A central thesis has been that complex intellectual achievements can be understood as the culmination of learning that begins with simple S–R connections. Robert Gagné (1968, 1970) has made one of the most ambitious attempts to construct an S–R model of this sort. Gagné has proposed that individual and chained S–R associations make possible the learning of multiple discriminations. These discriminations, in turn, provide the basis for the learning of concepts; concepts make possible the learning of simple rules regarding the concepts; and simple rules can be combined to form complex rules. While Gagné acknowledges that there may be "stages" or "levels" of learning with respect to a particular type of problem, he holds that such stages occur at particular ages only because learning takes time. Thus, the age at which correct conservation responses emerge is assumed to be determined neither by biological factors nor by the evolution of logical structures, but by the amount of time required for learning all the necessary responses, chains, concepts, and rules.

Another tenet of Gagné's approach is that "the process of cumulative learning can involve and be contributed to by the operations of inductive and deductive thinking" (Gagné, 1968, p. 189). Although he acknowledges that his model does not provide a theory of thinking, and he states that "each structure may also build upon itself through self-initiated thinking activity" (p. 190), Gagné attempts neither to show how thinking—deductive, inductive, or otherwise—develops from cumulative learning, nor how thinking affects learning or is affected by it. As with many other S–R attempts to account for complex achievements, a question therefore arises as to the origins of intellectual processes not traceable exclusively to environmental inputs. If it is assumed that self-initiated thinking, as well as inductive and deductive reasoning, influence learning without being explicable in terms of S–R histories, then the apparent parsimony of explaining development in terms of learning from environmental contingencies is lost. Furthermore, the invocation of "learning" vs. "thinking" processes to explain specific achievements becomes quite arbitrary.

The Organismic–Developmental Paradigm

What I call the organismic–developmental paradigm encompasses several approaches sharing the general assumption that the processes of psychological development are similar to the processes of organic development. According to this assumption, what develops are not merely new responses to environmental stimuli, but new *structures*—distinctive forms of psychological organization—that function like physical structures. Whereas the physical structures of the body contribute specific biological functions to the total body system, psychological structures are well-organized procedures that contribute to the organism's overall adaptive activity.

Another assumption of this paradigm is that the sequence of behavioral and psychological development, like that of organic development, is *invariant* in the sense that more advanced levels can never precede more primitive levels. Although environmental inputs are needed to actualize each successive step, the influence of the environment at any given time depends upon the existing level of the organism's development.

Whereas the S–R paradigm grew out of the empiricist–associationist tradition of epistemology, the organismic–developmental paradigm grew out of an epistemological tradition that can be loosely described as *nativist–structuralist*. This tradition holds that knowledge is never a direct copy of external reality, but is always structured according to inborn characteristics of the human mind. Important exponents of this view include Plato and Kant. Darwin's theory of the evolution of traits distinguishing one species from another is also an important forerunner of the organismic–developmental paradigm. Organismic–developmental theorists postulate that developmental changes in individuals (*ontogenetic* changes) are governed by principles of adaptation like those governing the evolutionary development of species (*phylogenesis*). This does *not* mean that the development of the individual necessarily replicates the history of his species, i.e., that ontogeny recapitulates phylogeny. Rather, it means that development consists of progressive physical and behavioral reorganizations oriented toward more effective adaptation, just as do changes in species over the course of evolution.

Particular levels of organization are often designated as "stages" by organismic–developmental theorists, as well as by the psychodynamic theorists to be discussed later. However, even Piaget, whose theory is often described primarily in terms of developmental stages, stresses that development is a continuous rather than a discontinuous process and that stage concepts are rather arbitrary divisions of a continuous sequence into segments that emerge gradually from preceding segments.

As an illustration of the concept of a developmental stage, consider a child's transition from crawling to walking. One of my children had shown only a few tentative attempts at using furniture to pull herself up to a standing position, until, one day, with no furniture to pull on, she got to her feet and took several steps. From that day on, walking was her preferred mode of locomotion. The maturational processes culminating in her ability to walk were continuous—muscle cells gradually matured; nerve fibers gradually acquired myelin coverings and began to function efficiently; trial-and-error interactions with the world taught her about balance and the effects of gravity. However, at a particular moment in time, the confluence of all these gradual, continuous processes brought about a complex new organization of behavior which had not previously occurred, but which now enabled her to do things that had been impossible a short time before.

Rather than being an isolated achievement, the new upright position and mode of locomotion brought a drastic reorganization of other aspects of the child's behavior—it changed her relationship to the physical world by giving her new ways of seeing, hearing, touching, and influencing the world. Among other things, the child could now see and grab what was on top of tables, could look down upon and attempt to pick up the family cat, and could attempt to imitate people while she stood upright. The new achievement also brought a change in the child's relationships to other people. And, as parents discover, the thrill of seeing their child walk is soon superseded by a host of new anxieties and prohibitions as they seek to protect the child from the dangers suddenly made accessible.

Not all children make the transition to walking so suddenly—many mix crawling and tentative walking in gradually changing proportions over a period of months until walking finally predominates. Yet, even if the transition requires several months to complete, a marked contrast in behavioral organization is evident when the beginning and end points of the transition are compared. The differences in behavioral organization between prewalking and walking graphically illustrate what most organismic–developmental theorists have in mind when they speak of differences in levels or stages of organization. However, these theorists vary according to whether they define stages in terms of *behavior* characteristic of a given age or in terms of inferred *psychological structures*. Arnold Gesell represents the former extreme, while Heinz Werner and Jean Piaget represent the latter extreme.

Gesell's Approach

Referring to developmental psychology as "the embryology of behavior," Gesell (1954) modeled his research on procedures for tracing the differentiation of the growing embryo. Gesell's strategy was to observe and document every aspect of the behavior of infants and children at successive ages. On the basis of these observations, he assembled standardized tasks for eliciting behavior and then accumulated age norms for responses to the tasks. He referred to the typical behavior of a given age as a "stage," but his concept of stage went little beyond the description of the behavior characteristic of the age. The negativistic behavior of 2-year olds, for example, was part of the "2-year-old stage" simply because Gesell found it to be characteristic of most 2-year olds. Child-rearing advice stemming from this view often consisted of assuring parents that the child would "grow out of it" as he advanced to the next stage of behavior. While more theoretically inclined developmentalists have looked askance at the apparent circularity of ascribing behavior to a stage merely because the behavior typically appears at a specified age, the norms embodied in Gesell's infant tests have proven useful in evaluating the development of children throughout the world.

Werner's Theory

Like Gesell, Werner took embryology as a model for developmental psychology, but he was much more ambitious than Gesell about the scope of developmental principles. Werner (1957) proposed that developmental psychology is not restricted "either to ontogenesis or phylogenesis, but seeks to coordinate within a single framework forms of behavior observed in comparative animal psychology, in child psychology, in psychopathology, in ethnopsychology, and in the general and differential psychology of man in our own culture" (p. 125).

Werner postulated what he called the *orthogenetic principle,* that developmental changes consist of progressions from undifferentiated functioning to functioning that is differentiated, specialized, and *hierarchically integrated.* By *hierarchic integration,* Werner meant that various specific behaviors become coordinated within higher levels of organization. For example, early speech consists largely of one-word labels for separate objects, while later speech consists of multiword utterances in which individual words function as components of higher order grammatical structures, such as subjects and predicates. Subjects and predicates, in turn, are integrated within sentences, which are still higher in the hierarchy of grammatical organization.

Werner (1957) considered his orthogenetic principle to be a heuristic concept rather than a hypothesis subject to empirical confirmation or disconfirmation. As a heuristic concept, its theoretical status is no different from such concepts as the "stimuli," "responses," and "learning" of S–R theories, the "assimilation," "accommodation," and "schemes" of Piagetian theory, and the "id," "ego," and "superego" of Freudian theory. All these concepts embody untestable assumptions about how behavioral phenomena should be divided up for study. The value of such concepts is that they suggest testable hypotheses about relationships among measurable behaviors. The more hypotheses that are confirmed, the more valuable are the heuristic concepts.

While the heuristic concepts of other theories are no more testable than Werner's orthogenetic principle, Werner's principle has not been used to generate hypotheses as specific as those generated by most of the other heuristic concepts. Instead, Werner's strategy was to employ a variety of data on organic development, psychopathology, behavior in brain-injured patients, anthropology, and his own experiments to *illustrate* the orthogenetic principle. The illustrations were intended to demonstrate the ubiquity of the principle rather than to identify specific and predictable courses of development. Since he maintained that the specific course of development may vary from situation to situation and species to species, Werner applied his theory primarily to general phenomena such as symbol formation (Werner and Kaplan, 1963) and to defining the dimensions along which development proceeds.

Wernerian research.   One body of research growing out of Werner's theory has been directed at demonstrating parallel developmental changes in ontogenesis, microgenesis, and pathogenesis. *Microgenesis* refers to the short-term development of a specific percept, concept, or behavior, while *pathogenesis* refers to the development of psychopathology. Werner believed that his developmental principles governed microgenesis and pathogenesis as well as ontogenesis. As an illustration, Figure 2-2 portrays responses to Rorschach inkblots by normal adults viewing the blots tachistoscopically at progressively longer exposures and by children and disturbed adults viewing the blots under normal exposure times (Werner, 1957). The graphs show that the percentage of responses based on details rather than on global, undifferentiated percepts increased with exposure time, illustrating the *microgenesis* of percepts as the duration of perception lengthened. The figure also illustrates the *ontogenesis* of percepts as age increased, and the contrasts in levels of percepts between diagnostic groups hypothesized to be developmentally primitive (hebephrenic and catatonic schizophrenics), developmentally intermediate (paranoids), and developmentally advanced (normals).

The most extensive application of Werner's approach has been to research on a dimension of cognitive style ranging from *field inde-*

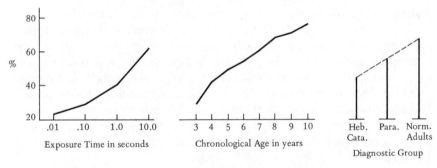

Figure 2-2. Percentage of responses based on details of Rorschach inkblots by normal adults at tachistoscopic exposures, and by children and various diagnostic groups at full exposure. (Werner, 1957.)

pendence at one extreme to *field dependence* at the other extreme. Herman Witkin has been a leader in this research, which typically employs the Rod-and-Frame Test and the Embedded Figures Test to measure the influence of contextual distractions on perception. In the Rod-and-Frame Test, subjects sitting in a darkened room are asked to judge the uprightness of a luminescent rod when the only visible context is a luminescent frame surrounding the rod, the frame itself being tilted at an angle. The Embedded Figures Test consists of cards which display simple designs and cards displaying complex designs in which the simple designs are hidden. The subject's task is to pick out the simple design hidden within each complex design. *Field dependence* is defined as poor performance on these tests, caused, presumably, by a person's excessive dependence upon the surrounding context or "field." Field dependence decreases between the ages of 8 and 17, but the rank order of individuals' scores remains relatively stable from age to age, suggesting stable personality or cognitive differences (Witkin, Dyk, Faterson, Goodenough, and Karp, 1962).

Piaget's Theory

Jean Piaget is currently the most prominent of the organismic–developmental theorists. While he shares with Werner and Gesell a basically organic model of development, he has gone much further in specifying stages of development and in testing specific hypotheses. He is primarily interested in answering the epistemological question of how knowledge is created. His strategy is to elucidate the nature of human knowledge by identifying the successive procedures developed for obtaining knowledge during ontogenesis.

Calling his enterprise *genetic epistemology* ("genetic" being used virtually as a synonym for "developmental"), Piaget regards it as embracing many fields of study, including logic, mathematics, and biology, as well as the traditional subject matter of developmental psychology. This is because he believes that the conceptual abstractions created by man in the form of mathematical and logical systems have their forerunners in the earliest forms of sensory–motor behavior and that even the earliest forms of behavior serve epistemological functions like those of abstract logical thought. Furthermore, Piaget believes that logic and mathematics can provide models for representing the cognitive competence attained during the more advanced developmental periods.

According to Piaget, the organism's initial behavioral equipment includes not only reflexes such as sucking, but general modes of functioning that serve to promote progressively more effective adaptive techniques. The modes of functioning are *accommodation*—the tendency to alter one's behavior in response to environmental realities—and *assimilation*—the tendency to construe environmental input in ways that make it comprehensible and usable. The adaptive techniques ultimately developed by members of a particular species are a joint function of the genetically transmitted growth plans of the species and the particular environment encountered.

Piaget hypothesizes that intellectual development begins with progressive modification of reflexive behavior as the infant adapts his reflexes to the world he meets. For example, the innately determined sucking reflex becomes coordinated with looking, grasping, and other behaviors needed to assimilate aspects of the environment (breast, bottle) providing nourishment. At the same time, the infant accommodates his sucking to the environment by focusing his mouth more and more precisely on the object that yields nourishment, rather than sucking randomly at whatever his lips touch.

Like S–R theorists, Piaget divides behavior into units. However, he calls his basic unit a *scheme* rather than a response. A scheme is not just a specific response to a specific stimulus, but a coordinated series of actions that can be applied to many different components of the environment. For example, when the infant has reached the point where he can effectively spot something suckable, grasp it, focus his lips precisely on it, and begin sucking as it enters his mouth, he has a *sucking scheme*. Piaget regards organized procedures of this sort, adaptable to many complex stimulus situations, as the essential units of behavior. In effect, the behavioral schemes evident during the *sensory–motor period*, the first 18 months of life, are the first psychological structures.

The major developmental changes following the sensory–motor period consist of translations of *sensory–motor* schemes into progressively more abstract *mental* schemes. Toward the age of 18 months,

Piaget hypothesizes that the child becomes capable of activating sensory–motor schemes on a progressively more covert level. One aspect of this new capability is that the child can mentally recreate images of things he has seen. According to Piaget (1951), these images begin as subtle imitative activities—it is as if the child can recreate for himself something he has seen by replicating the activities of the stimulus object or replicating the eye movements involved in perceiving the object.

Between approximately 18 months and 2 years of age, the representational activity becomes progressively more independent of concrete stimulus inputs, to the point where the child can create mental images that are not mere replicas of perceptual experiences, but that include new and purposeful combinations of images. For example, lusting after a cookie jar placed out of reach, the 2-year old can look around the room and envision a sequence beginning with pushing the family cat off a kitchen chair, carrying the chair to the kitchen counter, climbing on the chair, reaching for the cookie jar, removing its lid, and consuming his ill-gotten gains.

The figurative aspect of thought.   With the advent of mental representation, a feature of Piaget's theory which distinguishes it from other theories becomes crucial. This is Piaget's (1977) distinction between the *figurative* and *operative* aspects of thought. The figurative aspect comprises mental signifiers, such as images, symbols, and words, that stand for particular stimuli. These signifiers are very much like the covert speech and other mediating responses hypothesized by S–R mediation theorists, in that they consist of mental contents which function in a fashion analogous to external stimuli. Piaget calls these covert signifiers *schemas*, in contrast to the *schemes* described earlier. (The terms *schema* and *scheme* have been used interchangeably in many translations of Piaget's work, but in the 1960s Piaget made it clear that *schemas* are components of the figurative aspect of thought, whereas *schemes* are components of the operative aspect.) Prior to about the age of 18 months, the only schemas are hypothesized to be percepts elicited by stimuli from the external world. After about 18 months, however, mental schemas can be generated with increasing independence of perceptual input.

The operative aspect of thought.   What distinguishes Piaget's theory from other theories is that, beside the figurative aspect of thought, comprised of schemas, he posits an *operative* aspect of thought, comprised of mental schemes—organized mental activities analogous to overt sensory–motor schemes. Whereas sensory–motor schemes are physical actions by which the infant manipulates objects in his environment, *mental* schemes are conceptual activities by which the child manipulates the contents (schemas) of thought. In the case of the child plotting his course toward the cookie jar, the mental schemes consist of conceptually carrying out the activities needed to reach his goal, e.g., directing his attention to the cat, chair, and cookie jar, imagining the disposal of the cat and the moving of the chair, judging the heights and distances involved, and determining that the sequence will attain the goal. The figurative schemas consist of the child's images of each specific stimulus, e.g., the cat, chair, chair-against-the-counter, etc.

Operative development.   The mental activities described so far are merely conceptual enactments of physical activities. However, once the child becomes capable of mentally enacting physical activities, Piaget hypothesizes that further development consists of changes in the types of mental schemes that can be constructed. From the ages of about 2 to 6 years, the operative aspect of thought is limited primarily to schemes resembling actions that can be carried out physically and applied to schemas representing static aspects of the physical world. But, by around the age of 6, most children succeed in solving problems, such as those posed by the conservation tasks, in ways suggesting that their thinking is no longer modeled so exclusively upon physical activities and stimuli.

Piaget hypothesizes that the new mental schemes emerging around the age of 6 reflect an integrated system of logical operations. Rather than responding merely to the way things look, the child now gives precedence to logic over appearances. Even though the quantity *looks* greater in the narrow container than in the wide container, the child asserts that it is not *really* greater. More importantly, he supports his assertion with one of several logical arguments: The quantity poured from one container to another must still be the same as the comparison quantity because nothing has been added or taken away; the increase in height compensates for the decrease in width; or returning the quantity to its original container would show that it still rises to the original level. The child's concept of quantity has thus changed from one based exclusively upon static appearances to one based upon relationships among operations such as addition and subtraction. Because systematic use of logical operations is not evident in the child's thinking until about the age of 6, Piaget refers to the period between the ages of 2 and 6 as the *preoperational period.*

From about the ages of 6 to 11, the emergent systems of logical operations remain focused upon concrete real-world content, such as quantities and classes of objects. Piaget therefore calls this the *concrete operational period* of development. He has proposed an array of conceptual models, called *groupings*, for portraying the logical relationships implicit in the concrete operational child's thinking. While Piaget acknowledges that children are not consciously aware of basing their thinking on systems of logic, he maintains that the groupings exhaustively summarize the set of operations available to children during the concrete operational period.

The *formal operational period*, beginning at about the age of 11, is distinguished from the concrete operational period by the adolescent's capacity to apply logic-based schemes not only to concrete content, such as quantities and classes of objects, but to things that are themselves abstractions, such as moral principles, ideals, and hypothetical constructs. The ability to apply formal logic to abstractions enables the adolescent to conceptualize a problem in terms of an array of possible solutions logically deducible from the initial terms of the problem. For example, in one test of formal operations, the child is given four glasses of colorless liquid and a small bottle of liquid with a medicine dropper. The experimenter presents another glass of colorless liquid and demonstrates that drops from the small bottle will turn its contents yellow. The child is then told to produce the yellow color by using the liquid in the small bottle and the liquids in the glasses.

Subjects who have reached the formal operational period recognize that the problem can be solved by trying out all the possible combinations of the liquid in the bottle with the liquid in Glass 1, Glass 2, Glass 3, Glass 4, Glasses 1 and 2, 2 and 3, etc., until they obtain the appropriate mixture. In other words, regardless of any previous experience with similar problems, they translate the problem into an array of possible relationships and deduce that trying out all possible combinations must inevitably lead to the solution. Concrete operational subjects, by contrast, employ only a few combinations or mix the chemicals randomly, because they cannot conceptualize the problem in terms of all possible relationships.

Causes of development. Piaget hypothesizes four general contributors to developmental change:

1. organic *maturation;*

2. *experience* gained through interactions with the physical world, whereby the child not only observes things happen but engages in experimentation to find out *how* things happen;

3. *transmission of information* from other people by language, example, and inadvertent as well as deliberate teaching;

4. *equilibration.*

While other theories contain various versions of the first three contributors, the fourth contributor, equilibration, is a keystone of Piaget's theory having no direct counterparts in other theories.

The concept of equilibration is based upon Piaget's assumption that intellectual development is determined neither by genetic factors nor by environmental contingencies alone, but involves instead the progressive *construction* of new ways of knowing. Changes in the way the child represents the world to himself come about as the child discovers problems he cannot solve and seeks to understand them by inventing new mental representations. While Piaget acknowledges that learning can take place through conditioning, he maintains that major changes in thinking, especially in the transitions to concrete and formal operations, occur when a system of mental representation reaches a point where its limitations become evident to the child.

As an example, Piaget (1964) cites an experience recalled from childhood by a mathematician friend. While playing with some pebbles, the future mathematician placed them in a row and counted them. He then put the pebbles in a circle and counted them again. No matter how he arranged them, the number always remained the same! Since his preoperational conception of quantity was based upon appearances, he could not comprehend the fascinating regularity with which the number was preserved despite the changes in appearance. His discovery of the relationships between number and appearance created a disequilibrium in his accustomed way of thinking about quantities. This disequilibrium could only have come about when he had reached the point where his preoperational representations of quantity and his awareness of number were advanced enough to enable him to notice the contradiction between the changes in the appearance of the stones and constancy of their number.

The future mathematician's resolution of the problem is a prime example of what Piaget means by equilibration—he realized that, no matter what the arrangement of the stones, their number *must* always be conserved. He had thus reached a new equilibrium in his understanding of number, based upon an operational concept of numerical relationships rather than upon a concept of number restricted to appearance. This new concept could then be applied to many numerical relationships.

In sum, equilibration is the process whereby the various contributors to development are brought together in the construction of higher-order cognitive structures from lower-order structures. To use a computer analogy, cognitive structures are like computer programs, whereas schemes are like subroutines of these programs, and schemas are like the codified data which the programs operate upon and transform. However, unlike computers, living organisms are endowed with equilibration processes whereby they construct new and more powerful programs when old programs reach their limits.

The Psychodynamic Paradigm

The psychodynamic paradigm originated primarily with Freud's theory of neurosis. While his theory of neurosis is still influential in the study of psychopathology, only the developmental aspects of psychoanalytic theory are relevant here. Beginning in the mid-1890s, Freud sought to construct a general psychological model that would explain normal as well as pathological functioning. As his work progressed, two distinct theories of behavioral change evolved. One was his *theory of psychosexual development*, concerning successive stages in the distribution of *libidinal* (sexual) energy to the oral, anal, and phallic zones. Freud appears to have believed that the changes in libidinal focus from one erogenous zone to another were biologically predetermined and universal. Elements common to all human cultures helped make the conflicts arising during the first three libidinal phases more-or-less universal, although the exact form, intensity, and outcome of the conflicts could vary according to both the family and cultural environments. For example, the loss of the father or the presence of multiple mothering persons could affect the outcome of the Oedipal conflict. Freud later added the construct of an aggressive drive, or "death instinct," but the developmental course of the aggressive drive has received much less attention than that of the sex drive.

Freud's other theory of behavioral change was his *theory of motivation and learning*. He hypothesized that behavior was motivated primarily by the instinctual drives of sex and aggression. Behaviors that yielded pleasure through the discharge of instinctual impulses would be learned and repeated. Furthermore, objects (including people) that facilitated tension reduction became positively valued. This was essentially a drive-reduction learning theory, whereby learning results from reduction of organically based tensions. However, Freud's portrayal of learning also included many concepts of nineteenth-century associationist theory, according to which ideas become associated with one another in the mind through having been experienced at the same moment in time or through being similar in some way. Thus, a drive state could elicit a whole complex of indirectly associated ideas in addition to an idea that had previously accompanied reduction of the drive.

Freud hypothesized that thinking and other ego functions originate in the child as defensive mediators between the id's instinctual impulses, which seek immediate gratification, and the reality to which the child must adapt in order to survive. According to Freud's model, the infant in an intense drive state—such as hunger, a component of the sex drive—hallucinates the object—breast or bottle—previously associated with reduction of the drive state. Such hallucinations provide temporary gratification when the outside world does not immediately meet the infant's needs. The hallucinations constitute the first mental images and are the source of later thought processes. The subsequent development of thinking, other ego functions, and the superego was likewise attributed to the child's need to circumvent direct conflicts between his instinctual impulses and environmental realities. Tension arising out of conflict was thus seen as the primary instigator of development.

Psychoanalytic Ego Psychology

As the ego gained increasing attention in psychoanalytic theory, Heinz Hartmann (1939) proposed that many of the ego's functions develop independently of conflicts between id drives and reality. Among these ego functions are thinking, language, perception, memory, motor development, and learning processes. Hartmann hypothesized that the potential for developing these functions is, like id drives, innate. Nevertheless, Hartmann agreed with Freud that the energy powering these functions is derived from the instinctual drives, although he expanded Freud's concept of the "neutralization" or rechanneling of libidinal energy into ego functions to include neutralization of aggressive energy and a permanent rather than temporary neutralization of instinctual energies (Hartmann, Kris, and Loewenstein, 1949). In effect, Hartmann granted ego functions a developmental course of their own, rather than ascribing their origins to defensive reactions, but he still believed that their motive forces originated in the instinctual drives of sex and aggression.

Anna Freud has also been a major contributor to psychoanalytic ego psychology. She has provided detailed theoretical analyses of how defense mechanisms reflect the adaptive functions of the ego (1946) and has attempted to integrate diverse aspects of psychoanalytic theory within a developmental framework (1965).

As a result of the shift toward ego psychology in psychoanalytic theory, the most notable recent attempts to apply the psychodynamic paradigm in developmental research have dealt with the development of ego functions, rather than with unconscious conflict, symptom formation, or psychosexual development. Some of this work is directed at comparisons of psychoanalytic theory with Piaget's theory (Décarie, 1965) and will be discussed in chapter 3. Most of the rest of the work is oriented toward Erik Erikson's neo-Freudian theory of psychosocial development.

Erikson's Theory

Erikson's (1963) theory of psycho*social* development differs from Freud's theory of psycho*sexual* development in that developmental stages are defined not only in terms of the ascendant erogenous zones, but also in terms of the *modes of action* employed by the child and the *modalities of social interaction* which grow out of interpersonal exchanges occurring around the child's modes of action. For example, as portrayed by Erikson, the initial stage of development is dominated by a general incorporative mode which includes incorporation of stimuli through the various sense organs, as well as through the mouth. He therefore refers to this stage as the *oral–sensory stage*, rather than just the oral stage, as Freud called it. Since the infant is oriented toward incorporation of input from the outside world, the social modality he will learn at this stage, if all goes well, is called *getting*—because it involves getting others to provide what he needs and receiving what they give him. The four subsequent psychosocial stages are a second oral–sensory stage in which more active incorporation is the mode and *taking* is the modality; the *anal–urethral–muscular stage*; the *locomotor and infantile genital stage*; and the *rudimentary genital stage*.

While Erikson does not appear to hypothesize any specific cause of movement from one stage to the next, he does maintain that failure of the appropriate mode to become dominant within a stage will disrupt subsequent stages. For example, if an infant repeatedly vomits food after intake, this premature dominance of the *eliminative mode*, not normally dominant until the anal–urethral–muscular stage, may interfere with the child's learning of the social modality of getting. This, in turn, will affect later personality development.

In addition to the sequence of psychosocial stages, Erikson has hypothesized that humans experience a sequence of developmental crises or *nuclear conflicts*. The first nuclear conflict, associated with the two oral–sensory stages, concerns the development of *basic trust or mistrust*. Its resolution depends upon the success of the mother in satisfying the child's needs, thereby instilling in him a sense of trust in her and in the world she represents. Subsequent conflicts are over *autonomy vs. shame and doubt*, relating largely to toilet training during the anal–urethral–muscular stage; *initiative vs. guilt*, centered in the harnessing of aggression and the resolution of the Oedipal situation during the locomotor–genital stage; *industry vs. inferiority*, occurring in the latency period prior to puberty and concerning the development of skills necessary for mature adult roles; and *identity vs. role confusion*, the conflict arising at puberty when the adolescent is faced with the need to integrate the upsurge in libidinal demands with previous identities, basic aptitudes, and the social-role opportunities available to him. During adulthood, three additional nuclear conflicts arise that, like the earlier conflicts, are each influenced by the outcomes of all preceding conflicts. These three conflicts are over *intimacy vs. isolation*, concerning the formation of mature love and friendship relationships; *generativity vs. stagnation* in childrearing, work, and creative accomplishments; and *ego integrity vs. despair*, which the aged must face as they lose youthful social roles and confront death.

Throughout development, Erikson's focus is upon the interplay of the ego and its social context, especially in terms of the ego identities assumed at each period. Accordingly, the research generated by Erikson's theory is concerned primarily with identifying ego identities and nuclear conflicts within various age groups. Ciaccio (1971), for example, used Erikson's descriptions of the first five nuclear conflicts to devise a scoring system for stories told by 5-, 8-, and 11-year-old boys in response to pictures presented under standardized conditions. Each theme within a story was scored as to whether it reflected concerns relevant to any of the five nuclear conflicts and whether the concerns were positive (e.g., reflected a sense of autonomy) or negative (e.g., reflected shame and doubt). On the basis of Erikson's theory, it was predicted that the 5-year olds would show the greatest concern with autonomy vs. shame and doubt; 8-year olds would show the greatest concern with initiative vs. guilt; and 11-year olds would show the greatest concern with industry vs. inferiority.

As shown in Figure 2-3, the 5-year olds indeed gave the most responses indicative of the second Eriksonian conflict, the 8-year olds the most responses indicative of the third conflict, and the 11-year olds

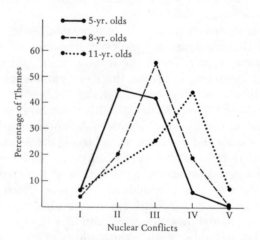

Figure 2-3. Percentage of themes reflecting five Eriksonian conflicts in 5-, 8-, and 11-year-old boys. (Adapted from Ciaccio, 1971.)

the most responses indicative of the fourth conflict. However, 87 percent of the negative responses across all three age groups concerned the second nuclear conflict, over shame and doubt. Ciaccio concluded that, while Erikson's sequence of nuclear conflicts was evident, problems with shame and doubt remained prominent in children who had supposedly reached the more advanced conflicts.

Longitudinal studies of college students, using questionnaire and interview measures, have also yielded evidence for changes with age in concerns about the more advanced nuclear conflicts. In these studies, too, the negative aspects of certain conflicts, especially identity diffusion, remained prominent over several years, while concern with other conflicts rose and fell (Constantinople, 1969; Waterman, Geary, and Waterman, 1974). Erikson's theory thus appears to offer a useful source of concepts for research on personality development, although it does not provide precise explanations for progress along either normal or deviant courses of development.

The Ethological Paradigm

Ethology originated primarily with Darwin's evolutionary analysis of the survival value of animal behavior in its natural environment. Although Darwin (1872, 1877) also applied his analyses to human behavior, it was not until the late 1960s, following the refinement of animal ethology into a methodologically rigorous discipline, that the ethological approach to human development became prominent.

Rather than being a model of how behavior changes during ontogenesis, the ethological paradigm consists of a set of assumptions and methods for analyzing the survival value of specific behaviors. A basic assumption is that many behaviors are genetically determined and that behavioral traits, like physical traits, evolve through the survival and successful reproduction of individuals carrying the traits. It is not assumed that every genetically determined behavior has continuing survival value, but that most behavior patterns had survival value at some point in the history of the species or are by-products or fragments of patterns that had survival value. In a sense, *phylogeny*, the evolutionary development of the species, *determines ontogeny*, the developmental course of the individual, although ontogeny does not necessarily *recapitulate* phylogeny. While acknowledging the influence of learning, thinking, and social environments on human behavior, ethologists point out that several million years of natural selection shaped our inheritance before the emergence a few thousand years ago of our techniques for subsisting in ways other than by hunting and gathering food.

The ethologists' assumption that behavior patterns can be best understood in terms of their adaptive function dictates a methodology that begins with careful observations of a species in its natural habitat. These observations are catalogued into an *ethogram*, a thorough description of the typical behavior of the species. Although an ethogram is devoid of causal inferences about why particular behaviors occur, it requires decisions as to the units of behavior to be catalogued. Ethologists therefore seek to identify the most basic organized behavioral sequences manifested by most members of a species.

Designated as *fixed action patterns* (FAPs), these behavioral sequences occupy a place in the ethological approach similar to that of responses in the S–R approach and schemes in Piaget's approach. However, FAPs differ from the responses of interest to S–R theorists in that they are considered to be genetically organized adaptive units that function—or at one time functioned—to enhance survival of the species, rather than being learned products of the experiential history of the individual. FAPs also differ from Piaget's schemes in that schemes are hypothesized to be constructed from an amalgam of individual experience and genetically determined potentialities through the process of equilibration.

When observations have been catalogued in an ethogram, the ethologist seeks to identify the functional significance of each FAP and the conditions controlling it. Environmental stimuli triggering FAPs are called *sign stimuli* or *releasers*. In order to determine precisely what aspect of the environment serves as a releaser and under what conditions it does so, an ethologist may experimentally manipulate environmental stimuli. For example, herring gull chicks have been observed to beg for food by pecking at the tip of their parent's bill. The parent responds by regurgitating food onto the ground, picking up a little, and giving it to the chicks. The parent's bill is yellow, but has a red spot on it. By experimentally presenting chicks with dummy bills having spots of various colors in various locations, Tinbergen (1951) found that both the color and location of the spot were critical in making it a releaser for the chick's FAP of pecking.

While FAPs consist of preprogrammed behaviors evolving through natural selection, Lorenz (1965) has hypothesized that the ability to learn from experience is likewise a product of evolutionary adaptation. However, being genetically determined, learning is constrained by other aspects of an organism's species-specific inheritance. Learning may therefore be limited to promoting behavioral change with respect only to a particular class of behaviors at certain developmental stages. Thus, a bird species makes innately determined nestbuilding movements, but individual birds must learn which materials in their environment can be used for this purpose. Likewise, what ducks learn when they follow their mother depends upon what moving object happened to become their "mother" by being visible during the critical period shortly after hatching when ducks imprint.

Human Ethology

The extension of the ethological paradigm to human behavior has taken a number of forms. One form has been a critical attack on laboratory–experimental psychology for studying very limited aspects of behavior in contrived situations. The ethological argument has been that laboratory experiments based upon preconceived theories rather than upon observations in natural habitats obscure the integrated and adaptive nature of behavior (e.g., Hutt and Hutt, 1970). A related attack has been made against environmentalist biases. As Hess (1970, p. 1) states it:

> Man is an animal. He is a biological organism with an evolutionary history. Nevertheless, when it is suggested that, in common with other animals, man may manifest inherited, or genetically programmed behaviors, dissent often comes quickly from behavioral scientists. Indeed, it is unfashionable these days to investigate such genetically determined behavior in humans. . . .
> If we look at the behavior of *all* animals on this earth, we reach three inescapable conclusions.
> 1. Innate behavior is the necessary and *sufficient* condition for the survival of most organisms.
> 2. Learned behavior, alone, is the necessary and *sufficient* condition for the survival of none. . . .
> 3. Innate, or genetically programmed behavior is necessary for the survival of *all* animals.

Another way in which ethology has been extended to humans is by extrapolating to humans ethological findings on nonhuman species. While this has produced best-sellers such as *The naked ape* (Morris, 1967), many ethologists now deplore the unsupported extrapolation of findings from one species to another species, especially to humans.

Although attempts have long been made to *interpret* human behavior from an ethological perspective, ethological *research* on human development is a more recent phenomenon. In one of the most direct applications of ethological methods to humans, McGrew (1972) made detailed written and videotape records of behavior in nursery schools during free-play periods each day for several months. The data were then coded into units like those comprising an ethogram of animal behavior, although McGrew called the units *behavioral elements* rather than fixed action patterns. For example, among facial gestures, two behavioral elements were *narrow eyes* and *grin face. Narrow eyes* was defined as: "The eyelids are brought closer together than normal"

(p. 46). *Grin face* as: "The lips are spread wide and the mouth corners are retracted; both rows of teeth are visible and usually close together. The expression is reflexive and fleeting in appearance." (p. 44).

In addition to cataloguing behavioral elements and comparing them to behaviors observed in other species, McGrew analyzed *agonistic* (combative) interactions between children. For each agonistic interaction, he identified a winner, the child who gained or retained possession of an object or space, and a loser, the child who lost or failed to gain possession of an object or space. From tabulations of dyadic interactions between boys which ended in one winning and one losing, McGrew constructed a male dominance hierarchy. (Girls did not display enough agonistic interactions to permit construction of a female dominance hierarchy.) It can be seen from Figure 2-4 that most of the fights were between the most dominant males, listed in the upper left quadrant, and that boys high in the hierarchy almost always defeated boys lower in the hierarchy, as indicated by the predominance of dots above the diagonal. The dominance rankings also correlated significantly with adults' ratings of the boys' aggressiveness, activity, and sociability.

McGrew interpreted his findings as suggesting the existence of a well-defined dominance structure comparable to those found among nonhuman species. He also analyzed interactions during the formation

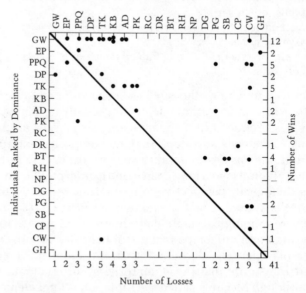

Figure 2-4. Graphic representation of male dominance hierarchy. Each dot represents a dyadic fight over possession. For a child's wins, read across; for a child's losses, read down. (Adapted from McGrew, 1972.)

of the nursery group at the beginning of the school year, changes of behavior after the introduction of a new child, the relation between group density and social behavior, and periodicities (daily, weekly, monthly, yearly) in behavioral changes. Although these analyses revealed a number of suggestive relationships that would probably not be revealed by other approaches, much further work is needed before the generality and significance of these relationships are known.

Infant attachment. Attachment behavior of infants toward their mothers has been the focus of more ethologically guided research and theory than has any other area of human behavior. Unlike McGrew's effort to begin with an ethogram of behavior, most of the work on attachment has been based on deductions from ethologically based theory. John Bowlby (1969, 1973), for example, hypothesizes that human attachment functions in certain ways like imprinting in fowl and even more so like attachment behaviors in nonhuman primates. According to Bowlby, attachment consists of genetically determined behavioral systems which emerge independently of one another but become coordinated so as to promote proximity between the child and a specific mothering person. Two of the behavioral systems—crying and smiling—function as signals that elicit mothering behavior from adults. The other three systems—sucking, following, and clinging—are means by which the child actively attains proximity. In Bowlby's theory, however, attachment refers to more than just the observable attachment behaviors. It refers to the hypothetical construct of an *attachment bond*—the disposition of a child to maintain proximity to a particular person. This disposition is assumed to differ in strength and specificity among individual children and within the same child at different developmental periods. The attachment bond is not merely the sum total of the observed attachment behaviors, but is inferred from the attachment behaviors.

While a child's choice of a person for attachment is environmentally determined by the person's availability and behavior, the attachment behaviors result from an evolutionary history in which these behaviors promoted survival. Unlike the S–R and psychoanalytic drive-reduction theories, both of which ascribe attachment to the secondary reinforcement value a mothering person acquires through reducing primary drives, Bowlby hypothesizes that attachment behavior functions like a *goal-corrected control system.* By this he means that, when threatening stimuli or separation elicit behavior aimed at promoting proximity to the mother, proximity-seeking is terminated by visual, auditory, and/or physical contact with her. Furthermore, the type and intensity of contact needed to terminate proximity-seeking depend upon the intensity with which the behavior system was activated.

Summary

All research is shaped by conceptual paradigms, whether implicit or explicit. *Paradigms* consist of schematic models for representing phenomena and the relations among them, whereas *theories* are designed to provide explanations for particular phenomena. While several theories may share the same general paradigm, the theories may differ in the *hypothetical constructs* they employ. Constructs employed by developmental theories include *drive states, mediating responses, developmental stages, libido,* and *attachment bonds.*

The major paradigms in developmental psychology include the *S–R, organismic–developmental, psychodynamic,* and *ethological* paradigms. While most psychological research now shares the *methodological behaviorism* that originated in the S–R paradigm, the four major paradigms are distinguished by the ways they categorize behavioral phenomena, their models of behavioral change, and the nature of the specific theories based upon them.

S–R theories include *operant conditioning, mediation theory, modeling theory,* and *cumulative–hierarchical* learning theory. The organismic–developmental paradigm is shared by the theories of Gesell, Werner, and Piaget. The psychodynamic paradigm originated with Sigmund Freud's theory of psychosexual development and includes later extensions of it to ego psychology, as well as Erikson's theory of psychosocial development. The ethological paradigm, originating in naturalistic studies of animal behavior, is just beginning to generate specific theories of human behavior, such as Bowlby's theory of infant attachment.

3 Comparison of the Major Viewpoints

THE MAJOR PARADIGMS overlap considerably with respect to the phenomena they focus upon, but differ in the way they portray such phenomena and in the programs of research they imply. It is therefore important to examine their mutual interfaces in the context of actual research. Piagetian theory and Freudian theory, as the most influential versions of the organismic–developmental and psychodynamic paradigms, respectively, will serve as the representatives of these paradigms.

The major viewpoints all concur that both learning from experience and biological factors are important determinants of behavioral development. They also concur that evolution by natural selection has shaped the genetic codes for the biological equipment and principles of learning that characterize each species. However, they disagree about the relative impacts of biological and environmental determinants on behavioral development, about how biological and environmental influences shape development, and about what it is that develops. In some areas, there is essentially no intersection among the viewpoints, either because they deal with different subject matter or because one approach simply precludes issues of interest to another approach. Rather than discussing every aspect of development from each viewpoint, it may therefore be more helpful to begin with a schematic summary of how the viewpoints differ in their fundamental components. Table 3-1 provides such a summary.

The "primary units of data" referred to in Table 3-1 consist of the observations on which each viewpoint rests, although other kinds of data may also be collected to test hypotheses suggested by the viewpoint. Key assumptions about the starting point from which postnatal development begins are summarized as "views of the infant." Sum-

TABLE 3-1. Basic Components of Four Views of Development.

	S-R	Piagetian	Psychoanalytic	Ethological
1. Goals of theory	explain and control behavior	explain the nature and origins of knowledge	explain personality and treat psychopathology	explain adaptive behavior
2. Primary units of data	stimuli, responses, reinforcements	behavioral schemes	free associations, self-reports	fixed action patterns, releasers
3. Views of infant	*tabula rasa*	constructor of knowledge	polymorphously perverse	programed for survival
4. Hypothetical constructs	habits, mediating responses	cognitive schemas, schemes, structures, stages	id, ego, superego, instinctual energies, defense mechanisms, psychosexual and psychosocial stages, fixations	attachment, feedback systems
5. What develops?	stimulus-response associations	schemes, schemas, structures	ego, superego, redistribution of instinctual energies, defense mechanisms, fixations	adaptive behavior
6. Developmental processes	learning	accommodation, assimilation, equilibration, organization	channeling of instinctual energies	genetic programing, environmental releasers
7. Determinants of greatest interest	environmental contingencies	maturation, experience, social transmission, equilibration	instinctual impulses, innate ego potentialities, id-reality conflicts	natural selection
8. Predominant research strategies	extrapolate from responses made to experimental manipulations	infer structures and mechanisms of change from reactions to cognitive challenges	infer unconscious influences from clinical observations	describe behavior in natural environs and infer adaptive functions

marizing the S–R view as "tabula rasa" means only that the primary focus is upon how input from the environment causes behavioral change, not that there are no biological factors in development. Likewise, summarizing the psychoanalytic view of the infant as "polymorphously perverse" (Freud, 1905) reflects the assumption that the infant seeks direct and immediate gratification of his instinctual impulses, unmodulated by reality, guilt, or past learning. Development then consists largely of rechanneling the unmodulated instinctual impulses through a succession of biologically determined foci, on the one hand, and through environmentally influenced modes and modalities of behavior, on the other. Most analysts also credit the infant with innate potentialities for the development of ego functions such as thinking, language, and memory. The other categories in Table 3-1 are self-explanatory.

Research Intersects of the Paradigms

Paradigms are too often treated by their adherents and opponents alike as if they were independent languages, unrelated to the languages embodied in other paradigms. Yet, excessive separation among paradigms can prevent findings and methods evolved within one paradigm from being used by adherents of other paradigms. As aids to the search for knowledge, paradigms are most useful when viewed in terms of their relative advantages and disadvantages for representing particular phenomena. The most creative research is often that which combines aspects of two or more paradigms into a new and more productive synthesis. The following studies illustrate the ways in which different paradigms intersect in actual research and some of the problems encountered in such research.

S–R and Piagetian Theory: Attempts to Train Conservation

Piaget's early books (e.g., 1928) on children's concepts of the physical and social worlds earned him an international reputation by 1930. Yet in the United States, Piaget received little notice between the early 1930s and the late 1950s. This was probably because the dominant S–R methodology precluded approaches that either relied as much on "clinical" questioning or focused as much on mental processes as did Piaget's. However, the rebirth of cognitive psychology during the late 1950s rekindled interest in Piaget's work. By this time, Piaget had moved beyond the "clinical method" for studying children's thinking and beyond his early impression that mental development consisted largely of a decline in egocentrism as a result of social interaction and the learning of language.

By the late 1950s, Piaget had not only evolved much of his theory of cognitive development, but had also published a great deal of research on children's responses to tasks designed to test deductions from his theory. Administered according to what Piaget christened the "revised clinical method," these tasks employ standardized materials and procedures which the experimenter supplements with flexible questioning to obtain the fullest possible picture of the child's thinking. Although Piaget's work recaptured the interest of American psychologists, many of his findings were attributed to artifacts of his methods. Consequently, replication studies were undertaken to verify the findings, especially with respect to conservation (e.g., Elkind, 1961). In most cases, these studies confirmed that children failed to conserve until surprisingly late ages, even when rigorous methodology and simplified questioning were employed.

Once the basic findings were replicated, S–R psychologists focused on *why* children failed such seemingly simple tasks. While children's failures to conserve are of much greater importance to Piagetian theory than to S–R theory, the emergence of conservation in a stage-like fashion posed a challenge for S–R explanations of behavioral development. As a result, numerous attempts were made to demonstrate that conservation could be trained. From the S–R point of view, if children who failed conservation problems could be taught correct responses, this would show that conservation was merely an outcome of learning, rather than reflecting a "stage" of development.

Training studies have also been inspired by two other goals. One was to answer what Piaget has called "the American Question," because so many Americans ask it: "Even if there are developmental stages, how can we speed them up?" The other goal was to elucidate the transition to concrete operational thought by finding out what could and could not be taught and what behaviors had to be present before others could be taught. The latter strategy is of interest to developmental researchers of many persuasions, including Piaget, because it employs research on learning as a tool for exploring the ways in which development may proceed. Several studies have demonstrated that children can indeed be trained to give correct answers to conservation problems. However, teaching a child to say "same" rather than "more" when he is asked to compare a perceptually transformed quantity to an untransformed quantity does not meet a very stringent criterion for conservation. According to Piaget, the more critical issues concern the persistence of the child's answers long after training, his logical explanations for conservation, and the transfer of his conservation responses to new stimulus materials.

An S–R training study. In one of the few S–R training studies to meet Piaget's criteria for conservation, Gelman (1969) hypothesized that children fail to conserve because they rely on irrelevant cues while ignoring the relevant quantitative attributes. Consequently, she predicted that reinforcing children for attending to the relevant quantitative attributes and for ignoring irrelevant cues would induce conservation. As a test of this hypothesis, kindergarteners who failed tests of length, number, substance, and liquid conservation were trained to discriminate lengths and numbers. This was done by presenting each child with discrimination learning problems involving three stimuli, one of which differed quantitatively from the other two. For example, one row of three chips was presented with two rows of five each, and one 10-inch stick was presented with two 6-inch sticks. The experimenter rearranged the stimuli from trial to trial as done in conservation problems, e.g., by stretching out one row of chips.

On half the trials, the child was asked to point to two stimuli that were the same; on the other half, he was asked to point to two that were different, *viz.*, the odd stimulus and either one of the others. Correct responses were rewarded with a trinket. By being thus reinforced, the child was expected to learn a set to discriminate relevant quantitative attributes from irrelevant transformations of stimuli. In order to ascertain the effect of reinforcing attention to the quantitative properties, Gelman included two control groups. Children in one control group received the same procedure as the experimental group, but no reinforcement or feedback as to the correctness of their responses. The second control group received a similar procedure except that the odd stimulus on each trial differed from the other two in *shape* rather than length or number and the children were reinforced for discriminating among the shapes.

All children were retested on conservation of length, number, substance, and liquid quantity immediately after training and again two to three weeks later. On both the immediate and the delayed post-training test, the trained children gave far more correct conservation reponses than either of the control groups. Furthermore, among children who gave correct answers, more trained than control children gave logical *explanations* for conservation, e.g., "they're the same because nothing has been added or taken away." The predictions from the S–R hypothesis were thus borne out—nonconserving children could be trained to attend to quantitative properties while disregarding irrelevant cues; when they were so trained, their conservation performance and explanations improved greatly; the improvement generalized to properties that had not been trained; and the improvement lasted for at least two to three weeks after training.

But did this prove that conservation is merely an outcome of training rather than being dependent upon cognitive stages? Gelman herself argued against this interpretation on the grounds that the children's improvement was so rapid as to suggest that training merely provided feedback about the conservation task requirements—in effect, training told the children to respond to quantitative invariance rather than teaching them what it was. Thus, the improvement in conservation may have occurred because the children were induced to apply cognitive structures they already possessed.

This explanation becomes especially compelling when it is noted that the trained subjects were from upper middle class homes (Gelman, 1967) and had a median age of 64.5 months. Although IQ scores were not reported, the mean IQs of upper-middle-class children are typically in the 115 to 120 range. Assuming the mean to be 115, the mean mental age of the children was 1.15 × 64.5 months = 74 months, not far below the mean chronological age of about 7 years typically cited by Piaget for conservation by Swiss children. Other successful efforts to train conservation explanations, transfer to other stimuli, and persistence on delayed post-tests have also employed children with mental ages of 6 or higher (e.g., Hamel and Riksen, 1973).

A Piagetian training study. The finding that children can be induced to give conservation responses is not necessarily incompatible with Piaget's theory of stage-like changes in cognitive organization. Piaget (1974) has himself cited with approval certain studies in which conservation was trained. In these studies, the training procedures were designed to induce disequilibrium in nonconservers' concepts of quantity by demonstrating contradictions between the children's expectations about what happens to quantities when they undergo various perceptual transformations. For example, in a study by Piaget's coworkers, Inhelder, Sinclair, and Bovet (1974), equal quantities of colored liquid were poured into the containers A and A' pictured in Figure 3-1. Children were then asked to allow an equal amount of liquid to flow from containers A and A' into containers B and B'. Nonconserving children—equating amount with level in the container—allowed containers B and B' to fill to the same level, thus leaving some liquid in container A'. They then expected the quantities from B and B' to fill containers C and C' to the same level.

Inhelder et al. hypothesized that the discrepancy between the children's expectations of equality in C and C' and their observations of the contrast in levels to which C and C' were filled would create a disequilibrium in their thinking. The disequilibrium could be resolved by noticing that the quantity missing from C' was still in A' and then recognizing that the total quantity remained the same regardless of the perceptual transformations. To further help the child recognize the conservation of quantity, he was also asked to compare the flow of liquid from A to C and A' to C' when B and B' were hidden by a screen. It was expected that, when the child saw that the quantities from A and A' remained equal, he would begin to subordinate perceptual changes to the conservation principle that quantity does not change unless something is added or taken away. Post-training tests of conservation revealed little progress in children who had consistently failed pretests of conservation, but much progress in children who initially vacillated between conservation and nonconservation. It was therefore concluded that training *could* induce conservation, but only in children who already had rudimentary operational structures.

Surprise and eye movements as indices of cognitive structures. While the success in training children who seem cognitively advanced is compatible with Piaget's view, further research is needed to empirically delineate the cognitive structures Piaget hypothesizes to be necessary for successful training. A training study by Wilton and Boersma (1974) suggests how this might be done. In this study, not only were children's judgments and explanations for conservation scored,

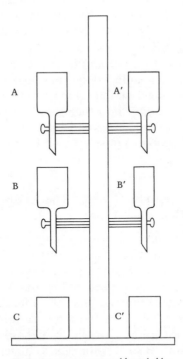

Figure 3-1. Apparatus used by Inhelder, Sinclair, and Bovet (1974) for training conservation of liquid quantity.

but their reactions to contrived violations of number and length conservation were judged for surprise, and their eye movements toward the stimuli were photographed with a special camera. Number conservation was violated by surreptitious addition of chips to one row as it was spread out for comparison with another; for length, a strip of cardboard was surreptitiously lengthened as it was moved for comparison with another strip.

Natural conservers and nonconservers successfully trained with Gelman's (1969) procedure were surprised at the contrived violations and their eye movements showed systematic scanning of the stimuli. By contrast, untrained nonconservers were not surprised at the violations and their eyes tended to fixate or "center" on the larger-appearing stimulus. Children who received training but still failed the conservation tests were intermediate between untrained and successfully trained children with respect to surprise and systematic scanning. This suggests that surprise and systematic scanning may reflect a rudimentary awareness of conservation that precedes correct performance on standard conservation tasks. If this is indeed the case, then a test of Piaget's hypothesis that initial level of cognitive organization determines the outcome of training could be made by comparing the effects of training on children who initially show neither surprise to conservation violations nor systematic scanning, and on those who do show surprise and/or scanning indicative of more advanced cognitive organization.

In sum, while S–R training studies have demonstrated that conservation responses can be induced in some children, their findings also seem consistent with Piaget's contention that learning is constrained by cognitive development. On the other hand, such studies have contributed to a clearer empirical focus and methodology which can be used to operationalize Piagetian constructs and to test the processes he hypothesizes.

S–R and Psychoanalytic Theory: The Existence and Etiology of Psychoanalytic Character Types

Although psychoanalytic concepts have generated a good deal of research, the theory rests primarily upon inferences from clinical observations of patients during therapy. Since Freud himself did not treat children, the developmental aspects of his theory were derived largely from his patients' recollections of their childhoods. As a consequence, one line of research has been directed at determining whether character traits cluster as predicted by Freud's hypotheses about various psychosexual fixations and, if so, whether such clusters are correlated with the childhood experiences hypothesized to cause the fixations.

One of the most intensively studied personality clusters is that of the anal character, described by Freud (1908) in terms of the *anal triad* of traits—obstinacy, parsimony, and orderliness. Freud hypothesized that the anal character results from the repression and sublimation of anal erotic impulses in reaction to conflicts over toilet training. As Freud saw it, excessively early or severe toilet training or unusually great pleasure in bowel functioning can lead to a fixation on anal eroticism. The anal personality traits then develop as defenses against this eroticism.

An S–R study of the anal character.   Noblin, Timmons, and Kael (1966) used operant conditioning to test the psychoanalytic hypothesis that anal personalities are more resistant to the influence of authority figures than are oral personalities, whom Freud described as being dependent, compliant, and submissive. On the basis of their reponses to the Blacky Test, an objectively scored projective test, college students were selected who had either anal or oral personalities. Half the students of each type then received operant conditioning with favorable comments as reinforcers and half with negative comments as reinforcers.

Each subject was given 120 cards on which were printed one first- and one third-person pronoun, plus sentence fragments that could be completed using either type of pronoun. The subject was to read each sentence fragment aloud, completing it with whichever pronoun he chose. The first 30 cards served as a baseline measure of the subject's spontaneous use of the two classes of pronouns. On the next 60 cards, for half the subjects the experimenter made mild affirmatory responses (e.g., "um-hmm") to 75 percent of the cards on which the subject made a "correct" choice. (Without their knowledge, half these subjects were being reinforced for using first-person pronouns and half for third-person pronouns.) The other half of the subjects received negative comments (e.g., "um-no") according to the same pattern as the subjects receiving positive comments. The final 30 cards constituted an extinction phase during which no reinforcements were given.

As Figure 3-2 shows, the oral subjects increased their "correct" responses when receiving favorable comments and decreased them when receiving negative comments, while anal subjects showed exactly the reverse pattern. These results thus supported the hypothesis that oral and anal personalities respond oppositely to inputs from authority figures. In addition, they indicate that what is a positive reinforcer for one type of person can be a negative reinforcer for another.

Development of the anal character.   If there is indeed a cluster of traits corresponding to Freud's description of the anal character, the critical developmental question is whether this cluster *results* from a fixation on anal eroticism arising during toilet training. To answer this question, data are required from the period of toilet training as well as

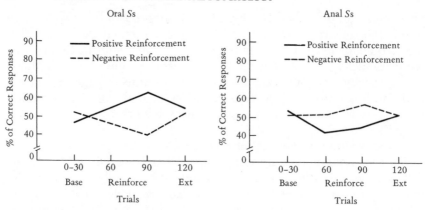

Figure 3-2. The opposite effects of positive and negative comments on responses by oral and anal subjects. (Adapted from Noblin, Timmons, and Kael, 1966.)

from later developmental periods when the hypothesized rechanneling of anal erotic impulses into character traits has already occurred. In one attempt to answer the developmental question, graduate students filled out a questionnaire test of anal traits and their mothers were interviewed to obtain toilet training data (Beloff, 1957). Because there was no correlation between the students' scores and severity of training, Beloff rejected the psychoanalytic hypothesis as to etiology.

Although her data are not very persuasive against the psychoanalytic hypothesis, Beloff reported a further finding that suggests an alternative explanation of the etiology of anal traits: She found that the students' scores on the anality questionnaire correlated significantly with their mothers' scores on the same questionnaire. Taking a social learning theory approach, Hetherington and Brackbill (1963) interpreted Beloff's finding as indicating that identification with the parent and direct learning via parental rewards and punishments may be more influential in the formation of anal traits than is toilet training per se. Toilet training may, in fact, be no more influential than numerous other learning situations in which the child's behavior is shaped by the socialization practices of his parents.

To test their hypothesis, Hetherington and Brackbill constructed ten behavioral measures for 5-year-old children and a questionnaire for measuring the parsimony, orderliness, and obstinacy, as well as the toilet training practices, of the children's parents. Four of the children's measures were designed to measure obstinacy, as manifested in stubborn persistence at monotonous tasks and resistance to changing a response despite its increasing inappropriateness and pressure from an adult experimenter. There were three measures of parsimony, one obtained by giving each child ten pennies and observing how many he later donated in response to a moving appeal for contributions; the second consisted of the number of crayons shared with classmates who had none; and the third was the amount of useless gravel the child hoarded when given free access to it over a one-week period. The measures of orderliness consisted of the number of symmetrical inkblots each child chose in preference to asymmetrical inkblots in ten pairs; ratings of how neat each child kept his nursery school locker; and ratings of how clean each child attempted to remain while finger painting.

The intercorrelations among tasks were found to differ for the boys and girls. This may have been an important finding in its own right which points up a flaw in the studies cited above—they did not include separate analyses for each sex and, in some cases (e.g., Noblin et al., 1966), did not even report the sex of their subjects! The correlations among various measures of each trait and correlations among the total scores for the three traits were higher and more consistently positive for girls than for boys. Since the correlations of the three traits measured by questionnaires were also higher for mothers than for fathers, this suggests that there are persistent sex differences in the patterning of these traits.

For the girls and their mothers, total scores for obstinacy and parsimony correlated significantly with total scores for orderliness, although the correlations of obstinacy with parsimony were not significant. For the boys and their fathers, there were no significant correlations between obstinacy, orderliness, and parsimony. In fact, two of the three correlations for the boys and one of the three for their fathers were negative. Thus, insofar as there was any clustering of anal traits, it occurred only for females and was significant only with respect to the correlations of obstinacy and parsimony with orderliness.

As to the etiology of the anal traits, no significant correlations were found for either sex between age of beginning, time to complete, or age of completion of toilet training, on the one hand, and the three traits, on the other. A significant correlation was found between severity of toilet training and a composite score for the anal traits among girls, but, being negative, this correlation contradicted the Freudian hypothesis that severe training intensifies the traits.

The learning theory hypothesis received some support in that 9 of the 16 correlations between mothers' and daughters' scores for obstinacy, orderliness, parsimony, and a composite of the three were significant. The boys' scores, however, showed no more than chance correlations with their parents' scores. Further analysis revealed a positive correlation of .35 between the composite trait scores for fathers and sons from father-dominated homes and a negative correlation of −.36 between scores of fathers and sons from mother-dominated homes. Although neither was significant, these correlations did suggest that boys learned personality traits from their fathers only in homes where the father was the dominant parent.

In summary, there appeared to be a clustering of anal traits only in females and no support for the hypothesis that extreme toilet training intensifies such traits. The alternative hypothesis that anal traits are learned from parents received support for girls, but, at best, only suggestive support for boys. From the psychoanalytic viewpoint, the study can be criticized for not taking account of individual differences in instinctually based anal eroticism that might determine the impact of training. However, since three of the eight correlations between training indices and children's personality traits were negative, training practices per se seemed not to have played the role predicted from analytic theory. While contradicting Freud's hypothesis, the moderate evidence in favor of the S–R hypothesis is quite compatible with the views of neo-Freudians such as Fromm (1947), who hypothesized that the "hoarding" character, similar to the anal character, is a product of general socialization experiences rather than of repressed anal eroticism.

S–R and Ethological Theory: The Effect of Maternal Responsiveness on Infant Crying

One of the few areas in which the S–R and ethological approaches have been empirically compared is that of mother–infant interactions. Based largely on the S–R views of J. B. Watson, child-care manuals for many years admonished mothers that picking up a baby whenever he cried would teach him "that crying will get him what he wants, sufficient to make a spoiled, fussy baby, and a household tyrant whose continual demands make a slave of the mother" (U.S. Children's Bureau, 1924, p. 44). While couched in more sophisticated language, later S–R theory concurred that the frequency of an infant's crying could, like any other response, be increased if it were reinforced with attention. According to ethological theory, however, infant crying is an innately determined attachment behavior which functions to maintain proximity to the mother. Genetic selection for crying is hypothesized to have occurred because infants who maintained the proximity of their mothers through crying were more likely to survive the dangers of predators, cold, and hunger.

Taking an ethological approach, Bell and Ainsworth (1972) longitudinally studied the relations between mothers' responsiveness to crying and later rates of crying in their infants. S–R theories would predict that maternal responsiveness to crying early in infancy should increase crying later in infancy. By contrast, the ethological view implies that consistent success in bringing the mother should reduce crying, because the proximity-maintaining function of the crying is successfully fulfilled. In the Bell–Ainsworth study, 26 mother–infant pairs were observed in their homes at three-week intervals throughout the first year of life. The observers noted the frequency and duration of crying, the number of cries ignored by the mothers, and the length of time the baby cried without obtaining a response from the mother. Scores were computed for each quarter of the year by averaging scores obtained during the four visits in the quarter.

It was found that individual infants were highly variable in the frequency and duration of their cries, but that each infant's crying tended to stabilize during the last six months of the first year. This was reflected in the fact that the only significant correlations between crying from one quarter to the next were between the third and fourth quarters, where the correlation for frequency was .43 and for duration .39. In contrast to the lack of stability in infant crying, the percentage of cries ignored by each mother and the duration of each mother's unresponsiveness to crying were quite stable over the entire year. Nearly all correlations of these variables from one quarter to all the succeeding quarters were significant. The greater stability of mothers' than of infants' behavior suggested that mothers' responsiveness to crying was determined more by individual differences among the mothers themselves than by differences in the infants to whom they were responding.

The long-term effect of maternal responsiveness was assessed by calculating correlations between the percentage of crying episodes ignored by each mother in the first, second, and third quarter, and the frequency of her infant's crying in each of the succeeding quarters. Table 3-2 shows that all 12 correlations between mothers' behavior in a quarter and infants' crying during the next quarter were positive, eight of them significantly so. Thus, mothers who were *most unresponsive* to their children's crying in early quarters had children who cried the most in later quarters.

TABLE 3-2.   Relations between Mother's Unresponsiveness and Child's Crying in Successive Quarters.[a]

Child's Crying	Mother's Unresponsiveness					
	1st Quarter		*2nd Quarter*		*3rd Quarter*	
2nd Quarter	.56	.45				
3rd Quarter	.21	.40	.39	.42		
4th Quarter	.20	.32	.36	.65	.52	.51

Data from Bell and Ainsworth (1972).
[a]Correlations on left side of each cell are between crying episodes ignored by mother and frequency of crying by infant; those on right side of each cell are between duration of mother's unresponsiveness and duration of child's crying. All correlations ≥ .39 are significant.

Although the evidence certainly contradicts the admonition against responding to babies' crying, Bell and Ainsworth acknowledged that crying may be extinguished when it is completely unsuccessful in eliciting attention, as occurs in institutional environments where babies soon become quiet and apathetic. More detailed S–R analyses also suggest that maternal unresponsiveness of the mild to moderate degree observed by Bell and Ainsworth may create a schedule of intermittent reinforcement whereby the child receives reinforcement to only some of his cries, especially those of long duration (cf. Maccoby and Masters, 1970). Since intermittent reinforcement is known to make responses exceptionally resistant to extinction, this might explain the increase in crying by infants with relatively unresponsive mothers. However, mothers' responses increased from a mean of 54 per cent of crying episodes in the first quarter to 63 percent in the fourth quarter. Since the percentage of "reinforcement" was thus increasing rather than decreasing, no extinction conditions were being instituted and the potentially greater resistance to extinction caused by intermittent reinforcement does not seem relevant. Neither the decline in mean crying duration from 7.7 minutes per hour in the first quarter to 4.4 minutes in the fourth quarter nor the increases in crying by infants of unresponsive mothers seem easily explainable in terms of S–R theory.

Piagetian and Psychoanalytic Theory: Development of the Object Concept and Object Relations in Infancy

Since they both portray development in terms of stages, while focusing on the cognitive and affective aspects of development, respectively, it would seem natural for the Piagetian and psychoanalytic theories to be brought together in developmental research. However, there has been little research designed to relate them empirically. In one of the few existing studies, Décarie (1965) constructed a scale of infant test items designed to measure development of the "object concept" as portrayed in Piaget's theory and a second scale designed to measure development of "object relations" as portrayed in psychoanalytic theory. She then employed the items of both scales to test children at the ages of 3, 6, 9, 12, 16, and 20 months, 15 at each age.

Measurement of the object concept. The object concept scale consisted of tasks designed by Piaget to trace the infant's progress during the sensory-motor period from a lack of any concept of external objects to a mental representation of objects that permits inferences about their locations even when they have undergone a sequence of hidden displacements. The items of the scale are outlined in Table 3-3. For all 90 subjects, the patterns of successes and failures were found to conform to

TABLE 3-3. Décarie's (1965) Object Concept Scale.

1. Child visually searches for a ball dropped in front of him.
2. Child continues to reach for object after it has been partially hidden.
3. Child actively searches for an object after it has been completely hidden.
4. After seeing object placed under one screen and removed to a second screen, child searches under the first screen and then under the second.
5. Same as in Item 4, except that child searches immediately under second screen without looking under the first.
6. Examiner shows child safety pins in a box, dumps the pins out behind a screen, places the empty box within child's reach, and asks, "Where are the pins?" Child scored as passing if he searches for pins under the screen.
7. Same as Item 6, except that box is placed beneath one screen and then visibly moved to a second screen, where pins are removed. Child scored as passing if he searches under second screen without searching under first screen.
8. Examiner places hand containing small doll under each of three screens in succession, showing doll after first and second screens and empty hand after third. Child scored as passing if he searches only under the third screen.

Piaget's theory of an invariant developmental sequence—i.e., no subject passed an advanced item while failing a less advanced one.

Measurement of object relations. While Piaget's theory refers to the concept of physical objects, the psychoanalytic theory of object relations refers to emotional investments in things other than the self. The emphasis in psychoanalytic theory is upon the development of affectionate feelings—known as *libidinal cathexes*—toward people, but the concept of object relations is restricted neither to positive feelings nor to feelings directed toward people. Because psychoanalytic writings on object relations have been so diverse and have been based neither on consistent definitions nor upon operational measures, Décarie attempted to base her scale on the hypotheses of a few orthodox Freudian analysts. The measures she chose are outlined in Table 3-4.

Unfortunately, even when the theoretical basis was limited to the work of a few analysts, the lack of clearly specified behavioral distinctions between such aspects of cathexis as the libidinal and aggressive, and between stages of development made it impossible to operationally define stages in terms of expected levels of performance on the measures. Furthermore, unlike Piaget's theory, psychoanalytic theory does not imply an invariant ordering of performance, because deviations can be interpreted as pathological aberrations rather than as violations of a necessary developmental sequence. However, Décarie did identify three series of items which the theory implies should emerge in invariant order. For example, because cathexis of persons should pre-

TABLE 3-4. Décarie's (1965) Object Relations Scale.

1. When put in feeding position, child shows anticipatory reactions, e.g., opening mouth, turning head, sucking.
2. Child smiles to mother and/or examiner in response to their smiles.
3. Child smiles to mother but not to unfamiliar examiner.
4. Child stops crying for at least 30 seconds when he sees mother.
5. Child reacts positively to mother playing with him and negatively when she stops.
6. Child reacts negatively when toy is taken from him.
7. Child actively responds to mother's request for kiss or hug.
8. Child gives up objects when asked to do so.
9. Child complies with prohibition against taking attractive objects.
10. Child reacts positively to mother clapping and saying, "Oh . . . oh . . . oh," in an astonished and joyful voice.
11. Child reacts negatively to mother frowning, shaking finger threateningly, and saying, "Tut . . . tut . . . tut."

cede cathexis of inanimate objects, negative reactions to an interruption of play with the mother should be observed before negative reactions to loss of a toy. Nevertheless, no clearcut support was obtained for any of the three sequences, partly because of frequent deviations from the implied order and partly because the range of item difficulty did not permit a decisive test of the sequence.

Décarie had hoped to assess the relation between the Piagetian object concept scale and the psychoanalytic object relations scale by calculating the correlations between the highest level achieved on each of them. Because 46 of the 90 children failed items considered to come earlier on the object relations scale than items passed, overall scores for these children were obtained by having three people rate the level of attainment suggested by the children's patterns of successes and failures. The averages of the three ratings were then correlated with scores on the Piagetian scale. The correlation between the object concept scores and the object relations scores was found to be .82, indicating a high degree of relationship.

Since the two scales correlated .86 and .79, respectively, with chronological age, and .92 and .86, respectively, with mental age on an infant ability test, it is possible that their correlation with one another may have resulted from their mutual correlations with general developmental level. If this were the case, would the significant relationship between the object concept scale and the object relations scale tell us anything about the relationship between cognitive and affective development per se?

The answer to this question depends upon the degree to which the theories of cognitive and affective development uniquely dictate the particular measures employed and predict particular relationships among them. If all theories imply the same measures and the same relationships among them, no particular theory is supported by confirmation of the relationships. In Décarie's study, the Piagetian measures were taken directly from Piaget's work. Moreover, not only the prediction of a unique ordering of successes, but the surprising nature of some of the predicted behaviors—e.g., the child's searching under a screen where an object was previously found rather than where he saw it being hidden—add to the power of the object concept scale as a test of Piagetian theory. Complete confirmation of the ordering of successes and the appearance of the surprising behaviors both lend specific support for Piagetian theory.

The situation is more problematic with respect to the object relations scale. Previous psychoanalytic work provided neither specific measures nor specific definitions on which to base an object relations scale. Décarie was forced to make many interpretations from inconsistent writings by one group of analysts while ignoring others who had written on the same topic. Once she had selected measures of the variables portrayed in psychoanalytic theory, considerable ambiguity remained as to what relationships among them would support or contradict the theory. Décarie's rather arbitrary identification of three series of items that might be expected to be mastered in invariant order did not provide so strong a test of the theory that disconfirmation of the order can be taken as contradicting the theory. Although disconfirming results are often interpreted as indicating flaws in procedure rather than flaws in a theory, it is not clear in the present case that *confirming* results would uniquely *support* the theory any more than the disconfirming results contradict it. Thus, while the substantial correlation of the affective measures with the Piagetian scale, chronological age, and the infant ability scale suggest that affective development is closely related to other aspects of development, the nature of psychoanalytic theory makes it difficult to conclude anything about the theory of object relations per se.

Piagetian and Ethological Theory: Relations between Person Permanence, Object Permanence, and Infant–Mother Attachment

Furth (1974) has attempted to clarify the different roles ascribed to experience in different theories by distinguishing between (a) *species experience* derived from aspects of the environment that are *typical* for members of a species, and (b) *individual experience* derived from the *particular* environmental contingencies encountered by individual organisms. S–R theories generally make no distinction between species and individual experience, and they tend to explain all behavioral change as if it resulted from individual experience. Piagetian and ethological theory, on the other hand, are both concerned with species experience. The ethological view is that species experience has its effects mainly through natural selection, thus determining the individual's behavioral organization by means of heredity.

The Piagetian view is that species experience has its organizing effect as much during the development of each individual as during phylogeny, because behavioral organizations are constructed by each individual around materials provided in his species-typical environment. Although Piaget maintains that the general sequence of development will be similar in all members of a species possessing the same genetic dispositions and living in environments that possess the same basic properties (e.g., three-dimensional objects), he credits experience deriving from particular environmental contingencies with playing an important role in certain aspects of development.

In one of the few studies relating Piagetian and ethological theory, Bell (1970) tested Piaget's (1954) suggestion that, because of the great saliency of human caretakers, infants typically develop a concept of person permanence prior to a concept of object permanence. This developmental disparity between the concept of independently existing humans and of inanimate objects is an example of what Piaget calls a horizontal décalage—a lag between the ages at which a particular concept (that of the permanent object in this case) comes to be applied to different types of content. (Piaget's contrasting term vertical décalage refers to a lag between the development of different levels of thought, rather than the application of a particular concept to different contents.)

In Piaget's view, the concepts of object and person permanence originate in the interaction between genetically guided maturation and experience with objects and people, but specific environmental variations can affect the rate at which these two variants of the object concept emerge. While Piaget thus acknowledges that environmental variations can contribute to horizontal décalages, he denies that environmental variations can affect the ordering of vertical décalages. Because each successive level of thought is constructed from the previous level, no levels can be skipped or interchanged.

To determine whether there is a décalage between object and person permanence, Bell tested 33 infants at 8 months of age, again one week later to obtain a reliability check, and again at 11 months of age. The tests for object permanence assessed the infants' responses to the partial and complete covering of objects and to the movement of objects from one hiding place to another. Tests for the concept of person permanence were exactly parallel to those for object permanence, with the mother being the person hidden and screens mounted on wheels being used to hide her. Babies were given credit if they reached toward the appropriate screen. Of the 33 infants tested, 23 obtained more advanced scores on person permanence than on object permanence, while seven showed a *décalage* in the opposite direction, and three showed no significant differences. Thus, person permanence usually, though not always, preceded object permanence.

Attachment behavior and the 'décalage'. Granted that species experience common to all the babies was responsible for the eventual development of object and person permanence, what aspects of individual experience could account for the individual differences in the sequence of object and person permanence? Bell hypothesized that the *décalage* in favor of person permanence would be related to the security of the infant's attachment to his mother, with securely attached infants being most likely to show the *décalage*. Furthermore, Bell hypothesized that mothers' behavior toward their babies could be responsible for differences in security of attachment.

To test these hypotheses, the 33 infants were observed through one-way mirrors following brief separation episodes in an experimental room. On the basis of their attempts to maintain contact, proximity, and/or interaction with their mothers, the infants were classified into three groups: Group A comprised five babies who showed little attachment behavior and actively avoided their mothers during reunion episodes; Group B comprised 24 babies who showed strong attachment behaviors following separation; and Group C comprised four babies who did not explore the environment prior to separation, seemed upset by the situation itself, and seemed ambivalent upon reunion with their mothers. Group B babies were considered to be securely attached, while Groups A and C were not.

A strong relationship was found between security of attachment and the precedence of person permanence over object permanence: All 23 of the babies who were more advanced in person permanence were from Group B, while the remaining Group B baby showed no difference between person and object permanence. By contrast, four of the Group A babies and three of the Group C babies were more advanced in object than person permanence, while the other baby in each of these groups showed no difference between object and person permanence.

To determine whether environmental conditions influenced security of attachment, and, in turn, the *décalage* between person and object permanence, Bell compared interview and observational data from the mothers of each group of babies. Whereas the groups did not differ in amount of experience with hide-and-seek games resembling the person permanence tests, mothers of the babies who were advanced in person permanence took their babies on more frequent outings, had fewer daily separations from them, commented more on their babies' positive features, and never showed physical rejection or mistreatment of their babies, in contrast to mothers of the other babies. It thus appeared that differences in maternal behavior could ultimately be responsible for the differences in rate of development of person permanence, although development of object permanence did not seem to be similarly affected. The general Piagetian model for the development of person and object permanence was upheld, but the classification of children as to attachment behavior contributed a great deal to the overall picture of relations between socially oriented behaviors and what Piaget has portrayed primarily as cognitive achievements.

Psychoanalytic and Ethological Theory: The Development of Attachment Behavior

In several of his works, Freud proposed that the infant's relationship with his mother is based on dependency, or, in Freud's (1914) own term, it is *anaclitic* (from the Greek *anaklinein*, "to lean upon"). By this Freud meant that the libidinal investment the infant makes in his mother arises from his dependency on her for feeding and protection. In his final work, Freud (1940) reiterated that "love has its origin in attachment to the satisfied need for nourishment" (p. 45). However, he also stated that:

> . . . the phylogenetic foundation has so much the upper hand over personal accidental experience that it makes no difference whether a child has really sucked at the breast or has been brought up on the bottle and never enjoyed the tenderness of a mother's care. In both cases the child's development takes the same path; it may be that in the second case its later longing grows all the greater. (pp. 45–46)

From the contrasting implications of the first and second statements have arisen two different psychoanalytic hypotheses regarding the development of object relations. One hypothesis is held by analysts who stress that the development of object relations is linked to the development of ego functions (e.g., A. Freud, 1965; Hartmann, Kris, and Loewenstein, 1946). Their hypothesis, implied in Freud's first statement, is that the infant becomes attached to his mother *because* she gratifies his basic needs. Like drive-reduction learning theory, this hypothesis holds that the mother becomes discriminated, mentally represented, and desired by the infant because of her repeated association with reduction of primary drives. In learning theory terms, the infant acquires a *learned* or *secondary drive* to be with his mother as a result of her association with primary drive reduction.

The contrasting hypothesis, implied in Freud's second statement and adopted by psychoanalytic object relations theorists (e.g., Fairbairn, 1952), holds that instinctual drives are innately focused toward human objects. While this position implies that the selection of an attachment object does not result from secondary reinforcement, it does retain the concept of instinctual drive as a motivator of attachment behavior.

In his ethologically based theory, Bowlby (1969, 1973)—originally a psychoanalyst of the object-relations school—has rejected both types of drive reduction as explanations for attachment. Instead, he depicts attachment in terms of a behavior control system innately programmed so that increases in distance from the attachment object elicit attachment behavior directed at restoring proximity. Primary drives are thus unnecessary for either the establishment or maintenance of attachment behavior. Because ethical constraints preclude experimental man-ipulation of human infant care to determine whether the feeding situ-ation is indeed the source of infant attachment, Bowlby supports his hypothesis largely with evidence from animal experiments. Many studies have shown that imprinting in fowl occurs independently of feeding, but two findings with primates appear more relevant to human behavior. One is Harlow's (1961) finding that rhesus monkeys fed from a nipple mounted on a wire imitation "mother" spent most of their time clinging to a nonfeeding cloth "mother" and became anxious when she was removed, even though the wire mother remained.

While it might be hypothesized that the cloth mother reduced a primary drive for tactile stimulation that was less easily satisfied than the hunger drive, a second finding provides further evidence against the drive reduction theory: This finding was that even when "mothers" were sources of severe punishment, infant monkeys showed strong attachment behavior toward them. In an experiment by Rosenblum and Harlow (1963), the "mothers" were terrycloth imitations equipped with nozzles through which compressed air could be blasted. A buzzer warned of each impending blast, but, rather than leave their "mothers," the infants clung more tightly, thereby suffering intense blasts on the face and belly. In another experiment, infant monkeys continued to seek contact with monkey mothers who, themselves reared without mothers, violently abused their infants and showed no positive behavior toward them (Seay, Alexander, and Harlow, 1964). Attachment behavior toward mother-like objects thus persisted despite punishment and a total lack of nurturance.

The Schaffer and Emerson study.   The closest approach to a test of the secondary drive hypothesis with humans has been through com-parison of attachment toward primary and nonprimary caregivers. Schaffer and Emerson (1964) carried out a longitudinal study of attach-ment behavior by interviewing the mothers of 60 infants at four-week intervals. In each interview, the mothers were questioned about their child's protest behavior in well-defined situations, such as being left alone in a room and being put down after being held.

On the basis of the interview material, each child was scored for intensity of attachment and the number of people who evoked separation protests. Since the primary data were obtained through interviews rather than direct observations, the interview data were checked by comparing mothers' reports with observations of their children's behavior in separation situations arising spontaneously while the interviewer was present. In addition, a separation situation—having the child remain with a stranger while the mother left the room—was enacted after the mother's final report had been obtained. Because there was 92 percent agreement between mothers' reports and the spontaneous observations, and 89 percent agreement between mothers' reports and behavior in the contrived separation situation, it was concluded that the mothers' reports were reasonably valid.

The interviewer also assessed fear of strangers at the beginning of each home visit. Each child's fear responses were scored as the interviewer first remained motionless in the child's presence and then gradually increased his overtures until he picked up the child and sat him on his knee.

Contrary to the psychoanalytic drive-reduction hypothesis, no significant relation was found between the number of principal caretakers who fed, changed, and bathed the child and the number of people to whom the child generalized attachment behavior. Thus, being cared for more-or-less exclusively by the mother and/or one other person did not preclude the child showing attachment to other people, nor did being cared for by three or more people insure that the child would show attachment behavior toward all of them. In fact, one-fifth of the children showed attachment behavior principally toward people who did not participate in their care at all. The fear-of-strangers measure also showed that children with many attachment figures did not necessarily generalize their attachment behavior to other people. On the contrary, children who had three or more attachment figures showed significantly more fear of strangers than children who had only one or two attachment figures.

Thus, the somewhat indirect evidence obtained by Schaffer and Emerson is consistent with Harlow's evidence from monkeys that attachment does not result from the repeated association of a caretaker with reduction of primary drives such as hunger. While Bowlby's formulation of the contrast between his theory of attachment and the psychoanalytic drive-reduction theory has been severely criticized by psychoanalysts (e.g., Engel, 1971), these analysts have yet to formulate and test specific empirical implications of their theory that would make possible a clear comparison between it and the ethological hypothesis.

Summary

The S–R, Piagetian, psychoanalytic, and ethological viewpoints were compared with respect to their theoretical goals, primary units of data, views of the infant, hypothetical constructs, and predominate research strategies, as well as their concepts of what develops, developmental processes, and determinants of development. Because paradigms are most useful when viewed in terms of their relative advantages and disadvantages for representing particular phenomena, intersections of pairs of paradigms were examined in the context of specific studies.

The intersection of the S–R and Piagetian viewpoints in attempts to train conservation demonstrated that, while S–R theories have not provided adequate explanations for the development of conservation, they can contribute methodologically and conceptually to more precise strategies for studying the phenomena discovered by Piaget. The intersections of the S–R and psychoanalytic viewpoints in studies of psychoanalytic character types have supported psychoanalytic observations that such character types may exist, but have also suggested that psychoanalytic theory is inaccurate with respect to the developmental mechanisms involved. In a study comparing the S–R and ethological viewpoints, high maternal responsiveness to infants' crying was followed by long-term reductions in the infants' crying. This finding indicated that the operation of reinforcement principles may be constrained by the innately determined functions of certain behavior.

A comparison of the development of the object concept as depicted by Piaget and object relations as depicted by psychoanalytic theory showed that the two types of development were generally correlated, but that the lack of precision in the psychoanalytic theory of object relations prevented a valid test of it. The ethological theory of infant attachment and Piaget's hypothesis that person permanence typically precedes object permanence were found to be mutually complementary in explaining the relations between attachment behaviors and *décalages* in person vs. object permanence. Data on the development of infant attachment behavior have generally supported the ethological view over the psychoanalytic drive-reduction hypothesis, but the lack of a testable formulation of the analytic hypothesis makes a decisive comparison of the two difficult.

4 Research Strategies

IF ALL KNOWLEDGE is shaped by the conceptual paradigm of the knower, how is objective knowledge possible? It is for the purpose of seeking objectively valid knowledge that "scientific" (from the Latin *scire*, to know) research has been evolved. In seeking knowledge about development, we can refer to guidelines that have been devised for scientific research in general, to adaptations of these guidelines for psychological research, and to the still more specific adaptations necessary for developmental research. The purpose of this chapter is to provide an overview of guidelines for developmental research and of research strategies derived from them. While many of the strategies are linked to particular statistical techniques, we will focus upon the logic of research rather than upon statistical techniques per se.

In applying scientific guidelines, it is important to distinguish between the initial generation of ideas, on the one hand, and the confirmation of their implications, on the other. The initial generation of ideas is essentially a subjective process for which even the most completely formalized sciences have no rules. Referred to by philosophers of science as the *context of discovery*, this aspect of scientific activity encompasses the generation of observations, questions, tentative answers, theories, insights, and trial-and-error thinking about how the world works. Such activity may occur prior to, during, or following the execution of specific research studies. Without this kind of activity, there would be no science and no research. However, once a researcher has hit upon a question he wishes to answer or a hypothesis he wishes to test, he must translate his subjective impressions into testable form. The phase of scientific activity in which ideas are formulated in a testable manner and evidence is systematically gathered in order to test them is known as the *context of confirmation* or *context of justification*. It is to the empirical *confirmation* or *justification* of ideas that the more formal

74

standards of scientific research apply. If ideas are not tested against these more formal standards, we can never know whether they are genuine "discoveries" or just wrong guesses.

From Idea to Research

To be scientifically testable, an idea must specify relationships between attributes that can be observed either directly or through their effects on other attributes. Because a relationship between attributes can be identified only by finding out whether one attribute changes as the other changes, attributes of interest to science are typically referred to as *variables*—i.e., attributes whose values can vary.

While much scientific activity is concerned with quantitative measurement of variables, variables that are measurable only in present-vs.-absent or categorical fashion are also important. Suppose, for example, that you want to find out whether open classrooms facilitate learning to read. Reading skill is quantifiable in terms of the number of words recognized on a standardized test, but the variable of classroom type is not quantifiable in the usual sense. Yet if you merely study children educated in open classrooms, you cannot determine whether open classrooms facilitate reading, because you have no other "value" of the classroom variable to provide a basis for comparison. You could, however, test the effect of open classrooms by comparing the reading skill of children educated in open classrooms with that of children experiencing a different "value" of the classroom variable, e.g., traditional classrooms. If children from open classrooms were superior in reading skill, then it might be concluded that, *compared to traditional classrooms*, open classrooms facilitate the acquisition of reading. In short, ideas become researchable only when they are translated into statements about *relationships* among variables—e.g., the relationship between classroom type and reading skill—as shown through a correspondence between particular values of one variable and particular values of another variable.

Operationally Defining Variables

If a researcher has a hunch that, say, high anxiety interferes with the development of creativity in adolescents, one of the first steps he must take to move his hunch into the context of confirmation is to decide how to measure "anxiety" and "creativity." Whatever his private notions about the ultimate nature of anxiety and creativity, the operations with which he chooses to measure these variables serve to define the variables for purposes of testing his hunch and for communicating to others what he means by anxiety and creativity. His *operational definitions* might consist of observers' ratings of classroom behavior, personality test scores, readings on instruments designed to measure physiological functioning, ratings of subjects' drawings, or almost any other type of measure. If others wish to replicate or extend his findings, they can employ his definitions of anxiety and creativity by employing the same measurement procedures, whether or not they share his concepts of anxiety and creativity or his hunch about the relations between them.

Most behavioral variables can be operationalized in more than one way. Scholastic aptitude, for example, is often operationally defined by IQ. However, there are numerous IQ tests, differing in items, method of administration, and the samples of children on whom norms for performance are based. Other types of measures—such as grade-point average—are also used to assess scholastic aptitude. Since there are so many possible operational definitions of scholastic aptitude, none of them is likely to be agreed upon as *the* definition. Instead, the worth of each must be judged according to the function it is to serve. For some purposes, several different measures may be combined, as when college admissions offices employ weighted combinations of high-school grade average and scholastic aptitude test scores to predict college grades. For most behavioral research, two kinds of criteria must be considered in choosing an operational definition for a variable in any particular situation. These criteria involve the *reliability* and the *validity* of the measurement operations.

Reliability

Reliability is the degree to which a measure consistently yields a particular value for a variable when the true value of the variable does not change. Sources of unreliability include characteristics of the measuring procedure, of the variable being measured, and of the people doing the measuring. The reliability of an IQ test, for example, can be affected by whether the instructions for administering and scoring it are explicit enough to enable different examiners to proceed in exactly the same way. The reliability of the test can also be affected by momentary fluctuations in the attention and motivation of the subject and by the ways in which different examiners affect subjects' performance. In practice, the problem of reliability has been broken down into the following three categories.

Test–retest reliability. This form of reliability refers to the degree of agreement between scores obtained when the same measure of a variable is applied twice within an interval brief enough that the true value of the variable is not expected to change. It is an index of short-term fluctuations in what is being measured and of uncontrolled variations in the measuring procedure. Because experience with a measuring procedure may influence a subject, test–retest reliability is sometimes measured with *equivalent forms* of a procedure. The equivalent (or "alternate") forms are designed to measure exactly the same variable with items different enough so that experience with one form does not influence performance on the other form.

Split-half reliability.   If a measuring procedure is comprised of a number of items, as is true of most psychological tests, the correlation between scores for each half of the measure can be calculated to determine how well the halves agree with each other. In order to equalize warm-up, fatigue, and other factors that may affect performance at various points in the procedure, the odd-numbered items are typically compared with the even-numbered items to obtain a measure of *split-half* reliability. This is usually more convenient than devising equivalent forms. However, there are two sources of bias in estimates of reliability based on split-half correlations. Split-half correlations may be greater than test–retest or equivalent-form correlations because unreliability due to fluctuations in subjects and conditions from one occasion to another is not reflected in the split-half correlation.

On the other hand, since each item has its own biases and sources of unreliability, a score based on *all* items of a measure is affected less by the idiosyncrasies of individual items than is a score based on *half* that many items. To compensate for the decreased length, statistical formulas—such as the Spearman–Brown "Prophecy Formula" (cf. McNemar, 1969)—have been devised for estimating what the split-half reliability would be if each half were as long as the entire test. However, because these formulas cannot take account of fluctuations in subjects and conditions from one occasion to another, split-half reliability really only indicates the *internal consistency* of a measure, rather than its consistency over time.

Interobserver reliability.   A third kind of reliability, *interobserver* or *interjudge reliability,* concerns the degree of agreement between two or more people in their scoring of a variable. Interobserver reliability is important when people serve as the measuring instruments, as when two clinicians rate a person's anxiety after observing him. It is also important when two people score data obtained with instruments, as when two trained raters independently score records of changes in heart rate where there is room for interpretation as to how large a change from a subject's baseline heart rate should be scored as a response.

Validity

Whereas reliability refers to how consistent a measure is, *validity* refers to how *accurately* a procedure measures what it is supposed to measure. Like reliability, validity can be conceptualized in several different ways.

Content validity.   In some cases, validity is merely a matter of deciding whether the content of a measure includes what we want to measure. For example, if we are interested in whether children can tie shoes, having them try tying a few shoes would be a measure with high *content validity* (also called *face validity*). Likewise, an achievement test with high content validity would be one that contains a representative sample of items that school officials want children to learn.

Criterion-referenced validity.   A second type of validity concerns the degree to which a measure agrees with an independent criterion of what is being measured. For example, the criterion validity of a kindergarten reading readiness test may be evaluated in terms of its accuracy in predicting whether children's reading test scores are at grade level by the end of the first grade. If the readiness test accurately predicts such scores, then its validity with reference to this criterion is high.

Criterion-referenced validity can be subdivided according to the time intervals between the measure and the validity criterion. *Predictive validity* refers to accuracy in predicting a future criterion, as in the prediction of first-grade scores from a kindergarten test. *Concurrent validity* refers to the agreement between a measure and a validity criterion that is assessed concurrently with it, at the same point in time. *Postdictive validity* refers to accuracy in reflecting something that has already happened. A personality test that accurately indicated whether adults had experienced psychological trauma in childhood, for example, would have high postdictive validity.

Construct validity.   For purposes of developing and testing theoretical concepts, one of the most important but elusive aspects of validity is *construct validity*. Construct validity refers to the accuracy with which a measure reflects a hypothesized variable when there is no better measure of the variable to use as an ultimate criterion. Because there is no single criterion measure, the theoretical conception of the variable, as well as the measurement operations, must be perfected in order to attain construct validity. Confusion often arises around differences between construct validity and other forms of validity. Debates over the meaning of IQ test scores, for example, frequently revolve around the question of whether the IQ validly measures "intelligence." There is plenty of evidence that the IQ scores of children above the age of about 6 have moderately high *predictive validity*, in that they correlate with later grade-point averages, achievement test scores, and adult occupational status (cf. Achenbach, 1974, chapter 7, for a review). They also have moderately high *concurrent validity*, in that IQ scores obtained on various tests correlate significantly with one another. But do they measure *intelligence*?

When Binet and Simon (1905) set out to construct what later became the first IQ test, their goal was to identify children who would not benefit from regular schooling so that these children could be placed in special classes. Binet and Simon began by assembling test items that would measure the kinds of thinking required in school without requiring knowlege that depended upon previous schooling. Advancing no theory of the nature or cause of "intelligence," Binet and Simon explicitly denied that the abilities measured by their test were necessarily inherited, permanent, or immutable. Nevertheless, the Binet test and its successors have come to be regarded as far more than predictors of school performance.

What, then, is the "something more" connoted by the IQ score? "Intelligence," of course, but what's that? At one time, under the influence of a now bygone movement in physics known as "operationism," some insisted that the meaning of any variable be restricted exclusively to its operational definition. According to this view, "intelligence is what intelligence tests measure"—no more, no less. But the less than perfect correlations among IQ tests, their differing content and procedures, and their inability to predict artistic and manual accomplishments leave one with a plethora of definitions for "intelligence." Furthermore, the lack of content validity in these tests with respect to major theories of intellectual development leaves a large gap between the tests and much research on "intelligence." While operational definitions are essential to the conduct of research and the objectification of knowledge, the choice of measurement operations depends upon the conceptual paradigm of the researcher. Controversies over what IQ tests "really" measure expose the disparity among conceptual paradigms lurking behind the term "intelligence." If the construct purportedly measured by IQ tests were defined merely as the potential for earning good grades under standard school conditions, rather than as "intelligence," there might be far less debate about whether such tests really measure it.

Since much research is designed to develop and test theoretical explanations for phenomena, the meaning of many constructs depends upon networks of relationships among hypothesized variables and measures of them rather than upon a correlation with a single criterion such as school performance. In Hull's (1952) theory, for example, the construct of drive was sometimes quantified in terms of the number of hours a laboratory rat had been deprived of food. Yet drive states could also be operationally defined in terms of water deprivation, fear arousal, and—for human subjects—motivation for money, social interaction, and praise. Moreover, the meaning of drive as a construct rested as much on the behaviors that occurred during hypothesized drive states as it did on the deprivation assumed to create these drive states. Likewise, the cognitive structures hypothesized by Piaget cannot be completely defined with any single measurement procedure. Instead, a variety of procedures must be used to measure these constructs in different ways. If Piaget's theory of concrete operations is correct, then a variety of measurement procedures should produce results converging upon the conclusion that synchronized changes occur in children's thinking about a variety of different problems. The construct validity of each measure of concrete operational structures would be enhanced to the degree that it showed the changes in performance predicted by the theory and that it correlated with other measures hypothesized to reflect the same structures.

In summary, the construct validity of a measure depends upon how the results it yields fit into a network of predictive, postdictive, and/or concurrent relations among variables specified by the theory of which the construct is a part. If the results obtained with a particular measure do not fit into a chain of reasoning that is ultimately supported by other observations, it is often not known whether to blame the measure for inaccurately reflecting the hypothesized variables or to blame the research hypotheses for being wrong. Much of the fascinating interplay between the context of discovery and the context of confirmation consists of trial-and-error tinkering with ideas, on the one hand, and measures, on the other, to obtain replicable networks of relationships.

Internal and External Validity

Beside applying to the accuracy of specific measures, the concept of validity also applies to the accuracy of conclusions drawn from research. The conclusions drawn from a study have *internal validity* only if alternative explanations for the findings can be ruled out with confidence. Among the factors that threaten the internal validity of psychological research are uncontrolled characteristics of the subjects, such as their personal hypotheses about a study that may influence their behavior in ways unrecognized by the researcher; faulty research equipment and data analysis that produce erroneous results; and errors of logic in drawing conclusions about why the subjects behaved as they did under the conditions studied. As will be repeatedly evident in chapter 7, maximizing internal validity is one of the fundamental concerns in the choice of research methods and settings.

External validity refers to the accuracy with which conclusions can be *generalized* to other subjects and other conditions where the same determinants are believed to operate. Despite being internally valid, conclusions from a study may be limited in external validity by such factors as biased sampling of subjects—which limits the findings to very restricted groups of people; biased or unnatural situations—which restrict generalizations to similarly atypical situations; and procedures that cause subjects to behave in ways not representative of their usual behavior. An extensive survey of threats to external validity has been compiled by Bracht and Glass (1968).

Independent and Dependent Variables

Since much research is inspired by questions of the form "Does *X* affect *Y*?," variables are often divided into those believed to influence other variables and those expected to be influenced. The variables whose values depend upon those of other variables are referred to as *dependent variables*, typically symbolized by the letter *Y*, whereas the variables expected to influence the dependent variables are referred to as *independent variables*, symbolized by the letter *X*. Although the question, "Does *X* affect *Y*?" may seem simple, many of the stickiest problems of scientific research involve isolating variables that actually do affect other variables.

Suppose, for example, that we want to test the effects of a drug education course (the independent variable) on the subsequent use of drugs by teenagers (the dependent variable). No clearcut conclusions can be reached about the effects of drug education per se unless we compare a group receiving drug education and a similar group that does not receive drug education. Assuring similarity between the groups with respect to all variables except drug education is, therefore, an important prerequisite for the research. If their parents were to decide which teenagers would receive drug education, differences between them and other teenagers in later drug use might result from differences in parental attitudes, role models, or socioeconomic status (SES), rather than from differences on the independent variable of drug education. In this case, parental preferences, rather than drug education per se, might be more appropriately regarded as the independent variable.

To complicate matters further, parental preference per se, while potentially *correlating* with drug use, is unlikely to play a *causal* role. Instead, it may merely be correlated with other parental behaviors that are the true influences on drug use by teenagers. Nevertheless, since these other behaviors may be much more difficult to measure than is parental preference for drug education, parental preference might be treated as a convenient proxy for the true independent variables for purposes of predicting drug use. In practice, factors may be identifiable as independent variables in the sense that they precede and *predict* variation in other variables without being rigorously demonstrated to *cause* variations in the dependent variables in any mechanical, one-to-one sense.

Experimental Research

One way of preventing extraneous differences between groups of subjects from biasing the evaluation of drug education would be to start with two groups of pupils who are similar in all respects and to deliberately assign drug education to only one of the groups. By deliberately controlling the assignment of drug education, we are *experimentally* manipulating the independent variable. Research is truly experimental only if the researcher systematically manipulates the independent variable in order to observe its effects on the dependent variable.

Randomized Groups Designs

One general strategy for experimental research is to employ a *randomized groups design*. In this design, pupils would be randomly assigned to the drug or no-drug education condition. The purpose of random assignment is to create groups that are as similar as possible by avoiding selection biases that might lead to the piling up of more subjects possessing a particular characteristic in one condition than in the other. The principle is that, if the number of subjects is large enough, random assignment is likely to produce approximately equal distributions of important subject characteristics in each experimental condition. A common technique for randomly assigning subjects is to arbitrarily assign each subject a number and then to assign the subjects to one condition or the other according to the order in which their numbers appear in a random number table.

Matched Groups Designs

A second strategy for experimental research is to employ a *matched groups design*. In this design, the experimenter attempts to insure similarity in the groups receiving each condition by *matching* their members on variables that may potentially influence the independent variable. For example, an experimenter might want to insure that the groups receiving each experimental condition had the same distributions of IQ. Rather than risking the possibility that random assignment might by chance produce dissimilar distributions of IQ in the two conditions, he locates pairs of subjects having approximately the same IQ and assigns one member of each pair to each condition. However, even when the experimenter can form pairs of subjects matched on potentially important variables such as IQ, the large number of other potentially important variables on which the subjects may be dissimilar makes it necessary to employ a random procedure for determining which member of each pair will receive each experimental condition. Because of the necessity for randomly assigning matched subjects to their treatments, this design is also known as a *randomized blocks design*—each "block" consists of the two (or more) subjects who are initially matched and are then randomly assigned to different treatments.

When important subject characteristics that may influence the dependent variable are known in advance and when subjects matched for these characteristics can be randomly assigned to the different treatments, the randomized blocks design may be more efficient than the randomized groups design because it prevents the disproportionate assignment of certain types of subjects to treatment conditions, as can occur by chance with a purely random procedure. Recall, for example, that in Klaus and Gray's Early Training Project for Disadvantaged Children, purely random assignment of children to the two experimental and proximal control conditions resulted in groups differing enough in initial IQ to make subsequent IQ differences difficult to interpret (see Figure 1-1). If random assignment to the three conditions had been made from triads of children initially matched for IQ, the groups receiving the three conditions would probably have been more similar in IQ. Any differences at the end of the study could then have been more confidently ascribed to differences in treatments.

The randomized blocks design also permits statistical procedures that take account of the correlations arising because each subject has a matched counterpart in each experimental condition. These procedures are sometimes more powerful in detecting experimental effects than are procedures that do not take account of correlations between subjects who have received different treatments. However, attrition of subjects during the experiment can reduce this advantage over a randomized groups design, because, if one member is lost from a matched block of subjects, then no comparison can be made among the members of that block across all the experimental conditions. In the Klaus and Gray study, only a few subjects were lost, but it may have been enough to negate the advantages of a randomized blocks design over the randomized groups design actually employed. The choice between randomized groups and randomized blocks designs depends on many specifics of the research to be undertaken, such as the feasibility of identifying matching variables in advance, the expected rate of attrition, the number of subjects available, and the possibility of substituting new subjects or of averaging data from other subjects to replace those who are lost.

Within-subjects Designs

As an alternative to assigning similar groups to different conditions, the effects of certain independent variables may be assessed by studying the behavior of the same subjects under different values of the independent variable. This is called a *within-subjects* or *repeated measures design*, because the dependent variable is repeatedly measured in relation to different values of the independent variable *within* individual subjects rather than *between* groups. For example, the effect of teachers' attention on nursery school children's aggression can be studied by recording amount of aggression as teachers alternate between giving much attention and little attention according to a predetermined sequence. If the dependent variable (aggression) increases whenever the independent variable (teachers' attention) is increased, and decreases when the independent variable is decreased, this indicates a systematic relationship between the independent and dependent variables.

Within-subjects designs have been widely used in operant conditioning, often with only a single subject. In such applications, the dependent variable (e.g., aggressive behavior) is first measured during a *baseline period* before any experimental manipulation is made. The dependent variable is measured again while the experimental manipulation is in effect; again during a period when the manipulation is temporarily suspended; and again when the manipulation is reinstated. Letting *A* designate a baseline period and *B* a period during which the experimental manipulation is in effect, this sequence is described as an *ABAB* sequence. If the dependent variable changes consistently from the *A* to *B* condition and back again, it can be concluded that manipulation of the independent variable causes change in the dependent variable. Designs like the *ABAB* design that involve a series of manipulations of a variable over time are also called *time series designs*. Those that specifically involve reversals of the experimental manipulation are called *reversal designs*.

Time series designs of the type just described would, of course, be inappropriate for studying dependent variables that could not be expected to change after they had reached a certain level. For example, if we were interested in the effects of various programmed teaching materials on the learning of multiplication, a time series design would be inappropriate because multiplication skills are not likely to decrease as the teaching materials are successively changed. A comparison of the effects of the different teaching materials on different groups would therefore be more appropriate, as in the randomized groups or randomized blocks designs. On the other hand, where applicable, a time series design may maximize precision in defining just what the independent variable is. If children's aggression changes in unison with alternations in attentiveness by teachers, then the changes in aggression are pretty certain to be a function of the teachers' attentiveness per se. By contrast, if a group comparison design were used to study the same relationships—even if bias were avoided in the assignment of teachers as well as children to attentive and nonattentive conditions—being consistently attentive or inattentive might cause teachers to be generally categorized as "nice" or "not nice" by the children, over and above the intended differences in attentiveness. The children's general view of a teacher might then become the variable influencing their aggressive behavior regardless of the teacher's attentiveness.

Factorial Designs

So far, "design" has referred to procedures for assigning subjects to experimental conditions in order to compare the effects of two or more values of a single independent variable on a single dependent variable. Another aspect of research design concerns the number of independent variables or *factors* being studied. The illustrations so far have merely involved comparisons of the effects of two or more values or *levels* of a single factor. However, few independent variables of interest to behavioral scientists are likely to have completely straightforward effects, uninfluenced by other independent variables. Much research is therefore directed at finding out how two or more factors simultaneously affect a particular dependent variable. As an example, suppose you wanted to compare the effects of two curricula for teaching science. Since the effectiveness of each curriculum might depend upon the type of classroom structure within which it was taught, it would be important to compare the effects of the curricula within different types of classroom. Thus, if your dependent variable was performance on a science achievement test, you might want to compare the scores of children receiving Curriculum A in traditional classrooms, Curriculum B in traditional classrooms, Curriculum A in open classrooms, and Curriculum B in open classrooms. The most efficient way to compare the effects of the two factors (independent variables) is to employ a design like that portrayed in Table 4-1.

Whenever two or more factors are "crossed" for simultaneous testing as shown in Table 4-1, the design is referred to as *factorial*, in contrast to the *single factor* designs discussed previously. Factorial designs are typically described in terms of the number of factors and number of levels of each factor being tested. Thus, the design represented in Table 4-1 is a "2 × 2" design, because it has two factors, each with two levels. If one of the factors had three levels (e.g., three curricula), it would be a "3 × 2" design. If the design had three factors, each with two levels, it would be a "2 × 2× 2" design. This would occur, for example, if each group of subjects was divided in half and each half was given instruction for a different length of time in order to evaluate the effects of length of instruction. Any number of factors having two or more levels can be crossed.

If 20 children were randomly chosen for each cell of the 2 × 2 design portrayed in Table 4-1, the effects of Curriculum A versus Curriculum B can be compared on 40 children at the same time as the effects of traditional classroom structure are compared with the effects of open classroom structure on 40 children. This is obviously more efficient than conducting one experiment to test the effects of curriculum and a second to test the effects of classroom structure. More importantly, the factorial design permits analysis of *interactions* between the effects of the two factors. An example of an interaction would be that children in traditional classrooms perform better with Curriculum A than Curriculum B, whereas children in open classrooms show the opposite pattern. In other words, the effects of one factor (curriculum type) interact with the effects

TABLE 4-1. A 2 X 2 Factorial Design in which the Type-of-Curriculum Factor is "Crossed" with the Type-of-Classroom Factor, with 20 Subjects per Cell.

	Curriculum Type	
Classroom Type	A	B
Open	Subject 1	Subject 41
	2	42
	.	.
	.	.
	.	.
	20	60
Traditional	Subject 21	Subject 61
	22	62
	.	.
	.	.
	.	.
	40	80

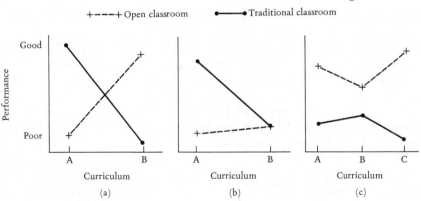

Figure 4-1. Three kinds of interaction between the effects of type-of-curriculum and type-of-classroom on academic performance.

of the other factor (classroom type) so that the effects of each depend upon the level of the other. Figure 4-1(a) graphically portrays an interaction of this sort.

Figures 4-1(b) and 4-1(c) illustrate other kinds of interactions that may occur between two experimentally manipulated variables. In Figure 4-1(b), Curricula A and B are portrayed as yielding equal results in open classrooms, whereas in traditional classrooms Curriculum A is superior to both curricula in open classrooms and to Curriculum B in traditional classrooms. In Figure 4-1(c), a complex interaction between three types of curriculum and two types of classroom is portrayed.

There are many variations on the principle of crossing factors in order to study the effects of various combinations of independent variables, although designs having more than four factors may be difficult to interpret because so many interactions are possible among the factors. An extensive survey of factorial designs can be found in Cochran and Cox (1957), while Winer (1971) provides advanced, authoritative coverage of statistics, primarily analyses of variance, for analyzing them.

The Solomon and Lessac Design for Experimental Studies of Development

Solomon and Lessac (1968) have proposed an especially powerful design for comparing behavioral changes in groups of subjects experiencing different experimental manipulations. They illustrated their design in a study of the effects of environmental deprivation on behavioral development in animals (Lessac and Solomon, 1969), but the design is applicable to any research in which behavioral changes are to be compared in more than one group from a pretreatment to a posttreatment testing. Because testing may itself have an effect on future behavior, the design specifies that one group undergoing each experimental condition should be tested prior to the experimental treatment, while a second group undergoing each condition should not be pretested. The effects of pretesting are subsequently revealed by post-treatment comparisons of the pretested and nonpretested groups.

Lessac and Solomon employed the design to study the effects of environmental deprivation on beagles. They compared beagles raised in isolation cages between the ages of 12 weeks and 1 year with those raised under normal stimulation. Half the beagles in each group were pretested at the age of 12 weeks on several measures of reflexes, anxiety, and learning. All the beagles were tested on these same measures at the age of 1 year. Table 4-2 shows the results on one measure, the mean number of seconds required by each of the four groups to jump out of a box in which they received electric shocks.

Even though there were no differences in perception of pain, as indicated by the amount of shock required to produce yelps and leg flexions, the isolated groups were significantly slower to escape than the control groups. The effect of pretesting was also significant in that the two groups (Groups 2 and 4) that received no pretest took longer to escape than did the two pretested groups (1 and 3). Comparison of the pre- and posttest scores of Group 1 shows that isolation did not cause a deterioration of escape behavior. Instead, this group improved slightly, from a mean of 16.59 seconds to 14.96 seconds. However, comparison with the very poor posttest performance of Group 2 indicates that the pretest experience must have protected the level of development reached by Group 1 at age 12 weeks. Thus, stimulus deprivation was much more debilitating for animals that lacked the experience afforded by pretesting. On the other hand, comparison with the much better posttest performance of Groups 3 and 4 indicates that, although the 12-week performance of Group 1 was protected by pretesting, normal experience would have greatly improved performance, especially in animals that were pretested. If the study had been conducted with only an isolated and a normal group that were similar with respect to pre-

TABLE 4-2. Mean Number of Seconds Taken by Beagles to Escape from Shock

	Isolated Groups		Control Groups	
	1	*2*	*3*	*4*
Pretest	16.59	No pretest	15.14	No pretest
Posttest	14.96	43.86	1.10	9.22

Data from Lessac and Solomon (1969).

testing, the important effects of pretesting on the subsequent experimental manipulations would not have been detected.

Natural Experiments

Practical and ethical constraints often rule out experimental manipulation of important variables. However, naturally occurring conditions that approximate experimental designs can sometimes by utilized for research purposes. It it were not possible to deliberately assign similar groups of students to drug education or no drug education, for example, it might be possible to find schools in which this had occurred accidentally. Such a situation could arise if a school system decided to implement drug education for all students but initially limited it to a few classrooms in a given grade, because not enough qualified teachers were available. However, valid conclusions about the effects of drug education would require that potentially influential variables such as the achievement levels and SES of the students were uncorrelated with assignment to drug education. Natural experiments that actually approximate the precision of true experimental designs are extremely rare, although procedures have been devised for increasing the rigor of conclusions drawn from various approximations to natural experiments. Campbell and Stanley (1963) have provided a handy guide to these procedures.

Correlational Research

A great many questions cannot be answered with experimental methods. In some cases, this is because there is little possibility of controlling the independent variables or of finding natural experiments in which groups have been conveniently equated on all variables except the independent variable of interest. In other cases, attempts to manipulate variables would create artificial situations in which the true relationships among variables would be hopelessly distorted. In still other cases, the ideas to be tested concern relationships among variables without any distinct hypothesis about the direction of influence among the variables. Research in which independent variables are not systematically manipulated is generally referred to as *correlational* because the co-relationship between the values of one variable and the values of another variable is studied, rather than the causal relationship implied when changes in a dependent variable occur in unison with manipulations of an independent variable.

Group Comparisons

Some correlational research designs are similar to experimental factorial designs in that two or more groups differing in what is believed to be an independent variable are compared with respect to a dependent variable. However, the independent variable on which the groups differ is not manipulated by the researcher. Comparisons between groups differing in age, sex, IQ, and SES, for example, can be made only in correlational fashion because these variables are preexisting characteristics that cannot be experimentally manipulated. In effect, correlational group comparisons resemble natural experiments except that the comparison groups in a natural experiment are assumed to differ only with respect to the independent variable, whereas in correlational group comparisons, the differences on the independent variables may be accompanied by a host of other differences as well. Independent variables of this type are generally referred to as *classification variables*, rather than as experimental variables, because they merely represent ways of classifying subjects.

In many experimental studies, classification variables like age, sex, IQ, and SES are used to define dimensions of comparison that are crossed with dimensions defined by two or more values of an experimentally manipulated independent variable. As an illustration, Asher and Markell (1974) tested the hypothesis that low motivation may be what causes boys to perform more poorly than girls on most tests of reading skills. After having fifth graders rate their interest in various topics, the authors gave each child written passages about the topics he or she rated most interesting and the topics rated least interesting. Words were omitted from each passage and the child was to guess what the missing words should be. The dependent variable was the number of missing words correctly supplied for the interesting and uninteresting materials. The effects of the independent variables of type-of-reading material and sex-of-subject were assessed with a 2 × 2 factorial design. The independent variable of type-of-reading material was experimentally manipulated to provide within-subject comparisons—i.e., performance by the same subjects was compared on interesting and uninteresting material. The other independent variable, sex, was a classification variable.

Mean scores obtained by children of each sex for the high- and low-interest passages are portrayed in Figure 4-2. The figure shows that the sexes did not differ much on high-interest material. However, with the low-interest material, boys performed much worse than they did with high-interest material and much worse than girls with either type of material. This interaction between the effects of sex and reading material was statistically significant according to an analysis of var-

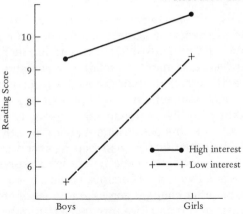

Figure 4-2. Reading scores obtained by boys and
girls with high- and low-interest reading materials.
(Data from Asher and Markell, 1974.)

iance. (The data could also have been analyzed with other statistics, but
the logic of research design rather than the specific statistical method is
of interest here.) Comparisons of individual cells showed the boys'
scores for low-interest materials to be significantly poorer than scores in
any other cell. Disinterest in the content of standard reading tests may
thus account for the frequent finding that boys read more poorly than
girls. While lack of experimental control over the variable of sex makes it
impossible to conclude precisely *what* it is about being a boy or girl that
leads to the effect, the finding nevertheless suggests that boys' apparent
inferiority in reading might be overcome by teaching and testing them
with more interesting materials.

Coefficients of Correlation

The purpose of the single-factor research design is to identify co-
relationships between the values of a dependent variable and a few
preselected values of the independent variable. However, preselection
of a few values of a variable is often undesirable or impossible because
the values of the variable cannot readily be divided into meaningful
categories having enough subjects in each one. A different approach to
assessing the co-relationship between two variables is to see whether
individual scores on one variable increase or decrease consistently in
relation to scores on the other variable. For example, to determine
whether there is a relationship between reading speed and achievement
test scores, one could draw a graph in which reading speed is plotted
along one axis and achievement along the other axis. Unlike grouping

subjects arbitrarily into categories by reading speed (e.g., high, middle, low) in order to see whether achievement differs among the groups, plotting the scores on a graph would show whether there is a consistent relationship between increments in reading speed and achievement. If one found that each increase in reading speed was accompanied by a uniform increase in achievement, one could predict any subject's achievement score from knowing his reading speed. Conversely, one could predict his reading speed from his achievement score. In other words, there would be a perfect correlation between reading speed and achievement.

The function of a correlation coefficient is to express the degree of relationship between two types of scores, based on the degree to which one changes as the other changes across a number of observations. The degree of relationship is typically expressed as a number that can range from -1.00 (perfect negative relationship) to $+1.00$ (perfect positive relationship). If achievement scores were scattered around to such a degree that there was no relationship at all between reading speed and achievement level, then the correlation between reading speed and achievement would be .00.

R **correlation.** Specific statistical methods for obtaining correlation coefficients will be discussed in chapter 5. However, at the level of research strategy, there are many ways to apply correlational methods. Expressing the degree of relationship between two variables, such as reading speed and achievement, as they are each measured in a number of subjects is the most common approach and is known as R *correlation.* (A word of caution—the letter R is also used in various forms to denote specific correlational statistics, to be discussed in chapter 5, that can be applied in ways other than to express the relationship between variables across individuals.)

It should be noted that, although an R correlation expresses a relation between two variables, the size of the coefficient depends upon the particular sample of subjects on whom the scores were obtained, rather than upon an intrinsic relationship between the variables that can be expected to hold in all populations. The obtained correlation coefficient is, therefore, only generalizable to groups like the sample studied. A high correlation between reading speed and achievement in surburban fifth-grade girls, for instance, says nothing about the relationship between reading speed and achievement in urban fifth-grade boys. Furthermore, since an R correlation expresses a relationship across individuals measured at a particular point in time, it does not necessarily indicate that a change in the value of one variable for an individual predicts a change in the value of the other variable for that individual. For example, even if there is a high correlation between reading speed and achievement in a group of fifth graders, this does not necessarily mean that a decrease in a particular child's achievement must be accompanied by a decrease in his reading speed or vice versa.

P **correlation.** The degree of relationship between two variables *within an individual* is expressed with a correlation calculated between the person's score on the two variables measured at different points in time. Thus, if a child's IQ and achievement test percentile for his age were both measured each year for 12 years, the correlation between the 12 pairs of scores would express the degree to which the two variables rose and fell together. Known as *P correlation*, this approach may be more appropriate than *R* correlation for expressing relationships between variables that (a) change within individuals over time, and (b) have different patterns of change from one individual to another. For example, fear of failure might be especially high in some people during developmental periods when their achievement motivation is high, whereas in others fear of failure might be low when achievement motivation is high. An *R* correlation between fear of failure and achievement motivation across subjects would be low, but this would mask the fact that the two variables were related differently in different subjects. If the two variables were similarly related in all subjects, then *R* correlations would yield the same findings as *P* correlations.

Q **correlation.** Whereas *R* and *P* correlations express the relationship between two *variables,* *Q correlations* express the similarity between two *persons,* calculated across variables. That is, when two subjects have scores on each of, say, 20 variables, the *Q* correlation summarizes the degree to which subject *A*'s profile of scores on the 20 variables is similar in shape to subject *B*'s profile of scores. For *Q* correlations to be valid, all the variables must be scored on scales having similar means and variances. Otherwise, correlations between subjects may arise merely because the numerical similarities and differences among the variables cause uniformities in the shapes of all subjects' profiles of scores.

If *Q* correlations are calculated between each pair of people in a group, clusters of people who correlate highly with one another can be regarded as representing "types." Personality types can be identified through *Q* correlations of personality measures, but "stages" of personality and cognitive development may also be potentially identifiable through *Q* correlation. For example, if children were given measures of variables hypothesized by Erikson (1963) to vary as psychosocial development progresses, *Q* correlations among the children might reveal whether there were groups who manifested patterns like those ascribed to various psychosocial stages. Table 4-3 presents an overview of *R, P,* and *Q* correlations.

TABLE 4-3. *R*, *P*, and *Q* Correlational Strategies.

R Correlation
(between two variables measured in N persons)

Variables:	A	B
1	a_1	b_1
2	a_2	b_2
3	a_3	b_3
.	.	.
.	.	.
.	.	.
n	a_n	b_n

Persons

P Correlation
(between two variables measured N times in 1 person)

Variables:	A	B
1	a_1	b_1
2	a_2	b_2
3	a_3	b_3
.	.	.
.	.	.
.	.	.
n	a_n	b_n

Occasions for 1 person

Q Correlation
(between two persons measured on N variables)

Persons:	A	B
1	a_1	b_1
2	a_2	b_2
3	a_3	b_3
.	.	.
.	.	.
.	.	.
n	a_n	b_n

Variables

Correlation and Causation

It has become a truism that "correlation does not imply causation." Merely because one variable consistently increases or decreases in unison with another does not mean that one causes the other. This is true whether the correlation between the variables is identified by comparing the value of one variable in groups differing in scores on the other variable or by calculating a correlation coefficient between two variables across a number of individuals. If we find, for example, that grade-point average correlates highly with IQ, we cannot conclude either that differences in IQ cause differences in grades or that differences in grades cause differences in IQ. It is possible that a third variable, such as achievement motivation, determines both IQ and grades. Or perhaps teachers' awareness of pupils' IQ scores creates a self-fulfilling prophecy ("Pygmalion effect"), as Rosenthal and Jacobson (1968) have claimed. In either of these cases, improvement in IQ test performance by itself would not affect grades nor would improvement in grades affect IQ.

While correlation does not necessarily imply causation, correlations between unmanipulated variables often provide leads to causal relationships. If no correlation exists between two variables, then a causal relationship between them can pretty well be ruled out. If a correlation does exist, and if a causal relationship could plausibly run in only one direction, then tentative causal inferences might be made, subject to further test in other ways. For example, if a significant correlation were found between height and popularity among adolescents, the inference that height influences popularity would be far more plausible than the opposite inference. Such an inference of causality would, however, still not have the strength of an inference made from changes in a dependent variable occurring when an independent variable is manipulated. Since people's height cannot be experimentally manipulated, a causal inference could be strengthened only by progressively ruling out alternative explanations for the obtained correlation. Because such variables as SES and biological maturity may be correlated with both popularity and height, it would be important to demonstrate that height is correlated with popularity among individuals who do not differ in SES and biological maturity.

Partial correlation. Special statistical techniques can be used to aid in moving from correlational findings to causal inferences. In one, known as *partial correlation*, the potential contributions of other variables to the correlation between two variables of interest can be partialled out in order to determine whether the correlation between the two remains significant. Accordingly, if SES and biological maturity were each found to correlate with both height and popularity, partialling out the correlation of each of these variables with height and popularity would show whether height and popularity remained correlated when the effects of the other variables were removed. If the remaining ("partial") correlation between height and popularity were significant, this would suggest that the correlation was not accounted for by the effects of one of the other variables. However, other explanations for the correlation between height and popularity might still need to be ruled out before a causal inference could be defended with confidence. Once the relevant correlations have been obtained, computation of partial correlations are quite simple, as demonstrated in Section A-1 of the Appendix.

Cross-lagged panel correlation.   Another strategy for using correlational methods to identify causal relationships is to compare the correlations among variables from one point in time to another. As an illustration, correlations have often been reported between various types of parent behavior, on the one hand, and children's test scores, on the other. Simple correlations between parent and child behavior do not, however, tell us whether one causes the other. It might seem more plausible that parent behavior causes child behavior, rather than the reverse, but there is plenty of evidence that different children elicit different behavior from adults, including their parents (e.g., Yarrow, Waxler, and Scott, 1971). In order to choose between the hypothesis that a particular type of parent behavior causes a particular type of child behavior and the opposite hypothesis, correlations of each variable with the other variable can be compared from one point in time to another. Thus, if the correlation of parent behavior at Time 1 with child behavior at Time 2 is substantially higher than the correlation of child behavior at Time 1 with parent behavior at Time 2, it is more likely that parent behavior is determining child behavior than the reverse.

Campbell has formulated this strategy in terms of what he calls the *cross-lagged panel correlation technique* (Campbell and Stanley, 1963). It is called "cross-lagged" because it involves correlations across a time lag (Time 1 to Time 2) and "panel" because it entails forming a panel of the relevant variables at Time 1 and a second panel of them at Time 2. Figure 4-3 portrays a cross-lagged panel analysis of relationships between amount of maternal social attention and children's mental test scores at the ages of 11 and 17 months (Clarke-Stewart, 1973). From simply looking at the correlation of .45 between test score and maternal attention at age 17 months (right-hand side of Figure 4-3), it would be impossible to determine which of the variables influenced the other or whether their mutual correlation resulted from the joint influence of a third variable.

The fact that the correlation between test scores and maternal attention at the age of 11 months was .00 (left-hand side of Figure 4-3) suggests that between the ages of 11 and 17 months some new causal relationship emerged. Because the cross-lagged correlation of .60 between maternal attention at 11 months and test score at 17 months was significantly greater than the cross-lagged correlation of -.04 between test score at 11 months and attention at 17 months, it appears more plausible that maternal attention influenced test scores rather than the other way around. Furthermore, the greater correlation between maternal attention at 11 and 17 months than between test scores at 11 and 17 months (.70 versus .26) indicates that maternal attention was relatively stable from 11 to 17 months, whereas test performance was not. The cross-lagged panel technique thus makes it possible to coordinate a series of correlations between unmanipulated variables in order to choose among causal hypotheses.

Caution is nevertheless in order with respect to causal inferences. It is still possible that a third variable influenced both maternal attention and test scores at 17 months while influencing only maternal attention at 11 months. In particular, Clarke-Stewart found that black mothers gave their children significantly less attention than white mothers. Since the black children's test scores were also lower than those of white children at 17 months, it is possible that something related to race—e.g., amount of distraction in the home—influenced maternal attention at both times and mental test scores at 17 months. Partial correlations could have been used to test this possibility. If race were scored as 1 for white and 2 for black, it could be treated as a variable whose contribution to the correlation between attention and test scores could be partialled out. If the correlation between attention and test scores remained significant with race partialled out, this would indicate that, regardless of race, maternal attention did indeed influence test score. Further methods for eliminating competing interpretations of cross-lagged panel data have been proposed by Sandell (1971) and by Rozelle and Campbell (1969), while Kenny (1975) has provided a good overview of the strengths and weakness of cross-lagged panel analysis.

Another approach to determining whether maternal attention

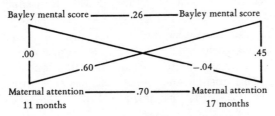

Figure 4-3. Correlations between children's Bayley mental test score and mothers' social attention at ages 11 and 17 months. (From Clarke-Stewart, 1973.)

enhances children's test performance would be to experimentally manipulate maternal attention. If mothers were taught to give their infants' extra attention, and if their infants proved superior at 17 months to a control group not receiving extra attention, this would be good evidence for a causal relationship between maternal attention and children's test performance. Various combinations of correlational and experimental methods can thus be used to move from the initial isolation of co-relations among variables to choices among competing hypotheses, and, ultimately, to convergent evidence for causal relationships.

Time Span of Research

Longitudinal studies, where the same subjects are repeatedly tested or observed, would appear to offer the most natural way to trace behavioral development. However, because of their cost and the continuity of researchers, resources, and subjects required, longitudinal studies comprise only a small proportion of developmental research. One shortcut to longitudinal research is to relate current behavior to retrospective data on past behavior, either by having people recall past behavior or by employing documents, such as school records, in which behavior was recorded when it occurred.

Unfortunately, retrospective studies are vulnerable to many biases that cannot be identified as easily as in prospective longitudinal studies, where data are collected on subjects as they age. Recollections of the past, either by subjects or by people who know them, are vulnerable to memory distortion, while documentary evidence may be subject to unknown selective factors influencing the original data and the current availability of subjects. For example, in a retrospective study it might be found that more schizophrenic adults than normal adults from the same school repeated a grade. Yet, since not all the schizophrenic or normal adults from the school are likely to be found, it may well be that the apparent difference in school failure results from the fact that only the most successful normals and the least successful schizophrenics, especially those in hospitals, can be found for follow-up. While these two groups may indeed have differed in school performance, this difference says nothing about childhood differences between most people who as adults are normal and those who are schizophrenic. Possible selective factors thus limit the external validity of any conclusions about schizophrenia per se.

Much research on changes with age follows a cross-sectional strategy, in which individuals of different ages—i.e., cross-sections of the age continuum—are compared. This strategy is based on the assumption that, if an older age group is drawn from the same population as a younger group, the behavior of the older group indicates how the younger group will eventually behave. According to this assumption, the relationship between earlier and later behavior can be determined without having to wait for development to occur.

Although longitudinal conclusions are often drawn from cross-sectional data, the validity of these conclusions must be carefully assessed. As an example, the norms of the Wechsler Adult Intelligence Scale ("WAIS"; Wechsler, 1955) were based on cross-sectional samples of men and women at ages 25–34, 35–44, 45–54, and 55–64 who were representative of the U.S. population with respect to geographic region, urban vs. rural residence, white vs. nonwhite race, occupation, and education. Because it was found that the older groups performed more poorly than the younger groups, it was concluded that people's WAIS performance typically declines with age. However, this conclusion has been called into question by findings that, when the *same* adults are tested at different age levels, their performance on the WAIS does not decline, but *improves* significantly with age (Kangas and Bradway, 1971). While the effect of repeated testing can bias longitudinal data, this is unlikely to have been responsible for improved performance in the Kangas–Bradway study, as the longitudinal testings were twelve years apart. The vulnerability of the WAIS to differences in education, cultural experiences, and other factors correlated with historical epoch of development, rather than with age per se, may therefore have been responsible for the poorer performance of the older adults in Wechsler's normative samples.

Even though longitudinal studies may expose the effects of sampling biases in cross-sectional findings, longitudinal research is also vulnerable to sampling biases. Subjects for longitudinal research are often selectively chosen for expected long-term availability. When attrition does occur, it may be related to subject characteristics that bias the ultimate subject sample still further. Moreover, it has been demonstrated that cultural–historical effects like those differentiating between cohorts (age groups) studied cross-sectionally can also affect longitudinal findings, in that the developmental course of a particular cohort may differ from that of cohorts born earlier or later. In a two-year longitudinal study of adolescents, for example, Nesselroade and Baltes (1974) found that cultural changes from the beginning to the end of the study had more influence on personality changes than did age changes within the participating cohorts. The cohorts ranged from 13 to 16 years in initial age and 15 to 18 in final age, but all four cohorts showed declines in superego strength, social–emotional anxiety, and achievement, such that the youngest subjects resembled the oldest subjects at the end of the study rather than resembling the oldest as they *had been* at the beginning of the study. If a single cohort had been studied longitudinally, it might erroneously have been concluded that the changes in personality were a function of age per se, whereas comparison of the cohorts showed that the changes were occurring simultaneously in all four cohorts.

Combining Longitudinal and Cross-Sectional Strategies

Because sampling, cultural–historical, and age effects may be confounded with one another in purely cross-sectional and purely longitudinal designs, Schaie (1965) has proposed that effects due to cohort, age of measurement, and date of measurement be separated as explicitly as possible. As an aid to separating these variables conceptually, the relevant relationships between cohort, age, and date of measurement are illustrated in Table 4-4. Consider first the possible confounding of effects in a purely cross-sectional design. Table 4-4 shows that a cross-sectional study comparing 5-, 7-, and 9-year olds, in say, 1978, would require children from cohorts born in 1973, 1971, and 1969, respectively. A threat to the internal validity of this design is that differences found between the 5-, 7-, and 9-year olds might be attributable to cohort characteristics other than age. For example, even if all the subjects lived in the same town, SES might differ because available housing was relatively cheaper when the families of the oldest cohort moved to town. A threat to external validity is that any similarities or differences among cohorts might not be generalizable to earlier or later points in time, because of cultural–historical changes.

Now consider the possible confounding of effects in a longitudinal study of, say, the 1975 birth cohort at ages 5, 7, and 9. This would require studying this cohort in 1980, 1982, and 1984, as illustrated in Table 4-4. The internal validity of this design is vulnerable to the possibility that differences found from 1980 to 1982 and 1984 might be due to cul-

TABLE 4-4. Interrelationships Among Time and Age Variables Involved in Developmental Analyses.[a]

Birth Cohort	Age Studied				
	5	7	9	11	
1969	1974	1976	1978	1980	Cross-sectional
1971	1976	1978	1980	1982	Longitudinal
1973	1978	1980	1982	1984	Time-lag
1975	1980	1982	1984	1986	

[a]Figures in table are the years in which each birth cohort would be studied at each age listed above the table.

tural–historical changes rather than to aging per se. The external validity may be weakened by possible peculiarities of the cohort that distinguish it from cohorts born earlier or later.

A design employed specifically to identify cultural–historical effects, the *time-lag design*, entails comparing subjects from different cohorts when they have reached the same age–e.g., the 1969, 1971, 1973, and 1975 cohorts when they reached age 11 in 1980, 1982, 1984, and 1986, respectively, as illustrated in Table 4-4. This approach, of course, confounds possible differences in cohort with differences in year of measurement.

In short, the conventional cross-sectional, longitudinal, and time-lag designs all tend to confound effects due to cohort, age, and time of study. To overcome this confounding, the following strategies have been proposed for combining longitudinal and cross-sectional approaches.

Longitudinal–sequential designs. The Nesselroade–Baltes (1974) study of adolescent personality, described earlier, combined aspects of cross-sectional, longitudinal, and time-lag strategies in what the authors called a *longitudinal–sequential* design. In this design, different birth-year cohorts are compared over the same longitudinal period. This makes it possible to do cross-sectional comparisons of cohorts at any point during the study, comparisons of the longitudinal course of development in each cohort over the course of the study, and time-lag comparisons among cohorts as they reach a particular age in successive years. It can thus be determined whether changes in behavior are attributable to cultural-historical changes, age changes, or an interaction between the two.

Longitudinal–sequential designs also make it possible to obtain longitudinal data on relatively long periods of development in less time than it takes the development to occur, as illustrated in Table 4-5(a). If, for example, you wish to study changes in Variable X occurring over the four years between the ages of 5 and 9, but have only two years in which to do it, you could study Variable X in three cohorts: One that ages from 5 to 7; one that ages from 6 to 8; and one that ages from 7 to 9 over the two years. If age changes on Variable X are found within cohorts over and above any time-related changes common to the three groups, then inferences about age changes in Variable X between 5 and 9 can be drawn as follows: Children from the youngest cohort having a score of 100 on Variable X at age 6 and 110 at age 7 can be expected to eventually obtain the same score on Variable X at age 8 as found for the middle cohort children who also obtained 100 on X when they were 6 and 110 when they were 7. By looking at the scores obtained in the youngest cohort when they were 5, it is possible to infer the relationships among scores from the age of 5 to the age of 8. Likewise, children from the middle cohort who had scores on Variable X of 110 at age 7 and 120 at age 8 can be expected to obtain the same score on Variable X at age 9 as found for children in the oldest cohort who had obtained a score of 110 on X when they were 7 and 120 when they were 8. By looking at the scores obtained by the children in the middle cohort when they were 6, it is possible to infer the relationships among scores from the age of 6 to the age of 9. In sum, by finding children in the youngest cohort comparable to children in the middle cohort and, in turn, children in the oldest cohort comparable to these same children in the middle cohort, conclusions may be drawn in two years about a four-year period of development.

Cross-sectional–sequential designs. A second way to combine aspects of the cross-sectional and longitudinal approaches is to study cross-sectional samples from several birth cohorts at successive points in time. Known as the *cross-sectional–sequential design*, this entails much the same pattern of observations as the longitudinal–sequential design in that data are obtained on subjects of two or more ages, from different cohorts, at two or more points in time. The difference is that, in the cross-sectional–sequential design, the observations are not repeated on the same members of a cohort from one occasion to the next, but are made on *different* members of the cohort. In other words, new samples are drawn from each cohort for each successive set of observations.

When applied to the study of Variable X between the ages of 5 and 9, a two-year cross-sectional–sequential design would entail studying in Year 1 a sample of children from the 5-year-old, a sample from the 6-year-old, and a sample from the 7-year-old cohort. In Year 2, a *different* sample would be studied from each of the same cohorts, now aged 6, 7, and 8, respectively. And in Year 3 (after the elapse of a total of two years), a *third* sample would be studied from each cohort, now aged 7, 8, and 9. This cross-sectional–sequential design is illustrated in Table 4-5(b).

Cross-sectional–sequential designs have the advantage over longitudinal–sequential designs of not requiring preservation of the same subject samples from one observation period to the next. As a consequence, the effects of being studied, attrition from the samples, and initial selection for expected stability do not threaten the validity of conclusions. On the other hand, cross-sectional–sequential designs have the disadvantage that changes in individuals cannot be identified over time. Furthermore, complete congruence among successive samples from a cohort may be threatened by uncontrollable random fluctuation in sampling and by factors such as death which alter in unknown ways the composition of the cohort from which the samples are drawn.

Time-lag–sequential designs. Just as the longitudinal–sequential and cross-sectional–sequential designs are extensions of simple longitudinal and cross-sectional designs, the *time-lag–sequential design* proposed by Buss (1973) is an extension of the time-lag design to include observations on successive samples from two or more cohorts. Recall that the simple time-lag design entails observations on successive cohorts as they reach a particular age in different years. In contrast, the time-lag–sequential design entails making observations on *two or more samples from each cohort* as they reach two or more age levels in different years. As illustrated in Table 4-5(c), such a design could be employed to study the behavior of the 1971, 1972, and 1973 birth cohorts as they reach the ages of 7, 8, and 9 in 1978 through 1982, respectively. It would reveal the behavior of 7-year olds, 8-year olds, and 9-year olds from the three different cohorts.

TABLE 4-5. Longitudinal–Sequential, Cross-Sectional–Sequential, and Time-Lag–Sequential Designs.[a]

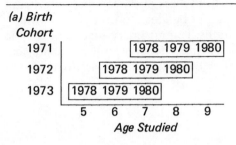

(a) Birth Cohort

(a) Longitudinal–sequential design in which three 2-year longitudinal studies are coordinated to study development between ages 5 and 9. The same subjects within each cohort are studied on three occasions from 1978 to 1980.

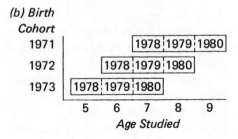

(b) Birth Cohort

(b) Cross-sectional–sequential design in which three samples are drawn from each of three cohorts on three occasions from 1978 to 1980.

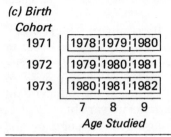

(c) Birth Cohort

(c) Time-lag–sequential design in which three samples from each of three cohorts are compared on three occasions from 1978–1980, 1979–1981, and 1980–1982, respectively.

[a] ▢ indicates cohort.

▢ indicates separate samples within cohort.

The time-lag–sequential design does not require repeated observations on the same subjects as do longitudinal designs, but it does permit comparisons between the effect of time of observation and the effect of age at which behavior is studied. For example, suppose it were found that 9-year olds from the 1971 cohort, 8-year olds from the 1972 cohort, and 7-year olds from the 1973 cohort—all studied in 1980—were more similar to each other than were 7-year olds from each cohort studied in 1978, 1979, and 1980, respectively. This would imply that the *time* effect was greater than the *age* effect. Or suppose that, despite being studied in 1978 and 1980, respectively, 7-year olds from the 1971 cohort were more similar to 9-year olds in the same cohort than they were to children of any age in the other cohorts. This would imply that the *cohort* effect was stronger than the *age* or *time* effects. However, time-lag–sequential designs—like cross-sectional–sequential designs—are vulnerable to variations in samples from the same cohort and they do not typically yield information that cannot be gleaned from longitudinal– and cross-sectional–sequential studies. Their primary advantage may be to yield information specifically on the effects of cultural–historical changes with fewer observations than the other designs would require to get the same information.

Summary

Guidelines and strategies were presented for scientific research on development. Scientific standards for research apply primarily to the *context of confirmation* wherein ideas evolving from the *context of discovery* are tested. Ideas are most effectively tested when the variables they specify are *operationally defined* in terms of *reliable* and *valid* measurement procedures. Research designs must be *internally valid* before accurate conclusions can be drawn from them and *externally valid* before the conclusions can be generalized beyond the subjects actually studied.

The basis for causal inferences is generally strongest when *experimental manipulations of independent variables* are made in order to assess their effects on *dependent variables*. *Randomized groups designs* and *matched groups (randomized blocks)* designs are employed to insure that subjects experiencing different values of an independent variable are comparable with respect to extraneous variables. *Within subjects (repeated measures) designs* are employed to compare the effects of different values of an independent variable on the same subject or subjects. *Factorial designs* permit the simultaneous testing of the effects of two or more independent variables and the *interactions* between them. The *Solomon and Lessac design* is used to detect the effects of pretesting on subsequent behavior. Naturally occurring differences in the value of an independent variable sometimes make it possible to approximate experimental designs by means of *natural experiments*.

Correlational research portrays relationships between variables without experimental manipulations. *Correlational group comparisons* take the same form as some experimental designs, but the independent variables are *classification variables* rather than being experimentally manipulated. *Coefficients of correlation* express the strength of the relationship between two sets of scores without any indication of causal relations between them.

The most common application of correlation—*R correlation* —expresses the degree of relationship between two variables, each measured in a number of people. *P correlations* express the degree of relationship between two variables, each measured several times in the same person. *Q correlations* express the similarity between two people in the patterns of scores they obtain on several variables.

While correlations between variables do not imply causal relationships, evidence for causality must often be gathered without experimental manipulation of independent variables. *Partial correlation, cross-lagged panel correlation*, and various combinations of other methods can aid in making choices among competing explanations for findings.

Since developmental research concerns age changes in behavior, the ages and times spanned are crucial aspects of research design. *Longitudinal, cross-sectional,* and *time-lag designs* provide the simplest approaches to the study of development. However, because effects associated with cohort, historical time of measurement, selective sampling, and repeated observations may all affect the validity of findings obtained with these designs, more complex designs have been proposed for separating the effects of cohort, age, and time of measurement. These include the *longitudinal–sequential, cross-sectional–sequential,* and *time-lag–sequential designs*, all of which extend the simpler designs to simultaneous comparisons of cohort, age, and time of measurement.

5 Statistical Issues

NEARLY ALL behavioral research involves statistical concepts of one sort or another. Even where formal statistical tests are not reported, as in much of Piaget's work, findings must be evaluated within a statistical frame of reference. That is, conclusions about the age at which a behavior emerges, about the sequence of behavioral change, and about factors that influence behavior are based upon samples of subjects assumed to be representative of larger populations. It is to provide a systematic basis for *describing samples* and for *making inferences from samples to populations* that statistical methods have been developed. As it is assumed that the reader is already familiar with the *t* test, analysis of variance (ANOVA), chi square, and Pearson product-moment correlation, the purpose of this chapter is to introduce issues and approaches pertinent to developmental research but usually omitted from general statistics courses.

Some Basic Concepts

In their descriptive function, statistics are used to summarize the characteristics of samples. The mean (arithmetical average), median (50th percentile), and mode (most frequent score) each describe samples in terms of a single representative score. The *variance* (average of the squared differences between each score and the mean of the sample) and the *standard deviation* (square root of the variance) each describe the amount of dispersion of scores around the mean. Correlation coefficients describe the strength of relationships between two variables in a sample.

Whereas the numbers used to describe characteristics of samples are known as *descriptive statistics*, the values of these same characteristics in entire populations are called *parameters*. Statistics that describe samples may be used to *infer* parameters of the parent populations from which the samples are drawn. Statistical tests are designed to estimate the probability that a sample statistic truly reflects a parameter of the population from which the sample is drawn. Tests for the significance of the difference between two samples, for example, are designed to estimate the probability that the two *populations* sampled really differ. Thus, if a t test of the difference between samples from two populations is significant at $p < .05$, this indicates that a difference this large could arise by chance in only 5 percent of samples drawn from the two populations, if the populations did *not* in fact differ from one another. Analogously, tests for the statistical significance of a correlation between two variables in a sample provide an estimate of the probability that the variables really are correlated in the population sampled.

Harris (1975, p. 1) has succinctly summarized the role of statistics in research as follows:

> Statistics is a form of social control over the professional behavior of researchers. The ultimate justification for any statistical procedure lies in the kinds of research behavior it encourages or discourages. . . . In their descriptive applications, statistical procedures provide a set of tools for summarizing efficiently the researcher's empirical findings in a form which is more readily assimilated by his audience than would be a simple listing of the raw data. . . . The inferential applications of statistics provide protection against the universal tendency to confuse aspects of the data which are unique to the particular sample of subjects, stimuli, and conditions involved in a study with general properties of the populations from which these subjects, stimuli, and conditions were sampled.

Scales of Measurement

In order to apply statistics to a variable, the variable must be scored in a way that reflects the values of the variable in some quantitative form.

Nominal scales. The simplest form of quantification is merely to count the number of times each value of a variable occurs in a sample. Statistics can be applied to nonquantitative variables such as sex merely by counting the subjects of each sex in a sample. When this is done, the relationship between two nonquantitative variables, such as sex and answering "Yes" to the question, "I like dolls," can be assessed by counting the number of each sex in a sample who answer yes and the number of each sex who do not. When the values of a variable are thusly scored in terms of categories instead of quantitative gradations, the values are said to form a *nominal scale*, because, even if numbers are used to label the categories, the numbers function merely as names for the categories. Variables scored on nominal scales can be statistically assessed only in terms of the frequency of occurrence of each score. Thus, the distribution of a variable scored on a nominal scale can be summarized only in terms of the mode—the most frequent score. Statistical tests applicable to nominally scaled variables are those—such as the chi square—that indicate the probability that scores could by chance be distributed in the proportions observed in a particular sample or samples, if the parent population(s) were not really distributed in the same way as the sample(s).

Ordinal scales.   More diverse statistical methods are possible if the values of a variable can be rank ordered, as when a teacher is asked to rank her pupils from most to least aggressive. Because it is assumed that the ranks merely reflect an *ordering* of quantities, rather than quantitative intervals of equal size from one rank to another, scales of this type are called *ordinal* scales.

Interval scales.   Scales that do in fact reflect equal intervals from one score to another are known as *interval scales.* The centigrade and Fahrenheit scales are both interval scales for measuring temperature, even though they differ in the sizes of their respective intervals and their definitions of the zero point. Many measurement scales used in psychology fall somewhere between ordinal and interval scales with respect to quantitative precision. As an example of one of these "quasi-interval" scales, a five-point scale for recording judgments of aggressiveness is not likely to reflect exactly equal intervals of aggression. However, it may be quantitatively stronger than an ordinal scale, because it allows distributions of scores other than the flat distribution yielded by ordinal scaling whereby one individual is placed at each rank.

Ratio scales.   While they are more truly quantitative than either nominal scales or ordinal scales, interval scales lack one feature that would qualify them for the full range of quantitative operations. The missing feature is a true zero value that makes it possible to derive quantitative ratios of the properties scaled and to speak of "twice as much" or "one-third as much" of a property. Scales that have equal intervals and true zero points—such as scales of time, weight, and length—are known as *ratio scales.* Needless to say, few behavioral variables are measured in terms of ratio scales.

Statistical Problems in Developmental Research

Behavioral research draws upon a large body of statistical theory and methodology developed by mathematicians and specialists in various fields where statistics are needed for practical purposes. Many statistical methods used in behavioral research were originally developed for research related to agriculture. Thus, it was for research related to the production of beer that William S. Gosset, a statistician employed by the Guinness brewery in Dublin, invented the well-known t test for the significance of the difference between two means. (Because Guinness forbade its employees to publish the results of their work, the t test was published under the pseudonym "Student," and is often known as "Student's test.")

The basis for extending agricultural statistical methods to behavioral research is that both focus on variables in populations of individuals that differ from one another in many unknown and uncontrollable ways. Furthermore, since research on entire populations is rarely feasible in either field, population characteristics must be inferred from samples. Thus, the different effects of fertilizers A and B on the weight of potatoes is assessed by randomly assigning plots (samples) of potatoes to receive the different fertilizers. Randomization is employed to control for possible differences in soil fertility, moisture, sunlight, etc., that might affect potato weights over and above the effects of the two fertilizers. If at the end of the experiment a t test shows potatoes receiving fertilizer A to be significantly heavier than those receiving fertilizer B, it is concluded that the population of potatoes defined by the fact that they receive fertilizer A will be heavier than the population of otherwise identical potatoes receiving fertilizer B.

In more elaborate studies, where several fertilizers might be compared under various conditions of fertility, moisture, or sunlight, a factorial design would be appropriate. An ANOVA—basically an extension of the t test to comparisons of multiple samples—would then be employed to test the significance of the differences among the potatoes receiving the various conditions.

Like agricultural researchers, behavioral researchers often employ statistics that compare differences in scores from one sample to another and from one time to another. For example, the number of words learned under various reinforcement conditions or the differences in attitude scores obtained by people hearing different communications can be analyzed in same way as the effects of fertilizer on potatoes. The use of correlation coefficients to portray relationships between variables is likewise similar in agricultural, behavioral, and many other areas of research. However, this statistical tradition may handicap developmental research that is not easily analyzable in terms of group differences on a single quantitative variable or correlations between individual variables. One source of difficulty for traditional statistical approaches is that developmental changes in behavior often make it necessary to use different methods of measurement for subjects of different ages. A second problem is that many developmental differences may be better viewed in terms of integrated patterns of functioning than in terms of isolated variables whose values merely increase or decrease with age. In the following sections, we will consider these problems in more depth and then discuss potential statistical solutions.

Age Changes in Measurement Possibilities

Suppose we hypothesize that high activation during infancy is predictive of aggressive behavior problems and inefficient learning in later life. Even if we do not know what determines activation level, a finding that it *predicts* later problems would provide a basis for further research on the causal relationships and on prevention of these problems. Because prediction from earlier to later characteristics is sought, a longitudinal strategy must be employed, be it a conventional longitudinal design or a longitudinal–sequential design. Since the independent variable of activation level cannot be experimentally manipulated, a correlational approach is adopted with the intention of making cross-lagged panel analyses (cf. chapter 4). The possibility that activation level may be congenitally determined makes it desirable to obtain observations from birth onward.

Infant activation level can be measured in a variety of ways. The child can be placed in a small crib mounted on a stabilimeter—a device resembling a grocery scale and designed to measure the amount of movement in the crib. Other devices, resembling self-winding wrist watches, can be placed on the child's wrists, ankles, and back to record specific body movements. Trained observers can employ rating scales to score activity level. These methods may remain useful until 8 or 10 months of age, when the child's increased mobility makes the stabilimeter unusable. The child's increasing curiosity, personal preferences, and dexterity may also reduce the usefulness of the wrist and ankle devices because they become vulnerable to destruction and may cause the child to behave atypically when he is wearing them. The presence of raters may also begin to influence the child's behavior. Even if this potential source of bias is overcome by hiding the raters or getting the child thoroughly accustomed to them, the type of behavior they rate changes radically.

As the subjects age, many changes must be made in how the independent variable of activation is defined and measured. The dependent variables of aggression and efficiency of learning are unlikely to be meaningfully measurable at all until long after activation can first be measured. Measures of these may progress from observational ratings, to standardized behavioral tests, to paper-and-pencil tests. Even when exactly the same measures can be used at two or more age levels, the distribution of scores is likely to change greatly as subjects mature.

Consequently, the meaning of any particular score may change as an above-average score at one age becomes a below-average score at a later age. A subject whose behavior remained perfectly stable from one age to another would be changing greatly in rank order compared to his peers. Furthermore, a measuring scale in which no subjects obtain the top score at one age may have to be replaced at another age because many subjects obtain the top score and some would obtain still higher scores if the limits of the scale did not impose a *ceiling effect* by artificially curtailing the distribution of scores. Thus, identification of stability and change in behavior over long periods is likely to require coordination of changing methods of measurement, changing measuring scales, and changing meanings for particular scores over time.

Changes in Variables vs. Changes in Individuals

In the typical application of statistics, variables are treated as if they, rather than individuals, are the essential realities to be studied. For some purposes, individuals are similar enough that statistically significant relationships between variables within a sample validly portray all members of the sample and the population from which it is drawn. However, when populations are comprised of complex individuals, relationships that hold true for large enough proportions to produce statistically significant findings do not necessarily hold true for every individual in a population. In developmental research, this may mean that certain characteristics at a particular age are predictive of later characteristics in *some* people, but not in others.

The problem is not merely that individuals progress along a particular path at different *rates* or that they differ in the *size* of their responses to environmental conditions. Individual differences in rate of development and in size of responses to environmental conditions exist in potatoes just as much as in humans, and individual variation of this sort is what requires agricultural researchers, like behavioral researchers, to employ samples of subjects rather than single subjects. The problem of individuality in development, however, goes beyond individual variation in specific variables. It concerns individual differences in the *organization* of behavior and the possibility that much development involves changes in patterns of organization that can be identified better in terms of typologies of individuals than in terms of isolated variables averaged across many individuals. Consider, for example, this vignette from the Berkeley Guidance Study, in which personality development was studied longitudinally from infancy to the age of 40:

> One of the subjects, at age 30, was a bright, articulate, talented, prize-winning architect, and the father of two bright children. Our early records

through his preschool and grade and high school years showed him to be a toneless, inarticulate, withdrawn child, held over several terms in school, and graduating from high school without adequate college recommendation. He had consistently obtained relatively low IQs through year 18. To quote him at age 30: "You have to admit I was a listless odd ball." While we were trying to ferret out with him in a long series of interviews the many factors he felt were associated with the marked changes from his first twenty years, he interrupted to say, "You personality birds could profit from an intensive art course in design. You would discover that what makes a good design, and the possibilities are almost infinite, is that combination of atypical or offbeat elements which grabs one's attention and enough compensating strengths to hold the total in balance, even precarious balance. People, too, come in an almost infinite variety of designs with unique individuality and compensating strengths, which, in my case, were very slow in developing." (Honzik and Macfarlane, 1970, pp. 1–2)

Block (1971, pp. 10–11) puts the implications for developmental research as follows:

Developmental psychology has been hampered in its progress to date because . . . it has staked much on and clung too long to the potent assumption of uniformity of relationships. The massive influence of this expectation on the strategy of empirical research in developmental psychology may be seen in two ways: across people and across time. Across people, the presumption in its pure form asserts that *all* people develop in essentially the same way. There may be differences in initial or terminal status and in the rate or timing of development, but these differences pose no conceptual problem so long as the sequence or direction of development remains constant. Across time, the hypothesis of uniformity suggests that relationships or qualities observed at one time may be expected to apply later as well. . . .

Across people, it is often recognized that the sexes may mature differently. Within like-sexed groups, however, there usually is reluctance to abandon the paradigm of relationship uniformity for a Pandora's box of so many different lawfulnesses that their aggregation appears conceptually unmanageable. The idea of different developmental paths—different in kind and in direction, rather than simply different in rate of traversal—is anathema to the nomothetic view that seeks universal laws applicable to one and all.

Nomothetic vs. idiographic views. In referring to the "nomothetic view," Block raises an issue that has sparked controversy in many branches of psychology. *Nomothetic* approaches (Greek *nomos*, law) seek general laws that are assumed to govern all individual cases. *Idiographic* approaches (Greek *idio*, personal, separate), by contrast, seek to portray the behavior of particular individuals. According to the idiographic view, even if there are general principles of behavior, each individual represents a unique outcome of the interaction of these principles. Since it may be impossible to determine the precise nature of all the interactions involved, it is contended that the best way to predict an individual's behavior is to identify patterns that are peculiar to him. This is the point made by the subject in the Berkeley Guidance Study.

While nomothetic and idiographic approaches have both had their defenders and detractors, the two approaches are not mutually exclusive. In applying nomothetic physical laws to the design of a bridge, for example, an architect may face a situation that is unique with respect to ground conditions, load requirements, and available materials. The bridge he designs must be uniquely structured to do the job, and the size, strength, and placement of the components depend upon their roles in the overall structure. Nevertheless, no matter how unique the structure, it cannot violate general physical laws. Thus, while the bridge exists as a structure differing in many respects from all others, and while the role of each component may be understood better in an idiographic fashion as part of the whole than as an isolated variable, the whole and all its components are governed by the same nomothetic principles that apply to all physical structures. Because idiographic analyses are always constrained in this way by nomothetic principles, the value of an idiographic approach must be judged according to whether it increases understanding of how component variables are organized into wholes and whether identification of these wholes can improve our overall understanding of the phenomenon under study.

In his contention that developmental psychology has been hampered by too great a reliance on nomothetic approaches, Block is criticizing the assumptions that relationships between variables from one age to another are similar in all people and that relationships between variables are similar from one period to another. In confronting the issue raised by Block, it is important to distinguish between *theoretically* based assumptions of uniformity, on the one hand, and assumptions of uniformity made for *methodological* purposes, on the other. In actuality, some of our prominent theories of personality–social and cognitive development emphasize differences rather than uniformities in the organization of variables during different developmental periods. According to Erikson's (1963) theory of psychosocial development and Piaget's (1970) theory of cognitive development, for example, development consists more of qualitative changes in overall mental organization than of quantitative changes in isolated variables. These theories in effect define each stage of development in idiographic terms, as a coherent system rather than as a collection of isolated variables.

While the idiographic aspect of Piaget's theory is constrained by the assumption of uniformity among people in the nature and sequence of cognitive stages, Erikson allows for individual variations in the outcomes of what he considers to be universal developmental crises. Proceeding from a different set of assumptions, S–R theorists argue that individual differences in development can be as great as the environmental variations encountered. Some of our major theories thus emphasize idiographic differences among periods and people at least as much as uniformity with respect to basic principles of functioning.

On the other hand, certain features of behavioral *methodology* may mold developmental research into a quest for uniformities far more narrow than our theories of development imply. Such features arise in part from the statistical heritage that guides most behavioral research. Because a basic criterion for a "finding" is that a statistically significant relationship be obtained from observations on samples assumed to be broadly representative, it is too often implied that such findings apply uniformly to all members of the population sampled. However, unless the relationships are identical for all subjects—in which case statistics may be unnecessary—it is possible that statistically significant results reflect relationships among variables in some individuals but that the variables are unrelated or even oppositely related in at least a few individuals. Likewise, a finding of no significant relationship among variables in a sample may mask the fact that the variables have strong positive relationships in some individuals but strong negative relationships in others. Thus, both because statistical relationships among variables in groups may mask differences among individuals, and because identification of organized systems of variables may be more productive than analyses of isolated variables, it is important to consider ways of adapting statistical methods more effectively to the needs of developmental research. The purpose of the following sections is, therefore, to present statistical methods that may be of special value in developmental research. The emphasis will be upon the logic and diversity of potential approaches to analyzing developmental data rather than upon the mechanics of computation. *Brief computational procedures are presented in the text, but more extended procedures and tables not readily available in general statistics texts are in the Appendix in fourteen sections, referred to in the text as, e.g., Section A-1.*

Parametric Statistics

Statistical methods are often divided into parametric and nonparametric. Although there is no unanimity on how to distinguish between the two categories, parametric methods in general depend more heavily upon assumptions about the distributions of the variables to which they are applied. The *t* test, for example, is regarded as a parametric method because it is based upon the assumption that scores on the variables tested are distributed according to a normal curve. The accuracy of the p value obtained for a particular value of t depends on the degree to which the population sampled is indeed normally distributed and its parameters are accurately estimated by the mean and standard deviation of the sample. The "parametric" nature of the t test thus inheres in the fact that its validity rests upon parameters of a theoretically defined distribution. The ANOVA and the test for the significance of the Pearson product-moment correlation are also parametric tests.

In order to be normally distributed, a variable must be measured according to a ratio scale, an interval scale, or a quasi-interval scale. A variable "measured" on only a nominal scale obviously cannot form a normal distribution of scores ordered by size. While a variable measured on an ordinal scale does form a distribution of scores ordered by size, the distribution cannot be normal because each rank does not represent a uniform quantitative interval and because there is only one score at each rank, except for tied scores. Although a group of tied scores can be given the average of ranks they would have obtained if they differed slightly, the true distribution of scores on an ordinal scale is assumed to be flat—i.e., there is one score at each rank from the highest to the lowest, forming a straight-line distribution of frequencies, rather than the bell-shaped distribution of the normal curve. In effect, then, the assumption of a normal curve also implies an assumption about the type of measurement scale employed.

Some parametric tests entail still further assumptions beyond the assumption of normality. The t test for comparison of two sample means assumes that both populations sampled have similar standard deviations, while the ANOVA entails the same assumption for all the populations sampled. However, despite the seemingly restrictive assumptions on which parametric tests are based, "Monte Carlo" studies have shown tests such as the t and ANOVA to be minimally affected by certain deviations from their assumptions. (In a Monte Carlo study, a computer is used to generate large populations of numbers distributed according to certain predetermined criteria, e.g., nonnormal distribution, specified standard deviations, etc. By performing a statistical test on many samples drawn randomly from such populations, it can be determined whether the number of statistically significant outcomes corresponds to that predicted by the theory of the test.) It has been found that deviations from normality and differences among samples in standard deviations do not greatly distort the number of significant ts and Fs obtained, *provided that* the samples being compared are similar in size and not too small (Boneau, 1960; Box, 1954; Donaldson, 1968).

The Pearson product-moment correlation, designated as r, is not itself a parametric statistic, because the size of the coefficient expresses the degree of relationship between paired scores in a sample no matter what their distribution. However, the validity of the test for the p value of r depends upon parametric assumptions. If, for example, one variable is extremely skewed in one direction, while the other variable is oppositely skewed, the maximum r obtainable will be less than 1. Since the test of significance for r assumes that the correlation can range from −1 to + 1 (McNemar, 1969), the p value obtained for an r from a sample in which opposite skewness of the two variables limits the size of r may be invalid. Other deviations from normality may also affect the validity of p values obtained for r. Using Monte Carlo methods, Norris and Hjelm (1961) found that repeated samples from markedly nonnormal distributions produced inappropriate numbers of correlations having significant p values when the true correlations of the populations were high, although not when the true correlations were very low. Since the direction of deviation from the proper number of significant correlations depended on the way in which the population deviated from normality, no generalizations could be made about whether deviations from normality make the standard p values for r too liberal or too conservative.

A second weakness of r is that it reflects only linear correlation. If two variables are related in some nonlinear fashion, r will typically be small. There is, however, another correlational statistic, the *correlation ratio*, designated as η (Greek letter *eta*), that reflects the accuracy with which one variable (call it Y) can be predicted from a second (call it X), even if their relationship is not linear. It does this in terms of the proportion of variance in Y that is categorizable according to values of X. The rationale for eta is like that of the ANOVA: Both yield a p value indicating whether the Y scores differ significantly more *between* groups that differ in X than *within* groups that are similar on X. Since the overall ratio reflects any consistent differences in the magnitude of Y scores from one value of X to another, it does not matter whether Y increases or decreases from one particular value of X to another. Curvilinearity of correlation between X and Y is indicated if eta is greater than r for the same data. Computational procedures and methods for evaluating the size of the difference between eta and r are found in Appendix, Section A-2.

Eta may generally be more useful than r in determining the significance of the relationship between age and variables that change with age in a nonlinear fashion. As an example, children's preoccupation with a particular Eriksonian conflict would be expected to begin at a low level, rise with age to a peak, and then fall again. The Pearson r could not detect a curvilinear relationship like this, but eta could. However, the exact shape of the relationship must be identified by other means, such as graphical portrayal. Because eta indicates the degree to which one variable can be predicted from another, two etas can be calculated for each set of paired scores—i.e., the eta portraying the predictability of Y from X and of X from Y.

Nonparametric Statistics

If developmental research dealt only with variables scored on quasi-interval, interval, or ratio scales and distributed in ways compatible with parametric statistics, there might be little need to look beyond parametric statistics. However, age changes in measurement possibilities and the potential importance of qualitative differences in individuals and in developmental levels make it important to consider statistical models other than the parametric. There are also many situations outside of developmental research in which data are simply not amenable to parametric statistical analysis. To meet these needs, statistical techniques known as *nonparametric* or *distribution-free* have been developed. To paraphrase Conover (1971), a statistical method is nonparametric if it satisfies any of the following criteria:

1. It may be applied to data scored in a nominal fashion.
2. It may be applied to data scored in an ordinal fashion.
3. It may be applied to data scored in an interval or ratio fashion regardless of the shape of the parent distribution.

Its exceptional clarity makes Siegel's (1956) textbook, *Non-parametric methods for the behavioral sciences*, the most helpful source for the reader interested in further details of most of the methods to be discussed. However, if Siegel's book cannot be obtained, the books by Conover (1971) and Hollander and Wolfe (1973) are useful alternatives, while Mosteller and Rourke (1973) provide in-depth treatment of non-parametric statistics for advanced students.

Statistical Tests for Nominal Data

The most widely used nonparametric test is the chi square, and its computational procedures are covered in general statistics courses. In the 2×2 chi square, the data typically consist of two samples of subjects scored on some variable that can have either of two possible outcomes. For example, it might by hypothesized that more 12-year olds than 16-year olds answer "true" to a particular true–false item on a personality test. The chi square merely indicates the probability that the proportions of trues and falses found for each age differ significantly from those expected if there were in fact no difference between the populations from which the samples were drawn. The chi square can also be used to test relationships between two variables each of which is scored in more than two categories and to test the deviation of observed outcomes from theoretically predicted outcomes of a single categorically scored variable.

For 2 × 2 comparisons of samples that are too small for a valid chi square test (expected frequencies are less than five subjects in one or more cells), a handy alternative is *Fisher's exact test*. This test provides the exact chance probability of any combination of frequencies found in a 2 × 2 analysis. For the small sample sizes for which it is most useful, no computation at all is necessary because tables of the probabilities for each possible outcome have been constructed. Appendix, Section A-3 presents p values for sample sizes up to 13 in each group, together with instructions for using Fisher's test.

Another handy test for which tables of probabilities make computations unnecessary is the *binomial test* for the significance of various proportions of outcomes in a single dichotomously scored variable. If a particular distribution of outcomes is expected by chance (e.g., 50 percent true and 50 percent false responses to a true–false item), the tables provide the p value for the distribution of responses actually obtained in a given number of observations. Section A-4 provides p values for sample sizes up to 90. When observations on a dichotomously scored variable are paired in some way, as when comparing successes and failures by the same subjects on two items, the binomial test can also be employed to determine whether the proportion passing the first and failing the second (+ − pattern) significantly exceeds the proportion showing the reverse (− +) pattern. For example, if you wished to determine whether children pass item A on a test before they pass item B, you could treat the + − pattern (pass A, fail B) as one outcome, the − + pattern (fail A, pass B) as the opposite outcome, and drop all subjects with + + and − − patterns. If the + − outcomes significantly exceed the − + outcomes (as shown by the table of p values in Section A-4), then item A is easier than item B for the population sampled.

If, instead of comparing the proportion of successes and failures on two items, you wished to compare the proportions on three or more items, then *Cochran's Q test* can be employed, as shown in Section A-5. The purpose of this test is to compare three or more sets of dichotomous scores that are related by virtue of being obtained on the same or matched subjects, as in the single factor randomized blocks design presented in chapter 4. Thus, beside comparing the responses to several items by the same subjects, it can be used to compare the dichotomous scores obtained on a single item by matched groups of subjects who have received different experimental conditions. For example, the number of successes and failures on a conservation task could be compared for groups that had been randomly assigned to different training conditions.

Statistical tests that assume ordinal or interval measurement cannot be applied to nominal data, but tests designed for nominal data can be applied to data scored quantitatively. Some of the tests for nominal data go under different names when applied to quantitative data. The 2×2 chi square, for example, is known as the *median test* when applied to a quantitative variable dichotomized at the median. The binomial test is known as the *sign test* when the two possible outcomes of a variable are defined in terms of "greater than" or "less than." This would be true, for example, when comparing the number of subjects who obtain higher scores on their second try at a task than on their first try. The binomial test is known as the *quantile test* when the two outcomes are defined as being greater or less than some specific score—e.g., a score ≤ 21 is considered to be one category of outcome, while a score > 21 is considered to be the other.

Because a parametric test is more sensitive to the quantitative properties of data than is a nonparametric test, the parametric test will usually be more "powerful." That is, if the parametric assumptions are adequately approximated, the parametric test is more likely to yield statistically significant relationships with a particular sample size. However, quantification of psychological data is often quite arbitrary, such data rarely satisfy the criteria for true interval or ratio scaling, and many relationships may be nonlinear. Recasting data into forms amenable to nonparametric analysis may therefore reveal relationships not evident when they are analyzed with parametric statistics. For example, a Pearson product-moment correlation may show no significant relationship between ratings of activity level in the first days of life and number of signs of brain damage reported for children at the age of 3. However, if the children's scores for activity level were divided into three groups and if each group were in turn divided into three categories according to the *types* of neurological signs exhibited, a 3×3 chi square might show a significant relationship between activity level and type of sign, even though a parametric analysis which treated both variables in a linear fashion revealed no relationship.

Measures of Correlation for Nominal Data

Measures of correlation between categorically scaled variables can be obtained from the chi square. The *phi correlation* (designated as r_P or φ) is calculated from the chi square (χ^2) value for a 2×2 table by the formula $r_P = \sqrt{\chi^2/N}$ where N is the total number of subjects in the table. The phi correlation is equal to the Pearson product-moment correlation obtained on the same dichotomous data, and its p value is that of the χ^2 derived from the same 2×2 table.

A second measure of correlation, the *contingency coefficient* (C), is derived from χ^2 by the formula $C = \sqrt{\chi^2/N + \chi^2}$. An advantage of the contingency coefficient is that it can be used to portray the strength of relationship between two variables scored in terms of more than two categories, i.e., for χ^2 tables larger than 2 × 2. A disadvantage is that the size of a particular C is comparable only to Cs on other tables having the same number of rows and columns. This is because the number of cells in the table sets an upper limit on the size of the C obtainable, with larger Cs possible in larger tables. The value of C obtained for a 2 × 2 table is smaller than the r_P obtained for the same table to a degree shown by the formula $C = \sqrt{r_P{}^2/1+r_p{}^2}$. Although calculation of the exact p value for C is cumbersome, an adequate estimate of the p value for C is given by the p value for the χ^2 calculated on the same table.

Statistical Tests for Ordinal Data

Comparisons of two distributions.   Statistical methods meeting Conover's (1971) second criterion for nonparametric statistics make use of the relationships "greater than" and "less than" among scores. Whereas the median test, sign test, and quantile test apply to dichotomous divisions of scores into "greater than" or "less than" one particular value, other ordinal methods make use of the greater quantitative precision obtainable with more extensive rank ordering. The *Mann–Whitney test,* for example, is designed to compare two samples of scores in a manner analogous to the two-sample *t* test. It is nearly as powerful as the *t* test when all the assumptions of the *t* test are met and is much more powerful than the *t* test when the data violate the assumptions of the *t* test, e.g., when samples of unequal size are markedly skewed and/or when the standard deviation of one sample is two or more times greater than that of the other sample. To perform the Mann–Whitney test, the scores from both samples combined are rank ordered, with tied scores being given the average of the ranks they span. The test then compares the sum of the ranks from one sample with the sum of the ranks with the other sample. The computational formula and the *p* values for differences between sample sizes up to 20 are provided in Section A-6.

The *Wilcoxon matched-pairs signed ranks test* employs ranking in a different way to compare two sets of scores obtained either on the same individuals or on pairs of matched individuals. Whereas the Mann–Whitney test is appropriate for comparisons like those made with the *t* test for two independent samples, the Wilcoxon test is designed for comparisons like those made with the *t* test for matched pairs. To perform the Wilcoxon test, the difference between the scores in each pair is first calculated. These differences are then ranked according to their magnitudes and a plus or minus is assigned to the rank of each difference, depending on whether the first or second score in the pair is greater. To determine whether one set of scores differs from the other, the sum of the differences given plus signs is compared to the sum of the differences given minus signs, as shown in Section A-7.

The *Kolmogorov–Smirnov test* employs yet another approach to ranked data. Using this test, the cumulative frequency of subjects obtaining each of a series of ranked scores is compared either to a cumulative frequency of scores predicted by a theoretical distribution (one-sample test) or to a cumulative frequency of scores obtained by a second sample of subjects (two-sample test). Because it compares the *shapes* of two distributions, the Kolmogorov–Smirnov test is called a test of *goodness of fit.*

Suppose, for example, you wished to determine whether children of two ages performed similarly on a measure that is scored on a scale of 1 to 5. You are interested not only in whether the average score at one age is higher than at the other age, but whether there are differences in the proportions obtaining any of the five possible scores at each age. Figure 5-1 illustrates cumulative frequency distributions for two groups. To apply the Kolmogorov–Smirnov test, the proportions of subjects at each ranked score are calculated for each of the two distributions. The score showing the largest difference between the distributions is then identified, as indicated by D in Figure 5-1, and a p value for this difference is obtained as shown in Section A-8. The test is thus sensitive not only to a difference in the means or medians of two distributions, but to a difference at any point in the distributions. Consequently, two distributions having similar means and/or medians may still be shown to differ significantly because of differences in the proportions of subjects obtaining particular scores.

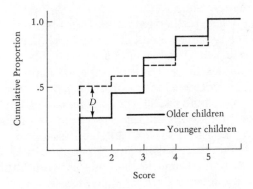

Figure 5-1. Comparison between cumulative proportions of scores obtained by two age groups.

Comparisons of multiple distributions.   In addition to tests for two distributions of ordinal data, certain nonparametric tests are designed to function like the ANOVA. The *Kruskal–Wallis one-way analysis of variance*, based on ranks, functions like a single-factor ANOVA in which several unrelated samples are compared with respect to their scores on one variable. However, the Kruskal–Wallis test can be used with smaller samples than the ANOVA and may be more powerful than the ANOVA if the sample sizes differ considerably and the variances and/or shapes of the distributions also differ considerably. Section A-9 provides the method for assessing the significance of the differences among the average rank orders obtained by three or more samples.

The median test can also be extended to function like a single-factor ANOVA by calculating the median of the scores across all groups to be compared. Chi square is then computed on the table formed by dividing each group into two cells, one containing the number of scores from that group above the median, the other containing the number below the median. The number of subjects in each group need not be equal. Such an approach may be especially useful when comparing various groups of subjects on a measure that is so skewed as to make parametric ANOVAs and those based on ranks inappropriate. As an example, frequency of glances at an experimenter by a child who has been given a task to work on is sometimes used as a measure of dependency on cues from other people or "outerdirectedness" (e.g, Achenbach and Weisz, 1975a). The distribution of frequencies is often highly skewed, with a large proportion of subjects making one or no glances and progressively fewer making greater numbers of glances. In a comparison of the glances made by children of four ages, the overall median might be found to be one glance. The children in each age group can be divided into those making one or no glances and those making more than one glance, and a chi square can be computed on the resulting 2 × 4 table (median split on glances × four age levels).

Wilson (1956) has further extended this approach to analysis of two-factor designs based on median splits. As shown in Section A-10, his procedure makes it possible to analyze the *interaction* of the two independent variables, as well as their separate main effects. Thus, sex could be added as a dimension to form a 2 × 2 × 4 (median split on glances × sex × age) analysis. The chi square can also be used in other ways to analyze interactions among more than two independent variables (cf. Goodman, 1970; Winer, 1971). In effect, most nonrepeated measures designs previously reserved for parametric ANOVAs can now be analyzed with nonparametric methods as well, although analyses with more than three factors are cumbersome.

Repeated measures designs in which scores are obtained from the *same* or *matched* subjects under several conditions (randomized block designs) can be analyzed with the *Friedman two-way analysis of variance*. This test functions like Cochran's Q test does for dichotomous data and like a single-factor repeated-measures ANOVA for data that qualify for parametric analyses. In applying the Friedman test, the scores for each subject (or "block") are rank ordered, the resulting ranks are summed within each condition, and a p value is obtained for the differences among the sums of ranks in each condition, as shown in Section A-11.

Measures of Correlation for Ordinal Data

The degree of correlation between two sets of ranked scores can be expressed with *Spearman's rank-order correlation*, designated as r_s, rho, or ρ (the Greek letter rho). If there are no ties among the ranked scores, the size of r_s is the same as that of the Pearson r calculated on the same ranked data, but r_s is not greatly affected by ties. As shown in Section A-12, the p value of r_s is computed differently from that of r. A slightly larger r_s is needed to obtain the same p value, although r_s is easier than r to compute. When it is important to know the p value for large correlations in populations having markedly nonnormal distributions, r_s may be preferable to the Pearson r because nonnormality can distort the p values for r, especially when r is large (Norris and Hjelm, 1961). If the data are scaled in quasi-interval, interval, or ratio form, they would, of course, have to be transformed to ranks.

While r_s portrays correlations between two sets of scores, Kendall has developed a correlation coefficient for portraying the degree of association among several sets of ranked scores on the same subjects. Known as the *Kendall coefficient of concordance* and designated by the letter W, this statistic is based upon the differences in rankings received by each subject when the subjects have been ranked on several variables or several times on the same variable. The larger the differences in the mean rankings, the stronger the association among the sets of ranks. For example, suppose that eighth-grade English, mathematics, history, science, and art teachers were all asked to rank 20 students on creativity. If agreement among the teachers were high, then a student ranked 1 by one teacher would tend to be ranked close to 1 by the other teachers. Likewise, a student ranked 20 by one teacher would tend to be ranked close to 20 by the other teachers. As a result, the average ranks received by the 20 students would range from about 1 to 20. On the other hand, if agreement among the teachers were low, a student ranked 1 by one teacher might be ranked 20 by a second teacher, 15 by a third, 5 by a fourth, etc. In this case, the average rank received by each student would be close to the middle of the 20 possible ranks and the difference among the students in mean rankings would be low.

The W obtained for a series of rankings has a linear relationship to the average of the r_s calculated on every pair of rankings, as expressed in the equation: average $r_s = (kW-1)/(k-1)$ where k is the number of rankings. However, unlike r_s, W ranges only from 0 to $+1$, rather than from -1 to $+1$, because there cannot be complete disagreement between more than two sets of rankings considered together. Computational procedures and a table for the significance of W can be found in Section A-13.

Scalogram and Related Methods

Beside focusing on co-relationships between variables and subjects, developmental research focuses upon the *sequence* in which behaviors emerge. While the ultimate purpose for studying such sequences may be to identify causal relationships, rigorous description of a sequence is often an important accomplishment in itself. Furthermore, theories of development make specific predictions about the order in which behaviors should emerge. These predictions can be tested by determining whether behaviors predicted to emerge late in a sequence are in fact evident only in individuals who also manifest all the behaviors predicted to emerge earlier in the sequence. The most general method of testing for ordered sequences—known as *scalogram analysis*—was illustrated in chapter 1 (see Table 1-1) with Schwartz and Scholnick's (1970) study of the sequence of judgments involved in conservation.

Scalogram analysis is purely descriptive. It merely portrays the number of responses in a sample that conform and fail to conform to a particular ordering, without yielding a value for the probability that the items form a scale in the population sampled. The inventor of scalogram analysis, Louis Guttman (1950), proposed that the degree to which a sample of responses approximates a unidimensional scale be assessed in terms of a *coefficient of reproducibility* (Rep). This consists of the proportion of responses in the sample that can be reproduced from the overall ordering of subjects into a pattern that most nearly approximates a uniform order. For example, consider the patterns of positive and negative responses portrayed in Table 5-1(a) for six subjects on five items. When the items are listed in an order that maximizes the scale-like consistency of the responses, the number of responses conforming to the ordering is divided by the total number of responses to yield the Rep. As shown in Table 5-1(b), the 30 responses (five by each of six subjects) can be ordered so that only one response is out of order—subject B's positive response to item 4. The Rep is thus 29/30 = .967.

While the general strategy of ordering items of behavior according to whether they are positive or negative (present or absent) is well suited to

TABLE 5-1. Positive and Negative Responses to Five Items by Six Subjects.

(a) Raw Distribution by Item and Subject

Subject	1	2	3	4	5
			Item		
A	−	−	−	−	+
B	−	−	−	+	+
C	+	−	−	−	+
D	+	−	+	+	+
E	+	−	−	+	+
F	+	+	+	+	+

(b) Scaled Order of Responses

Subject	2	3	4	1	5
			Item		
F	+	+	+	+	+
D	−	+	+	+	+
E	−	−	+	+	+
B	−	−	+	−	+
C	−	−	−	+	+
A	−	−	−	−	+

developmental research, there are several problems with Guttman's procedure. A minor problem is evident in Table 5-1(a): Because equal numbers of subjects gave positive responses to items 1 and 4, a 2–3–1–4–5 ordering of items would yield the same Rep as the 2–3–4–1–5 ordering shown in Table 5-1(b). According to the former ordering, subject C would have a − − + − + pattern, whereas subject B has this pattern when the latter ordering is used. Since this merely means that items 1 and 4 are equal in difficulty, the choice between the two possible orders is arbitrary.

Another problem is that Guttman's procedure is cumbersome and somewhat subjective, especially if there are many subjects and/or items. Furthermore, the overall proportion of positive and negative responses determines the Rep obtainable by chance. At the extremes, if all responses were either positive or negative, there could be no violations of order and the only possible Rep would be 1.00.

Green (1956) has proposed methods for simplifying computation and for evaluating Rep in light of the minimum reproducibility obtainable with particular overall frequencies of positive and negative responses. Green's computational method merely entails ranking each item according to how many positive responses it received. The rank ordering of items provides the scale, which is then tested for Rep as shown in Section A-14. Green's procedure for evaluating the Rep, also shown in Section A-14, entails calculating the Rep expected if items receiving the obtained number of positive and negative responses were totally independent of one another. Green called this Rep_{Ind} (the Rep obtainable if the items were independent of one another). It is also known as the *minimum marginal reproducibility*, because it is the minimum reproducibility possible with the observed number of positive and negative responses. What Green calls an *index of consistency* (I), or *coefficient of scalability*, is then calculated by the formula $I = Rep - Rep_{Ind}/1 - Rep_{Ind}$. An I of 1.00 indicates perfect scalability, whereas an I of .00 indicates scalability no higher than expected by chance for the obtained totals of positive and negative responses. An I of well above .60 is regarded as indicating that a scale is unidimensional (Nie, Hull, Steinbrenner, and Bent, 1975). One widely available package of statistical programs for computers, the Statistical Package for the Social Sciences (SPSS; Nie et al., 1975) contains a program for scalogram analysis and the index of consistency. Although scalogram analysis deals with dichotomously scored items, dichotomous cutting points can be established on items originally scored in more numerous categories. With the aid of a computer program such as that in the SPSS, the cutting points can be juggled to obtain maximum scalability with a given set of data.

Developmental sequences sometimes involve not only the addition of new behaviors but the disappearance of old ones (e.g., counting covertly to oneself may replace counting on one's fingers). Because negative responses to items preceding those that elicited positive responses are counted as violations of a scale in Guttman's procedure, Leik and Matthews (1968) have devised scalogram procedures that are not weakened by a series of negative responses preceding a series of positive responses. According to the Leik and Matthews procedure, shown in Section A-14, only those negative responses occurring to items located between items eliciting positive responses from a particular subject are counted as violations of a scale. Because the rank ordering of positive responses elicited by each item is not used to provide a unique (or nearly unique) ordering, subjective decisions are required to select the most useful scale ordering. However, tests are provided for the statistical significance of the various orders obtainable with a given set of data.

Identification of Multiple Scales

Scalogram analysis is designed to determine whether a series of items can be consistently ordered along a single dimension. Yet in much research, the intrinsic nature of the phenomena or the difficulty of designing unidimensional measures makes it desirable to identify sub-sets of items each of which might be orderable into a scale, even though the subsets do not collectively form a single scale. For example, in a study of Piagetian tasks, a consistent pattern of successes and failures might occur among conservation tasks for number, length, and weight, while a consistent pattern also occurs among seriation tasks for number, length, and weight, without the two patterns meshing into a single dimension. Thus, even if all subjects showed either a $- - -$, $+ - -$, $+ + -$, or $+ + +$ pattern on the conservation tasks, and similarly scal-able patterns on the seriation tasks, it is possible that many would show patterns across the six tasks that did not conform to a uniform overall scale. Some subjects might pass number conservation, fail number seri-ation, pass length conservation, and fail the remaining tasks. Others might fail all three conservation tasks while passing one or more seri-ation tasks.

An ordering theoretic method.   One way to identify orderings of positive and negative responses without restricting the possibilities to a unidimensional scale is merely to order items by pairs according to the proportion of subjects passing and failing each pair. Referring to their approach as an *ordering theoretic method*, Bart and Airasian (1974) have proposed that, within a series of items, a pair of items be regarded as occurring in sequential order if no more than a preselected percentage of subjects (e.g., 5 percent) fail to conform to a particular ordering of passes and fails on those items. If no more than, say, 5 percent of the subjects show either the $- +$ or $+ -$ pattern—i.e., most subjects show $- -$ or $+ +$ patterns, then the items are considered to be logically equivalent to one another. If each possible pattern $(+ +, - -, - +, + -)$ is shown by more than 5 percent of the subjects, then the items are considered to be logically independent of one another.

In applying their method to seven Piagetian tasks administered to 30 high-school freshmen, Bart and Airasian employed a preselected level of 1 percent (in effect requiring that no subjects out of 30 violate a pattern), with the results shown in Figure 5-2. As can be seen in the figure, passing Task 3 was concluded to be a precondition for passing all the other tasks, and Tasks 1 and 2 were concluded to be logically equivalent preconditions for passing all the remaining tasks. Tasks 4 and 6 were concluded to be logically independent of one another, but preconditions for passing Tasks 5 and 7, which, in turn, were concluded to be logically equivalent to one another.

As Bart and Airasian point out, their procedure, like Guttman's, does not yield an estimate of the probability that the ordering obtained in a sample also prevails in the parent population. The preselected levels for the percentage of order violations to be tolerated is not equivalent to a *p*

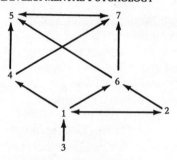

Fig. 5.2. Relationships among
responses to seven Piagetian tasks
as portrayed with Bart and Airasian's
(1974) ordering-theoretic method.

value, because the percentage is not based on the sampling distributions
of any particular statistic. Furthermore, unless sample sizes are quite
large, a preselected tolerance level can only be roughly approximated.
Because 1 percent of 30 is .03 subjects, the actual tolerance level
employed by Bart and Airasian was 0/30 violations. Judgments based
solely on whether there are 0 responses in one or more cells will sometimes be statistically very stringent and sometimes lenient. For example,
using Bart and Airasian's tolerance level, both distributions of responses
shown in Table 5-2 would be interpreted as showing item A to be a
precondition for item B. However, the lefthand distribution, where only
three subjects showed a + − pattern is far weaker evidence for an A→B
pattern in the population than is the righthand distribution, where all 30
subjects showed a + − pattern. According to the binomial distribution,
the 0/3 proportion shown in the + − and − + cells of the lefthand
distribution yields an insignificant two-tailed p value of .25, whereas the
two-tailed p value for the 0/30 proportion shown in the righthand table
is < .001. The value of the descriptive ordering proposed by Bart and
Airasian would be greatly enhanced if the interrelationships among
items were assessed statistically in this way and the p values for each
relationship entered on the appropriate arrow in a diagram like that in
Figure 5-2.

Multiple scalogram analysis. Lingoes (1963) has developed a
method for repeatedly applying scalogram analysis to a set of data in
order to identify subsets of items, each of which may form a Guttman
scale. After items have been rank ordered according to number of positive responses, the item with the largest number of positive responses is
selected. Two-by-two arrays like those in Table 5-2 are then formed in
which relations between the first item and each item having fewer

TABLE 5-2. Two Possible Distributions of
Responses to Items *A* and *B*.

		Item *B*				Item *B*	
		−	+			−	+
Item *A*	+	3	13	Item *A*	+	30	0
	−	14	0		−	0	0

positive responses are examined to find the item having the "smallest distance" from the first item. The smallest distance is defined as the largest sum of − − and + + patterns and the smallest sum of − + and + − patterns, where the number of + − patterns is greater than the − + patterns. In other words, the item is sought that is most like the first item in eliciting positive and negative responses, except that the second item elicits fewer positive responses than the first. This second item is then placed in a 2 × 2 table with each remaining item until the item having the smallest distance from it is found. The procedure is repeated until one of several cutoff points specified in Section A-14 is reached. When a cutoff point is reached, the remaining item receiving the most positive responses is employed to begin the formation of a new scale with any remaining items that qualify, and so on, until no items remain that are close enough to any other item to form a scale. The end result is one or more Guttman scales, each of which can be tested for Rep if desired. In this way, several different scales can be identified within a set of items that would not conform to a single Guttman scale.

Problems in Measuring Change

Measurement of behavioral change is one of the cornerstones of developmental research. In some cases, the objective is to measure naturally occurring change within a group of subjects from one age to another; in other cases, it is to measure changes accompanying experimental manipulations; in still others, it is to *compare* changes occurring either in naturally differing groups or in groups receiving different experimental manipulations. Unfortunately, a number of statistical and empirical problems complicate the measurement of change.

Regression Phenomena

One of the most pervasive problems arises from something Francis Galton (1885) originally observed as what he called "regression towards

mediocrity in stature." In studying heredity, Galton examined the relationship between the mean height of pairs of spouses (called *midparent*
height) and the mean height of their mature offspring. To his surprise, he
noticed that the height of the offspring of tall parents averaged *less* than
that of their parents, whereas the height of offspring of short parents
averaged *more* than that of their parents. It was this tendency for extreme
parents to have offspring more like the population average that Galton
called "regression toward mediocrity."

Galton's discovery was to have two momentous implications for the
future of statistical thinking. On the one hand, the regression phenomena proved to have great generality across many domains and to
greatly complicate what otherwise appears to be a very simple problem
of measurement. On the other hand, Galton observed that, when the
median offspring height was plotted for each midparent height, the
medians formed a straight line, with offspring heights distributed symmetrically around each median on the line. Conversely, when the
median midparent height was calculated for each offspring height, the
midparent heights formed a second straight line, with the midparent
heights being symmetrically distributed around each median. Figure
5-3 illustrates the way in which two different "regression" lines are
produced by plotting median offspring height for each midparent
height, and vice versa. Galton's discovery of how the relationship between two variables was exposed by these two lines led him to formulate
the concept of correlation as a joint function of the "regression" of each
variable on the other. It was this brainchild of Galton that Karl Pearson
put into the computational form known as the Pearson product-moment
correlation.

Variations in errors of measurement.   Returning now to the regression phenomenon itself, this phenomenon stems from the fact that, in
any measurement, the obtained score is a sum of the "true" score and the
errors of measurement. Errors of measurement comprise not only mistakes in the measurement procedure, but uncontrolled variation in what
is being measured—in short, measurement error is everything that
decreases the reliability of measurement. As objective as the
measurement of height may seem, it is nevertheless subject to unreliability stemming from variations in the measuring procedure and the
variable being measured. A person measuring another person with a
standard measuring device may tilt the device differently on successive
occasions, may look at the unit markings from slightly different angles,
and may err in recording the measurement. The person being measured
may also vary in how erect he stands and in whether he stands flat on his
feet or with slight inclinations on the ball or heel of his foot. If measurement of height is subject to so many sources of unreliability, you can

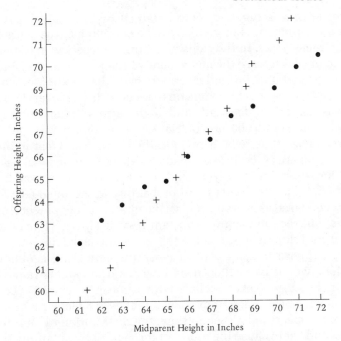

Figure 5-3. Regression lines found when median offspring height is plotted for each midparent height (dots) and median midparent height is plotted for each offspring height (crosses).

imagine how much more susceptible psychological measures are to these effects. However, for the sake of simplicity, we will continue to use height for our illustration of regression effects.

Errors of measurement tend to be normally distributed around the "true" value of the variable measured. Consequently, on any given measurement, the probability of obtaining a score far above or far below the true value is smaller than the probability of obtaining a score close to the true value. This means that, if an extremely high or low score is obtained on one occasion, the next measurement of the same variable is likely to yield a score closer to the true value than one as extreme as the initial score. Thus, if 1000 people who are all really 6 feet tall are each measured once, the actual scores obtained might range from 5 feet 10 inches to 6 feet 2 inches, with a mean of 6 feet. If they are measured again, it would be found that people who obtained extremely high or low scores the first time now obtained scores closer to the mean of the group as a whole—i.e., that their scores had "regressed" toward the mean—merely because ordering six-footers according to their initial scores was, in effect, ordering them according to random errors in their scores. Since the most probable errors in any measurement are those close to the true score, the score obtained by any individual on the second measurement is more likely to be close to his true score than to either extreme. Thus, individuals who initially received extreme scores appear to regress toward the mean merely because the improbable errors of measurement that initially earned them their extreme scores are replaced by more probable errors on the second trial. If everybody in the sample is actually 6 feet tall, and if the errors of measurement are random, there should be no correlation between the first and second measurements—those who were initially recorded as 5 feet 10 inches or 6 feet 2 inches are as likely as anybody else to be recorded as 6 feet on the second measurement. (Conversely, because those who scored 6 feet on the first trial share the same small probability of scoring 6 feet 2 inches on the second trial as everybody else, the number of people scoring 6 feet 2 inches will remain roughly constant from trial to trial, even though different individuals will receive this score on each trial.)

Now suppose that, instead of a sample composed exclusively of six-footers, we measure 1000 people whose true heights range from 5 feet 5 inches to 6 feet 7 inches, with a mean of 6 feet. The actual measurements may range from 5 feet 3 inches to 6 feet 9 inches. If each person were measured a second time, the distribution of measurement errors would again cause the scores of those initially obtaining the most extreme scores to regress toward the mean of the entire sample. However, because in this sample there are true differences in height, a person whose true height is 6 feet 7 inches and who scored 6 feet 9 inches on the first trial would be far more likely to score 6 feet 7 inches than 6 feet on the second trial. In other words, even though the most extreme scores are due to improbable measurement errors that are replaced on the second trial by more probable errors, the fact that differences in the true heights persist from the first to the second trial means that a correlation will be found between the first and second measurements—people who scored 5 feet 3 inches on the first trial are likely to score 5 feet 5 inches on the second trial, but are far less likely to score 6 feet 7 inches than are people who scored 6 feet 9 inches on the first trial, and vice versa.

Variations in true scores. Galton's original problem had a further complication that is also present in much developmental research: Not only did regression effects arise from the random distribution of measurement errors despite a correlation between the first and second scores, but the "true" first and second scores were likely to differ. In Galton's problem the first score in each pair was midparent height, while the second score was the height of the mature offspring (corrected for sex differences). Even assuming that heredity causes a correlation between parent and child heights, many factors other than errors in the measurement of height are likely to affect the correlation. These include nutrition and disease, plus the likelihood that parents do not pass the same genotype for height to all their children.

As it turned out in Galton's case, and in many subsequent empirical problems, the extraneous influences on the true scores tended, like errors of measurement, to be randomly distributed. Thus, even if there were no error of measurement and perfect one-to-one correspondence between parent and child *genotypes* for height, the shortest parents would have offspring whose heights averaged somewhat more than their own, whereas the tallest parents would have offspring whose heights averaged somewhat less than their own. This is because, if environmental influences on height are randomly distributed, the shortest parents are those who not only have genotypes for short stature, but who experienced the most adverse environmental effects on height, and conversely for extremely tall parents. Even if the offspring of each extreme type of parent inherited exactly the same genotypes as their parents, the low probability of their experiencing the same extremes of environment would cause their heights to be closer to the population mean than the heights of their parents, despite the fact that parent–offspring heights are correlated.

The practical implications of regression phenomena can intrude into nearly all aspects of research on changes in individuals from one occasion to another and on relations between scores of individuals who are linked in some way. For example, in many longitudinal studies, comparisons are made between scores obtained at one age and scores obtained at a later age, as was done with IQ in the Fels study described in chapter 1. In that study, children whose IQs were exceptionally high at one age were subsequently found to decline in IQ. Attempts were made to explain this decline in terms of characteristics of the children and their parents. However, the possibility must always be considered that the decline was attributable to regression effects. Since an IQ score is the sum of the "true" IQ and the measurement error, the very highest scores obtained at the earlier testings are likely to have contained more IQ-inflating errors than IQ-deflating errors. At subsequent testings, the most extreme IQ-inflating errors are likely to have been replaced by smaller errors of measurement, which caused the obtained IQs to be closer to the "true" IQs.

Change Scores

It would seem logical to employ the difference between an initial score and a later score to measure behavioral change over time or in response to a particular manipulation. For example, the change between pre- and posttutoring test scores might be employed to compare the effect of different tutoring methods on children with reading disabilities. However, the size of each change score depends not only upon the effects of tutoring, but upon the initial true score and the errors of measurement in the initial and final scores. Thus, children initially obtaining extremely high scores may not appear to benefit much from tutoring, because regression effects from the first to second testing would work against any effects of tutoring on their change scores. Conversely, regression effects might inflate the change scores of initial low scorers.

Even though regression effects may differentially influence change scores of individual high and low scorers, this would not bias an overall comparison between tutoring conditions, provided the groups receiving the different conditions had the same distributions of pretutoring scores. However, if one group initially scored higher than the other, regression effects in that group might attenuate the apparent effects of tutoring on its change scores while enhancing the apparent effects of tutoring on the change scores of the initially lower group.

Other factors also argue against testing the effects of experimental manipulations with groups differing in initial scores on the dependent variable. Even if regression effects can be adequately controlled, ceiling effects in measuring instruments might attentuate change scores of an initially higher scoring group. On the other hand, when an initially high scoring group does improve, there is cause to wonder whether the improvement is as meaningful as the same size improvement in an initially low scoring group. The same absolute change from two different levels of a variable may represent very different percentages of change and may account for different proportions of variance in groups initially scoring at the different levels.

Considerable attention has been devoted to the artifacts arising in the measurement of change and in potential techniques for avoiding them. A variety of viewpoints and solutions have been presented by Harris (1963). Cronbach and Furby (1970) have reviewed the typical situations in which change scores are employed, the statistical risks encountered in these situations, and some compromise statistical techniques to use when the benefits of using change scores appear to outweigh the risks. However, because change scores mask both the initial size of scores and regression effects, most experts agree that their use is to be avoided whenever possible.

Some Alternatives to Change Scores

In cases where the effects of two or more experimental conditions are compared—as in the example of the tutoring programs cited above—the best alternative is initially to equate subjects by random or matched assignment to the experimental conditions and to compare their final scores, rather than their change scores. If final scores are to be compared in groups that differ in initial scores, then it may be possible to partial out the effect of the initial differences by means of *analysis of covariance* (ANCOVA). ANCOVA is basically an ANOVA in which the effect of an unwanted variable (the *covariate*) is partialled out of the relationship between an independent variable and a dependent variable in a manner analogous to partial correlation. In the tutoring example, tutoring condition would be the independent variable, posttutoring reading scores would be the dependent variable, and pretutoring reading scores would be the covariate partialled out. ANCOVA provides less precision of interpretation than comparison of groups who are similar in initial scores, and its validity is weakened if the regression of the dependent variable on the covariate differs much among the groups being compared. However, if the statistical assumptions for ANCOVA are met, it is vastly better than artificially equating groups after the fact by selectively comparing subjects from one group who happened to match subjects from the other group on initial score. When this is done, unrepresentatively high subjects from one group and unrepresentatively low subjects from the other group are compared. Regression effects therefore work in opposite directions in the two samples. Furthermore, because the samples are unrepresentative of their larger populations, findings cannot be generalized to the larger populations.

Much developmental research is focused upon changes in a particular variable across more than two occasions, whether they be different age points or different points in a series of experimental manipulations. Because of the problems raised by change scores, such data are often analyzed with a repeated-measures ANOVA in which the levels of one factor consist of the scores obtained by the same subjects on each of several occasions. Thus, an ANOVA with a single repeated-measures factor might be performed on the reading scores obtained by children at each of three points during a curriculum. An ordinary ANOVA that treated the three sets of scores as if they were on different subjects would not be appropriate because, being on the same individuals, the scores are likely to be correlated from one occasion to another. The repeated-measures ANOVA is designed to take account of these correlations among occasions. A significant F value for the repeated measures ANOVA would indicate that the average scores differed significantly from one testing to another. If two randomly selected samples received two different reading curricula, the comparison between the groups on three occasions could be added as a "between groups" factor to form a 2×3 ANOVA, with "occasions" being a repeated-measures factor. Such an analysis might be superior to merely comparing the two groups at the end of their respective curricula, because it could reveal an interaction between the effects of curriculum and occasions, in case one curriculum showed its greatest effects earlier than the other curriculum.

However, applying a repeated-measures ANOVA to observations made on only two occasions does not avoid the problems inherent in change scores. As pointed out by Huck and McLean (1975), a repeated-measures ANOVA in which one set of initial scores and one set of final scores comprise the repeated-measures dimension will produce exactly the same results as an analysis of the change scores obtained by subtracting the initial from the final scores.

Although moderate deviations from normality and homogeneity of variance do not invalidate ANOVA, the repeated-measures ANOVA requires the additional assumption that the correlations between scores be approximately equal for each pair of occasions. This assumption may be fulfilled under some circumstances, but it is unlikely to be met where experimental manipulations have their effects on different subjects at different points in time and where subjects are studied across age periods separated by substantial intervals. In the latter case, correlations between successive ages are likely to be greater than correlations between the earliest and latest ages studied. Great inconsistency in the correlations of scores between different intervals can produce an excessive number of significant F values. Solutions to this problem include use of nonparametric tests such as the Friedman two-way ANOVA, described earlier, and correction procedures designed to produce more appropriate p values for the Fs obtained with the repeated-measures ANOVA (cf. McCall and Appelbaum, 1973; Wilson, 1975).

Summary

Statistics are used to *describe samples* and to *make inferences about population parameters*. The type of scale employed to measure a variable determines the type of statistical procedures that can be applied to it. Nonparametric statistics are available for all types of scales, whereas *parametric statistics* are generally restricted to *quasi-interval, interval*, and *ratio* scale data that approximate certain assumptions about the shapes of their distributions. Changes in measurement possibilities with age and the potential importance of qualitative patterns of functioning make it essential that developmental research not be restricted to analysis of linear relations between individual variables. The correlation ratio, *eta*, can be used to detect nonlinear relations among pairs of variables.

Nonparametric statistics such as the *chi square, Fisher's exact test*, and the *binomial test* can be used to test hypotheses about the distribution of variables scored on nominal scales, while the *phi correlation* and *contingency coefficient* can be used to express the strength of relationship between such variables. *Cochran's Q test* is designed to test the relations among dichotomous scores on a variable in three or more sets of matched observations. The *sign test*, *median test*, and *quantile test* are all adaptations of the binomial test to quantitative data.

Data scored on ordinal scales can be analyzed with the *Mann–Whitney test* for comparing two independent samples and the *Wilcoxon test* for two dependent samples. The *Kolmogorov–Smirnov test* can be used to identify differences between the cumulative frequency distribution of a sample and a theoretically predicted distribution, or between two samples. Nonparametric tests for comparing three or more groups in a fashion similar to the one-factor ANOVA include the *Kruskal–Wallis one-way analysis of variance* and the *extension of the median test* to multiple groups, while Wilson has adapted the median test to two-factor ANOVA designs, with provision for testing interactions. The *Friedman test* is used to compare three or more matched sets of observations, as is done with the one-factor repeated measures ANOVA for randomized blocks designs.

The strength of relationship between two ordinally scaled variables can be expressed with *Spearman's rank-order correlation*, and between more than two ordinal variables scored on matched individuals with *Kendall's coefficient of concordance*.

Guttman's *scalogram analysis* is designed to identify a cumulative response dimension. It has been supplemented by more refined procedures for judging the generalizability of single dimensional scales, for identifying scales in which early items may be replaced by later items, and for identifying multiple scales.

The measurement of change presents a host of statistical problems, many of which are due to *regression effects*. Use of change scores may confound the initial magnitude of scores with differential regression and ceiling effects. Among the alternatives to change scores are comparison of final scores on individuals similar in initial scores; analysis of covariance to remove the effects of initial differences on final scores; repeated-measures ANOVA; and nonparametric tests.

6 Multivariate Statistics

Most of the statistical methods considered so far are regarded as being "univariate" in that they deal with single relationships between two variables. Multivariate statistics, by contrast, deal simultaneously with relationships among more than two variables. ANOVAs involving more than one independent variable occupy a somewhat ambiguous position, but are traditionally considered to be univariate. If, as proposed by Harris (1975), multivariate statistics are operationally defined as those that require matrix algebra, then ANOVAs employing multiple independent variables and a single dependent variable clearly fall into the univariate group because they do not require matrix algebra. The following discussion focuses on the rationale and general application of multivariate methods. Because computations are typically performed by computer, they will not be discussed in detail here, but an introduction to the computational procedures can be found in *A primer of multivariate statistics* (Harris, 1975).

Multiple Regression and Discriminant Analysis

A *multiple correlation* is a correlation between several "predictor" (or independent) variables, on the one hand, and a single "outcome" (or dependent) variable, on the other. Designated as R, the multiple correlation coefficient is obtained by a formula that weights the predictor variables so as to maximize the correlation of their sum with the outcome variable. Whereas an ordinary Pearson r is a function of the regression relationship between two variables, the multiple R is a function of the regression relationship between the outcome variable and the *weighted sum* of the predictor variables. The strength of the regression relationship can be stated in terms of the percentage of variance in the outcome variable that is shared by or "accounted for" by the predictor variables. This percentage of variance is equal to the square of the multiple R (i.e., R^2), and is known as the *multiple regression coefficient.*

Multiple correlation and regression coefficients are large when there is little disparity between the scores actually obtained on the outcome variable and the scores predicted by the regression of the outcome variable on the weighted sum of predictor variables. For example, many college admissions offices use multiple regression to predict the grade-point average (GPA) that applicants are likely to achieve if they are admitted. To do so, they first compute the regression of current students' college GPAs on their high school GPAs and Scholastic Aptitude Test (SAT) verbal and quantitative scores. These serve as predictor variables for the outcome variable of college GPA. When the regression of college GPA is computed on high school GPA and SAT scores, the regression equation yields values, called *beta weights*, by which any individual's scores on the three predictor variables can be multiplied to obtain his predicted college GPA. This predicted score is the score that lies on the regression line illustrated in Figure 6-1. The "optimal" weighting of the

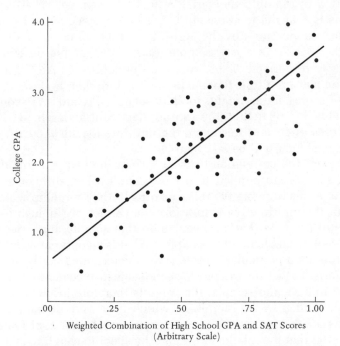

Figure 6-1. Regression of college GPA on weighted combination of high school GPA and SAT scores. Regression line indicates predicted college GPA for each value of the combined predictor variables. Dots represent obtained college GPAs.

predictor variables is that weighting which minimizes the sum of the squared differences between the scores actually obtained and the predicted scores lying along the regression line. The smaller the sum of squared differences, the larger the regression and correlation coefficients. To predict the GPA of new applicants, each new applicant's high school GPA and SAT scores are multiplied by the beta weights obtained for these variables from the regression of the current college students' GPA on their high school GPA and SAT scores.

The optimal weighting of variables in order to maximize their relationships with one or more other variables is a basic feature of all multivariate methods. These methods share with multiple regression the "least squares" criterion for determining what is an optimal weighting. That is, the weights chosen for each variable are those which collectively result in the smallest possible sum of squared differences between the scores predicted for each individual in a sample and the scores actually obtained.

A second characteristic that other multivariate methods share with multiple regression is evident in what typically happens when the weights derived for predictor variables in one sample are applied to the prediction of the outcome variable in a new sample. What typically happens is that the relationship between the outcome and predictor variables, as measured by the multiple correlation or regression coefficient, is weaker in a new sample than in the sample on which the weights were derived. Thus, suppose the college GPA of last year's freshmen had a multiple R of .60 (R^2 = .36) with their high school GPA and SAT scores. If the weights for high school GPA and SAT scores that yielded the R = .60 in this group are applied to the high school GPA and SAT scores of current freshmen, the multiple R with the GPA of the current freshmen will be less than .60.

Why does the correlation "shrink" when the beta weights derived in one sample are applied to a new sample? The shrinkage occurs because, in maximizing the relationships in the sample to which it is applied, the multiple regression formula cannot distinguish between aspects of the data that are peculiar to that sample and aspects that would remain stable in other samples. What is an optimal weighting of predictors for a particular sample is thus determined partly by chance characteristics that are unlikely to be the same in a second sample. When applied to a second sample, the weights therefore produce a smaller multiple R than in the sample on which they were derived. Because multivariate analyses capitalize on chance characteristics of a sample, it is essential that the relationships and the specific weightings be taken with a grain of salt until the findings are *cross-validated* (i.e., replicated) in new samples.

The prototypical nature of multiple regression for other multivariate methods—and for ANOVA—is clearly demonstrated in Kerlinger and Pedhazur's (1973) excellent introductory handbook on multiple regression. Especially useful for developmental research is their discussion of the application of multiple regression to categorically scaled variables. Multiple regression can be used to analyze the relations of categorical and/or quantitative predictor variables to a single dependent variable in a manner resembling ANOVA, where an ANOVA would be uninterpretable because the predictor variables are too numerous, are divided into too many levels, or are correlated with one another. As an example, prediction of college GPA might be improved if the effects of socioeconomic status (SES), sex, and public vs. private high school were added to high school GPA and SAT verbal and quantitative scores. To do this, all six predictor variables can be put into a single multiple regression equation. The categorical variables of sex and type of high school are each treated as "dummy" variables—i.e., the two categories of each are simply given different numbers, such as 0 and 1, as if they were quantitatively scaled variables. (Kerlinger and Pedhazur also provide methods for coding categorical variables that are divided into more than two categories.) The ordinal variable of SES is put into the equation without transformation, as are the variables of GPA and SAT scores, each of which is scored on a quasi-interval scale.

Most standard computer programs for the resulting multiple regression equation calculate the amount of variance each of the predictor variables uniquely contributes to the prediction of the outcome variable, as well as tests for the statistical significance of each of these contributors. Most programs also have an option for portraying the contribution of the predictor variables in a "step-wise" fashion—i.e., separate regression equations are calculated for each combination of the predictor variables so as to show how much each predictor uniquely contributes in the presence and absence of each other predictor. The results are thus simpler to interpret than an ANOVA employing the same six predictor variables. Furthermore, for an ANOVA, the predictor variables of GPA and SAT scores would have to be divided into a small number of levels unless the sample were so enormous as to include enough subjects to form adequate cells at each value of each of the six factors.

Discriminant Analysis

Another variety of multiple regression is known as *discriminant analysis* (Cooley and Lohnes, 1971). In discriminant analysis, the outcome variable is scored in a categorical fashion, and the regression equation (known in this context as the *discriminant function*) supplies weights for the predictor variables that will optimize prediction from an individual's scores on these variables to his membership in one of the categories of the outcome variable. In the prediction of performance in professional schools, for example, the outcome variable may merely be scored in terms of obtaining or not obtaining a degree. The purpose of a discriminant function in this case would be to optimally weight predictor variables so as to maximize the accuracy of predicting which group of students an applicant most resembles—those who typically do or those who typically do not obtain a degree. The discriminant function is thus designed to discriminate between discrete categories of the outcome variable rather than to predict specific scores on an outcome variable measured in linear fashion.

Path Analysis

Closely related to multiple regression in computational procedures but differing in rationale is an approach known as path analysis. Although the general concept was proposed by a geneticist long ago (Wright, 1921), path analysis has only recently begun to be applied to behavioral research. Like multiple regression, path analysis is designed to determine the amount of variance in a single dependent variable that can be accounted for by a number of independent variables. However, unlike multiple regression, path analysis has the further aim of determining whether the pattern of shared variances among independent and dependent variables is compatible with particular causal pathways hypothesized by the researcher.

As an illustration, consider the relationships among parent behavior, achievement motivation, and IQ found in the Fels longitudinal study discussed in chapter 1. In the Fels study, increases in IQ between the ages of 6 and 10 were positively related to achievement motivation and parental efforts to train mental and motor skills prior to age 6. Although the relationships were not presented in terms of correlations, let us suppose that there was a correlation of .60 between achievement motivation before age 6 and subsequent IQ increases; a correlation of .58 between parent behavior and IQ increases; and a correlation of .70 between parent behavior and achievement motivation. Either achievement motivation or parent behavior, or both together, might thus be hypothesized to affect IQ. How can we determine what the causal sequence is?

Several causal pathways involving the three variables are plausible. Path analysis is designed to aid in choosing among them. The first step in a path analysis is to diagram the causal pathways among which a choice is to be made. One plausible sequence is that parent behavior affects achievement motivation and that achievement motivation, in turn, causes IQ changes, as diagrammed in Figure 6-2(a). A second possibility, shown in Figure 6-2(b), is that achievement motivation and parent behavior both independently cause IQ changes. A third possibility, shown in Figure 6-2(c), is that parent behavior directly affects both IQ and achievement motivation, but that achievement motivation has little effect on IQ. In this case, the correlation between achievement motivation and IQ changes would be due to the fact that they are both caused by parental behavior.

All three of the sequences diagrammed in Figure 6-2 are compatible with the obtained correlations between achievement motivation, IQ changes, and parent behavior. Other causal relationships are also compatible with the obtained correlations but can be ruled out on logical grounds. For example, because the IQ changes occurred between the ages of 6 and 10, whereas the measurements of achievement motivation and parent behavior were made prior to age 6, the IQ changes could not have caused the differences in achievement motivation and parent behavior.

To move from the correlations among the three variables to tests of the three hypothesized causal pathways, *path coefficients* are computed for the relationships between the dependent variable (IQ) and the independent variables (achievement motivation and parent behavior). A path coefficient is the proportion of variance in the dependent variable for which an independent variable is uniquely responsible, with the effects of all other independent variables partialled out. Path coefficients

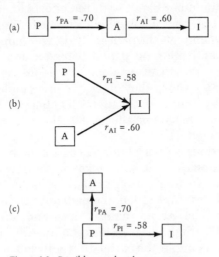

Figure 6-2. Possible causal pathways among achievement motivation (A), parent behavior (P), and IQ changes (I).

are really regression coefficients obtained by transforming the independent variables and the dependent variable into standard scores that have mean = 0 and variance = 1 (z scores), and computing the regression of the dependent variable on each independent variable in turn, with all the other independent variables partialled out. This can be done with an ordinary computer program for step-wise multiple regression. Because all variables are initially converted to standard scores, each coefficient (beta weight) obtained for the regression of the dependent variable on an independent variable will be between -1.00 and $+1.00$. Furthermore, if all the variance in the dependent variable is accounted for by the independent variables in the regression equation, the regression coefficients (with signs omitted) will add up to 1.00. This is because, being computed on variables transformed to standard scores having variance equal to 1.00, the partial regression coefficient of each independent variable indicates what percent of the variance in the dependent variable it accounts for when the effects of all the other independent variables are partialled out. Thus, if the standardized partial regression coefficient of independent variable A is .20, this means that the dependent variable will increase .20 for every increase of 1.0 in variable A.

To return to our example from the Fels study, we first transform scores for parent behavior, achievement motivation, and IQ changes to standard scores, and then compute the regression of IQ changes on the two independent variables. Suppose we find the path coefficient (p) for achievement motivation to be .36 and that for parent behavior to be .00. This means that, with the effects of parent behavior partialled out, achievement motivation still accounts for 36 percent of the variance in IQ changes. On the other hand, with the effects of achievement motivation partialled out, parent behavior accounts for none of the variance in IQ changes. To complete the path analysis, we compute the regression of achievement motivation on parent behavior and find the path coefficient to be .49. What can we conclude about causality? The path diagram in Figure 6-3 shows that, of the two independent variables, only achievement motivation directly affects IQ changes. The diagram also shows that parent behavior affects IQ changes only by affecting achievement motivation.

Certain limitations on causal inference from path analysis should be noted. First, path analysis at best makes it possible merely to choose among several competing causal explanations for a set of obtained correlations. In the example cited, the path analysis made it possible to choose one of the three causal explanations portrayed in Figure 6-2, but the findings were also compatible with other causal explanations. For example, the correlation between parent behavior and child achievement motivation might result from the fact that highly motivated children elicit intensive training from their parents rather

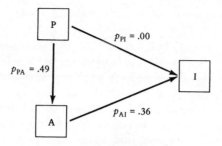

Figure 6-3. Path diagram showing that the obtained path coefficients (designated as p) are compatible with the hypothesis that parent behavior (P) affects achievement motivation (A) which, in turn, affects IQ changes (I).

than that parents' training elicits achievement motivation in their children. Such a reversal of the hypothesized causal relationship would not invalidate the conclusion that achievement motivation affects IQ, but it would invalidate the conclusion that parent behavior affects achievement motivation.

A second limitation is that other variables might have accounted for more variance in the dependent variable. These other sources of variance either might be independent of the variables already identified or might themselves account for the apparent contribution of the identified variables. If SES were included, for example, it might obtain a significant path coefficient of its own in addition to the one obtained by achievement motivation. On the other hand, its presence might reduce the contribution of achievement motivation because this apparent contribution is actually due to the effects of SES. The effective use of path analysis thus requires the formulation of clearcut and comprehensive causal models among which choices can be made on the basis of the obtained data. As most path analyses entail more variables and greater complexity than the one illustrated here, the reader intending to use path analysis may find it helpful to seek more detailed guidelines in a source such as Kerlinger and Pedhazur (1973).

Factor Analysis and Cluster Analysis

In a complex area where many variables are potentially relevant, a fundamental goal of research is to sort out relationships among the variables in order to obtain clearcut descriptions of important phenomena. One of the cornerstones of modern botany, for example, was the organization of plant characteristics into a comprehensive taxonomy by Linnaeus during the eighteenth century. Unlike botanical taxonomy, however, descriptive efforts in the behavioral sciences are handicapped by the fact that behavioral characteristics do not remain fixed in place, readily observable with high reliability by anyone who chooses to look. Instead, there are countless ways of dividing up behavior according to the situations in which it occurs, the definitions of the behavioral units, and the degree of inference and expertise needed to assess them. As a result, multivariate methods are often used for organizing observations on large numbers of variables into more manageable units.

The primary statistical methods for reducing a large number of variables to a smaller number of descriptive entities are based upon correlations. Suppose, for example, that a longitudinal study of the origins of psychopathology begins with parents' reports of 100 kinds of behavior problems in their children. If the correlation of each item with every other item were calculated, there would be $(100 \times 99)/2 = 4950$ correlation coefficients. Even if one could meaningfully consider the correlations between each pair of variables, it would be humanly impossible to glean from all these correlations the ways in which the variables form larger groupings.

R Factor Analysis

One general approach to this problem is to employ R *factor analysis*, a multivariate procedure that summarizes a matrix of correlations among variables in terms of a limited number of "factors." Each factor is a vector composed of weights for all the variables in the correlation matrix. The weights are known as *loadings*, and they can range from -1.00 to $+1.00$. In the computation of the first factor, loadings are assigned to each variable in such a way that they form a combination optimally weighted to account for as much as possible of the variance shared by the variables. If a subject's scores on all the variables are multiplied by the loadings these variables received on the first factor, the sum of these products would be an optimally weighted summary of his scores. This summary score is called the subject's *factor score*.

Because a single factor usually accounts for only a portion of the variance in a correlation matrix, additional factors are computed to provide vectors of item loadings that will account for the remaining variance. Each factor is determined primarily by a group of items that intercorrelate highly with one another. It is these items that have the highest loadings on the factor. Table 6-1 illustrates the way in which the results of a factor analysis are typically displayed, with the loadings of every item on a factor forming a vector that represents the factor.

A *factor score* can be computed for each subject on each of the obtained factors. For example, in a factor analysis of 100 behavior prob-

TABLE 6-1. Illustration of Results of an *R* Factor Analysis of Ten Types of Behavior Problems.[a]

Item	Factor Loadings Factor I	Factor II	Factor III
1. Fighting	.93	−.06	−.16
2. Stealing	.87	.01	−.19
3. Truancy	.65	−.13	−.08
4. Firesetting	.49	.16	.12
5. Hyperactivity	.15	.29	.86
6. Bedwetting	.13	.14	.44
7. Insomnia	−.11	.71	.21
8. Speech problems	−.21	.17	.59
9. Shyness	−.28	.89	.16
10. Fears	−.31	.69	.18

[a]The boxes around loadings on each factor indicate the *items* that have the highest loadings on the factor. These items thus form a cluster that defines the factor.

lems, ten factors might be found. A subject's pattern of problems could then be summarized in terms of his factor scores on these ten factors, providing a far more parsimonious description than his scores on 100 variables. To illustrate with the ten variables displayed in Table 6-1, suppose the behavior problems had been scored on a 0–1–2 scale. If a child had received a score of 1 for the first item, "Fighting," the loading of .93 for fighting would be multiplied by 1; if he had been scored 2 for the next item, "Stealing," the loading of .87 for stealing would be multiplied by 2, and so on for all the loadings on Factor I. The sum of the products obtained by multiplying the child's score on each item by the item's loading on Factor I is the child's factor score for Factor I. The same procedure would be followed to obtain the child's factor scores on Factors II and III. Each factor can then be treated as a variable and subjected to statistical analysis.

Simple structure. The most useful factor analytic results are usually those in which several factors each have a few items with very high loadings and many items with low loadings. In such results, each item typically has high loadings on just a few of the factors and low loadings on the rest. When factor analyses yield several concentrations of high loadings like this, they are said to approach the ideal of *simple structure*—i.e., they describe the correlations among variables in terms of a few clearcut dimensions.

A number of mathematical procedures have been developed to "rotate" the results of factor analyses into arrangements of loadings that most nearly approximate simple structure. Rotation of a factor matrix merely refers to transforming all the loadings in some uniform way. For example, a *varimax* rotation is accomplished by a formula designed to approximate simple structure by maximizing the variance among the squares of the loadings. Some rotational procedures, including the *varimax* rotation, produce *orthogonal* factor solutions in which each factor is uncorrelated with the others. This means that, if portrayed graphically, the vectors of loadings that comprise each factor would be at right angles to ("orthogonal to") one another—i.e., the loadings of items on one factor would not correlate with the loadings of the same items on any other factor. Other procedures, such as the *oblimin* and *oblimax* rotations, produce solutions that are known as *oblique* because factors may be correlated with each other. If portrayed graphically, the vectors of loadings on correlated factors would be at less than right angles, i.e., they would be oblique to one another. (A good introduction to many types of factor analysis can be found in Comrey, 1973, while more advanced presentations can be found in Gorsuch, 1974, Harman, 1967, and Mulaik, 1972.)

Q Factor Analysis

Although groupings of variables may provide a much more meaningful description of data than does a large matrix of correlations among single variables, these groupings do not necessarily represent "types" of subjects. However, types of subjects can be identified by finding subjects whose profiles of factor scores are similar in shape. One way to do this is to transform subjects' factor scores so that scores on each factor have the same mean and variance, e.g., by using z scores, and then to compute Q correlations between factor scores for each pair of subjects. Thus, if ten prominent factors emerge from a factor analysis of 100 variables, the correlations can be calculated between subject A's factor scores on each of the ten factors and subject B's factor scores on the ten factors. If the resulting Q correlation is large, then the two subjects can be regarded as similar "types."

A more direct application of Q methodology to factor analysis is to compute Q correlations of each subject's standardized scores on the 100 variables with every other subject's scores on these variables. The matrix of correlations between every pair of subjects is then factor analyzed. This is called *Q factor analysis* (or *inverse factor analysis*) to distinguish it from the factor analysis of R correlations among variables. The resulting factors consist of each *subject's* loading on each factor, as illustrated in Table 6-2. Thus, Factor I indicates that subjects A, B, and C have similarly shaped profiles of scores, while the profiles of the remaining subjects are of different shapes. The high loadings of subjects D, E, and J

TABLE 6-2. Illustration of Results of a *Q* Factor Analysis of Ten Subjects.[a]

Subject	Factor Loadings		
	Factor I	*Factor II*	*Factor III*
A	.88	.05	.13
B	.72	−.16	.08
C	.49	.17	.00
D	.20	.76	.23
E	.11	.74	−.01
F	−.07	.02	.71
G	−.12	.18	.60
H	−.14	−.06	.10
I	−.18	.00	.65
J	−.23	.51	.04

[a]The boxes around loadings on each factor indicate the *subjects* who have the highest loadings on the factor. Subjects A, B, and C are similar to one another, as are subjects D, E, and I, and subjects F, G, and I. Subject H does not resemble any of the other subjects.

on Factor II show that their scores form similarly shaped profiles. Because subject D has the highest loading, he is the purest representative of this group.

Braun (1973) has demonstrated how Q factor analysis can be employed to identify stage-like differences in profiles of responses. He first obtained responses by subjects aged 15 to 64 on 477 items of an attitude questionnaire. For each item, he then calculated the average response score for subjects at each of the 50 ages. After being converted to standard (z) scores, the average scores for each age group on the 477 items were Q-correlated with the averages obtained on the 477 items by each other age group. Thus, the 477 scores for the 15-year olds were Q-correlated with the 477 scores for the 16-year olds to give the degree of similarity between the profiles of the 15- and 16-year olds. The same thing was done with the 15- and 17-year olds, 16-, and 17-year olds, etc. In effect, each of the 50 ages was treated like an individual subject whose similarity in profile of responses to each other age was reflected in their mutual Q correlation on 477 items. The resulting matrix of $(50 \times 49)/2 = 1225$ correlations was then factor analyzed to identify the groups of ages that correlated most highly with one another.

Each of the factors was composed of loadings for each of the age groups, as portrayed in Table 6-3. The factor loadings were examined to determine which factor showed the highest loading for each age level. As can be seen in Table 6-3, the highest loadings for ages 15 through 18 were all on Factor I. This suggested that the responses of subjects at these

TABLE 6-3. *Q* Factor Analysis of Average Responses by 50 Age Groups to Attitude Questionnaire Items.[a]

Age years	I	II	III	Age group
15	−0.97*	0.17	0.09	youth 15–18
16	−0.84*	−0.10	−0.07	
17	−0.84*	−0.10	−0.07	
18	−0.62*	−0.35	−0.10	
19	−0.45	−0.48*	−0.11	young adult 19–26
20	−0.25	−0.70*	−0.01	
21	−0.16	−0.75*	−0.08	
22	0.04	−0.89*	0.01	
23	−0.05	−0.63*	−0.31	
24	0.07	−0.59*	−0.28	
25	−0.03	−0.45*	−0.44	
26	0.14	−0.53*	−0.41	
27	0.05	−0.25	−0.51*	adult 27–39
28	0.05	0.05	−0.51*	
29	0.07	−0.37	−0.53*	
30	0.16	0.04	−0.41*	
31	−0.01	−0.02	−0.64*	
32	0.14	0.12	−0.50*	
33	0.36*	−0.13	−0.16	
34	0.20	0.08	−0.53*	
35	0.17	0.25	−0.39*	
36	0.12	0.29	−0.35*	
37	0.14	0.46	−0.51*	
38	0.04	0.13	−0.34*	
39	0.20	0.35	−0.46*	
40	−0.11	0.68*	−0.29	middle aged 40–52
41	−0.11	0.57*	−0.40	
42	0.02	0.60*	−0.22	
43	0.19	0.31*	−0.08	
44	0.28	0.29*	−0.08	
45	0.20	0.26*	0.25	
46	0.25	0.27*	0.03	
47	0.20	0.46*	0.02	
48	0.01	0.63*	−0.15	
49	0.13	0.45*	0.00	
50	0.14	0.40*	0.18	
51	−0.04	0.46*	0.24	
52	0.02	0.65*	0.11	

TABLE 6-3. Continued.

Age years	I	II	III	Age group
53	0.22	0.22	0.45*	senior 53-64
54	0.19	0.39	0.42*	
55	0.24	0.15	0.58*	
56	0.27	0.17	0.31*	
57	0.37	−0.05	0.64*	
58	0.04	0.24	0.54*	
59	0.24	0.19	0.62*	
60	0.21	0.23	0.57*	
61	0.46	−0.07	0.54*	
62	0.24	0.13	0.53*	
63	0.29	0.08	0.61*	
64	0.24	0.07	0.57*	

Adapted from Braun (1973).
[a]Asterisk indicates highest loading for that age.

ages were more similar to one another than they were to any other age.

The fact that the loadings for ages 15 to 18 were all negative has no bearing on the interpretation of their interrelationship. Factor analytic procedures somewhat arbitrarily determine whether specific loadings on a factor will have positive or negative signs. What indicates similarity among items—in this case, age groups—is the size and similarity in sign of the loadings, whether the sign be positive or negative. However, as is evident in Factors II and III of Table 6-3, a factor sometimes includes a group of items with high positive loadings *and* a group with high negative loadings. Age groups 19 through 26 had their highest loadings (negative in sign) on Factor II, while age groups 40 through 52 also had their highest loadings (positive in sign) on Factor II. While the sign of the loadings is not in itself important, the *opposite* signs of the loadings obtained by these two groupings means that they responded oppositely to the same items. The same sort of negative relationship between two age groups is evident on Factor III where the 27- to 39-year olds (except the 33-year olds) had high negative loadings and the 53- to 64-year olds had high positive loadings. Braun interpreted the "bipolar" nature of these factors as indicating that the attitudes of the 19- to 26-year olds were specifically in conflict with those of their parents' generation (the 40- to 52-year olds). Likewise, the attitudes of the 27- to 39-year olds were in conflict with those of *their* parents' generation, the 53- to 64-year olds. The fact that the 15- to 18-year olds had their highest loading on a factor different from all other groups suggested a unique attitudinal orientation that was neither close to nor opposite to that of the other age groups.

With the exception of age 33, the clearcut groupings of adjacent ages according to their highest factor loadings are indicative of stage-like organizations of attitude patterns. Once such stage-like organizations are identified, longitudinal–sequential strategies can be pursued to determine whether the "stages" are a function specifically of age, of cohort, or some combination thereof.

Monotonicity Analysis

Bentler (1971) has proposed a way of using factor analysis to identify developmentally ordered relationships among groups of behavioral items scored dichotomously. Called *monotonicity analysis*, Bentler's method employs a type of correlation coefficient based on a 2 × 2 table displaying the patterns of $+ -$, $+ +$, $- -$, and $- +$ responses obtained by a group of subjects (e.g., Table 5-2). This correlation coefficient, called a *coefficient of monotonicity* (m), represents the degree to which two variables are concordant with respect to being present or absent. If the $+ -$ cell is labelled A, the $+ +$ cell B, the $- -$ cell C, and the $- +$ cell D, then $m = (BC - AD)/[BC + AD + 2\sqrt{(ABCD)}]$. In order to identify clusters or dimensions of ordered items, a matrix of monotonicity coefficients is subjected to factor analysis. Because the formula for m is merely a special case of a more general formula for the concordance between two items, items scored on ordinal scales can also be subjected to monotonicity analysis. Where an instance of concordance is defined as a subject having a score on variable X that is greater than or equal to his score on Y, and discordance as $X < Y$, the general formula is: $m = (N_{concordant} - N_{discordant}) / [N_{con} + N_{dis} + 2\sqrt{(N_{con}N_{dis})}]$.

Employing artificial data scored so as to create monotonic relationships among several subsets of variables, Bentler (1971) has demonstrated that factor analysis of monotonicity coefficients identifies the subsets much more clearly than factor analysis of Pearson rs calculated on the same dichotomous or ordinal data. Because the groupings of items revealed by monotonicity analysis constitute scale-like orderings, monotonicity analysis may provide another approach to the goals of scalogram analysis, especially in the identification of multiple ordered scales.

Cluster Analysis

Like factor analysis, the various methods of cluster analysis are designed to summarize relationships among a large number of variables and/or subjects in terms of a relatively small number of groupings. However, cluster analysis differs from factor analysis in that it yields groupings composed of particular variables or individuals, rather than dimensions on which every variable or individual has a loading, be it large or small. Cluster analysis can be applied to correlations among variables or subjects, but it can also be applied to other measures of relationship, such as the sum of the squared differences between scores obtained on several variables by each subject. This measure of relationship is known as *Euclidean distance*. Cluster analysis has been less widely used and standardized than factor analysis, although the publication in recent years of textbooks (Anderberg, 1973; Everitt, 1974) and of readily available computer programs (Dixon, 1975) indicates that it is becoming a significant addition to our statistical armamentarium.

One of the most useful applications of cluster analysis to developmental research may be in the identification of groups of individuals who can be treated as types because they share similar patterns of scores across a number of variables. As demonstrated in Braun's (1973) study, factor analysis of Q correlations can be used in a similar fashion, but when the similarities among subjects are represented in terms of factor loadings, "types" of subjects must be selected on the basis of arbitrary cut-off points for factor loadings. Table 6-3 shows that the clearcut similarities of loadings for successive ages made this easy in Braun's study. However, suppose you wished to identify types of subjects within an age group in order to see whether they differed in subsequent development. In this case, you would have no independent ordering of subjects by age to guide decisions about the relative size of factor loadings to use in identifying groupings.

Most methods of cluster analysis differ from factor analysis in the way they handle cutoff points, because they construct clusters in a hierarchical sequence. This means that a subject is first paired with whichever other subject is most similar in terms of the Q correlation (or Euclidean distance) computed between their profiles of scores. A pair of similar subjects then serves as the nucleus of a cluster to which other subjects are added if they are sufficiently similar to the existing members of the cluster. The process continues until whole clusters are combined into ever larger clusters. Decisions are necessary as to which level of clusters in the hierarchy are to be retained, but these are based on the relative homogeneity of subjects within clusters rather than upon cutoff points for placement of individual subjects.

Methods of cluster analysis differ greatly in how they create their clusters. One of the most promising methods for clustering children on the basis of their scores on several behavioral traits is known as *centroid linkage* (Edelbrock, 1978). It constructs clusters in the following way: First the two subjects whose profiles of scores are most similar (as indexed either by Q correlation or Euclidean distance) are brought together to form the nucleus of a cluster. Then the average of their scores on each variable is computed in order to obtain a new profile called a *centroid*. The centroid serves to represent the cluster in the search for new candidate members. When another subject is found whose profile is highly similar to the centroid he is added to the cluster and the centroid is recomputed as the average of the profiles of this subject plus the others already in the cluster. The process can be stopped when there are no subjects whose profiles meet a preselected degree of similarity to the centroid of any cluster that has evolved.

The usefulness of any classification system depends on how well it discriminates among individuals who differ in important ways. The real test of any set of clusters is therefore in their ability to group individuals who are then found to differ on variables not included in the cluster analysis. Because the clusters formed by centroid linkage of profiles of children's behavior problems have been found to validly discriminate children whose behavior disorders subsequently improve from those whose disorders do not, it may provide a basis for identifying children who are at the highest risk for long-term psychopathology (Achenbach and Edelbrock, 1977).

Multivariate Extensions of Univariate Methods

In addition to multiple regression and factor- and cluster-analytic methods, a number of multivariate methods consist of direct extensions of univariate methods to several variables at once. The concepts are elementary for the reader who is familiar with the univariate statistics and the principle of optimal weighting employed in multivariate statistics. However, the computations are complex and are usually done by computer. We will therefore confine ourselves to an overview of the statistics and what they are intended to do.

Canonical Correlation

One of the most direct extensions of a univariate method is the *canonical correlation*. This is exactly like a univariate Pearson r except that the correlation is between two sets of variables, each variable weighted to maximize the correlation of its set with the other set. Thus, the correlation between several different measures of moral judgment and several measures of resistance to cheating can be assessed in a single canonical correlation between the weighted combination of judgment measures and the weighted combination of behavioral measures.

Hotelling's T^2

Univariate tests of group differences also have their multivariate counterparts. The multivariate counterpart of the t test is *Hotelling's* T^2, which is a t test of the difference between two samples on several measures optimally weighted so as to maximize the size of the t. Thus, if the cognitive functioning of preschoolers who had received two different enrichment programs were to be compared on a variety of measures, all the measures could be included in a single comparison by means of Hotelling's T^2 test, rather than performing an ordinary univariate t test on each measure separately. If each of the measures is considered to be an imperfect index of a central dimension of cognitive functioning, comparison of the groups on an optimally weighted combination of the measures is more likely to reveal a difference than is a series of comparisons on each variable separately.

Multivariate Analysis of Variance

Just as Hotelling's T^2 is an extension of the t test to multiple variables, the *multivariate analysis of variance* (MANOVA) is an extension of ANOVA to comparisons on multiple dependent variables. In the assessment of the effects of different preschool programs on multiple measures of cognitive functioning, a MANOVA could be substituted for Hotelling's T^2 if more than two programs were to be compared and/or if the effects of more than one independent variable (e.g., length of program, sex of subjects) on the multiple measures of cognitive functioning were to be assessed. Exactly the same kinds of designs can be analyzed with the MANOVA as with the ANOVA, the only difference being that the MANOVA first transforms a weighted combination of dependent variables into a single score.

Analysis of Covariance

The *analysis of covariance* (ANCOVA) combines the principles of partial correlation with ANOVA to partial out or "covary" the effects of unwanted differences in variables (covariates) that affect the relationship between the independent and dependent variables in an ANOVA. For example, suppose that in the comparison of the effects of preschool programs it was impossible to form groups initially equated on mental age (MA). Since MA is an index of general cognitive functioning, an initial superiority in MA might make one group's outcome scores higher than those of other groups even if the programs do not differ in effectiveness. To partial the effect of the initial differences in MA out of the ANOVA of the effects of the preschool programs on the outcome measure, the ANCOVA first employs a regression analysis of the relationship between initial MA and the outcome measure. From the regression analysis, a weighting is found for MA that makes it possible to control for its effects by subtracting the weighted value of each subject's MA from his score on the outcome variable. Once the outcome scores have been corrected for differences in initial MA, an ANOVA is performed on these corrected scores. However, the correction for MA is valid only if the regression of the outcome variable on MA is similar for all groups. If the regressions differ significantly, then the weighting for MA will under- or over-correct the outcome scores for some of the groups. This, in turn, could lead to inappropriate F values.

Just as the relationship between several predictor variables and a single outcome variable can be analyzed by means of multiple regression, the effects of several covariates can be partialled out of a single outcome variable by means of ANCOVA. Furthermore, ANCOVA can be extended to multiple outcome variables in the same way as MANOVA. The form of ANCOVA applied to multiple outcome variables is known as *multivariate analysis of covariance* (MANCOVA). It proceeds by first employing regression analysis to correct all the individual outcome measures for differences in the covariate(s) and then performing a MANOVA on the weighted combination of these corrected scores. The effects of one or more covariates such as initial MA can thus be partialled out of the MANOVA of several cognitive outcome measures following various preschool programs. However, as the numbers of covariates and outcome variables increase, the risks of differences in regression slopes and invalid F values also increase.

Application of Multivariate Statistics

Multivariate statistics are designed to describe complex data parsimoniously by combining multiple variables into units among which linear relationships are maximized. Valuable as this is, it may encourage "shot gun" approaches to research in which measures are indiscriminately added in the hope that multivariate analysis will produce significant findings despite a lack of clear focus in research design. It should not be forgotten that, in the process of maximizing relationships within a particular sample, multivariate statistics capitalize on chance variation peculiar to that sample. While significance tests are designed to take account of this fact, "shrinkage" of multiple regression and multiple correlation coefficients from one sample to another demonstrates the unreliability of weightings employed to maximize relationships within a sample. The value of these methods for describing relationships should not blind us to their weaknesses as inferential procedures. The best test of any statistical finding is replication, but the fact that multivariate statistics weight data according to characteristics of the particular sample makes replication even more important than when univariate statistics are employed.

In describing their own approach to multivariate data analysis, Cooley and Lohnes (1971) have used the term *multivariate heuristics* in preference to "multivariate inference." For developmental research, the greatest current value of multivariate statistics may be in their capacity to organize multiple measures into units that can then be treated heuristically as operational definitions of multifaceted variables for which no single measures are adequate. The quantitative combination of measures yielded by multivariate analyses can then be subjected to further test.

A study of relations between behavior at ages $2\frac{1}{2}$ and $7\frac{1}{2}$ provides an extended example of how multivariate methods can be used to organize developmental data. In order to obtain a summary description of peer behavior at $7\frac{1}{2}$, Waldrop and Halverson (1975) factor analyzed 12 measures including total number of hours spent per week with peers, number of hours with one peer, and number of hours with more than one peer. Also included were ratings by observers on *intensiveness* of peer relations (strength of relationship to a single friend); *extensiveness* of peer relations (amount of involvement with groups of children); importance of peers (amount of spontaneous conversation about them); desire to be playing with others; and social ease (degree of comfort and spontaneity in social situations).

For both sexes, the first factor found—the one accounting for the most variance in correlations among measures—showed large loadings on social ease, total hours with peers, and importance of peers. However, the boys' first factor also showed high loadings on *extensiveness* of peer relations and on number of hours with *more than one* peer. By contrast, the girls' factor showed large loadings on *intensiveness* of peer relations and on number of hours with *one* peer. This indicated that, while there was a generally similar dimension of social behavior for both sexes, social boys had predominately extensive peer relations, whereas social girls had predominately intensive peer relations.

Having obtained a factor for each sex that in effect summarized the various measures of peer behavior in terms of a single dimension, each subject's standing on this dimension was quantified by computing his factor score on it—i.e., by multiplying the score he obtained on each variable by its loading on the factor and then summing the resulting products of these multiplications. A child who scored high on the items having the highest loadings on the factor for his sex would obtain a high total score for peer relations. The factor scores were then intercorrelated with scores on a variety of measures obtained at age $2\frac{1}{2}$. For both sexes, factor scores on peer behavior at age $7\frac{1}{2}$ correlated *positively* with age-$2\frac{1}{2}$ ratings on originality, peer involvement, and effective coping with barriers, and *negatively* with fearfulness and withdrawal. Thus, behavior at age $2\frac{1}{2}$ correlated with a basic dimension of peer behavior at age $7\frac{1}{2}$ although boys and girls differed in the way they manifested this dimension at age $7\frac{1}{2}$.

Multivariate statistics could also have been used in other ways to summarize relationships among the large number of measures obtained at ages $2\frac{1}{2}$ and $7\frac{1}{2}$. While univariate correlations were calculated between individual measures obtained at $2\frac{1}{2}$ and factor scores at $7\frac{1}{2}$, a multiple regression could have been calculated to determine how well the various measures at $2\frac{1}{2}$ collectively predicted factor scores at $7\frac{1}{2}$. Or children could have been divided into those who were high and those who were low on sociability at age $7\frac{1}{2}$ in order to compute the discriminant function for predicting membership in these groups from the age-$2\frac{1}{2}$ measures. As part of the typical multiple correlation–multiple regression computer program, partial correlations between the age-$7\frac{1}{2}$ factor scores and each age-$2\frac{1}{2}$ measure could also be obtained with the effects of the other age-$2\frac{1}{2}$ measures held constant. If the partial correlations remained large, this would show that the univariate correlations between age-$2\frac{1}{2}$ and $7\frac{1}{2}$ scores were independent of one another. If the partial correlations were much smaller than the simple correlations, this would indicate that the simple correlations were redundant with one another. In the latter case, it is possible that the age-$2\frac{1}{2}$ variables reflected a unitary dimension. This possibility could be explored by factor analyzing the age-$2\frac{1}{2}$ scores. If a clearcut factor emerged, each child's factor score on it could be calculated and the correlation with age-$7\frac{1}{2}$ factor scores could be computed. A high correlation would indicate that the relationships between age-$2\frac{1}{2}$ and $7\frac{1}{2}$ behavior could be conceptualized better in terms of a stable dimension of behavior than in terms of predictions of an age-$7\frac{1}{2}$ dimension from several different age-$2\frac{1}{2}$ variables.

Rather than identifying dimensions by independent factor analyses at the two ages, a canonical correlation could be calculated between all the measures taken at age $2\frac{1}{2}$ and all those at age $7\frac{1}{2}$. Such a correlation would probably be greater than the correlation between factor scores, because it would optimally weight each variable to maximize the correlation. On the other hand, the factors, based as they are on the data of each age taken separately, might more clearly define the dimensions of variation at each age without respect to whether each measure comprising these dimensions predicted behavior across age.

To carry the multivariate possibilities still further, a 2×2 MANOVA could be computed to determine whether boys and girls at two levels of, say, age-$2\frac{1}{2}$ originality, differed significantly on a weighted combination of the 12 measures taken at age $7\frac{1}{2}$. Even though originality was found to correlate with peer behavior factor scores for each sex taken separately, the MANOVA might show that one sex was significantly higher on peer behavior overall, or that originality and sex interacted in affecting peer behavior. Since the measures taken at both ages might merely reflect cognitive developmental level, the degree to which they comprised a stable independent dimension could be ascertained by changing the MANOVA to a MANCOVA with MA partialled out as a covariate. Sex differences on the 12 measures at age $7\frac{1}{2}$ could also be examined directly by computing Hotelling's T^2 on the difference between the scores for each sex.

If only univariate methods were available for analyzing data like those obtained by Waldrop and Halverson, we would be faced with hundreds of separate analyses. Unless all the relationships were very strong and consistent with one another, it would be difficult to sort out the ones that were due to chance, the ones that represented reliable relationships of a single measure to another single measure, and the ones that jointly reflected relationships on underlying dimensions. However, the apparent efficiency of multivariate methods for extracting significant relationships may prove deceptive unless the findings are regarded as provisional until tested further in new samples.

Summary

Multivariate statistics deal simultaneously with more than two variables, typically employ matrix algebra, and weight variables so as to maximize the relationships among them. *Multiple regression* and *discriminant analysis* portray the relationships between several optimally weighted predictor variables and an outcome variable, while *path analysis* makes use of multiple regression to test causal hypotheses. *R factor analysis* identifies dimensions defined by groupings of intercorrelated variables, whereas *Q factor analysis* identifies dimensions defined by groupings of similar individuals. *Monotonicity analysis* identifies groupings of items in ordinally scored data. Various forms of *cluster analysis* are designed to identify clusters of variables or individuals on the basis of correlations and Euclidean distance.

Multivariate extensions of univariate methods include *canonical correlations* between two sets of variables; Hotelling's T^2, a *t* test of the difference between two sets of variables; *multivariate analysis of variance*, for conducting analyses of variance on multiple outcome measures; and *analysis of covariance* and *multivariate analysis of covariance* for partialling the effects of unwanted covariates out of analyses of variance and multivariate analyses of variance.

Because multivariate statistics capitalize on chance variation in the derivation of optimal weightings, they may be better regarded as heuristic rather than as inferential procedures until their results are cross-validated in new samples. If this limitation is recognized, they may be put to good use for organizing multiple developmental measures into summary variables and relationships. These variables and relationships should then be subjected to further test.

7 Research Methods in Developmental Psychology

THE VALUE of any research method depends upon the questions a researcher wishes to answer. The best method may often be one invented by the researcher to meet his specific needs or may be some combination of methods growing out of different conceptual paradigms. The purpose of this chapter is to present an overview of dimensions along which methods vary and to present potential sources of bias in the various methods. The methods can be roughly ordered according to the type of control imposed on the stimulus inputs to the subject and the type of behavioral units to be recorded. The developmental level of the subjects is, of course, always an important factor in the choice of methods, and the researcher must pilot test his chosen method with subjects of the level he wishes to study. A particular method may have very different effects on subjects differing in developmental level.

Types of Stimulus Control

Naturalistic Settings

Research settings range from those in which the researcher has no influence over the stimuli encountered by the subject to those in which rigorous control is imposed on stimulus input. At one extreme, attempts to study "natural" behavior often begin with observations in settings

161

chosen to typify the customary environments of the subjects. However, the choice of a setting for observation and the presence of an observer or other means for recording behavior inevitably constrain the type of behavior that can be observed. For example, data on the natural behavior of children have often been obtained by observers concealed behind one-way mirrors in university nursery schools. The researcher assumes that the nursery school setting is not altered by his research and that the children's behavior is the same whether or not observations are being made. Yet even if the nursery school teachers are not affected by the knowledge that they are watched, and even if the observation mirrors do not affect the children, the researcher must nevertheless accept significant constraints on the kind of data he can obtain. He will not observe behavior that may be peculiar to other everyday situations, such as mealtimes with the family, bedtime rituals, and interactions with siblings. Even if he wishes to capture the "natural" behavior of children, he is thus restricted to the behavior occurring in response to a very specific physical situation, with its own history and connotations for each child, in the presence of a particular set of other children and adults, at a particular time of day, during a particular developmental period.

The influence of situational variations even within the same environment has been amply demonstrated by having observers rate nursery school children when playing alone, playing with other children, participating in a group activity led by a teacher, and taking a test (Rose, Blank, and Spalter, 1975). On a variety of characteristics—such as temperament (manic vs. depressed) and ease of speaking—there was considerable consistency in ratings from one *occasion* to another within a particular situation. Between *situations*, however, there was little consistency, even though all the situations were in the same nursery school environment.

Probably the most ambitious effort ever made to reduce environmental constraints in the naturalistic study of human behavior was undertaken by Barker and Wright (1951, 1955). They employed trained observers to follow children from the time they awoke in the morning until they went to bed at night, writing down everything the children did and the situations in which they did it. While this offered a broad ecological scope for the observations, it nevertheless introduced the effect of the observer following the child around.

Another way of attempting to get at "natural" behavior is to have parents or others who are normally with the subject record their observations. Many studies of language development have employed mothers' reports of their observations, often coupled with tests of the children's language under more controlled conditions. This requires mothers to alter their behavior in order to collect the data, and differences among mothers can affect the data they record. However, it may yield data on behavior that would not occur at all in the presence of other observers.

Manipulations of Stimuli in Natural Settings

Because virtually any alteration of a subject's accustomed environment may influence his behavior, the effects of each research method must be carefully weighed in choosing a method best suited to the subject's characteristics and the researcher's purposes. Since human behavior can be studied only in some particular environment, rather than in a pristine natural state totally devoid of environmental effects, the important question is not *whether* a specific setting influences behavior, but *how* one setting influences behavior differently than another, and *how consistent* behavior is from one setting to another.

This being the case, much research is carried on in environments deliberately designed to insure certain types of stimulus inputs. In some instances, a researcher wishes to preserve a naturalistic setting as fully as possible while he manipulates a particular variable in order to study its effects. A research nursery school, for example, might be temporarily equipped only with highly sex-typed toys (e.g., trucks and dolls) in order to see whether children of both sexes choose them with equal frequency. Such a situation remains fairly naturalistic and there is not enough control to insure that each child will be exposed to the choice of toys under identical conditions of timing, presence of peers, etc., but one aspect of the environment is deliberately controlled in order to study a particular kind of behavior.

A similarly modest type of stimulus control is exercised in studies where a parent is asked to do something in a setting familiar to his child in order to permit observation of the child's response. In the Schaffer and Emerson (1964) study of separation anxiety described in chapter 3, for example, mothers were asked to leave the room while an observer recorded their child's reaction. Likewise, in studies of language development, the parent may be instructed to say certain things to the child so that the child's level of comprehension can be assessed. In such situations, the researcher attempts to control one aspect of the stimulus input (e.g., the parent's disappearance or words to the child), but many other aspects are not controlled.

Standardized Environments

Often a researcher wishes to study a particular behavior in its natural complexity but cannot do so because naturalistic observation of the behavior is impractical or because the behavior is too susceptible to extraneous environmental stimuli. One strategy is to standardize the environment in which the subjects are observed while still permitting the subjects' behavior to vary widely. For example, a standardized setting for studying parent–child interactions may consist of a playroom arranged in exactly the same way for all subjects. Depending on what the researcher wishes to study, the parents may be asked to do nothing or to behave in certain ways while their child is observed. In other cases, the parents and child are instructed to complete a specific task and the parents' behavior as well as their child's behavior is studied. Under these conditions, the physical environment is highly controlled, but differences among parents and differences in what their children focus on in the environment are uncontrolled, and a wide range of behavior is possible. Where children's interactions with other children are of interest, play groups or clubs may be formed and specific inputs manipulated, even though the effects of each child on the others cannot be controlled. Another variant of this approach is to expose subjects to standardized stimuli under standardized conditions but to observe the effects in naturalistic environments. In studies of the effects of television, for example, children's aggressive behavior in nursery school has been systematically observed after the children had been deliberately exposed to either violent or nonviolent television (Friedrich and Stein, 1973). The researchers thus insured that the subjects were exposed to the target stimuli, but they then studied the effects of the stimuli under naturalistic conditions like those to which they hoped to generalize their findings.

Standardized Procedures

Another way of controlling stimulus input is to administer tasks according to standardized procedures. Projective tests such as the Rorschach inkblot test and the Thematic Apperception Test (TAT) employ standardized stimulus materials and moderately standardized instructions to the subjects, but the examiner has considerable discretion in responding to the subject's responses. The tasks employed by Piaget offer somewhat more controlled situations in that the materials and basic questions are designed to pose exactly the same conceptual problem for all subjects, but the examiner encourages discursive responses and he probes in unstandardized ways in order to get a full picture of the subject's thinking.

Most American versions of Piaget's tasks are designed to provide greater standardization of the initial questions and of the examiner's responses to the subject's responses. In this respect, they involve about the same degree of stimulus control as do individually administered IQ tests. These measures precisely prescribe the questions asked and the materials presented to the subject, but allow for variations in ways of putting the subject at ease in order to optimize his performance. Personal characteristics of the examiner and characteristics of the larger physical environment may still vary considerably, however.

Pencil-and-paper tests given to children in groups provide another type of stimulus control if the children are old enough to read instructions and mark down their responses without much help. Such tests are rarely useful before the age of about 7, and their value at higher ages depends on careful calibration of their reading and writing requirements to the capabilities of the subjects. In using group pencil-and-paper tests, it is assumed that stimulus control is achieved by focusing the subjects' attention on instructions, questions, and response alternatives that are the same for everybody, although the larger physical environment is not usually standardized.

The most highly controlled research situations are those in which stimuli are presented mechanically to individual subjects, the subjects react by activating a mechanism or by making very specific verbal or behavioral responses, and the larger environment is the same for all subjects. Many researchers studying perception, learning, and physiological processes regard as ideal an air-conditioned, sound-proofed lab in which the subject responds to mechanically presented stimuli by pushing buttons or moving levers that automatically record his responses on tape which can, in turn, be fed into a computer for analysis. Laboratory trailers equipped in this way are widely used in research with children, because the trailers can be conveniently parked at schools and other settings from which child subjects are obtained.

Although the importance of minimizing extraneous variables might seem to argue unconditionally for maximally controlled situations like those just described, the unfamiliarity of such situations may arouse anxiety, boredom, or bewilderment. With child subjects, mechanical gadgetry may also induce passive mental sets whereby the child waits to see what will happen rather than actively trying to think about the stimuli to which he is exposed. On the other hand, such situations may heighten motivation, narrow the range of possible responses, or decrease distraction to the point where atypically high levels of performance are elicited. This is desirable for certain purposes, but for others it is preferable to obtain performance representative of the child's typical functioning.

In deciding how controlled, novel, or familiar a situation to use, the researcher must first decide how he wishes to generalize his results. Highly controlled situations may be necessary for studying behavioral processes that are otherwise difficult to observe, but they may produce results that cannot be readily generalized to everyday behavior. On the other hand, situations representative of the subjects' accustomed environment may make it difficult to identify the determinants of behavior but may produce results that are broadly generalizable. Unfortunately, if the determinants of the behavior are unknown, the limitations on generalizability will also be unknown, and subtle differences from one naturalistic situation to another may cause unexpected changes in behavior.

Because the determinants of human behavior are so complex, neither an exclusively laboratory approach nor an exclusively naturalistic approach is likely to be very informative by itself. Instead, it is usually more productive to generate hypotheses through naturalistic observation, to progressively isolate hypothesized variables under controlled conditions, and then to move from controlled tests back to more ecologically valid tests under naturalistic conditions. The more intensive the interplay between research under controlled and naturalistic conditions, the more likely are we to develop a science that is both methodologically sound and socially useful.

Other issues to be considered in the choice of research situations include the specificity with which variables are defined, the applicability of various methods for recording data, and the kinds of unwanted extraneous variables that might influence subjects' behavior under various conditions. Methods of measuring behavior will be discussed next, followed by discussion of important unwanted influences on behavioral data.

Types of Behavioral Units

In addition to deciding on the type of stimulus control to employ, the researcher must also decide on the type of behavioral units to be recorded. We will first discuss observational methods for recording the ongoing stream of behavior, and then methods for recording specific responses to specific stimuli. Observational methods can be subdivided into those that are "open," i.e., open to the recording of behavior without prior categorization; those that are relatively "closed," i.e., directed at recording the ongoing stream of behavior in terms of categories defined in advance; and those that entail obtaining observations from secondary sources.

Open Observational Methods

Specimen description. When Barker and Wright (1951, 1955) attempted to obtain complete descriptions of naturally occurring behavior, they wrote everything down in the form of narratives about the children's behavior and the situations in which it occurred. This is called a *specimen description* because it is intended to describe behavior during a predefined specimen time period. More recent studies have employed audio and video tapes to obtain specimen descriptions. However, once the ongoing behavior has been recorded, it must be coded and scored in terms of categories amenable to statistical analysis. Unless descriptions are reduced to analyzable categories, they cannot be meaningfully related to specific variables of interest. Anyone contemplating the use of large-scale specimen descriptions should note that Barker and Wright's (1951) description of one boy's behavior during one day filled 435 published pages! Thus, no matter how complete a record is initially obtained, the researcher must still make decisions about the units to be applied in reducing the data to analyzable form.

Diary description.   Perhaps the oldest method of collecting data on child behavior is the *diary description.* In 1877, Charles Darwin published a diary description of his son's behavior in uncontrolled situations and informal experiments designed to test various aspects of development. Piaget's (1951, 1954) illustrations of stages of infant development also derive from diary-like descriptions of his own children. Diary descriptions differ from specimen descriptions in that they focus on categories of events selected by the diary keeper over a long period of development, rather than aiming at total coverage within a limited specimen period. Diary descriptions are currently enjoying renewed popularity in the study of language development, where specimen descriptions might reach gargantuan proportions without including much language behavior and where the age of the children makes them poor subjects for highly structured methods of studying language. Such diary descriptions are most effective when well-defined rules for recording data are specified in advance and when more controlled methods are employed to test hypotheses suggested by the diary observations. For example, when a child has been observed to use a particular word under certain conditions, variations of these conditions can be deliberately created to determine what meanings the child attaches to the word (e.g., Nelson, 1973). In this way, naturalistic observations are employed to identify stimulus and response units appropriate for studying the particular child. These units are then imposed in a controlled manner to test the researcher's hypotheses.

Closed Observational Methods

The two methods described so far impose little structure on the behavioral units to be recorded. More structured or "closed" observational methods employ specific constraints on what can be recorded, when, and how. The objective is to define in advance the behavioral units of interest and to record them with maximum reliability and precision. Development of such methods typically begins with pilot testing of preliminary procedures in observational situations. Observers then practice scoring the same behavior, and interobserver agreement is calculated for the scoring of the predefined behavioral units. If agreement between observers is low, it may be because they require further training in scoring the units, because the scoring rules require improvement, or because the target behavior cannot be scored with sufficient objectivity.

As an example, a researcher may wish to study aggression in nursery school children. He must first decide whether to focus only on overt physical aggression or to include verbal aggression and the symbolic aggression implied by gestures. In order to study a broad range of aggression but be able to analyze each type separately, he may establish separate categories for physical, verbal, and symbolic aggression. Within each category, he will have to develop definitions of what will and will not be scored. Hitting another child would typically qualify for the category of overt physical aggression, but suppose the hitting appeared to be accidental or done in jest? Or suppose a child tried to hit another child but was restrained by a teacher? Decisions about how to record behavior in these various borderline areas need to be made and spelled out in rules that observers can use for what they see. In addition, the stream of observed behavior must be translated into quantitative scores. Four ways of doing this are described next.

Time sampling.   In the *time sampling* method, the observer records only what occurs within specified time intervals, e.g., every other 15 seconds. Each observation interval is typically separated from the next in order to make it easier for the observer to keep up and to reduce the redundancy incurred in repeatedly scoring a behavior if it lasts longer than one interval. To record his observations, the observer may employ a data sheet divided into rows and columns. Each row is designated for a general category of behavior—e.g., physical aggression, verbal aggression—or for specific behaviors, such as hitting, kicking, or biting. Each observation interval is assigned a column. A watch or small beeper connected to an earphone or a light activated by a timer signals the observer each time an observation interval begins and ends. During each observation interval, the observer puts a check in the row corresponding to any of the designated behaviors that occur. More than one category of behavior can be scored in one interval. If a behavior continues from one observation interval through a nonobservation interval and into the next observation interval, it is scored in both the observation intervals. Although this may produce some redundancy in scoring a particular behavior, this degree of redundancy may be of value in reflecting behaviors of exceptionally long duration.

Rather than filling out a data sheet by hand, an observer may employ a mechanical event recorder—a device in which paper is fed from one roll to another at constant speed. The paper is divided into intervals corresponding to the time sample intervals, and mechanical pens mark the paper whenever the observer pushes a button on a keyboard to record a particular category of behavior. Hand held electronic devices are also available that have keys for recording data on cassette tapes or in electronic storage units. The data can then be fed into computers for analysis.

Event sampling.   In contrast to time sampling, *event sampling* consists of recording each occurrence of a particular kind of behavioral event during an observation period. Thus, each act of physical aggression would be counted once, regardless of its duration. A disadvantage of event sampling for studying variables like aggression is that it may be difficult to reliably define the offset of one behavioral event and the onset of the next. If Child A is hitting Child B, and Child C intervenes, thereby becoming the target of Child A's attack, should Child A be scored for one aggressive act or two? On the other hand, event sampling may be more appropriate than time sampling for recording behavior that occurs in relatively well-delimited units, the duration of which is not important. As an example, the average number of words in a child's utterances has been used as a measure of level of language development (Brown, 1973). Time sampling of language output would yield only the total number of words spoken during the observation intervals, whereas scoring each utterance as an event—defined by the number of words it contained—makes it possible to calculate the mean length of a child's utterances independently of the amount or rate of his speech.

Trait rating.   A third method for recording observations in specified categories is to make *trait ratings*. When making trait ratings, an observer may take notes or narrative descriptions of what he observes, but, then, on the basis of his accumulated observations, he rates the subject on prespecified traits such as aggression. In this way, he can take account of the cumulative context and intensity of behavior more flexibly than he could if recording narrowly defined behaviors by means of time or event sampling. Trait ratings thus consist of the conclusions drawn by the observer from his observations, rather than being a record of the behavior observed.

Whereas time and event sampling require only the recording and summing of items, trait ratings require judgments of how high or low a subject is on a trait. This means that not only the definitions of units but also the response scale employed by the raters may influence reliability and validity. Rating subjects on a seven-point scale from very unaggressive to very aggressive, for example, may produce very different results from ranking subjects on their aggressiveness relative to one another. Ratings on a scale are vulnerable to the tendencies of individual observers to differ in their use of particular steps on the scale. On the other hand, rank ordering may obscure the fact that many subjects in a sample are so similar in the trait that differences among them cannot be reliably detected. To minimize both these problems, rating and ranking can be combined by having observers group subjects at various ranks, e.g., "the most aggressive 20 percent of the subjects," "the next most aggressive 20 percent," etc. This insures that the observers will not differ in the frequency with which they use the various steps on the scale, but it does not require them to make excessively fine judgments of rank order. Of course, rankings of any kind are likely to be more useful when all comparisons are to be made within a sample than when subjects from different samples are to be compared, because a particular subject might rank much higher in one sample than he would in another. Whichever scoring procedure is used, trait rating is typically most appropriate where the categories of behavior required for time and event sampling would be excessively narrow.

Q-**sorts.**   Observations on multiple traits or behaviors can be combined into more comprehensive descriptions of individual subjects by using Q methodology, as described in chapters 4 and 6. To do this, the observer sorts a collection of trait or behavior items into a specified number of categories ranging from "very characteristic of the subject" to "very uncharacteristic of the subject." The number of items to be sorted into each category is usually specified so as to approximate a normal distribution, with few items in the extreme categories and progressively more toward the center categories. Beside being desirable for statistical purposes, requiring items to be sorted into a normal distribution counteracts observer differences in preferences for certain categories.

In a specifically developmental adaptation of the Q-sort method, Schachter, Cooper, and Gordet (1968) constructed a pool of 113 items that can be varied according to the age of the subject to be described. The age levels are designated in terms of phases of psychosexual development as the Anal–Toddler Phase (1¾–3 years); Phallic–Preschool (3–4½); Oedipal–Kindergarten (4½–6½); School Age; and Adolescent–Maturity. An example of an item designed to be included at all levels beginning with the Toddler is: "Seeks out physical contact–Avoids physical contact." One designed only for School Age and Adolescent–Maturity levels is: "Has high aspiration for self–Has low aspiration level for self." To describe a subject, someone who knows him well sorts each item into one of seven categories. If the positive version of the item (e.g., "high aspiration") is considered characteristic of the subject, the item would be placed in category 7, 6, or 5, depending on whether it is very, somewhat, or slightly characteristic. If the negative version applies (e.g., "low aspiration"), the item would be placed in category 3, 2, or 1. Category 4 is reserved for statements that do not seem to characterize a subject one way or the other.

Structured data collection methods such as Q-sorts and trait ratings can be imposed upon data already collected by other means. However, when such data consist of written descriptions, they are severely limited by the writing skills, biases, and choice of words of those who write them. These problems are partly overcome with audio and video tape recordings, which now make it easier to impose time sampling, event sampling, Q-sorts, and trait ratings after the stream of behavior has been recorded.

Reports from Secondary Sources

Where direct observation of behavior is impractical, it is often necessary to obtain reports from people who are not trained as researchers but who know the subjects well, such as parents and teachers. Advantages of obtaining data from such people are that no alteration of the subjects' natural situation need be made and that broad spans of time and situations can be tapped. Disadvantages include biases and unreliability that may exceed those of trained observers who have no personal involvement with the subjects. Because most data from secondary sources are acquired after the target behavior has occurred, there is also a greater risk of memory distortion than when observations are recorded as the behavior is occurring. Checks on reliability can sometimes be made by comparing nonresearchers' reports with observations by trained observers. In Schaffer and Emerson's (1964) study of infant attachment behavior, for example, interviewers obtained mothers' reports of their infants' behavior, but the behavior was also observed directly on a few occasions. Good agreement was found between the mothers' and observers' reports.

Numerous questionnaires, rating scales, and behavior checklists have been devised to obtain data from secondary sources. In cases where the target behavior cannot be readily observed by anyone but the secondary source, it may not be possible to assess reliability through comparison with observations made by another observer. An estimate of reliability may nevertheless be made by having the source person fill out similar forms on two occasions or by having two different interviewers obtain reports from the same source. This was done by Graham and Rutter (1968) with an interview schedule designed to obtain data from mothers on their children's psychopathology. The mothers' reports remained highly consistent for well-specified behaviors, such as bed-wetting and temper tantrums, but were inconsistent for items requiring more subjective judgments, such as poor relationships with parents. Although inconsistency from one report to the next probably implies a lack of objectivity, high consistency does not by itself guarantee that the data are either objective or useful. As with data from other sources, the ultimate test of data from secondary sources is in the degree to which they relate to other variables of interest.

Unobtrusive Measures

Measures used with children are rarely presented in totally undis-guised form. Even if a researcher were to explain the exact purpose of his work and the function of the measures he uses, it is unlikely that he would be fully understood. Tasks used with young children are typ-ically introduced as "games," or "some things for kids to do." When children are old enough to recognize that they are being tested, however, it is certainly preferable to describe the procedures as tests or as "new tests that are being tried out," and to give as much information as will be comprehended, rather than transparently labeling the measures as "games." Failure to allay subjects' suspicions may leave them with hypotheses that will affect their behavior in unknown ways.

No matter what the researcher calls them or how he attempts to disguise their true purpose, most measurement procedures intrude upon subjects enough to potentially influence their behavior. In addi-tion to observation of ongoing behavior in uncontrolled and slightly controlled environments, a number of unobtrusive measures have been devised to collect data on specific variables without distorting behavior. Some of these measures are merely based upon things people have produced for their own purposes, such as pictures spontaneously painted by children. If systematic differences are found in paintings by children differing in age, for example, it might be concluded that these represent developmental differences in behavior, unconfounded with the possible effects of a research setting. On the other hand, differences in the "natural" conditions under which the children did their paintings could be responsible for the age differences. If the younger children had typically done their paintings in nursery schools, while the older chil-dren did them in art classes, the differences in settings might be respons-ible for the differences in paintings. The potential disadvantages of artificiality incurred in asking children to paint under standardized conditions might thus be less than the disadvantages due to differences in the natural settings in this particular case.

Unobtrusive measures also include disguised experiments in natural settings. While the experimenter does not have as complete control as he does in laboratory studies, he may be able to manipulate a particular variable and record behavior with considerable precision, without the subjects realizing that anything is being studied. With children, many procedures can be applied in relatively unobtrusive ways in standard settings such as schools. Page (1958), for example, had teachers write motivating comments on the papers of randomly selected students and found these students to be significantly superior in subsequent exam performance, with no students being aware of the experiment. A detailed survey of unobtrusive measures has been compiled by Webb, Campbell, Schwartz, and Sechrest (1966), although the majority have been used primarily with adults and some, including the one used by Page, raise ethical issues of the sort to be discussed in chapter 10.

Self-report Measures

In many kinds of research, subjects are asked to tell something about themselves. As pointed out long ago by the father of behaviorism, John B. Watson (1913), self-reports of feelings, thoughts, and attitudes constitute behavior and can therefore be studied like other kinds of behavior. However, such reports should not be regarded as being equivalent to the unobservable feelings, thoughts, and attitudes themselves.

Self-report measures range from unstructured interviews, where the subject is encouraged to follow his own train of associations, to highly structured questionnaires where the subject is asked to give very specific responses to direct questions, often in yes–no or multiple-choice format. Psychodynamically oriented clinicians and researchers tend to favor nondirective interviews in which the subject follows his own associations, with occasional questions by the interviewer to ascertain specific points and to find out how the subject reacts to particular comments. Since young children are not good subjects for strictly verbal interviewing, most interviews with young children are conducted in a playroom where the child is invited to do as he wishes with the toys. This is intended to put the child at ease and make possible "open" observations of his behavior before specific questions are asked. Of course, data from interviews must at some point be put into structured form for analysis. There is as yet little evidence that data gathered in nondirective interviews are either reliable or valid, although Rutter and Graham (1968) obtained reasonably reliable ratings of psychopathology in children from interviews that combined structured and nondirective approaches.

Most structured self-report measures are designed to be read to or by the subjects and responded to with specific answers. An example is the Children's Manifest Anxiety Scale (CMAS; Castaneda, McCandless, and Palermo, 1956), on which children are to respond by checking "yes" or

"no" to items such as "I blush easily," and "I worry most of the time."
While written self-report measures are rarely used with children
younger than about 7, a few have been designed to be read to younger
children who give their answers orally. Mischel, Zeiss, and Zeiss (1974),
for example, have developed a questionnaire to identify individual
differences in the degree to which preschoolers attribute the outcome of
events to their own behavior or to forces beyond their control. For each
item, the child is to choose either an answer that indicates internal locus
of control (a feeling of control by the self), or external locus of control (a
feeling of being controlled by others). As an illustration, one item is:
"When somebody brings you a present, is that because you are a good
girl (boy) or because they like to give people presents?" A second is:
"When you can't find one of your toys, is that because you lost it, or
because somebody took it?"

Because responses can be influenced as much by the format of self-
report measures as by their intended content, it is imperative that the
formats be designed to avoid systematic biases. This is especially true
with children, whose tenuous understanding of self-report measures
may limit their ability to respond accurately. It has been suggested, for
example, that the failure of scores on the CMAS to correlate with other
indices of anxiety is because the CMAS items—all keyed in the positive
direction—merely measure willingness to say deviant things about the
self (Wirt and Broen, 1956). Likewise, if the responses scored as "external" were the second alternatives in all items of the Mischel et al.
measure, a tendency to forget the first alternative could cause a child to
receive an unduly high score for external locus of control.

Sociometric measures, in which children are asked to name other
children in their group whom they like most or least, resemble self-
report measures in general format, but the responses are used to obtain
ratings of how well each child is liked by others. For example, to find out
whether sex preferences in the evaluation of peers change with age,
children of three age levels might be asked to choose from the names (or
photos) of their classmates the ones they would most and least like to
have as friends. The number of boys and girls chosen by each sex at each
age can then be compared, although here, too, interpretations can be
clouded by potential biases in the way the questions are asked.

Expressive Measures

Personality characteristics. Whereas self-report measures are
designed to obtain subjects' own reports of their thinking, feelings, and
experiences, expressive measures are designed to tap these same variables more indirectly. Projective tests, such as the Rorschach and
Thematic Apperception Test (TAT), require subjects to make verbal

interpretations of ill-defined or ambiguous pictorial stimuli. The assumption is that the subject will project various aspects of his own personality into his responses. Although projective techniques have inspired much research, little evidence has been adduced for the reliability or validity of generalized personality interpretations made from them (Suinn and Oskamp, 1969; Zubin, Eron, and Schumer, 1965). Moreover, the fact that there are consistent age changes in projective test responses indicates that they are influenced by developmental factors over and above any individual differences in personality that persist across ages (Ames, Learned, Metraux, and Walker, 1952).

As personality measures, projective techniques have been most successful when subjects' responses have been rated for very specific traits or motives according to clearly defined rules and when measurable validity criteria were employed. An example is the rating of achievement motivation according to rules for scoring stories told to TAT pictures. The construct validity of these ratings has been demonstrated through correlations with behavior in other situations (McClelland, Atkinson, Clark, and Lowell, 1953). Application of formal rules to the scoring of a text or story, as done with TAT responses, is called *content analysis*. Formal scoring systems have also been applied to subjects' drawings. Drawings of the human figure have been especially popular as a basis for personality interpretations, although no well-validated procedure exists for making these interpretations. Children's play in interview situations has likewise been scored for various personality characteristics. Like projective tests, this method has been most successful when behavior has been scored for well-defined variables that could be validated in terms of relationships to other measurable variables.

Cognitive level.   Expressive measures have also been put to use in the study of cognitive development. One approach has been to create contrived violations of physical or logical principles in order to see whether subjects are surprised. The assumption is that a subject will be surprised only if he was aware of the principle in the first place. As an example, in order to test their grasp of conservation of liquid without recourse to the elaborate verbal interchanges required by Piaget's tasks, children have been asked to assist in pouring a large quantity into a small container (Achenbach, 1969, 1973). Unknown to the children, the small container was partially emptied by a hidden drain. High interobserver reliability was found in judgments of whether subjects were surprised. This approach appears especially useful with children who are not motivated or able to express their thinking in the verbal terms required for Piagetian tasks. Some retarded children, for example, were surprised by the contrived violations even though they did not give adequate explanations for conservation on Piagetian tasks. By contrast, surprise reactions by normal children were closely correlated with their verbal performance on conservation tasks. Contrived violations of physical principles have also been used to diagnose stages of object concept development in infants through the trick substitution of a new object for an object the infant has seen being hidden (LeCompte and Gratch, 1972).

Performance Measures

Performance measures are designed to measure how well or under what conditions subjects accomplish specific tasks. These include, of course, standardized ability and achievement tests that measure an individual's performance relative to normative samples. They also include measures of learning, problem-solving, memory, and perception devised for research on individual differences and on psychological processes in general. Many variations of discrimination learning tasks, for example, have been devised for studying the effects of developmental level, motivation, and feedback on learning processes. The measure of performance is usually the number of trials taken to reach a criterion of a specified number of successive correct responses, or a specified proportion of correct responses in a certain number of trials, or some other quantitative index of correct responding.

Although such measures as consistent choice of the correct stimulus in a discrimination learning problem are regarded as indicating mastery of the task, puzzling discrepancies often appear between children's verbal explanations for the task solution and their actual behavior. When asked how they know which stimulus to pick each time or why they picked a particular stimulus, it is not unusual for young children to reply, " 'Cause I'm smart," or " 'Cause I wanted the candy," rather than referring to the stimulus properties to which they had been consistently responding (e.g., the green one, the big one, the round one). However, Blank (1975) has shown that children as young as 3 can give correct verbal explanations if, after the child has reached the criterion for learning, the stimuli are placed out of sight and the experimenter asks the child to tell which stimulus is correct, e.g., "Which one has the candy?" When this is done, children respond in terms of the stimulus properties much more frequently than when asked, "How did you know . . . ?" or "Why did you choose . . . ?" Questions of the latter form are evidently interpreted by young children as referring to their motives or personal characteristics that led to their choice, whereas they clearly grasp the need to specify the relevant stimulus properties when asked which of the stimuli they chose.

Memory performance has been the focus of a great deal of research, much of it employing inaccuracies in memory as a basis for inferring the processes whereby people selectively encode, store, retrieve, and decode information. Not surprisingly, standardized measures show increases with age in the number of items correctly remembered. However, Piaget and Inhelder (1973) have added a new dimension to the study of memory by showing that children's memory for certain stimuli can be better several months after exposure to the stimuli than it was shortly after exposure to the stimuli, even though the children have not seen the stimuli again! Presented with a row of sticks in seriated order from longest to shortest, for example, 5-year-old children do not accurately reproduce the seriation in memory tests shortly after seeing the sticks. However, *without seeing the sticks again*, the same children can reproduce the seriation more accurately several months later. These findings contradict traditional views of memory as a process that, at best, preserves information and, more typically, involves loss of information.

How does Piaget explain the apparent improvement in memory? According to his theory, the improvement can be expected to occur when stimuli possessing certain properties are presented while the child is beginning to develop new conceptual representations of these particular properties. Five-year olds who are presented with seriations cannot accurately conceptualize them, but advances in the operative aspect of their thinking during the succeeding months enables them to progressively recode their original figurative images of the stimuli into more accurate reproductions of them. Although Piaget's explanation has been disputed, the surprising improvement in memory performance has been replicated by other investigators (cf. Liben, 1975).

Measures of perceptual performance have also been used to study development. It has been found that certain visual illusions—called *Type I illusions*—are stronger for young children than for adults, whereas other illusions—called *Type II illusions*—show the reverse pattern. Piaget (1969) has interpreted these age trends in the perception of illusions as manifestations of developmental changes in information processing strategies whereby perceptual functioning becomes progressively less "centered" and more flexibly "decentered." This means that the tendency of young children to fixate on individual components of a stimulus progressively gives way to more systematic and coordinated scanning of stimuli. According to this hypothesis, young children are most susceptible to Type I illusions because these illusions are heightened by fixation on individual components. By contrast, adults are most susceptible to Type II illusions because it is systematic scanning that heightens these illusions. Although agreeing with Piaget's hypothesis about Type II illusions, Pollack (1969) maintains that physical changes in the eye, rather than improvements in scanning, reduce the susceptibility to Type I illusions.

To test the hypothesis that age changes in a particular Type I illusion, the Mueller–Lyer, are due to changes in information processing patterns rather than to changes in the eye, Girgus, Coren, and Fraenkel (1975) obtained a series of six judgments at 30-second intervals from 7-, 9-, 11-, and 21-year old subjects. As illustrated in Figure 7-1, the subject could adjust the longer-appearing line (located to the right of center in the figure) until he thought it equaled the line to the left of center. The difference between the resulting lengths provided the measure of the illusion for that subject. If physical differences in the eye were responsible for the greater inaccuracy of the younger subjects, then this inaccuracy should remain as great on the sixth judgment as on the first judgment. On the other hand, if overcentered viewing by the younger subjects were responsible, repeated viewing might improve their accuracy. It was found that, with repeated viewing, the youngest subjects became as accurate as the oldest subjects by the sixth trial, thus indicating that their inefficient viewing strategies were responsible for their initial inaccuracy.

The rate, amount, or quality of accomplishment on performance measures can also be used to assess the effects of social and personality variables. Montemayor (1974), for example, sought to determine whether sex-typing of a game influenced first and second graders' performance on it. One group of each sex was told the game was intended for their sex, a second group was told it was for the opposite sex, and a third group was given instructions without reference to sex. It was found that each sex performed best when the game was described as being intended for their sex and worst when it was described as being for the opposite sex. The children's beliefs about sex-typing thus affected their performance on the game.

Psychophysiological Measures

Broadly construed, "behavior" includes any measurable activity of an organism, including physiological activity. Numerous measures of physiological functioning can be employed to obtain data on psychological variables, especially attention and arousal. Changes in heart

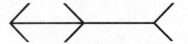

Figure 7-1. Mueller–Lyer illusion like that employed by Girgus, et al. (1975). The length of the righthand component could be adjusted until it appeared to equal the length of the lefthand component.

rate, respiration, and sucking are widely used to measure infants' attention to various stimuli. Heart rate is measured with electrodes taped on
the infant's chest; respiration by a device strapped around the infant's
chest or by a thermistor—a heat sensitive device taped near the infant's
nostrils; and sucking by a special nipple placed in the infant's mouth. If
heart rate, respiration, or sucking shows consistent changes each time a
particular stimulus is presented, this indicates that the subject is attending to the stimulus.

Suppose you wished to determine the age at which infants become
able to discriminate among particular sounds. One approach is to repeatedly present a particular sound until the infant *habituates* to it, i.e.,
he no longer shows changes in a physiological response such as sucking
when the sound is presented. If a change in sucking then occurs when a
different sound is presented, this indicates that the infant discriminates
between the two sounds. Using exactly this approach, subtle changes in
sound that convey meaning in adult speech have been found to elicit
significant changes in rate of sucking by one-month-old infants,
whereas comparable changes that do not convey meaning in speech fail
to affect sucking (Eimas, Siqueland, Jusczyk, and Vigorito, 1971). This
suggests that infants are especially attuned to aspects of sound that are
crucial for learning oral language.

The galvanic skin response (GSR) can also be used as an index of
covert responses. GSRs consist of changes in the electrical conductivity
of the skin, resulting from the activity of sweat glands in response to
physiological arousal. They are measured by placing electrodes against
the surface of the hands or the soles of the feet. GSRs may be advan-
tageous for studying physiological reactions in older children and
adults because they are less susceptible to voluntary control by the
subject than are heart rate, respiration, and sucking.

Other measures of physiological arousal include capillary dilation
—changes in blood flow through blood vessels, as measured with rubber
nipples placed over the fingers; evoked potentials—changes in electrical activity originating in the brain, as measured by elec-
troencephalographic (EEG) electrodes placed on the head; and changes
in pupillary size, as measured by a special camera.

Beside being used to measure arousal, certain physiological measures can be used to monitor covert behavioral processes. One such
measure is the electromyographical recording (EMG), the recording of
changes in electrical potentials of muscles by placing electrodes on skin
surfaces near the muscles. Garrity (1975), for example, used EMGs of
speech muscles located near the lower lip and chin to study relationships between covert speech and recall in preschoolers. She presented the children with pictures and asked them to recall the pictures a
short time later. The children were told not to talk aloud, whisper, or

move their lips until the examiner asked them to recall the pictures orally. It was found that subjects who showed the greatest EMG activity also recalled the most pictures, thus indicating that covert speech was linked to the process of remembering in children of this age. Furthermore, the highest IQ subjects showed substantial increases in EMG activity from initial presentation of the stimuli until they were asked to recall them, whereas lower IQ subjects showed decreases in EMG activity. Thus, it was the brightest children who apparently used covert speech most systematically as a memory aid.

By way of summary, Table 7-1 presents an overview of the degree of stimulus control and behavioral specificity most typically imposed by various research methods. Observational and unobtrusive measures tend to be used in situations where stimulus input is minimally controlled by the researcher; self-report and expressive measures in situations involving intermediate degrees of stimulus control; and performance and physiological measures in situations involving the highest degree of control. There are, of course, exceptions to these particular combinations of situation and method, but the assumed virtue of naturalism obtained with observational and unobtrusive measures is lost when they are employed in more highly controlled situations. Therefore, when it seems worth sacrificing naturalism to higher degrees of stimulus control, the more precise data yielded by structured behavioral measures typically makes them preferable to unstructured measures.

Sources of Bias in Collecting Data

Just as every environment influences behavior, every research method influences the data collected with it. Numerous sources of bias have been identified in behavioral measures. Some of these originate with subject characteristics, whereas others involve characteristics of the people or instruments that collect the data.

Demand Characteristics

If subjects are aware that they are being studied, they usually develop their own hypotheses about what is expected of them and may attempt either to fulfill or resist the expectations they ascribe to the researcher. The cues that govern a subject's perception of what is expected of him and of what the researcher hopes to find are known as *demand characteristics*. Sources of cues include things the subject has heard about the study, its setting, implicit and explicit instructions, characteristics of

TABLE 7-1. Degrees of Stimulus Control and Behavioral Specificity Typically Employed with Various Methods.

Data-Collection Method	Degree of Stimulus Control (S) and Behavioral Specificity (B)			
	None	*Low*	*Moderate*	*High*
Open observational	S	S B	B	
Closed observational	S	S B	B	
Secondary sources	S	S B	B	
Unobtrusive	S	S B	B	
Self-report		S B	S B	B
Expressive		S B	S B	B
Performance			S B	S B
Physiological			S B	S B

the researcher as a person, and the procedure itself. Orne (1969) has demonstrated that many subjects respond to demand characteristics by attempting to do especially well what they think the researcher really hopes they will do—in effect, these characteristics exert demands on the subject. Striving to figure out and do what the researcher wants may be less common among child subjects than among the college students employed in much of Orne's research. However, a host of other variables—such as attractiveness of the research materials, the friendliness, sex, size, and age of the researcher, and the opportunity to get out of class to participate in a study—may function as demand characteristics for children. Unwanted demand characteristics can often be identified through careful observation and interviewing of subjects during pilot testing and then reduced through changes in procedures.

Two effects related to demand characteristics have proved so powerful as to have earned names of their own. One, the *Hawthorne effect*, was discovered in studies of variations in working conditions in the Hawthorne plant of the Western Electric Company (Homans, 1958). A small group of employees was selected to work in a special room where changes in their productivity could be monitored as working conditions were systematically varied. It was found that virtually every experimental manipulation increased productivity. Furthermore, productivity continued to climb even when the experimental alterations were temporarily suspended! Interviews revealed that the workers felt that being part of an experiment was fun, that the company was interested in them, that what they were doing would benefit other employees, and that their group piecework wages were more affected by each worker's performance when they were in the small experimental group. Thus, the general effects of being in an experiment were greater than the effects of the deliberate experimental manipulations.

To avoid mistaking Hawthorne effects for the effects of the independent variables being studied, research on conditions that may be construed as potentially beneficial to the subjects should include a *Hawthorne control group*—a group of subjects receiving all the attention and ostensible benefits of the experimental condition *except* for the manipulations really being tested. Unless the performance of the true experimental group is found to differ significantly from that of the Hawthorne control group, it cannot be concluded that the experimental manipulation had an effect. In developmental research, intervention programs for the disadvantaged and innovative educational curricula are especially susceptible to Hawthorne effects. Because Hawthorne control groups are not always feasible in these situations, an alternative is to compare the effects of two or more different programs on similar groups of subjects. If the subjects have equally favorable attitudes toward the different programs, any differences in outcome should be attributable to program differences over and above Hawthorne effects. However, a no-treatment control group would still be desirable in order to determine whether the experimental treatments—even with the possible aid of Hawthorne effects—are actually producing better results than no special treatment. In intervention programs, Hawthorne effects may be valuable in themselves if they create favorable attitudes that in turn lead to lasting changes in behavior.

A phenomenon similar to the Hawthorne effect was discovered in experimental studies of drugs where patients often reported feeling better after being given substances having no physical effects. Bogus medications of this sort are called *placebos* (from Latin, "I shall please"). Since a placebo effect could make an ineffective drug seem beneficial, drug studies are unlikely to be valid without a *placebo control* condition—i.e., some patients receive the actual drug under test whereas others receive a similar appearing placebo. Unless those who receive the true drug improve more than the placebo control subjects, no effects can be ascribed to the drug itself.

Response Sets

Another biasing factor involves subjects' *response sets*—their dispositions to respond in certain stereotyped ways regardless of what they are asked to respond to. A type of response set especially prevalent on self-report measures is known as the *social desirability set*. This is a set to give only responses that conform to conventional standards of desirable behavior. To minimize the effects of this type of set, self-report measures can be designed either to exclude socially desirable response alternatives or to include equal proportions of socially desirable alternatives for each characteristic measured. When this is done, social desirability per se should not cause subjects to score differently on the different characteristics.

Measures that require yes–no responses are vulnerable to the tendencies of some subjects to consistently say yes (*yeasaying*) and of other subjects to consistently say no (*naysaying*), regardless of the content of the questions. Young children are especially prone to yeasaying, as shown by the responses of a 5-year old in a play interview (Yarrow, 1960, pp. 659–60):

> The child built an enclosure out of large blocks. The examiner asked, "Would you like to be in this all by yourself?" "Yes," replied the child. "Would you like your daddy with you?" "Yes." "Would you like your mommy in there with you?" "Yes." "Would you like to be in this all alone?" "Yes," this time with emphatic agreement.

Forced-choice questions that require the subject to choose one alternative or another instead of saying yes or no can minimize the effects of yea- and naysaying sets, if the questions are phrased simply enough to be understood. However, care must be taken to prevent the order of the alternatives from being confounded with the scoring of particular characteristics, as children tend to choose the second of two alternatives regardless of content (Mischel et al., 1974).

Multiple response categories or scales ranging from one extreme to another can be used to obtain more differentiated scoring of responses, but they are vulnerable to individual differences in tendencies to use extreme vs. intermediate categories. Because extreme responses have been found to decrease as age and intelligence increase, this type of response set may be partly a function of developmentally based ability to make fine discriminations (Katz and Zigler, 1967).

Another type of response set may affect observers' ratings of subjects' behavior as well as judgments given by subjects themselves. Known as the *halo effect*, this is the tendency for one aspect of what is being judged to color judgments of other aspects. It should not be surprising, for example, if features of female contestants other than diving skill create halo effects in male judges of diving contests. Likewise, teachers' evaluations of their pupils on various characteristics are often highly intercorrelated because a general impression of each child as a good or poor student influences all the teacher's judgments of the child. One way to reduce halo effects is to define rating dimensions so that both extremes have low (or high) social desirability. For example, in a five-step scale employed by Rose et al. (1975) for rating quality of attention in preschoolers, one extreme was defined as "obsessive," while the other extreme was defined as "flighty." Generally positive or negative feelings about subjects were, therefore, unlikely to push ratings in one direction or the other. Another way to reduce halo effects is to phrase rating scales in terms of frequency of occurrence of very specific behaviors, so that the respondent indicates how often the subject displays the behavior rather than whether the subject is high or low on a trait.

Subject Selection Factors

Ways of designing research to insure that subject samples are representative were discussed in chapter 4. Yet no matter how good a research design appears in the abstract, the researcher must be wary of unforeseen biasing factors that affect the selection of subjects. Whenever it is impossible to use all the members of a potential subject pool or to select subjects by procedures that guarantee representativeness, the risk arises that those who are studied differ significantly from the subject pool as a whole. If subjects select themselves by volunteering, the volunteers may differ in motivational and personality characteristics from those who do not volunteer (cf. Rosenthal and Rosnow, 1975). Where volunteering is not a factor, allowing teachers or others to choose the subjects may introduce selective factors, as was discovered too late in a comparison between 10,000 English school children receiving milk supplements and 10,000 not receiving supplements. Despite the huge samples, the study was ruined because teachers benevolently singled out the smallest and frailest children to receive the milk, thereby making the experimental and control groups hopelessly dissimilar (cf. McNemar, 1969).

Even if research begins with appropriately representative samples of subjects, the research procedures themselves may cause selective attrition which biases the results. If screening or pretesting procedures eliminate many subjects, then the results are generalizable, at most, only to subjects like those in the remaining subsamples. Loss of young subjects often occurs because of their reluctance to participate, refusal to speak, or failure to pay attention. While some attrition may be unavoidable, considerable ingenuity and pilot testing are necessary to insure that research situations are as pleasant and undemanding as possible, especially for young subjects. Since young children do not know what research is, pains must be taken to obtain a child's-eye view of the research situation and to reduce any causes for apprehension about it.

Longitudinal studies are vulnerable to selective attrition resulting from family moves, loss of cooperation from subjects, and, in some cases, death or illness. In order to reduce attrition through moves, subjects are often chosen for family stability, but this introduces a selective factor into the initial composition of the sample. The expense of longitudinal studies may make selectivity in composing samples preferable to risking loss of so many subjects that the data become useless, but it is important to identify the particular kinds of bias introduced so that limitations on the generalizability of the findings can be assessed.

Drawing longitudinal conclusions from cross-sectional comparisons of different age groups is vulnerable to sampling biases in other ways. As an illustration, a cross-sectional study of black elementary school children revealed that the mean IQs of the younger children were higher than those of the older children in the same schools (Kennedy, Van De Riet, and White, 1963). At first glance, this suggests that the children's IQs were declining with age due, perhaps, to poor schooling or to increasing cultural bias in the IQ test at higher ages. On the other hand, Schaefer (1965) argued that, because sampling was limited to elementary school children, the very youngest children were likely to be those who started school early because of exceptional ability, whereas each succeeding age group would contain more children who had been held back because of poor performance, to the point where the oldest elementary school children (up to age 16 in the Kennedy et al. study) would be the least able of all. Thus, because the sample was limited to only those 5-year olds who were in elementary school, rather than all 5-year olds, only the brightest 5-year olds would be included. Likewise, because the sample was limited to only those 16-year olds who were in elementary schools, only the least able 16-year olds would be included.

To test Schaefer's hypothesis that sampling biases were responsible for the apparent decline in IQ, Kennedy (1969) retested the same children five years later. He found that their mean IQs had indeed remained stable. Thus, the apparent decline in IQ indicated by cross-sectional comparisons of different age groups was probably due to differing biases in the selection of each age group, as argued by Schaefer, rather than to declines in the IQs of individual children as they grew older.

Even where sampling seems equally representative within two age groups of a particular subject pool, unrecognized biases can cause the groups to differ on variables other than age. If, for example, all the 6-year olds and all the 15-year olds in an entire town were compared on a variable such as IQ, it is possible that the 6-year olds might differ because new housing developments had attracted young families differing in socioeconomic status from the more established families of the 15-year olds. It is also possible that differences between the 6- and 15-year olds in motivation could be responsible for differences in obtained scores, even though the groups might not differ if they could be truly equated for motivation.

Instrument Bias

In addition to biases arising from subject characteristics, biases can also arise from characteristics of the instruments used to measure behavior. Suppose, for example, that parents were asked to indicate whether their child was *worse, unchanged, slightly improved, much improved,* or *cured* following psychotherapy. Assuming that there is some degree of error in responding and that the errors are randomly distributed, the fact that there are three positive categories and only one negative category would cause more erroneous responses to fall on the positive side on a purely statistical basis. Furthermore, on a "psychological" basis, respondents who feel neutral or have no opinion about an item tend to employ the center categories of a response scale. Since the center category is *slightly improved*, some responses might be placed in this category by parents who do not really have any conviction about whether their child had improved.

While it is typically better to provide equal numbers of positive and negative response categories for evaluative judgments, the value of a middle or neutral category depends upon the objectives of the researcher. The inclusion of a middle category generally makes a response scale easier to use, whereas scales having no middle category require the respondent to ruminate over whether he is inclined more toward the positive or negative side on items about which he has neutral or mixed feelings. However, in some situations, the researcher may wish to force a choice between the positive and negative sides because neutral responses may not be desirable for his particular purposes.

Virtually all measures are inherently biased in their sampling of behavior. No measure can record everything and there is rarely any way of knowing whether a perfectly representative sample of a particular behavior domain is being obtained. IQ tests, for example, might be better predictors of academic performance if they used items that have yet to be invented. In practice, choices of items are based on the researcher's ideas about how to measure a particular construct or domain, his success in actualizing his ideas in practical form, and a winnowing out of items according to the relationships they are found to have with various validity criteria.

Mechanical methods for presenting stimuli and recording responses are often subject to less error and variability than human data collectors. However, mechanical devices break down, they are never totally error free, and they do not absolve the researcher from having to make choices about how to control biases in stimulus situations and response modes. Videotaping, for example, records behavior far more accurately than written descriptions, but decisions must still be made about the most appropriate situations in which to record, how to assess the effects of the camera's presence on the subjects, the best categories to impose upon the data once it has been taped, and how to impose such categories reliably.

Researcher Expectancy Effects

Just as subjects' expectancies can influence their behavior in studies susceptible to Hawthorne and placebo effects, so, too, can *researchers'* expectancies influence what they convey to subjects and what they observe, record, and find in their data. Like placebo effects, certain types of researcher expectancy effects first became apparent in drug studies, and it was for drug studies that remedies were first devised. Even when a drug study includes a placebo control group, researchers who know which patients received the real drug might inadvertently bias the data obtained, because they may question the experimental and control patients differently and may be especially attentive to signs of improvement in the experimental patients. For this reason, drug researchers not only keep patients "blind to" (ignorant of) the experimental condition they are in, but also keep the people evaluating improvement blind as to which patients received the drug and which the placebo. Because the evaluators as well as the patients are blind to the experimental conditions, this is referred to as a *double blind placebo control* procedure.

Researcher expectancy effects have also been demonstrated in a variety of behavioral studies (Rosenthal, 1966). In these studies, some research assistants were told that a particular result was expected, while other assistants were told that the *opposite* result was expected. When the two groups of assistants then used identical procedures to test subjects, they obtained *opposite* results conforming to the opposite expectations they had been given. Although there is considerable debate about the actual strength and pervasiveness of researcher expectancy effects in otherwise well-designed studies (cf. Barber, Forgione, Chaves, Calverley, McPeake, and Bowen, 1969), there is no doubt that researcher expectancies can be a source of bias in a number of ways. These include designing studies so that the expected outcomes are inadvertently encouraged, behaving differently to subjects expected to act differently, and double checking data for mistakes only when the data contradict expected outcomes. The latter may be a perfectly innocent but common source of bias: Errors are inevitable, but those that bias results in favor of a researcher's expectancies are much less likely to be sought out and found than those that bias results against the researcher's expectancies.

Although automation of research procedures can reduce the direct effects of researcher expectancies on subject behavior and on the recording of data, the most certain solution is that adopted in double blind drug studies—i.e., to have data collected, analyzed, and checked by people who are blind to the critical variables. Since this is not always feasible, frequent reliability checks and systematic checking for all errors are necessary aids. The need for repeated or continuous reliability checks has been demonstrated by Reid (1970), who found that observer reliability was much higher when the observers knew they were being checked than when they believed they were not being checked.

Interactions between Subject and Researcher Characteristics

In addition to his expectancies about subjects' behavior, other characteristics of the researcher, such as his language and ethnic identification, may differentially affect subjects. While it is obvious that a test administered in a language not understood by subjects will not yield valid results, differences between the dialects spoken by minority groups and the language used in administering tests have too often been ignored. How much these differences affect performance is an empirical question that should be considered whenever there are dialect differences between researchers and subjects. To assess such effects on IQ test performance, Quay (1971) compared the scores obtained by black Headstart children tested in standard American English with those of similar children tested by an examiner speaking black dialect. No significant differences were found in performance, suggesting that the standard language did not bias the results. However, Quay's examiners were black males who may have obtained maximum performance from the subjects anyway, so that any effects of linguistic differences were minimized.

Unlike Quay, Marwit and Neumann (1974) compared the effects of examiner's race on the performance of both black and white children receiving standard and black dialect reading tests. In this case, race of examiner was found to interact significantly with race of subject and with the test language—black children unexpectedly performed best when the reading materials were in standard English and the examiner was white, whereas white children were not significantly affected by race of examiner or test language.

Overcoming the Effects of Bias

Despite precautions for reducing known sources of bias, the remaining potential for bias might seem so enormous as to make research futile. However, many types of bias stem not merely from irksome errors, but from important variables unrecognized by the researcher. The real question is not, therefore, whether all biases can be eliminated, but whether there is more than one plausible explanation for findings and whether an explanation other than the one favored by the researcher would be supported in further studies designed to choose between the two.

Logical as well as empirical issues arise in choosing between rival explanations for observed outcomes. The logical issues concern the inductive inferences drawn about general principles from specific situations. If several findings all seem consistent with a general principle, then we are apt to infer inductively that the principle will apply to all situations like those observed. However, the validity of such an inference is threatened by the fact that the observations may also be logically consistent with explanations other than the one we favor. Some of the rival explanations may attribute the results to biases in the data, whereas others may invoke principles that are of major interest in themselves. Whichever the case, scientific knowledge can never be achieved by inductive logic alone.

Where observations are equally consistent with two or more explanations, further *data* are usually needed to choose among the explanations. One step is to make additional observations under conditions or with measures in which the causal factors favored by the explanations rivaling the researcher's explanation are controlled—in other words, to attempt to *replicate* the original findings under new conditions or with new measures that will eliminate alternative explanations as thoroughly as possible. Another step is to determine whether there are any situations in which a theory and its rivals yield contrasting predictions. To do this, specific hypotheses must be deduced from each of the rival explanations and these hypotheses must be tested. If the researcher's theory is valid, then an empirical test should support the hypothesis derived from his theory and contradict the rival hypothesis. Testing a theory from a variety of angles to see whether the results converge in support of the theory is known as *triangulation*. When theories are tested by replication and triangulation, they must survive a variety of different biases. Since these biases work in various directions, repeated corroboration of a theory despite inevitable biases is what ultimately builds confidence in the theory. In fact, biases are often not even discovered until violations of predictions made by well-established theories induce researchers to seek them out.

Murphy's Law

In addition to all the systematic biases that can arise, even the best research is subject to what is probably the most universal law of human activity. Sometimes known as *Murphy's Law*, this hallowed principle states: *If anything can go wrong, it will*. Equipment failure, experimenter illness, subjects who fail to show up, computer errors, and misunderstandings among coworkers are but a few common examples of Murphy's Law. To minimize its effects, the prudent researcher will be certain to thoroughly pilot test his procedures with subjects and conditions as similar as possible to those of the actual study. He will also serve as a subject himself and ask colleagues to do likewise in order to ferret out possible trouble spots. And when the unexpected happens, he will be prepared to correct it in ways that preserve the validity of his study as fully as possible.

Summary

Research methods vary along two major dimensions—the type of control exercised by the researcher over the stimuli to which subjects are exposed and the type of units imposed on the behavior recorded. Researchers seeking a record of natural behaviors in the natural environment generally refrain from controlling stimulus input, whereas researchers seeking information about the operation of specific variables impose more controls over the stimulus input to their subjects.

Among data collection methods, *open observational methods* —including *specimen descriptions* and *diary descriptions*—impose the least specificity on the behavior recorded. Closed observational methods—including *time sampling, event sampling, trait ratings*, and *Q-sorts*—impose greater specificity on the behavior. The latter two methods can also be applied to observational data drawn from secondary sources. *Unobtrusive measures* are employed to obtain data on specific behavioral variables without the subject's awareness. *Self-report measures*, ranging from unstructured interviews to highly structured questionnaires, are designed to obtain subjects' own reports of their thinking, feelings, and experiences, whereas *expressive measures* are designed to tap these same variables more indirectly. The purpose of *performance measures* is to measure how well or under what conditions subjects accomplish specific tasks. *Psychophysiological measures* provide indices of arousal, attention, and covert behavioral processes.

Behavioral data can be biased by unwanted *demand characteristics* of the research situation, including subjects' motivation to please the researcher, *Hawthorne effects*, and *placebo effects*. It can also be biased by *response sets*, including *social desirability, yeasaying, naysaying*, and *halo effects*; by *subject selection factors*; by *instrument biases*; by *researcher expectancy effects*; and by *interactions between subject and researcher characteristics*.

Biases in research are best overcome by eliminating rival explanations through *replication* of findings with different measures under a variety of conditions, and through *triangulation* of theoretical explanations by zeroing in on hypothesized relationships from a variety of angles. However, all research—no matter how well designed—is subject to *Murphy's Law*.

8 Mission-oriented Research

MORE THAN MOST areas of behavioral research, research on children owes its origin to deliberate attempts to obtain socially beneficial knowledge. Starting in the 1880s, G. Stanley Hall—the acknowledged founder of child psychology in the United States (Kessen, 1965)—sought to base educational reforms on data he gathered by administering questionnaires to children. Following his lead, Hall's student, Arnold Gesell, in 1911 founded the Yale Clinic for Child Development to foster more systematic study of children. Like Hall, Gesell hoped to improve childrearing practices, and his group specialized in advice for parents.

Although other workers as diverse as the behaviorist Watson and the psychoanalytic followers of Freud freely offered prescriptions for childrearing, most of the early centers for child research concentrated on school curricula rather than on development per se. It was largely through the efforts of an economist, Lawrence K. Frank, that developmental research achieved an organizational identity of its own, independent of experimental education. Early in the 1920s, Frank proposed a national network of university-based institutes to do research that could guide childrearing and educational practice. His plan won the support of the Laura Spelman Rockefeller Foundation, which then granted funds for the establishment of child study institutes at Columbia in 1924, Minnesota in 1925, and Berkeley in 1927, and for the continuation of existing child study centers, including Gesell's Clinic and the Iowa Child Welfare Research Station, founded in 1917.

Despite the substantial Rockefeller grants, the institutes met resistance within the universities. The resistance grew largely from the feeling that studying children was a waste of time and that any money

191

should support existing departments. Even after the establishment of semiautonomous institutes open to participation by members of various departments, they were often shunned by departments of education and psychology, which regarded themselves as guardians of methodological purity. In reality, much of the research done in the institutes was not very interdisciplinary, was restricted to the counting of specific behaviors, and had no immediate application in childrearing or educational practice. Nevertheless, there was a sense of "mission" to it and a desire to make a better world for children. The sense of mission shared by the new groups of researchers was given organizational form in the Society for Research in Child Development, founded in 1933. Through it publications, *Child Development*, the *Monographs of the Society for Research in Child Development*, and *Child Development Abstracts*, the Society became the primary link among developmental researchers.

Despite the sense of mission shared by those who studied children, it was not until the late 1950s that the need for immediate practical knowledge of development became widely felt. The first significant stimulus was the success of the Russian Sputnik in 1957, which triggered national efforts to develop mathematical and scientific thinking. Thereafter, the National Institute of Child Health and Human Development was founded in 1963 to embody a permanent Federal commitment to research on children. The War on Poverty in the mid-1960s spawned Project Head Start, Project Follow Through, and a host of other health and educational programs for disadvantaged children. These were followed by greatly expanded daycare programs for children of all social strata and establishment of the Federal Office of Child Development to serve as an advocate for children. To great acclaim, Sesame Street harnessed the power of television for the benefit of children, while the potentially negative effects of television violence became a *cause célèbre* of a different sort.

In another area, a presidential commission challenged the nation to meet what it called the "crisis in child mental health" by overcoming the woeful inadequacy of services and research on behalf of disturbed children (Joint Commission on Mental Health of Children, 1969). Following belatedly upon the inception of a nationwide network of community mental health centers in 1963, Congress in 1975 mandated that these centers should offer services to children. Many states in the late 1960s and 1970s also passed laws designed to insure special educational services to children having a broad range of social, emotional environmental, or physical handicaps, and to strengthen protection of children from neglect and abuse. However, nearly all these efforts have been hampered by a lack of basic practical knowledge about how best to enhance children's development and well-being.

The Nature of Mission-oriented Research

The needs and opportunities created by new government programs in the 1960s, plus a new social activism among students and researchers alike, inspired interest in applying developmental research to the solution of social problems. At the same time, the increasing specialization of basic research on development made it difficult to translate the newest concepts and findings directly into coherent policies and programs. As a result, new approaches to research were needed to fulfill the "engineering" function of applying basic knowledge, theory, and methods to the solution of social problems. These approaches required not only a modification of existing research strategies and methods, but also new organizational structures for carrying out research that could not be mounted within the traditional university framework. As will become evident from the accounts that follow these organizational structures have played a central role in some of the most significant mission-oriented research.

Before considering case histories of mission-oriented research, it is important to note some differences between it and other kinds of developmental research. Although mission-oriented research draws on and may contribute to theory, and other research may have practical applications, the distinctions drawn here are between research designed primarily to provide data for social policy decisions and research designed primarily to extend or test theory. Many of the same distinctions can be drawn between "applied" and "basic" research, but what is here called mission-oriented research does not overlap completely with applied research. Applied research includes all research designed to answer practical questions, whereas mission-oriented research is that which is designed to affect social policy decisions. Because such decisions are affected by many factors beside research findings, the effects of mission-oriented research often depend upon how compelling a case the findings make to people who are themselves not researchers.

On Asking the Right Question

Can preschool programs break the poverty cycle by enhancing the development of disadvantaged children? Does watching violent television programs harm children? What is the best way to combat mental illness in children? Are open classrooms better than traditional classrooms? How can racial prejudice be reduced? How much does it cost to provide quality daycare for children of working mothers? These are some of the questions that have sparked major mission-oriented research efforts. The questions have been asked not merely out of curiosity, but because the formulation of legislation, government regulations, and social programs depended upon the answers.

In their initial form, most of the above questions are so general as to elicit only the most speculative of answers. One of the first steps in mission-oriented research is to translate socially significant questions into researchable hypotheses. For example, in order to determine whether preschool programs enhance development, operational definitions must be formulated for the aspects of development to be enhanced. Choices have to be made about whether the effects of preschool are to be judged over short periods or long periods, in terms of school achievement, social behavior, performance on tests of ability, creativity, specific skills, freedom from behavior problems, happiness, self-satisfaction, etc. These choices are always limited by the possibilities for measuring the variables in question.

Not only must the relevant aspects of development be operationally defined, but what is meant by a preschool program must be specified. Until the late 1960s, the researcher wishing to assess the effects of preschool education on disadvantaged children typically had to design and implement his own program before he had anything to assess. Considerable "engineering" was required to develop and try out curriculum materials and procedures based on various theoretical models of development. The question of whether preschool programs could be effective opened a Pandora's box of prior questions about how to translate developmental theories into practical procedures, at what age, for how long, and with what degree of intensity to apply these procedures, and how to strengthen them through parent participation and coordination with elementary school programs.

The Simplicity of Theories vs. the Complexity of the World

Translating policy-relevant questions into researchable hypotheses requires many of the same steps as theoretically oriented research. Both types of research require operational definition of variables and creation of conditions under which hypothesized relationships can be tested. However, theoretically oriented research aims for precise statements about the operation of isolated variables under conditions chosen by the researcher, whereas mission-oriented research must yield answers about behavior under conditions of naturally occurring complexity within deadlines for making policy decisions. Even in advanced physical sciences, which possess a large body of well-supported theory and precisely operationalized variables, the jump from theoretical models to practical tasks such as putting men on the moon requires a great deal of ad hoc engineering. Lacking well-supported theory, precisely operationalized variables, and a history of engineering applications, mission-oriented developmental research often confronts real-world complexities far beyond the capacities of existing models to represent.

Coupled with the limitations on subject selection, measurement possibilities, and time, the gap between existing theory and the complexities of situations to which answers must apply has given mission-oriented research a reputation for being "dirtier" than theoretically oriented research. Yet, because the need for data on which to base social policy decisions will continue to outstrip the advance of basic developmental theory, and because such theory may never be detailed and powerful enough for direct application to many practical problems, mission-oriented research is likely to remain the primary medium through which developmental research and theory influence social policy. Furthermore, mission-oriented research has and will continue to enrich the methodological repertoire of developmental researchers as well as exposing the gaps and ambiguities in existing theory.

Planned Variation in Project Follow Through

When research such as Klaus and Gray's Early Training Project for Disadvantaged Children (described in chapter 1) revealed that the benefits of preschool programs tended to disappear during elementary school, Project Follow Through was launched to extend Head Start services into the first four years of elementary school. Begun as a pilot project in the fall of 1967, it was mandated by Congress as "a program to be known as 'Follow Through' focused primarily upon children in kindergarten or elementary school who were previously enrolled in Head Start or similar programs and designed to provide comprehensive services and parent participation activities . . . which will aid in the continued development of children to their full potential" (Economic Opportunity Act, P. L. 90–92, Section 222a, 1967). Like Head Start, Follow Through was to provide not only for the education, but also for the emotional, physical, medical, dental, and nutritional needs of disadvantaged children. Parents were to participate actively in major decisions and in the operation of local programs.

Because Follow Through was initially an experimental program, research was authorized on the effectiveness of various approaches to working with disadvantaged children and their families. Known as "planned variation," the research strategy was to compare the performance of children receiving various types of curriculum models (planned variations) with that of children in the same communities who did not receive the special programs. As in much mission-oriented research, circumstances precluded a true experimental design whereby the children receiving each condition are equated through random assignment or matching procedures. A primary obstacle to an experimental strategy was that local parents and school systems were to choose their own Follow Through programs. This policy was based on the view that programs should be controlled by the people they are to serve. Despite the problems thus created for research design, it is unlikely that any program could receive a fair test if local parents, teachers, and administrators opposed it. Although a few small-scale intervention studies such as the Early Training Project have approximated an experimental design, it is rarely possible to evaluate highly publicized, politically significant programs with true experimental designs. In the planned variation research, conclusions about the relative effectiveness of programs depend largely upon a search for differences across conditions that are only roughly comparable, with tests of rival explanations for findings being made primarily through statistical manipulations of the data. The frustrations inherent in this type of research will be evident from the following account. The researcher must constantly ask himself how best to compromise between principles of good design and the realities of social programs, and whether meaningful research can be done under such conditions at all.

Types of Follow Through Program

Each of the groups responsible for local Follow Through projects initially chose from programs devised by researchers who served as sponsors and provided curriculum materials and supervision. The study of planned variation included ten types of programs, each of which had been in operation for at least two years. All of the programs shared some basic similarities. These included a focus on enhancing children's learning abilities; an emphasis on individual and small group interaction, with frequent interchanges between children and teachers; attempts to make learning interesting and relevant to the children's cultural backgrounds; and the encouragement of self-esteem, autonomy, and motivation to succeed. However, the programs differed in priorities assigned to the various objectives and the methods by which they were pursued. For purposes of comparison, the ten programs can be categorized into the three groups described below (Bissell, 1973).

Structured academic approaches. These programs stressed the teaching of academic skills through programmed instructional techniques. They were designed to promote specific behavioral objectives by reinforcing an ordered sequence of responses. One of the best known of these programs, the Engelmann–Becker Model for Direct Instruction, grew out of Bereiter and Engelmann's (1966) curriculum for disadvantaged preschool children. Sponsored by Siegfried Engelmann and Wesley Becker of the University of Oregon, it was designed to promote skills and concepts needed for reading, arithmetic, and language achievement through repetitive practice and the use of rewards and praise to reinforce specific behaviors. It represented perhaps the best developed and most extreme application of the S–R paradigm to compensatory education.

Discovery approaches. Rather than transmitting specific knowledge and skills, these programs were aimed at promoting autonomous learning through exploration and discovery in an environment responsive to the child's own initiative. Unlike the structured academic approaches, the discovery approaches stressed intrinsic motivation and the gratification children obtain through mastery. A positive self-concept, curiosity, independence, and the ability to cooperate with others were considered as important as cognitive growth to the child's total development.

An example of the discovery approach is the Responsive Educational Program developed by Glen Nimnicht of the Far West Laboratory for Educational Research and Development in San Francisco. Each child was encouraged to learn at his own pace and to explore the classroom environment, arranged to facilitate interconnected discoveries about the physical and social worlds. Self-correcting games and equipment were employed to enhance problem-solving skills, sensory discrimination, language ability, and enjoyment of learning.

Cognitive discovery approaches. Although more heterogeneous than the preceding two groups, these programs shared an emphasis on basic cognitive processes such as reasoning, classifying, and counting. Like the structured academic approaches, the cognitive discovery approaches directly taught academic skills and stressed engagement of children in verbal activities, but the focus was on the development of thought rather than on the production of specific responses, and autonomous discovery was encouraged. One of the most widely adopted of these approaches was the Cognitively Oriented Curriculum Model sponsored by David Weikart of the High/Scope Educational Research Foundation of Ypsilanti, Michigan. Based on Piagetian theory, this approach was designed to foster children's understanding of classification, quantity, causality, time, and space through experimentation, exploration, and constant verbalization, guided by detailed lesson plans. A home teaching program was also provided to involve parents in the education of their children.

Evaluative Research on Follow Through

As mentioned earlier, new organizational structures evolved during the 1960s to carry out mission-oriented research. Although special centers and projects were established in many universities, the need for rapid development and evaluation of national intervention programs could not be met by university researchers whose positions required teaching and the publication of basic research. The organizational innovations took a variety of forms. One was the diversification of existing organizations that specialized in fields related to those in which mission-oriented research was needed. The Educational Testing Service, of Princeton, New Jersey, for example, was already well established in the field of educational measurement, being best known for its College Board testing program. Although it had little previous experience in mission-oriented research on the development of young children, its experience in gathering nationwide test data made it a candidate for carrying out research in this area. It expanded its staff and activities in early childhood development and was awarded some of the first major contracts for evaluation of Head Start.

In addition to diversification by existing private firms, new firms were formed to develop the programs and carry out the research stemming from the Federal initiatives of the mid-1960s. The High/Scope Foundation, sponsor of one of the cognitive discovery approaches to Follow Through, has been among the most active of the new firms in mission-oriented research.

A third innovation was the establishment of educational research laboratories in various parts of the country by the U.S. Office of Education. The Responsive Educational Program for Follow Through, described earlier as an example of the discovery approaches, was a product of one of these laboratories, the Far West Laboratory for Educational Research and Development.

The effects of the planned variations in Follow Through were evaluated under Government contracts by two private social science research firms, neither of which was involved in implementing any of the programs. The Stanford Research Institute, of Menlo Park, California, was responsible for testing children in the Follow Through and nonFollow Through groups, while Abt Associates, of Cambridge, Massachusetts, was responsible for analyzing the data and reporting the findings. The most comprehensive findings were those on the cohort of children who entered kindergarten in the fall of 1971, and completed first grade in the spring of 1973 (Cline, 1975). Although evaluation of these children continued until they completed third grade, local program changes and attrition due to administrative decisions to remove children from Follow Through and the high transiency of disadvantaged families made identification of program effects even more difficult in the second and third grades than in the first grade.

The children. In order to identify the possible effects of initial differences in academic achievement, only children who had received the Wide Range Achievement Test when they entered kindergarten were included in the sample. The sample was further restricted to children who had entered first grade in 1972, had remained in their original Follow Through program, and had received the primary dependent measures—the word analysis, reading, and mathematics subtests of the Metropolitan Achievement Test—in Spring, 1973. Furthermore, sites were included for analysis only if they had at least 16 Follow Through and 16 nonFollow Through first graders who met the other requirements. These restrictions, plus a decision to retest only a portion of the available children, reduced the initial pool of 17,721 children who had entered Follow Through or comparison nonFollow Through kindergartens in 1971 to a total of 2168 Follow Through and 1313 nonFollow Through children.

The attrition made it essential to determine whether the remaining children were representative of those who had begun each program or whether high or low achievers might have been differentially lost. Comparisons of the initial test scores, racial composition, and SES of the total initial samples with those of the remaining children within each site showed that in many cases the final samples were not representative of the initial groups. In addition to the differences among the sites in which the various Follow Through programs were implemented, selective attrition thus raised another obstacle to direct comparisons among the programs. As a result, the analyses were focused primarily upon how the first grade achievement scores of children receiving each type of program differed from the achievement of children in nonFollow Through classes within the same sites. Even these comparisons were made difficult, however, by differences in starting levels and differential attrition of Follow Through and nonFollow Through children within the same sites and by the fact that some nonFollow Through children received special services under other Government programs.

The analyses. Because it was important to partial out the effects of preexisting group differences in achievement test scores, the primary method of statistical analysis was the analysis of covariance (described in chapter 6). Many potentially important indices of group differences were considered for use as covariates. Among them were geographical region of the country, city size, population density, amount of special educational services, school size, degree of racial integration, student/teacher ratio, initial scores on the Wide Range Achievement Test, ethnicity, and preschool experience. Others were parental income, education, and occupational level. However, some of these variables could not logically be employed as covariates because they were not distributed properly across programs. Effects of geographical region, for example, could not be covaried out of achievement scores across programs because some programs were implemented in only one or two geographical regions. Other potential covariates were found to be uncorrelated with first grade achievement scores, meaning that they were unlikely to represent any significant effect extractable by covariance analysis. Still other potential covariates had to be excluded because data on them were missing in too many cases or because the data violated statistical requirements, such as uniformity of regression relations with the dependent variable, first-grade achievement score. Only the score on the initial kindergarten achievement test was ultimately retained as a covariate in the analysis of first grade achievement. Because such potentially important group differences as geographic area of the country, ethnicity, and socioeconomic status could not be equated across programs by statistical or other means, valid comparisons of program effects could only be made among groups that did not initially differ on these variables.

Findings. For three very different programs where valid comparisons between Follow Through and nonFollow Through children were possible, the consistent superiority of Follow Through children on the mathematics subtest of the Metropolitan Achievement Test indicated definite beneficial effects. Two of the programs were from the group classified roughly as structured academic approaches. One of these, the University of Kansas Behavior Analysis Approach, teaches basic academic skills by means of programmed instructional materials and token reinforcers exchangeable for desired activities. The second, the Language Development Approach sponsored by the Southwest Educational Development Laboratory, was originally designed for Spanish-speaking children. It stresses language development through structured drill techniques. Academic subjects are taught in the child's native language, while English is simultaneously taught as a second language. The third program was from the group classified as discovery approaches. Sponsored by the Educational Development Center, it differs radically from the structured academic approaches in being modeled on the open classroom concept of the British infant schools. Emphasizing growth in self-expression and self-direction, as well as academic and problem-solving skills, it encourages children to initiate activities, pursue their own interests, and assume responsibility for their own learning.

The effects of these programs on the word analysis and reading scores of the Metropolitan Achievemant Test were far more variable. The University of Kansas program, for example, appeared to produce strong positive effects on the word analysis subtest in three urban sites where the children were from very-low-income black families, but negative effects on word analysis and reading scores in a rural site where the children were from somewhat higher income white families. The effects of the Southwest Educational Development Laboratory Program were greatest with Spanish-speaking children at a Puerto Rican site in a large eastern city and a Mexican-American site on the West Coast, while a French language version employed at a Cajun French site in the South had a small positive effect on mathematics achievement, but a negative effect on reading achievement. The Educational Development Center approach, which deemphasizes reading and word analysis skills, showed strong positive effects on these scores in a predominantly black urban site, negative effects in a predominantly black small town site, and slight positive effects in a predominantly white site. In addition, comparisons of kindergarten and first grade scores showed that this approach had most of its effect in first grade and that it appeared to be most successful with children who had preschool experience. This suggested that a period of "intellectual socialization" may be necessary before the approach can produce benefits measurable on traditional achievement tests.

Three other programs appeared to produce significant effects on some measures in some sites, but the effects were so inconsistent from one site to another that no generalizations could be made about their effects across sites. No significant benefits were found for the remaining four programs. However, for all four of these programs, the comparisons with nonFollow Through children were clouded so much by uncontrollable preexisting differences between the children that definitive conclusions cannot be drawn. It was speculated that many of these differences were due not to chance but to the different impressions the programs made on parents and school personnel who, in turn, selected different programs for children differing in ethnic, socioeconomic, and achievement characteristics.

Implications for Social Policy

One of the most fundamental questions raised by the planned variation research is whether it is indeed worth doing. On the one hand, Follow Through, like Head Start, represented a drastic innovation in government policy. It was an attempt to bring about long-term improvement in the lives of the disadvantaged by means of educational enrichment extending over several years of early childhood. Rather than mandating from Washington the programs to be followed throughout the country, the government encouraged diversity, local control, and a commitment to empirically determining how various programs work in a largely uncharted domain.

On the other hand, the commitment to diversity and local control, the instability of many of the populations served, the often contradictory agendas of parents, school personnel, program sponsors, and others involved in implementation, and the lack of knowledge about how to enrich and evaluate development all militated against clean and precise research. The chief flaw in research design was, of course, the lack of comparability among groups receiving the various programs. Analysis of covariance and careful documentation of preexisting group dif- ferences were used to extract conclusions about the effects of at least some of the programs as they operated in a few sites, but little could be concluded about the other programs. As Campbell and Boruch (1976) have shown, inadequate initial matching of groups receiving and not receiving compensatory education frequently leads to underestimation of the effects of the special programs, because the least able children tend to be placed in such programs.

One alternative to the planned variation approach is to restrict research to relatively small studies employing random assignment or initial matching of groups receiving the various programs. Some of the programs for which no benefits could be found in the planned variation study had, in fact, previously yielded positive results in small experi- mental studies (e.g., Weikart, 1972). However, the generalizability of findings from such studies depends on how well the programs can be implemented outside controlled research settings and by the numerous variations in population and site that appeared to influence the effects of programs in the planned variation study.

A dilemma is thus posed by the need for knowledge about how large-scale social programs actually affect their target populations and the difficulty of applying well-controlled research to such programs. While solutions to the dilemma inevitably depend upon the particular programs, political forces, and resources involved, perhaps one of the most important missions of mission-oriented researchers should be to convince decision makers of the need for controlled assignment of individuals to treatment groups. Since decision makers ranging from parents to school personnel to government officials have their own biases toward each program, it is important for them to be aware of how little is known about the effects of the programs and to share a com- mitment to learning what these effects really are. As most parents want their children to get any possible benefits of new programs rather than being assigned to no-treatment control groups, the most viable approach may be to offer two or more programs within each of several localities and to accept for the programs any children whose parents apply, but

with the condition that assignment to a particular program be determined by a random or matching procedure. While differential attrition
from the programs cannot be prevented, significantly higher attrition
from one program than another may in itself be an important indication
of differential effects, provided that the groups in the programs were
initially similar.

Another alternative is to employ "waiting list" control groups. Since
organizational and financial limitations often prevent immediate deliv-
ery of a new program to all those eligible, selection from the pool of
eligible candidates could be done openly by means of a lottery so that
those who receive the program initially are as similar as possible to those
who must wait until the program expands. An extensive discussion of
further alternatives and of the pros and cons of research like that on
Follow Through by many of the sponsors, researchers, and government
officials involved in the Planned Variation Study can be found in Rivlin
and Timpane (1975). In addition, Cooley and Lohnes (1976) have shown
how other statistical approaches would yield different conclusions in
the Follow Through research.

Differential Effectiveness of Three Interventions with Disturbed Children

Although compensatory education has received far greater publicity,
the need for better approaches to helping disturbed children is also
beginning to receive attention. Until recently, most views of psychopathology in children were derived from theories of adult psychopathology. The meager research on child treatment was confined
primarily to extrapolation of adult treatment paradigms to children. As a
result, there has been little systematic comparison of the effects of
various treatment modalities on children's problems.

For many years, most of the money for children's mental health
services has been spent on psychotherapy, carried out primarily by child
guidance clinics and private practitioners. However, follow-up studies
have demonstrated no greater improvement in children receiving
psychotherapy than in untreated children (e.g., Levitt, 1971; Shepherd,
Oppenheim, and Mitchell, 1971; cf. Achenbach, 1974, chapter 17, for a
review). Whether or not psychotherapy as typically rendered is effective, many disturbed children cannot get meaningful help of any sort
(Joint Commission on Mental Health of Children, 1969). Although Congress in 1975 mandated that community mental health centers must
begin to offer children's services, the increasing scarcity of funds for
social programs, coupled with increasing demands for cost/benefit

analysis by public agencies, makes it more important than ever that the effects of various treatment approaches be determined. Simply extending traditional adult-based methods to children without evaluating their effects on children's development can no longer be justified.

Unlike the research on Head Start and Follow Through, research on interventions with disturbed children has been carried out largely through local projects in conjunction with existing clinical agencies. Because most such agencies are committed to a particular treatment paradigm, such as the psychoanalytic or behavioral, systematic comparisons of various forms of treatment have rarely been made within a single clinical population.

In one of the very few such studies, Love and Kaswan (1974) compared the effects of psychodynamically oriented child psychotherapy, parent counseling, and a treatment approach they called "information feedback." Subjects for the study were secured through an elementary school district serving a wide socioeconomic range in Los Angeles. When school personnel identified an 8- to 12-year-old child as having social or behavioral problems too severe to be handled through the school's usual services, the principal or counselor discussed the child's problems with the parents and told them that they could receive help at the Psychology Department Clinic of the University of California at Los Angeles. If the parents were interested, they gave the school permission to send the clinic a description of the child's behavior problems. All families referred in this way were offered treatment by the clinic. Fees were based on income and no one was excluded for financial reasons.

In order to equate the cases receiving each of the three types of treatment, treatments were assigned in a rotating order as families made their initial appointments with the clinic. However, deviations from the rotating order were occasionally made to insure that similar proportions of high, middle, and low SES families would receive each treatment within each of the two years of the study. Although not random, assignment of subjects to treatments was thus designed to create groups that were as similar as possible prior to receiving treatment. The resulting groups were similar in distribution of SES and IQs of the children, but the parent counseling group had a larger proportion of single-parent and step-parent families than the other groups, and the distribution of problems for which children were referred differed somewhat among the groups. While these differences were likely to have arisen by chance rather than through any systematic selective factors, they could have produced differences in outcomes not attributable exclusively to the treatments. Differential dropout rates, which ranged from 7 percent in the information feedback group to 21 percent in the child therapy group, could also have affected the composition of the groups in such a way as to produce posttreatment differences not attributable to the treatments per se. Thus, despite the high degree of control over assignment to treatments, so many child and family characteristics were potentially relevant to treatment outcome that complete identity among the groups could not be attained. As will be discussed later, attempts were made to analyze the effects of such characteristics on the overall findings. An unavoidable constraint on the external validity of findings was that, of the 152 families referred, only 91 (60 percent) accepted and kept an initial interview appointment. As a result, findings are generalizable only to similar families who actually accept treatment.

Treatment Procedures

Families did not know about the alternative treatment approaches being compared and they all received the same information and inputs from the clinic until they began treatment. Each form of treatment was rendered by different clinicians who believed in its effectiveness. This meant that differences among the clinicians were confounded with differences among the treatments per se, although having several different clinicians render each treatment was intended to reduce the effects of the clinicians' personal characteristics on the group outcomes. The alternative of having the same clinicians provide all three treatments might have introduced biases resulting from the clinicians' different sympathies, antipathies, and expertise with respect to each treatment approach.

Child therapy.   As is typical in child psychotherapy, the therapist saw the parents and child separately for initial interviews and then saw the child alone for succeeding interviews, with the option of occasional parent or family sessions when necessary. To make the length of treatment comparable to the twelve weeks originally planned for the information feedback condition, treatment was limited to twenty sessions spread over twelve weeks. When information feedback was found to require no more than eight weeks, the limits on child therapy were shortened to twelve sessions during the second year of the study. While these limits might have artificially curtailed the therapy, they exceeded the national average for psychotherapy, and the participating therapists were people who believed short term therapy to be effective.

Parent counseling.   Like the counseling offered in many family service clinics, this approach was designed to advise parents on how to handle their child's problems. After the child was interviewed and tested to determine the nature of his problems, the counselor met with the parents, usually for four or five sessions, but for up to 13 in difficult cases.

Information feedback. Whereas child therapy and parent counseling were traditional approaches to helping disturbed children, the information feedback condition represented a new approach designed to provide the child, his parents, and his teacher with feedback about their interpersonal perceptions, communications, and interactions. The goal was to promote objective scrutiny of behavior by showing how communications and interactions look and sound so that interpersonal differences in perception could be identified and a common frame of reference established. It was assumed that identifying stimuli for behavior would promote understanding and control of the behavior, and that relying on the family's own problem-solving abilities would promote feelings of competence and solidarity within the family.

Two consultants were provided for each family, one responsible for contacts with the adults, the second for contacts with the child. After a videotaped explanation of the treatment approach as being designed to help family members take a fresh look at how they talk and behave with each other, parents were given a behavior inventory to fill out describing their own behavior and that of their child. The parents and their child were also asked to rate one another and themselves on ten adjectives such as "patient," "active," "friendly," and "angry." At subsequent clinic sessions, the family members made adjective ratings of one another and themselves from videotapes of their interactions, and the consultants presented the previously gathered ratings. Each family member's adjective ratings were graphically superimposed on ratings by the other family members to reveal points of agreement and disagreement. Similar feedback sessions were provided for school personnel. Teachers were shown comparisons between their ratings of the target child, their ratings of the "average" child at that grade level, other teachers' ratings of children at that grade, their ratings of how the target child would rate them, and the child's actual ratings of them. Teacher and parent ratings of each child's behavior were also compared to point up differences between home and school. A final meeting between the parents, teacher, principal, counselor, and clinic consultant provided an opportunity for the parents and school staff to make joint plans for handling the child's problems.

Outcomes of Treatments

Objectively measuring improvement is one of the most difficult aspects of research on psychopathology. Unlike organic disorders, psychopathology cannot be detected or measured with physical laboratory tests. The subjectivity of judgments of outcomes made it essential that the judgments not be contaminated by knowledge of the treatment conditions. Because the Love–Kaswan project was oriented toward ameliorating problems of school behavior, the primary measures selected were school grade-point averages obtained after the children had moved on to new classes where the teachers had not been involved in treatment, plus ratings of school behavior made by observers who were unaware of the treatment conditions.

Grade-point averages.   A 3 × 4 repeated measures analysis of variance was performed on grade-point averages obtained by each of the three treatment groups, three semesters prior to treatment, one semester prior to treatment, one semester after treatment began, and three semesters after treatment terminated. This showed a significant interaction between treatment group and time, caused by the fact that the decline in grades occurring from three semesters to one semester prior to treatment for all three groups was reversed in the parent counseling and information feedback groups after treatment, but continued in the psychotherapy group. Overall, it thus appeared that parent counseling and information feedback had a positive effect on school performance, whereas psychotherapy did not. However, when grade changes from the semester before treatment to three semesters after treatment were compared for lower, middle, and upper SES subjects receiving each treatment, it became clear that parent counseling and information feedback had very different effects on children differing in SES. As Figure 8-1 reveals, in the group receiving information feedback, upper-class children improved considerably in grade average, whereas middle-class children did not improve and lower-class children continued to decline in grades. By contrast, in the group receiving parent counseling, *lower-class* children improved the most, middle-class children improved slightly, and upper-class children continued to decline. Thus, these two treatment approaches appeared to have *opposite* effects on upper and lower class children. As can be seen from Figure 8-1, all three socioeconomic groups receiving psychotherapy continued to decline in grades, with the greatest decline being in the upper socioeconomic group.

In seeking an explanation for the opposite patterns of effects on upper and lower class children, Love and Kaswan examined various aspects of parent involvement in relation to changes in grades. In the two-parent families, across all social strata there was a significant positive correlation of .55 between the number of father appointments and improvement in grades in the information feedback group, whereas there was a (nonsignificant) *negative* correlation of $-.26$ between father appointments and improvement in the parent counseling group. This indicated greater positive benefits of father involvement in the information feedback group than in the parent counseling group. It was also noted that there was a greater proportion of mother-only families in the

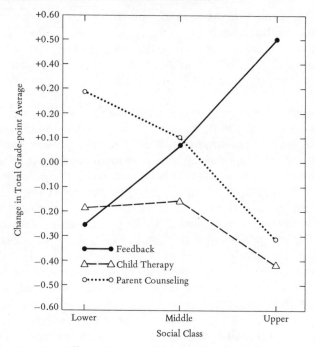

Figure 8-1. Differential outcomes of treatment in relation to socio-economic level of the family. (Love and Kaswan, 1974, p. 173.)

low socioeconomic group, that fathers seemed more responsive than mothers to feedback materials, and that mothers, especially lower SES mothers, seemed more responsive to directive counseling. These findings suggested that in upper-class families the father's reaction to treatment was pivotal, whereas in lower-class families the mother's reaction was pivotal. Furthermore, the higher verbal abilities of the upper-class parents, as shown on individually administered vocabulary tests, may have enabled them to utilize the information feedback better, while lower SES parents were influenced more by directive advice.

School observers' ratings.   After initial referral but prior to the first clinic contact, two observers rated the behavior of each referred child toward the teacher and toward peers in the classroom and on the playground. Ratings were made again nine to twelve months after termination of treatment. Without knowing which children were referred, the observers also rated nonreferred children who were matched to the referred children for age, sex, and SES. Ratings were made on the same ten adjectives employed by family members in rating each other in the information feedback condition.

Factor analysis of ratings made in various contexts showed two consistent factors. One, designated as *negative social impact*, included high positive loadings on "angry," "phony," and "rude," and a negative loading on "patient." The other, designated as *positive social impact*, included positive loadings on "controlling," "active," and "friendly," and a negative loading on "bored." Since there were consistent differences between the factor scores of referred and nonreferred children only on the first factor, these scores were used to evaluate behavioral changes following treatment. Results were statistically significant only for ratings of playground behavior, perhaps, as suggested by the authors, because restraints on the children's classroom behavior decreased the variability to which classroom ratings could be sensitive. A 2 × 3 repeated measures analysis of variance showed a significant decline in scores for negative social impact from pretreatment to posttreatment ratings. There were no significant differences among groups, although, as Figure 8-2 shows, the largest decrease was for the feedback group. Unlike the changes in grades, the changes in behavior showed no significant relationship to SES.

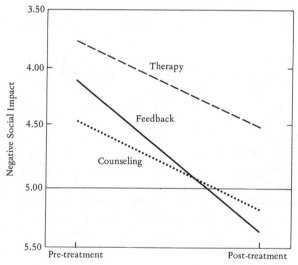

Figure 8-2. Ratings of negative social behavior toward peers on the playground. (Adapted from Love and Kaswan, 1974, p. 180.)

Implications for Social Policy

Public funds support most mental health services to children through direct subsidies to treatment centers, services rendered by schools, welfare payments for care, and grants for training and research. Related social problems such as juvenile delinquency, drug addiction, unmarried adolescent pregnancy, and child neglect and abuse are also of great public concern. Research like that of Love and Kaswan is necessary to determine how troubled children can most effectively be helped to adapt and develop constructively.

Although school performance and behavior toward peers are by no means the only criteria by which to judge adaptation and development, they represent two areas in which failure can create significant handicaps for future development. A child who fails to acquire the basic skills of reading, writing, and arithmetic and/or whose behavior has a negative impact on others is likely to develop a sense of incompetence that will interfere with long-term adaptation.

According to Love and Kaswan's findings, psychotherapy—the most common treatment for disturbed children—is not effective in reversing poor school performance, although it may be as effective as the comparison treatments in ameliorating negative behavior towards peers. Without a control group of disturbed children who received either no treatment or a placebo (or Hawthorne) condition, we do not know, however, whether behavior toward peers would have improved anyway without formal treatment.

On the other hand, the implications of the different outcomes in school performance seem clear. Not only was psychotherapy ineffective, but the effects of the other treatments depended upon the SES of the family. While it was not conclusively determined *why* the treatments had such different effects on families of different SES, it is clear that effective utilization of the treatments requires matching them to the appropriate types of families. Other factors not explored in the Love and Kaswan study are also likely to affect the outcome of various treatment approaches. Such factors include the age of the child, his specific problems, his general ways of coping with problems, and the types of problems existing within his family and school situations. If public mental health funds are to benefit children, they must support programs that are designed to match treatments effectively to each child's needs and to develop new approaches for children who are not well served by any of the existing methods.

The Surgeon General's Report on the Impact of Television Violence

Almost as soon as television became a household fixture in the early 1950s, concerns were raised about the potential effects of televised violence on children. In 1952, the Federal Communications Commission Subcommittee of the House of Representatives held hearings to determine the amount of crime, violence, and corruption in radio and television programming. These hearings were followed in 1954 by an investigation of the effects of television on juvenile delinquency, carried out by the Juvenile Delinquency Subcommittee of the Senate Judiciary Committee. The few empirical studies existing at that time showed that children with television sets averaged at least three hours per day of viewing, a figure that has not declined as the novelty of television has worn off. Surveys indicated that one-fifth to one-quarter of the viewing time between 4 and 10 P.M. in 1954 was taken up with themes of lawlessness (Committee on the Judiciary, 1956). These figures *excluded* boxing, wrestling, and other programs that might be considered violent but not lawless, such as documentary combat films.

Having established that children watched a great deal of television and that there was considerable lawlessness on television during children's viewing hours, the Subcommittee took testimony from social scientists, representatives of the broadcast industry, and other parties interested in the possible impact of television on children. While some evidence was presented that children with many frustrations in their lives and children from lower socioeconomic homes watched the most television, the testimony on causal relationships was confined mainly to personal opinion and anecdotal illustrations of how television violence either was or was not a cause of antisocial behavior. The Subcommittee concluded that television violence presented a risk to children and recommended that the Federal Communications Commission (FCC) and the television industry should set up definite standards for children's programming. The Subcommittee also noted that:

> The conclusions reached . . . are based upon scattered evidence and best opinion. There is no irrefutable body of research data, garnered through carefully designed and exhaustive research projects from which definitive cause and effect relationships can be identified.
>
> Until such research is undertaken, action in this field must, of necessity, be predicated upon opinion. Hopefully, during this interval weight shall be given to opinion derived from experience and evaluated by persons possessing training which might give them more than a "when I was a boy" basis for understanding human behavior.
>
> The subcommittee would like to call attention to the need for broad, carefully framed research efforts not directed to determining the effects of television only but rather to determining the extent and how the several media of mass communications may combine to make contribution, if any, to the development of antisocial behavior in children and youth. (Committee on the Judiciary, 1956, p. 53.)

Despite the Subcommittee's recommendations for FCC and industry policing, subsequent surveys of television programming in 1961 and 1964 revealed an *increase* in televised violence over the levels observed in the 1950s. The issue was rekindled in 1969 when surveys by the National Commission on the Causes and Prevention of Violence showed that 81 percent of prime time programs on the three major networks contained violence. The Commission recommended a reduction in televised violence, especially in children's cartoons. It also recommended research on the long-term effects of viewing television violence. In response, Senator John O. Pastore, Chairman of the Senate Commerce Committee, which oversees federal communications policy, wrote the Secretary of Health, Education, and Welfare that he was "exceedingly troubled by the lack of any definitive information which would help resolve the question of whether there is a causal connection between televised crime and violence and antisocial behavior, especially by children." Because of the contribution made by the Surgeon General's report on smoking, Senator Pastore requested that the Surgeon General appoint a distinguished committee to "establish scientifically, insofar as possible, what harmful effects, if any, [television] programs have on children" (Cater and Strickland, 1975, p. 1).

The Surgeon General's Scientific Advisory Committee

Following a precedent which he felt had strengthened the impact of the Smoking Committee's report, Surgeon General William Stewart included five industry representatives in his twelve-member Advisory Committee on Television and Social Behavior. While this in itself was enough to arouse suspicion among opponents of television violence, it was later revealed that a list of the prospective nonindustry appointees had been submitted to network executives for their approval. They were allowed to veto appointment of seven prominent researchers, including psychologists Albert Bandura and Leonard Berkowitz who had conducted much of the existing research on the effects of filmed aggression. Although this appeared to continue the tradition of assigning industry foxes to determine what's best for the consumer chickens, it must also be noted that President Nixon's enthusiastic endorsement of Senator Pastore's request aroused industry fears that it would be used in his campaign against the mass media. Political considerations thus loomed large in the Committee's work. To provide perspective on the sociopolitical context of mission-oriented research, this account will deal with the way in which the Committee's mandate was carried out, as well as with the research it sponsored. Cater and Strickland's (1975) book, *TV violence and the child: The evolution and fate of the Surgeon General's Report*, is the primary source of documentation on the Committee's work.

The twelve members of the final Committee, including the five industry nominees, consisted of three psychologists, two each psychiatrists, sociologists, and communication specialists, and one each anthropologist, specialist in early childhood education, and political scientist. Because the Committee decided to confine its role to assessing results rather than directing research, it was up to the Committee's staff to define the research needs and solicit proposals for meeting those needs. The gap between traditional ways of doing behavioral research and the requirements of targeted mission-oriented research is nowhere more evident than in the difficulties encountered in recruiting senior researchers to coordinate the staff's activities and in locating researchers to carry out the actual studies. In their search for a senior research coordinator, the Committee was turned down no less than 38 times!

A variety of factors prevent the rapid recruitment of established behavioral researchers for specific government projects. One is that most behavioral researchers work in academic settings where commitments to teaching are typically made a year in advance. A second is that positions on government projects are often for indeterminate periods and academically based researchers cannot move back into their old positions on short notice. A third is that the opportunities for individual visibility and publication, so essential to maintaining academic status, are limited by the need to carry out the mandate of a governmental body. Finally, diffusion of power and decision-making responsibilities often make the mandate vague and difficult to carry out effectively.

In the case of the Television Committee, the research coordinator ultimately chosen was a relatively junior academician who remained for only a short period after his proposal for a centrally coordinated research effort was rejected by the Committee in favor of open-ended invitations to researchers to submit diverse proposals. The rationale for this approach was that confining the research to a single coordinated effort would risk putting all the eggs in a basket that might later be discovered to be defective and that an open-ended invitation would encourage applications from researchers beside the few most prominent in the field. In fact, several invitations to senior researchers were turned down because of their commitments to other research. Of the proposals submitted, the Committee selected 23 for funding. Along with a review of previous findings, the results of these 23 projects formed the basis for the Committee's final report.

The Research

The research funded by the Committee fell into three general categories: Laboratory studies of the effects of television on children's behavior under well-controlled conditions; field studies of the effects of television under naturalistic conditions; and surveys of television content and the views of the industry personnel responsible for it.

Laboratory studies. One of the laboratory studies producing the clearest findings was carried out by Liebert and Baron (1972) with children at two age levels, 4–6 years and 8–9 years. In this study, each child was taken to a waiting room where the experimenter turned on a television which she suggested the child watch until she was ready for him. For all children, the first two minutes of programming consisted of videotaped commercials selected for their humor and attention-getting features. Thereafter, a randomly selected half of the children saw a violence filled 3½-minute sequence from "The Untouchables," while the remainder of the children saw a 3½-minute sports sequence.

In order to test the effect of exposure to the violent episode, the experimenter then escorted the subject to another room and seated him before an apparatus displaying two buttons and a white light. One button was labeled "help" and the other was labeled "hurt." The subject was told that the buttons were wired to a game in the adjoining room and that another (fictitious) child was about to play the game. It was explained that the game required the unseen child to turn a handle that would activate the white light. Whenever the light came on, the subject was to push either the "help" button–which would make the handle easier to turn and help the unseen child win the game–or the "hurt" button–which would make the handle hot and hurt the unseen child. The white light was then activated 20 times to produce 20 trials. The length of time the subject pushed the help and hurt buttons was automatically recorded. After the session, the subject was taken to another room containing nonaggressive toys plus a toy gun or knife and two large inflated plastic dolls. The subject was told he would be left alone for a few minutes and could play with any of the toys. Observers watching through a one-way mirror used a time-sampling procedure to score play with the aggressive toys and assaults on the dolls.

It was found that children of both sexes and both age levels who saw the violent television program pushed the hurt button for significantly longer durations across the 20 trials than did children who saw the sports program. Furthermore, significantly more aggressive play was observed among the children who viewed the violent program, with the effect being especially pronounced for the youngest boys. Exposure to a mere 3½ minutes of violent television thus appeared to *cause* aggressive behavior.

Field studies. The Liebert and Baron findings were clearcut and their experimental design provides a substantial basis for causal conclusions. But what about the external validity of the findings? Can it be concluded that the much more extended exposure to television violence experienced by many children increases their aggression toward real people in everyday situations? The field studies were designed to answer this question, some by means of experimental designs, some by means of correlational designs.

Friedrich and Stein (1973) conducted an experimental study of the effects of television content on the behavior of 3- to 5-year olds in a nine-week summer nursery school. Four nursery classes were formed with 25 children in each class, matched as closely as possible for age, sex, and SES distributions. For a two-week baseline period, observers scored each child for aggression, prosocial behavior (e.g., cooperation, nurturance), and self-regulation (e.g., tolerance of delay) using a time-sampling procedure. During the next four weeks, each class was divided into groups that viewed 20 to 30 minutes of violent television (Batman and Superman cartoons), prosocial programs (Mister Rogers' Neighborhood), or neutral films on varied topics. The groups were taken to separate rooms for the viewing on each of the three days per week they were in school, for a total of twelve times over the four-week period. Observers continued to score the children's class behavior during the four-week experimental period and for two weeks thereafter.

Changes in behavior were measured by subtracting the scores obtained in the two-week baseline period from the scores obtained during the four weeks of viewing and the two weeks after viewing. In order to determine whether the experimental conditions differentially affected aggressive and nonaggressive children, analyses were performed with children divided at the median on the aggression scores they obtained during the baseline period. Because these scores did not correlate perfectly with scores obtained during the later observation periods, regression effects could cause the children initially scoring high in aggression to decline in subsequent periods and the children initially scoring low to increase. This is exactly what happened—children initially above the median declined in aggression whereas those below the median increased in aggression. However, comparison of the groups exposed to the violent and neutral films showed that children initially high in aggression who viewed the violent films declined less in aggression than those who had viewed the neutral films. This difference between groups was apparently due to the difference in what they viewed.

On the measures of self-regulation, children exposed to the violent television showed declines in tolerance of delay, whereas children in the neutral and prosocial conditions increased in tolerance of delay. Another measure of self-regulation—task persistence—showed a significant effect for high-IQ children in that those viewing prosocial television increased in task persistence, whereas those in the violent condition decreased, but there was little effect for low-IQ children. The effects of the experimental conditions on prosocial behavior were found to interact with the SES of the child. Children who were *below* the median in SES and who viewed the *prosocial* television increased in prosocial behavior. However, among children who were *above* the median in SES, those in the *violent* and *neutral* conditions increased more in prosocial behavior than those in the prosocial condition. In sum, violent television appeared to have definite effects on tolerance of delay by children in real-life social situations, whereas the effects on other aspects of self-regulatory behavior, on prosocial behavior, and on aggression depended upon such characteristics of the child as his initial level of aggression, SES, and IQ.

Even if television has short-term effects on behavior in naturalistic settings, does it actually influence the development of long-term behavior patterns? Only a longitudal study could answer this question and the Surgeon General's Report could not wait the many years required to conduct such a study. However, it happened that, in a 1960 study, peer ratings of aggression had been collected for all the third graders in an upstate New York county. Parents' reports of the children's favorite television programs had also been obtained and the programs had been rated for degree of violence. The Surgeon General's Committee granted funds for a follow-up of the third graders, now aged 19, in which high-school classmates' ratings of aggressive behavior were obtained for 427 of the original 875 subjects. The subjects were also asked their favorite television programs, and these were rated for violence (Eron, Huesmann, Lefkowitz, and Walder, 1972).

For girls, a significant correlation of .47 was found between aggression in third grade and aggression ten years later, but there was no significant correlation between early preference for violent television and later aggression. For boys, third grade aggression and preference for violent television both correlated significantly with aggression ten years later. The cross-lagged panel correlations presented in Figure 8-3 show that preference for violent television in the third grade correlated higher with later aggression than with either third grade aggression or later

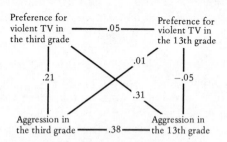

Figure 8-3. Cross-lagged correlations between aggression and preference for violent television in third grade and 10 years later ("13th grade".) (From Eron, Huesmann, Lefkowitz, and Walder, 1972, p. 257.)

preference for violent television. In addition, third grade aggression had a very low correlation with later preference for violent television, indicating that early aggressiveness does not cause a later preference for television violence. The correlations suggest that preference for violent television and aggression in the third grade may both be causally related to later aggression, but several rival interpretations are possible.

One of the most plausible rival interpretations is that aggressiveness in the third grade causes both preference for violent television and later aggression. To test this interpretation, Eron et al. recomputed the correlation between third grade preference for violent television and later aggression, with the effect of third grade aggression controlled by means of partial correlation. The remaining partial correlation of .25 indicated that preference for violent television in third grade was significantly related to later aggression, independent of third-grade aggression. Partialling out other variables, such as IQ, SES, parents' aggressiveness, and amount of television viewing in third grade, had little effect on the correlation of .31 between third-grade preference for violent television and later aggression. The significant correlation thus seems to indicate a definite, though far from perfect, long-term causal relationship.

Survey studies. Beside the research on the effects of television, the Committee also commissioned surveys of the amount of violence displayed in television programming and of views of personnel in the television industry. Content analysis of television programs from 1967 through 1969 showed declines in lethal violence and in the proportion of leading characters involved in violence, although the rate of violent incidents generally remained constant except for marked increases during children's cartoons.

Interviews with the producers, writers, and directors of violent television programs revealed that they considered violence to be essential for maintaining the credibility of dramatic action. Because people often do not pay full attention while watching television, the producers argued that violent action is necessary as an attention getter. They also felt that viewer satisfaction depends upon the strength of emotional build-up during a drama and the suddenness of its release. As one producer put it, "There must ultimately be some kind of physical settlement. The audience doesn't see a jail sentence. It will feel emotionally cheated and complain, 'Christ, what a dead ending that was '" (Baldwin and Lewis, 1971, p. 304).

Other points made by the producers were that violence created excitement and excitement increased viewing ratings, the prerequisite for holding sponsors; television violence allows viewers to vicariously express their own aggression; and exposure to violence may benefit children because it helps prepare them for reality. Despite the furor about television violence, it thus appeared that the networks would not take the initiative in reducing violent programming.

The Committee's Report

When it came time for the Committee to review the work it had commissioned, cleavages became apparent along several lines. Reports vary as to how severe the cleavage was between industry and nonindustry nominees to the Committee, but at least one of the industry representatives was especially insistent on hedging conclusions in with a great many qualifications (cf. Cater and Strickland, 1975). None of the research studies was entirely without flaws, of course, and differences of interpretation also arose along professional lines. However, the revelation of industry vetoes of prospective Committee members prompted the Committee to attempt to salvage its integrity by condemning the veto process as a serious error and by striving for conclusions that they could unanimously endorse. What they finally transmitted to the Surgeon General in January, 1972, was a 137-page report of their conclusions, plus over 2000 pages of research reports. Acknowledging that no single research study could be decisive by itself, the Committee summarized the overall evidence as indicating that:

> The findings converge in three respects: a preliminary and tentative indication of a causal relation between viewing violence on television and aggressive behavior; an indication that any such causal relation operates only on some children (who are predisposed to be aggressive); and an indication that it operates only in some environmental contexts. Such tentative and limited conclusions are not very satisfying. They represent substantially more knowledge than we had two years ago, but they leave many questions unanswered. (Surgeon General's Report, 1972, pp. 18–19.)

Reactions to the Report

Before the Report was officially released, the *New York Times* obtained a copy and announced in a front-page headline: "TV Violence Held Unharmful to Youth" (*New York Times*, 11 January, 1972). Beneath the headline the Committee's report was summed up in a lead paragraph:

> The office of the United States Surgeon General has found that violence in television programming does not have an adverse effect on the majority of the nation's youth but may influence small groups of youngsters predisposed by many factors to aggressive behavior.

While not as blatantly inaccurate as the headline, the article incorrectly reported that the Committee concluded the effects of violent television to be limited to small groups of youngsters. In actuality, the

Committee's report stated that the children adversely influenced might include either "a small portion or a substantial portion of the total population of young television viewers." Nevertheless the *Times* story unleashed a storm of controversy. Congressman John Murphy of New York charged that the Committee, "heavily loaded in favor of the industry," had produced a whitewash (Washington *Evening Star*, 18 January, 1972). The *Times* itself editorialized against televised violence whatever the precise scientific evidence and again erroneously reported the Committee's conclusion to be that "the majority of young people are not adversely affected," but only those "small groups" already "predisposed to aggressive behavior" (*New York Times*, 15 January, 1972).

Distribution of the *Times'* story by the National Association of Broadcasters aroused suspicions that the television industry had leaked selected portions of the Report to the *Times*. To counteract the misinterpretations, the Surgeon General announced that "The study shows for the first time a causal connection between violence shown on television and subsequent [aggressive] behavior by children" (Cater and Strickland, 1975, p. 80). The misinterpretations nevertheless continued, ranging from the Chicago *Daily News* at one extreme, "Dynamite is hidden in the surgeon general's report on children and television violence, for the report reveals that most children are definitely and adversely affected by television mayhem," to *Broadcasting* magazine's headline, "Violence on Air and in Life: No Clear Link," followed by, "A blue-ribbon committee of social scientists has concluded that there is no causal relationship between television programs that depict violence and aggressive behavior by the majority of children" (Cater and Strickland, 1975, p. 81).

Despite the conflicting interpretations by the press, Senator Pastore concluded that the Report represented a major breakthrough and he convened Senate hearings on what should be done about television violence. Calling the Surgeon General and various members of the Advisory Committee as witnesses, Senator Pastore elicited agreement from all of them that the research indicated a causal relationship between television violence and aggression, and that there was too much violence on television. Senator Pastore also solicited proposals from researchers, Committee members, Government officials, and others on what should be done to reduce televised violence. Although most witnesses felt it should be reduced, most also opposed Government censorship. One widely supported proposal was the development of a standard measuring procedure for televised violence so that the public, advertisers, the industry, and Government could be kept informed of just how much violence was being presented and who was presenting it.

While development of a violence index hardly seemed a very drastic measure, *TV Guide* ran a series blasting the Surgeon General's Report as "A million dollar misunderstanding," and concluding:

> You are now going to be presented with a "Violence Index." It will make most people yawn and tune in to *Mission Impossible*. But it will throw others into a panic because they'll assume that there would be no "Violence Index" without proof that TV violence is dangerous to young viewers. Be advised that the "Violence Index" has only one real meaning: It is a nonsolution to a nonproved problem produced by a noninvestigation of a nonresolved controversy over a nondefined threat to nonidentifiable people. (Efron, 1972, p. 36.)

However, each of the networks appointed a special vice-president in charge of children's programming and convened discussions of child experts with television experts and advertising executives. Citizen action groups also succeeded in getting some local stations to eliminate certain programs, and Leo Singer, President of the Miracle White Company, withdrew $2 million of his advertising from violent programs.

On the Government front, the National Institute of Mental Health (NIMH) held a conference that recommended development of a multidimensional profile to portray the types and contexts of violence rather than just the number of violent incidents. Sharply declining budgets for behavioral research and the departure of most NIMH staff involved in the television study left little evidence of a concerted effort to develop such a profile, but some research in the area was funded. To insure that the issue did not die, Senator Pastore convened a new round of hearings in April, 1974. Network representatives claimed that they were planning more variety and quality in children's programs, and there was indeed an increase in programs dealing with family life and personal relationships. There was also a reduction in "hard sell" commercials and in total time alloted for commercials on children's cartoon programs. Furthermore, during the 1975–76 television season, the networks and the FCC agreed to designate 7 to 9 P.M. as a family viewing period during which violence would be held to a minimum, although courts later ruled against the "Family Hour" on the grounds that it infringed the free speech of television writers and producers. Content analyses of television programming showed a decline in violence during the Family Hour, but significant increases during late evening hours and children's weekend programs raised the total number of violent incidents (Gerbner, 1977). Although Gerbner's analyses have been disputed by CBS (1976), which claimed a decrease in overall violence, Gerbner (1976) attributes the disagreement to the fact that CBS excludes humorous violence from its tabulations whereas he does not.

Implications for Social Policy

The history of the Surgeon General's Report is as instructive about the problems of interfacing behavioral research with social policy as about specific methods of research. Despite the difficulty of quickly obtaining definitive answers about the effects of television on development, the repeated findings of a positive relationship between exposure to television violence and aggression in studies differing in methodology and differing in their specific flaws certainly justified concern about television violence. Because all of the findings depended upon particular operational definitions of variables and upon various characteristics of the child and situation, no blanket statements about the effects of television on all children could legitimately be made. Whether or not the Committee's summary statement was overly cautious, the qualifications on the conclusions generally reflected the actual findings. Some critics of the summary portion of the Report justly maintain that it could have been written more clearly and concisely, but, since hardly anyone could be expected to read and assimilate the 2000 pages of research reports, there is no denying that an interpretive summary was necessary.

Could television programming be more decisively affected by better research or by better reporting of the research that was carried out? Even if the mechanisms had existed for immediately launching a more massive and better coordinated research effort, it seems unlikely that firmer conclusions about all the precise determinants of the effects of television violence could have been obtained in the 30 months from the initial formation of the Advisory Committee to the submission of its report to the Surgeon General. Establishment of firmer and more precise conclusions would have required at least one additional generation of studies to follow up on the complex findings of the first studies, plus longitudinal studies to determine the long-term effects of television under much more precisely defined and more varied conditions with more diverse populations than happened to have been available for the Eron et al. (1972) study.

If television violence was in fact harmful to any children, then delaying action until more detailed answers were obtained would not be justified. Furthermore, because direct Government action to control programming seemed out of the question, especially while fears of political censorship were rampant, the effects of any research findings depended more on the changes in attitudes they could induce than on direct translation into laws and regulations. The findings obtained were sufficient to induce at least some assent from the industry that television violence could be harmful, although certain elements of the industry seemed prepared to carry on guerrilla warfare against any attempts at reform, no matter what research might show. As for *public* attitudes—theoretically an important influence on the success of a capitalist enterprise—the decline in smoking after the Surgeon General's Report on Smoking showed that clearcut research findings could have an impact on the public, but that the impact tended to wear off despite constant reminders of the dangers of smoking.

Once research has demonstrated risks associated with such consumer behavior as smoking and watching violent television, the question of what should be done must be confronted almost entirely in the political arena. Researchers can determine the relationships between specified variables, but, having established relationships, their efforts to change public policy must be in their capacity as concerned citizens rather than as experts claiming special competence in deciding questions of social value.

Summary

Although developmental research was from its inception inspired by a sense of mission, it was not until the 1960s that much developmental research became mission-oriented in the sense of being designed to answer social policy questions. The impetus for such research was created by an increasing public concern for the needs of children and by a spirit of social activism among students and researchers. However, new opportunities for shaping social policy exposed the woeful gaps between basic theory and research, on the one hand, and such practical questions as how best to enhance the development of disturbed and disadvantaged children and how violent television affects children, on the other.

To answer questions of this nature, new approaches to developmental research and new vehicles for carrying it out have evolved. Experience with mission-oriented research has shown that social policy questions must typically be redefined in terms of operationally specifiable variables, that a great deal of work remains to be done in creating the "engineering" techniques needed to adapt developmental theories and methods to the study of practical problems, and that better ways must be found to maintain interfaces between developmental research and social policy.

9 New Directions in Developmental Research

IN MANY WAYS, the 1960s marked a major watershed in American developmental psychology. Not only was there a burgeoning of mission-oriented research, but interest in and support for basic developmental research increased greatly. Although the major paradigms described in chapter 2 have continued to guide much developmental research, new amalgams of interests and methods have led researchers in directions uncharted by the major paradigms. Exploration in these directions has greatly enriched our conceptual and methodological repertoire. The purpose of this chapter is to outline a few of the directions in which developmental research has expanded.

Some of the new amalgams have been initiated by specialists in other fields who turned to the study of development as a way of elucidating the phenomena that interested them. One of the most prominent of these has been the initiation of research on language development by workers more interested in language than in children per se. From the amalgamation of research on language and development emerged the new speciality of *developmental psycholinguistics*, which has since generated an array of concepts, methods, and findings pertinent to linguistics, cognition, and development. Now a well established component of the developmental field, developmental psycholinguistics is continuing to contribute new ideas to be discussed later in this chapter.

Another speciality emerging from the adoption of a developmental approach to issues outside traditional child psychology is that of

223

developmental psychobiology. The focus on the relationships between organic development and behavioral change has helped broaden developmental psychology to include organic bases for behavior across many species. Developmental concepts give promise of providing an integrative framework for such specialities as behavior genetics, the study of sex differences, relations between brain development and behavior, infant capabilities, and the evolutionary significance of various behaviors.

A third speciality emerging from the application of a developmental strategy is that of *developmental psychopathology.* Although adult psychopathology has long been hypothesized to have its roots in childhood, clinical theory has been based largely upon extrapolation to children of concepts derived from adult behavior and adults' recollections of their childhood experiences. However, it has become increasingly evident that an understanding of psychopathology in childhood and of the childhood origins of adult psychopathology requires direct study of adaptive and maladaptive development in children. When studied in relation to the normal developmental progression and the tasks to be mastered at various developmental periods, pathological behavior may be understood more fully than when it is treated merely as a disease entity independent of the developmental dimension.

In addition to the specialities emerging from the application of developmental strategies to new areas, the topics to be discussed include areas that, though long of interest to developmentalists, are receiving increased attention from new perspectives. The development of social behavior is one such area, now receiving renewed attention in the form of research directed toward integrating cognitive and social functioning and toward identifying the mutually reciprocal influences between children and adults.

While the paradigms outlined in chapter 2 will continue to guide research, and the ethological paradigm in particular is likely to play an increasing role, the most significant new direction emerging from the major paradigms is an amalgamation of the S–R paradigm and the cognitive versions of the organismic–developmental paradigm. Whether this will result in a new hybrid cognitive–behavioral paradigm or the assimilation of one of the existing paradigms by the other is not clear, but cognitive–behavioral approaches have become increasingly influential.

Beside the new kinds of research relating to children, another emerging feature of developmental psychology is the expansion of the developmental perspective to include the entire life span. To be discussed first because of its overarching transformation of the developmental perspective, *life-span developmental psychology* has added not only the entire life cycle to the subject matter of developmental research, but research strategies designed to untangle the separate contributions of the historical epoch and cohort-specific environments from whatever is consistent about the aging process from one cohort to another.

Life-span Developmental Psychology

The concept of life-span developmental psychology grew out of research on aging, which has gained importance as ever more people survive into the retirement years. No longer can the problems of old age be regarded as the relatively brief affliction of a small minority who may need little more than humane custodial care. The fact that most people will survive from 10 to 20 years beyond retirement is making the later years an increasingly important period of life.

In many ways, research on aging has been regarded as the mirror image of research on development between birth and maturity. Whereas research on the young is directed at the nature and timing of *increments* in functioning, research on the aged has been directed at the nature and timing of *decrements* in functioning. Cross-sectional findings that IQ test performance was negatively correlated with age beyond young adulthood helped establish the view of later adulthood as a period of "negative development." However, longitudinal studies in which the *same* adults were tested at repeated intervals have shown that IQ test performance continues to increase well into the middle adult years where cross-sectional studies had indicated declines. Furthermore, among people who are in good health, many aspects of test performance remain stable well into the 70s and 80s (Jarvik and Cohen, 1973).

Because cohort differences in education and acculturation, rather than declines from attained levels, accounted for the poor performance of older cohorts in cross-sectional studies, the need to separate effects due to cohort from those due to changes with age became acutely obvious to researchers on adult development and aging. This need stimulated development of research models in which age changes, cohort characteristics, and sociocultural factors related to time of measurement could be isolated (Baltes, 1968; Schaie, 1965). Several of the resulting research strategies, including cross-sectional–sequential, longitudinal–sequential, and time-lag–sequential, were described in chapter 4. These strategies are equally applicable to the study of changes with age at any point in the life cycle, whether the changes consist of quantitative increments or decrements, or of qualitative changes in behavior.

In addition to producing new models for the study of behavioral change, the life-span approach has spurred attempts to elucidate developmental changes in childhood by studying apparent reversals of these changes in later years. For example, it has been found that many elderly people fail Piagetian conservation tasks (Hornblum and Overton, 1976). One interpretation has been that neurological decrements in old age cause a loss of the cognitive structures required for logical thought. Regression in cognitive level, however, appears inconsistent with Piaget's theory that the operations of early stages become integrated with those of later stages and that the highest stages should remain intact. According to a Piagetian interpretation, the failure of elderly subjects to conserve may be due to their failure to use their full cognitive competence because such factors as inattention might interfere with performance. In support of this interpretation, Hornblum and Overton demonstrated that simple verbal feedback induced conservation by elderly subjects who had previously failed conservation tasks.

On the other hand, Rubin (1976) has shown that institutionalized elderly subjects who spontaneously give correct conservation responses readily relinquish them when presented with contrived violations of conservation. Since young spontaneous and trained conservers also revert to nonconserving responses when presented with contrived violations, whereas young adults do not, Rubin argued that the conserving responses obtained from elderly subjects by Hornblum and Overton may have represented superficial shifts in behavior rather than a firm grasp of logical operations.

The question is far from settled, however, as many factors other than a true decline from attained cognitive competence could be involved. It is possible, for example, that Rubin's experimental situation presented different demand characteristics for subjects of different ages. Thus, children and elderly people may have been more intimidated than young adults when a young adult experimenter confronted them with conservation violations that contradicted their earlier conserving responses. Likewise, Rubin's purely cross-sectional design may have reflected cohort differences related to educational background and selective factors within cohort, as the adults who performed worst—the institutionalized elderly—had the lowest educational level of the adult groups. While it is clear that life-span research will make an increasing contribution to developmental psychology, it is also clear that the issues raised by the life-span approach demand far more complex and sophisticated research designs than have typically been employed to study behavioral change. Not only must general effects due to age changes, cohort characteristics, and time of measurement be separated, but new varieties of demand characteristics, the increasing effects of illness with age, and variations in living conditions within and between age groups must be considered in constructing a life-span perspective.

Developmental Psycholinguistics

Prior to the emergence of developmental psycholinguistics, studies of child language consisted largely of parents' diary descriptions of their own children and tabulations of the words used at various ages. It was primarily Chomsky's (1957, 1965) linguistic theory and his attack on S–R views of language (Chomsky, 1959) that redirected research on language into what became known as developmental psycholinguistics. Chomsky proposed that every native speaker of a language has internalized a set of rules or a "grammar" that governs his language. Because all the grammatically correct sentences that could be uttered in the language and no grammatically incorrect sentences can be derived or "generated" from these rules, Chomsky called the hypothesized grammar a *generative grammar*. However, because actual speech is influenced by such factors as memory lapses, inattention, changes of thought in mid-sentence, and nonlinguistic aspects of a situation, the grammatical rules assumed to govern a language are not directly manifested in speech, but must be inferred from large samples of speech. The task of the linguist is to infer the internalized rules of a language from the observed utterances or "surface structures." An additional task, falling more into the realm of psychology, is to construct a model of how people actually produce sentences. This entails identifying the ways in which people transform the underlying meaning or "deep structures" of sentences into the observed surface structures. Chomsky's goal was to portray both the generative rules for the formation of deep structures and the rules by which the hypothesized deep structures are transformed into surface structures.

In presenting his views, Chomsky attacked the then prevailing paradigm for the study of language. According to this paradigm, the essence of language is not a generative rule system but the collection of words and phrases comprising the language, plus a set of rules prescribing the proper sequencing and usage of the words and phrases. Initial language acquisition is thus to be explained through the modeling and reinforcement of verbal responses. In perhaps the most extreme version of this view, Skinner (1957) attempted to explain not only the acquisition of language but all language behavior in terms of stimulus–response–reinforcement contingencies. According to Skinner's extrapolation of conditioning principles, language is to be understood as nothing more than a complex chaining of simple responses governed by reinforcement contingencies.

In attacking Skinner's theory, Chomsky (1959) argued that reinforcement contingencies cannot explain why some nonsensical strings of words seem to be perfectly grammatical sentences, whereas others do not. For example, "Colorless green ideas sleep furiously" would be accepted by native speakers of English as a grammatical sentence, but "Furiously sleep ideas green colorless" would not, even though both are nonsensical and the first is no more likely than the second to have become acceptable through a history of reinforcement common to speakers of English.

Other difficulties in accounting for language solely in terms of the content and arrangement of surface structures arise in the analysis of ambiguous sentences such as "Flying planes can be dangerous." Whether this sentence refers to the danger of operating a plane or to the danger that planes present to other people is not discernible from the surface structure of the sentence. Because exactly the same sentence may express either one of two thoughts, there must be something more to producing the sentence than stringing words together in an order determined by previously experienced reinforcements. It is to explain this "something more" that Chomsky proposed two constructs: (a) an underlying level of language (deep structure) which in this case might be expressed either as "Flying is dangerous" or "Planes are dangerous;" and (b) transformations by which the deep structure is translated into the surface structure of an actual utterance.

Chomsky's analysis might have been influential even if it had ended with his persuasive critique of the prevailing paradigm and his proposal for a generative–transformational paradigm. However, he maintained not only that deep structures and transformations underlie the surface structure of language, but that all languages possess the same underlying grammatical principles and that knowledge of these principles is innate! In the environmentalist atmosphere of the late 1950s, this was a far more radical proposal than the mere division of language into various levels of analysis. Nevertheless, whether because Chomsky's arguments against S–R explanations seemed so compelling or because his proposals coincided with an incipient interest in biological determinants of behavior, he quickly won vociferous supporters. Among them, Eric Lenneberg (1964, 1967) marshaled diverse findings to argue not only that the capacity for language is biologically determined, but that the capacity is unique to humans and that the rate and sequence of language acquisition follow a biologically programmed schedule.

Another disciple of Chomsky, David McNeill (1966) outlined a Chomskyan program for what he christened "developmental psycholinguistics." A cornerstone of this program was the portrayal of the developing child as a language acquisition device (LAD) containing knowledge of certain linguistic universals. One type of universal is a concept of language as a hierarchy of categories in which the lowest levels comprise word classes, such as animate vs. inanimate nouns, and the higher levels comprise progressively more general categories, such as subjects and predicates. A second type of linguistic universal was hypothesized to be the use of transformational rules for mapping deep structures onto the surface structures of actual utterances.

If the LAD is assumed to contain innate knowledge of linguistic universals, then the process of language acquisition consists of attempts by the child to infer the ways in which the surface structures of the language he hears reflect the universal characteristics of language. It is as if all children are born with a basic computer program for analyzing language, but each child needs priming with the data of a specific language to help him determine which subset of possible transformations are required for that language. Differing radically from the S–R view of language as a collection of instrumental responses governed by stimulus and reinforcement contingencies, this view implies that language acquisition can best be understood by identifying the grammatical rules governing successive levels of children's language.

As evidence that language acquisition begins with the child's imposition of categories on what he hears, McNeill cited findings that early two-word utterances consist of one word drawn from a relatively small class of "pivot" words, and a second word drawn from a larger "open" class of content words, mainly nouns and verbs (Braine, 1963; Brown and Fraser, 1964; Miller and Ervin, 1964). The words "allgone" and "bye-bye," for example, were both pivot class words that children joined to many open class words (e.g., allgone milk, bye-bye daddy), but not to each other (e.g., "allgone bye-bye" did not occur).

Because the pivot-open combinations were distortions of adult speech, they could not be ascribed to imitation of or reinforcement by adults. The pivot–open grammar thus appeared to reflect the child's selective imposition of his own grammatical categories on the language he heard. While not all developmental psycholinguists accepted the Chomsky–McNeill hypothesis that the child's grammatical structures are innate, it did appear that the key to language acquisition lay in the grammatical analysis of young children's speech. As a result, children's speech was painstakingly analyzed in search of the grammatical principles by which successive stages of language are organized.

Unfortunately, these efforts failed to uncover consistent grammatical relations in children's utterances longer than two words. Furthermore, longitudinal research showed that some children did not employ the pivot–open grammar in their two-word utterances (Brown, 1973; Nelson, 1973). It thus seemed that an account of language acquisition in terms of grammar, independent of the content of speech, would not be as productive as hoped. As a consequence, developmental psycholinguistics has turned more toward the semantic content and context of early language, and toward the relations between linguistic development, on the one hand, and cognitive and social development, on the other.

The Content and Context of Early Speech

According to Chomsky's (1965) theory, the rules of a language can be analyzed into three components. The *syntactic component* concerns the organization of units defined by their roles in sentences, such as subjects, predicates, and direct objects. It is the syntactic component that specifies the form which the deep structures of sentences must take—i.e., that they be organized according to interrelated categories such as subject and predicate—and the transformational rules by which the deep structure of a particular sentence is transformed into the surface structure of the sentence as it is ultimately expressed. Developmental psycholinguists initially focused on the development of syntax, because it appeared that what is unique, universal, and possibly innate about human languages inheres in their syntactic organization.

The other two components distinguished by Chomsky are the *phonological component*, which determines the sounds to be employed in expressing a sentence, and the *semantic component*, which relates the intended meaning to the syntactic structure of the sentence. Chomsky viewed the phonological and semantic components as being secondary to the syntactic component because they merely concern the materials of sound and meaning by which syntactic structure is actualized. However, one of the most significant shifts in developmental psycholinguistics has been toward the study of meaning in children's early language.

In one of the first such efforts, Bloom (1970, p. 2) "attempted to reach the 'meaning' of children's sentences by focusing on the correlation of linguistic and contextual features—on what the child said in relation to what he was talking about . . . ." Called *rich interpretation* (Brown, 1973), this approach differs from the *lean interpretation* of language which focuses only on the relationships among particular words in order to infer rules of syntax, as in McNeill's (1966) analysis of the pivot–open constructions.

Bloom argued that, although the meaning of a child's utterance may not be interpretable with complete certainty, more could be learned about the structure of early language by employing the nonlinguistic context as an aid to inferring the child's meaning than by merely analyzing word combinations. For example, Kathryn, one of Bloom's subjects, once said "Mommy sock" when her mother was putting Kathryn's sock on Kathryn. On another occasion, Kathryn said "Mommy sock" as she picked up her mother's sock. A lean interpretation, focused only on syntax, would treat both utterances as instances of a single grammatical construction. In contrast, a rich interpretation would treat them as reflecting two different meanings, one referring to what Mommy was doing with a sock, the second to the owner of a sock.

From her analysis of how three children formulated meanings in their early utterances, Bloom concluded that they employed different strategies of language learning and that no single preprogrammed approach to grammar could account for the language of all three. Furthermore, the fact that the children employed a single syntactic structure to express a variety of different meanings, as inferred from the context, suggested that their cognitive functioning was often ahead of their ability to differentiate syntactically among meanings. On the other hand, advanced syntactic forms were sometimes used when the context indicated that the child did not understand their meaning. The asynchronies between semantic and syntactic aspects of early language, and the apparent primacy of the semantic aspect in the communicative process, suggested that early child language is better understood in terms of general cognitive development than a specialized LAD.

In a subsequent study of the transition from single words to two- and three-word combinations, Bloom (1973) proposed that the initial ordering of words reflected relationships among the things they designated. Thus, the child learns that certain categories of things, such as Mommy, act upon objects, whereas other categories of things, such as doors, are acted upon. It is these *categories* of referents that provide the basis for what Bloom calls "semantic–syntactic structure" in early child language (Bloom, Lightbown, and Hood, 1975).

Going even further than Bloom in asserting the primacy of semantics in early language, Bowerman (1973, 1975) and Schlesinger (1971) have maintained that the order evident in children's two- and three-word utterances may be determined by the way in which the *particular* referents of the words are related to one another and not at all by superordinate semantic–syntactic categories such as subjects and predicates or agents and actions. They see no need for postulating deep syntactic structures underlying children's early language. Whether semantic functions are thus considered to have absolute or only relative primacy in early language, it is clear that the focus on content has moved the study of language development away from the preoccupation with the unfolding of syntax.

Social Aspects of Language Development

A major source of interest in social aspects of language development has been the debate over the differences between the language spoken by the dominant group in a society and that of disadvantaged minorities. In this country, an initial goal of many educational programs for disadvantaged children was to "improve" their language by making it conform more closely to standard American English (e.g., Bereiter and Engelmann, 1966). However, the view that the language of the disadvantaged might affect their educability was by no means confined to the United States, as the English sociologist Bernstein (1970) argued that the "linguistic code" of the English working class was more restricted than the "elaborated" linguistic code of the English middle and upper classes. By a restricted code, Bernstein meant that the language was context-bound and relatively undifferentiated in syntax, depending for communication more on shared extralinguistic experience than on explicit linguistic cues. Bernstein theorized that the differences in language resulted from differences in the personal relationships and cultural conditions characterizing different socioeconomic strata. As fostered by Bernstein, the study of the sociological implications of language differences became known as *sociolinguistics*.

Beginning with demonstrations that the dialects of disadvantaged children are not inferior to standard English when considered as communication systems within their appropriate social contexts (Baratz, 1969; Labov, 1970), the social context of language development has increasingly become a focus of research, for which the term *developmental sociolinguistics* has been proposed (Schachter, Kirshner, Klips, Fredericks, and Sanders, 1974). In a study intended as a prototype for developmental sociolinguistics, Schachter et al. evolved a system for scoring preschoolers' spontaneous communicative speech in terms of the children's motives for talking. The scoring categories were designed to cover motives for all spontaneous interpersonal statements, including personal motives, such as the expression of emotion (e.g., "Ouch!") and affirmation of possession (e.g., "That's mine"); social motives that involve a union between the self and another, such as "collaboration" (e.g., "I'll be the mommy and you'll be the baby"); and other motives not readily classified as either personal or social, such as "reporting" (e.g., "I'm making a monster"). Utterances within each category were also scored according to function, such as "continuation in conversation" and "modulation" (explanation, justification, attempts at verbal persuasion).

The scoring system was used to categorize the utterances of children in preschool settings during free play periods. The children included 2½-, 3½-, 4½-, and 5½-year-old advantaged whites, advantaged blacks, and disadvantaged blacks. Twelve three-minute language samples were obtained for each child by an observer who wrote down everything the child said. Each child's score for each speech category consisted of the total number of three-minute intervals in which there was evidence for that category of speech. The scores were analyzed to identify interactions between the developmental level of the children and sociolinguistic differences among them. As shown in Figure 9-1, the "modulation" scores manifested just such an interaction. The children differed little in modulation at age 2½, but the advantaged children of both races had much higher modulation scores at ages 4½ and 5½ than did the disadvantaged black children, whether they were of low or high IQ.

Because neither race nor IQ per se seemed to account for the differences in modulation scores, the difference was interpreted as reflecting sociocultural differences in the environments of the advantaged and disadvantaged children. Schachter et al. speculated that the verbal modulations may be the earliest manifestations of Bernstein's "elaborated" code. While consistent with Bernstein's theory about SES differences in use of the elaborated code, the data indicate that these differences are not present in very early speech, but emerge with age.

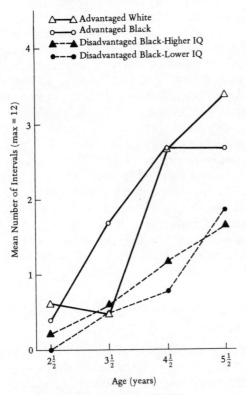

Figure 9-1. Mean number of three-minute intervals in which modulated speech was used by four socio-linguistic groups at four ages. (From Schachter et al.,1974, p. 61.)

Because the modulation scores of all the children increased with age, Schachter et al. proposed that greater modulation signifies more highly developed speech, a view at variance with Bernstein's egalitarian position that the elaborated code is not a more advanced form of communication than the restricted code. However, whether or not the linguistic differences are judged in terms of developmental level, Bernstein (1970) and Schachter et al. agree that failure to master the elaborated code can be a handicap in school, where it is stressed.

Developmental Psychobiology

The increased interest in biological determinants of language development that followed Chomsky's (1957, 1959) attack on environmentalistic associationism was one manifestation of a general rapprochement between behavioral and biological approaches to the study of development in the 1960s. Other manifestations included new interest in genetic determinants of development, in the interactions between environmental inputs and biological development, in cross-species comparisons of behavioral development, and in the nature of the infant's earliest capabilites. A major increase in research on sex differences in behavior also reflects the growth of interest in interactions between biological and environmental variables (Maccoby and Jacklin, 1974; Money and Ehrhardt, 1972; Waber, 1977).

The study of relations between behavioral and biological development is now broadly known as *developmental psychobiology*, and a journal of this name was founded in 1968. While most of what we shall consider is behavioral research that is linked to biology either through theory or through gross biological variables, such as differences between species and stages of maturation, it should be noted that behavioral development is being increasingly incorporated into the study of neurobiological development as well, under the name of *behavioral embryology* (cf. Gottlieb, 1973).

The Development of Higher Cognitive Processes in Nonhuman Species

One of the most intriguing innovations in developmental research is the study of higher cognitive processes in nonhuman species. Although S–R psychologists have long used laboratory animals to study learning processes believed to be similar across species, the usual assumption was that such processes in humans involved complex combinations of elemental principles that could be identified with greater precision in simple organisms under simplified laboratory conditions. It was hoped that, when a theoretical model succeeded in predicting the behavior of laboratory animals, the model could then be extrapolated to the far greater complexities of human behavior in its natural environment. Recent efforts to elucidate the development of higher cognitive processes by studying nonhuman species have generally moved in the opposite direction. Rather than beginning with simple animal behavior under highly controlled conditions and attempting to build precise models which could then be extrapolated to humans, developmentalists have begun with complex human behavior, have adapted the means for studying such behavior to nonhuman species, and have sought to elucidate developmental processes by comparing the course of these behaviors in humans and nonhumans.

One of the most famous subjects of this research is Washoe, a chimpanzee who learned the American Sign Language (ASL) for the deaf under the tutelage of Beatrice and Allen Gardner (1974). Despite the failure of early attempts to teach spoken language to chimps and the arguments of Chomsky's disciples that the capacity for language is uniquely human, Washoe's progress in ASL showed striking parallels with the acquisition of speech by human children. When surrounded by people who communicated in signs, Washoe not only imitated, but also generalized signs to appropriate new situations, combined signs in new and unique but appropriate ways, and employed signs to "talk" to herself when alone. She thus seemed to employ the sign system in a "creative" or "generative" fashion like human children acquiring spoken language.

Although there is still considerable debate about just how much more than the rudiments of linguistic competence Washoe achieved, her success opened up a host of new perspectives on language acquisition. For one thing, Project Washoe has placed a burden on nativists to be far more specific in defining what is innate about language acquisition. A second effect has been to provide methods for teaching ASL to nonspeaking humans such as autistic children (Fulweiler and Fouts, 1976). A further effect has been to stimulate the study of the general cognitive capacities that underlie language acquisition since, in the absence of evidence for a specific language ability in her species, these must be what account for Washoe's success.

In addition to studying language acquisition in nonhumans, developmentalists have employed adaptations of Piagetian measures to determine whether the invariant sequence of cognitive development hypothesized by Piaget can also be found in nonhuman species. Gruber, Girgus, and Banuazizi (1971), for example, adapted Piaget's methods to testing object permanence in cats. It was found that cats progress through stages like the first four stages of sensory-motor development reported by Piaget for human infants. Squirrel monkeys, however, have been found to succeed on adaptations of Piagetian object permanence tasks usually not mastered by humans until the sixth stage of sensory-motor development, at the age of about 18 months (Vaughter, Smotherman, and Ordy, 1972), and there is even evidence that they can pass tests of length conservation (Thomas and Peay, 1976). On the basis of the many parallels found between cognitive development in human and nonhuman primates, Jolly (1974) has proposed that understanding of infant adaptive competence can be greatly advanced through comparisons of the progress of various species through Piagetian stages.

Behavior Genetics

Probably no developmental issue has generated more heat and publicity than the controversy over genetic vs. environmental determination of IQ. Because the ethical and political implications of this issue loom so large, it will be taken up in detail in chapter 10. However, the furor engendered by the IQ controversy should not obscure the increasing efforts to objectively probe the relationships between genetic factors and behavioral development.

There are two general approaches to behavior genetics, distinguished from one another primarily by the types of characteristics on which they focus and differences in methodology appropriate for the different characteristics. One approach is known as Mendelian (Mather, 1971), because it focuses on categorically defined phenotypic traits analogous to the traits of color and skin texture of peas studied by Gregor Mendel. Phenotypic traits that occur in discrete categories are generally assumed to be controlled by individual genes that exert their influence according to such Mendelian principles as dominance–recessiveness. The genetic basis of these traits is inferred from the distribution of the traits in successive generations of related individuals, i.e., through the study of family "pedigrees."

Unfortunately, only a few behavorial characteristics occur in discrete categorical form. Most of these are forms of mental retardation associated with gross physical abnormalities. Some have indeed been found to occur in accordance with Mendelian principles. Phenylketonuria (PKU), for example, which is manifest in severe mental retardation, self-destructive behavior, and pale skin, is a Mendelian recessive trait. It is now known that the symptoms of PKU are not produced directly by a gene, but by an excess of phenylpyruvic acid. This excess results from a genetically caused failure to metabolize phenylalanine, a common component of normal diets. Environmental intervention in the form of a low phenylalanine diet beginning in infancy can prevent the neurological damage and subsequent retardation that otherwise result from the excess of phenylpyruvic acid in children having the genotype for PKU. Another trait manifested behaviorally in Mendelian fashion is Huntington's chorea, a degenerative disorder of the nervous system. Distributed as a Mendelian dominant, it does not usually appear until middle adulthood. However, IQ testing of individuals having a parent with Huntington's chorea has shown significantly poorer performance by those who later manifested the disorder than those who did not (Gottesman, 1974), suggesting a subtle interference with cognitive functioning long before the more acute symptoms appear.

The second general approach to behavior genetics focuses upon characteristics manifest on a continuum of gradations rather than in qualitatively discrete categories. Genetic influences on continuously distributed variables are generally assumed to involve complex interactions among multiple genes instead of one-to-one relationships between the observable trait and individual genes operating in Mendelian fashion. Called *biometric* or *quantitative* genetic analysis, the study of continuously distributed behavioral traits raises all the psychometric problems of reliability and validity encountered in attempts to measure behavior for other purposes as well.

The necessity for having psychometrically sound indices of behavior before genetic contributions are worth studying probably accounts for the fact that most quantitative behavior genetic research has concentrated on IQ and a few well-refined personality tests (e.g., Dworkin, Burke, Maher, and Gottesman, 1977). The cost and difficulty of doing quantitative behavior genetic research, which usually entails comparisons of the degree of correlation for traits in identical and fraternal twins, means that it will continue to be restricted to a few readily measurable traits. However, an approach of special interest to developmentalists is the quantitative study of genetic influences at various periods of development. Rather than assuming that a substantial difference in the correlations between scores for identical and fraternal twins at a particular age indicates a uniform degree of genetic influence on the trait across the life span, developmental behavior geneticists have begun to compare twin correlations on traits measured at successive ages. Because both environmental and genetic influences can change from age to age, a full understanding of genetic influences on a trait requires that the trait be traced over the course of development.

At both ends of the age spectrum, longitudinal twin studies have been employed to trace genetic contributions to a variety of abilities. Wilson (1972) compared the correlations between scores on the Bayley Infant Scale for identical and fraternal twins at ages 3 through 24 months. Despite substantial fluctuations for individual children from one testing to the next, the correlation between identical twins for overall score was .90 during the first year of life and .89 during the second year of life, both significantly higher than the also remarkably high correlations of .75 and .79 between fraternal twins' scores. Not only was there thus evidence for genetic influence on the overall level of the test scores, but the correlations between identical twins in *fluctuations* of scores were significantly higher than for fraternal twins. This indicated a genetic contribution to patterns of change in performance as well as to overall level of perfomance.

At the other end of the age spectrum, Jarvik, Blum, and Varma (1972) retested pairs of elderly twins on a variety of abilities over a 20-year period beginning when the twins were in their 60s. As estimated from the differences in correlations between scores for identical twins and fraternal twins, the genetic contribution to individual differences in certain types of performance, such as vocabulary, remained very high over the 20-year period. However, a marked decline in genetic influence was indicated on tasks involving speed, such as speed of tapping. The apparent differences in the course of genetic influence suggested that the effect of environmental factors, probably related to physical health, increased with age for performance involving speed, but not for performance involving accumulated knowledge.

Infant Capabilities

Research on infant behavior over the past 15 years has grown rapidly in terms of both quantity and technological sophistication. In the process, the barriers to communication with infant subjects have been remarkably reduced through ingenious methods for presenting stimuli and recording responses. While there is still considerable debate about the ability of newborns to acquire stable conditioned responses, short-term conditioning and habituation have been well enough demonstrated to indicate the existence of learning and memory processes in the first months of life (Appleton, Clifton, and Goldberg, 1975). The susceptibility of infants to conditioning and habituation has also made it possible to study their abilities to discriminate various types of stimuli. It has been found that, in at least the areas of speech and color perception, infants seem to employ the same perceptual categories as adults, indicating that these categories are biologically based rather than being acquired through culturally imposed learning.

With respect to speech perception, Eimas (1975) has shown that month-old infants respond with differential sucking when auditory stimuli change from what adults perceive as a p sound to a b sound, but not when the stimuli vary *within* the categories adults perceive as p and b. The same was found for stimuli perceived by adults as d and t sounds. As for color perception, Bornstein, Kessen, and Weiskopf (1976) demonstrated that 4-month olds who had ceased looking at (had *habituated to*) a repeatedly presented stimulus of one color (e.g., blue) began looking again if the stimulus wavelength was changed to one perceived by adults as belonging to a different primary hue (e.g., green). But they did *not* look at the stimulus again if the wavelength was changed by the same amount to one perceived by adults as belonging to the original hue category (e.g., a darker blue). The wavelengths of the boundaries of the color categories inferred for infants corresponded closely to the wavelengths of adult color categories identified by asking adults to name the colors of stimuli of various wavelengths.

In addition to evidence for biological determination of perceptual categories, there is evidence for biological determination of early imitative behavior. Meltzoff and Moore (1977) presented four gestures—lip protrusions, mouth opening, tongue protrusion, and finger movements—to 2-week olds, and had raters score videotapes of the infants' responses for evidence of similar behavior. Since the raters could not see what behavior was being presented to the infants, the ratings were unlikely to be influenced by experimenter biases. The frequency of each type of behavior by the infants was significantly higher following presentation of the same behavior by the adult than following presentation of the other behaviors. As no evidence was found for differential reinforcement of the infants' responses by the adult models, and as the infants were too young to have been previously reinforced for generalized imitation, it appears that there is a biological disposition to imitate at least certain classes of behaviors.

Developmental Psychopathology

Despite the pervasive belief that childhood experiences play a central role in adult psychopathology, most conceptions of psychopathology in childhood have until recently consisted of downward extrapolations of theories of adult psychopathology to children. Because models of etiology and treatment have been so heavily dominated by adult disorders and the needs of adult patients, the unique aspects of psychopathology in children have received little attention. However, the term "developmental psychopathology" is coming to designate the study of psychopathology in the context of developmental processes.

According to the developmental approach, psychopathology is best viewed in relation to the sequences of developmental milestones, the changes in adaptive capabilities, the developmental tasks to be mastered, and the environmental pressures that people experience as they grow older. A basic challenge is to determine "when a life crisis is a normal, predictable reorganization preceding a new level of development, and (how) to differentiate such crises from disintegrative or regressive reactions to stress" (Ricks, Thomas, and Roff, 1974, p. viii). This requires knowledge of normal development as a foundation for determining how the constitutional characteristics, environmental history, and developmental level of an individual jointly shape his behavior, both adaptive and maladaptive. Furthermore, it implies that treatment of child psychopathology must be aimed at facilitating the educational and social development necessary to long-term adaptation.

One of the biggest handicaps to research on the development of psychopathology has been the lack of diagnostic categories for childhood psychopathology. In the absence of a well-differentiated, objective, and reliable system for grouping children according to the type of disorder they manifest, it has been difficult to compare the etiologies, prognoses, and the effectiveness of different treatments for various conditions. Except for disorders with clearcut organic etiologies, the medical disease model for diagnosis has seemed inappropriate. Other diagnostic models employed for adult psychopathology, such as the psychodynamic model for neurosis, are of minimal reliability even when applied to adults who, unlike children, typically seek out their own treatment and participate actively in the diagnostic process. As an alternative to basing diagnosis on concepts of adult psychopathology, a number of researchers have employed factor analysis to identify clusters of behavior problems that characterize children (cf. Achenbach and Edelbrock, 1978). Disturbed children can then be grouped according to the clusters of problems they manifest. Unfortunately, many of these studies have lumped together children of all ages and both sexes. Classification of children according to clusters obtained in this way fails to reflect sex and developmental differences in behavior problems.

As an alternative to this approach, Achenbach (1978) has developed the Child Behavior Profile, based not only on factor analysis of behavior problems but on indices of social competence, such as skills, hobbies, participation in sports and organizations, school performance, and positive social relationships. The basic data are obtained from a behavior checklist filled out by parents. To reflect differences related to age and sex, different versions of the Profile have been constructed for different age groups of each sex. Rather than being categorized according to mutually exclusive syndromes, a child is scored on all the behavior problem and social competence dimensions appropriate for his age and sex to yield a Profile showing how he compares with normal children. The Profile portrays a child's pattern of behavioral problems and strengths in a standardized fashion that can be used clinically as well as for research on etiology, prognosis, and the effects of treatment.

Taking another approach to assessment of psychopathology in children, Chandler, Greenspan, and Barenboim (1974) tested the per-

formance of 8- to 15-year-old emotionally disturbed children on measures of role-taking and communication skills. The disturbed children
displayed markedly more egocentric responses than normal children on
both types of measures. In an attempt to overcome what appeared to be
developmental deficits in the disturbed children's role-taking, Chandler
et al. provided one group with a ten-week training program in which the
subjects acted out and videotaped brief skits that they could then view. A
second group received a ten-week program directed at enhancing communication skills through games in which cognitive conflict was
induced by providing the children with feedback about their inade-
quacies in communicating information to others. A third group served
as a no-treatment control.

Upon follow-up testing, both experimental groups were found to
have increased significantly more than the control group in role-taking
skills, but only the group receiving training in communication showed a
significant superiority in communication skills. Ratings of overall
improvements in behavior during the twelve months following treatment showed nonsignificant trends in favor of the treatment groups.
However, another study showed a significantly greater decline in delin-
quent acts by 11- to 13-year-old delinquents receiving the role-taking
program than by control groups (Chandler, 1973).

In addition to developmental assessment and treatment of maladaptive behavior in children, another developmental approach to psychopathology has been through the study of the life histories of people who
manifest psychopathology. Thomas, Chess, and Birch (1968), for example, conducted a longitudinal study of children in which they examined
relationships between parent behavior, temperamental characteristics
of the children, and the development of behavior disorders in the children. Except for a few very severe disorders of apparently organic origin,
most of the disorders seemed to result from mismatches between parents' expectations and the needs of their child at a particular developmental period.

Because the proportion of people who develop severe psychopathology is small, ordinary longitudinal samples do not usually
include enough severely disturbed subjects for meaningful study. One
alternative has been the *follow-back* method whereby data collected in
childhood, such as school and clinic records, are sought for adult psychiatric patients and matched controls (e.g., Watt, 1974). The assumption is that, if the records were made before it was known whether the
individual would develop psychopathology, then they should not be
biased by this knowledge. However, because many selective factors
affect the identification of adults as disturbed, differences found in
preexisting records can result from biases in the way disturbed adults
are located. For example, suppose a study starts with adults admitted to

a state hospital with the diagnosis of schizophrenia. Differences between the childhood records of state hospital schizophrenics and randomly selected comparison subjects may be due more to differing socioeconomic backgrounds than to early precursors of schizophrenia per se, since schizophrenics not admitted to state hospitals—because they can afford private care, receive no care, are in jail, etc.—are not included in the state hospital sample.

A second alternative is to employ a *follow-up* approach whereby information on everybody who had a particular type of childhood record is sought in order to determine relationships between childhood status and adult outcome. Because children manifesting problems are assumed to be at higher risk for later pathology than are randomly selected children, the usual starting points for follow-up research are records in child mental health agencies and juvenile courts. To avoid the type of bias resulting from the differential ease of locating particular types of subjects (e.g., state hospital schizophrenics), it is important to obtain information on a very high percentage of the subject sample. Studies in which nearly all the target subjects were located have, in fact, yielded valuable information about the long-term course of childhood disorders (e.g., Robins, 1970). However, if many of the subjects cannot be located for follow-up, it will not be known whether these subjects differ in outcome from those who can be located. Furthermore, even when information is obtained on most of the target subjects, the findings cannot be readily generalized to children who have had similar problems but were not seen by mental health agencies.

A third alternative is the longitudinal study of children who are known to be at high risk for a particular disorder, whether or not they manifest problems during childhood. Some of the most intensive research efforts of this sort are being directed at children who are at high risk for becoming schizophrenic in adulthood. These efforts have been spurred by the realization that decades of research on adult schizophrenics have repeatedly produced findings that were later recognized as artifacts of hospital diets and environments, selective biases in retrospective data, and other factors arising as by-products rather than causes of schizophrenia. To avoid these artifacts, Mednick in 1962 initiated a longitudinal study of children who, because they had schizophrenic mothers, were known to be at risk for becoming schizophrenic. Since the overt signs of schizophrenia are not typically evident until early adulthood, and since many children having schizophrenic mothers do not become schizophrenic, Mednick's strategy was to obtain data on behavioral and organic development that could eventually be compared for children who ultimately did and those who ultimately did not become schizophrenic. Both groups were also to be compared with control children matched for age, sex, and SES who had no schizophrenic relatives. In this way, Mednick hoped to determine what among children at risk for schizophrenia differentiates those who do from those who do not develop schizophrenia and what differentiates each of these groups from children who have no schizophrenic relatives.

Among Mednick's subjects who subsequently had mental break-downs as young adults, there was a much greater incidence of pre- and perinatal difficulties than among matched high-risk subjects who have not become schizophrenic and among matched low-risk control subjects (Mednick, Schulsinger, and Garfinkel, 1975). Other longitudinal research on children of schizophrenic parents likewise suggests early organic problems (Erlenmeyer-Kimling, 1974), although comparisons with children of mothers having nonschizophrenic psychiatric disorders indicates that an elevated incidence of pre- and perinatal difficulties may characterize them as well (Sameroff and Chandler, 1975). The addition of matched comparison groups of children whose parents have other serious psychiatric disorders is an important refinement that compounds the complexity of an already difficult research strategy, but should greatly increase the power of longitudinal high-risk studies now under way (e.g., Erlenmyer-Kimling, 1974; Neale and Weintraub, 1975).

Social Development

Although social behavior has long been of interest to developmentalists, the 1960s saw a far greater expansion of research on cognitive development than on social development. Since then, however, there has been an accelerating increase in work pertaining to social development. Four foci are especially notable, all of which to some extent reflect the influence of cognitive approaches. One focus is on the development of social thinking, while the second is on moral judgment. The third focus, which reflects the emphasis of cognitive approaches on young children's adaptive competencies, is upon the development of prosocial behavior. The fourth focus, reflecting the cognitive emphasis on the active partnership between the developing organism and his environment, is upon the interaction between the child's behavior and that of people around him.

Social Cognition

Piaget's hypothesis that the affective and social aspects of development are subject to progressive structuralization paralleling that of cognitive development has provided much of the framework for attempts to integrate social and cognitive development. In his earliest research,

Piaget studied children's concepts of social and moral issues as well as their concepts of natural phenomena. In fact, he at first believed that cognitive development resulted primarily from the process of social- ization through which the child is induced to take others' points of view and give up his egocentrism. According to Piaget's later theory of cog- nitive stages, however, the egocentrism evident in children's inability to imagine perspectives other than their own results from their lack of advanced logical operations. Progress in thinking about other people's perspectives should therefore be correlated with progress in solving problems of a purely logical nature. To measure children's ability to adopt multiple perspectives, Piaget and Inhelder (1956) asked them to identify pictures showing how a model mountain scene would look to a doll viewing it from several different positions. Because children did not attain much success before the age of 9, Piaget and Inhelder concluded that advanced operational development was necessary for even rudimentary role-taking.

Subsequent research on social cognition has followed a similar path, but has been designed to reduce obstacles that might cause children's perspective-taking abilities to be underestimated. Borke (1975), for example, allowed children to practice perspective taking by having them rotate a toy fire engine on a turntable to present the view seen by a doll looking at it from various angles. She found that 3- and 4-year olds could then rotate scenes to correctly portray the doll's perspective, although a mountain scene like that used by Piaget and Inhelder was much more difficult than the other scenes.

Further evidence for perspective taking by very young children was obtained by Mossler, Marvin, and Greenberg (1976), who showed brief videotaped sequences to children aged 2 through 6. In one sequence, a child was shown entering a house that the television narrator described as grandmother's house. After a subject had viewed the sequence and had been questioned to insure that he understood and remembered it, his mother was brought into the room. The sequence was then shown again with the sound turned off and the subject was asked about his mother's knowledge of what was going on, e.g., whose house the child on television was entering and why his mother did or did not know whose house it was. Although 2- and 3-year olds answered egocen- trically, 60 percent of 4-year olds, 85 percent of 5-year olds, and all the 6-year olds correctly answered the questions. It thus appears that sim- plified tasks enable children to adopt other perspectives at far younger ages than reported by Piaget and Inhelder.

Beside raising questions about the age at which children can display perspective-taking abilities, later research has cast doubt on the degree to which perspective taking represents the unitary ability implied by Piaget. When he tested children's abilities to assume another person's perceptual perspective, to assess another person's knowledge (cognitive perspective), and to judge another person's emotional state (affective perspective), Kurdek (1977) found minimal correlations among the different types of perspective taking. Similarly, Hollos (1975) used factor analysis to show that measures of perspective taking and measures of the theoretically necessary cognitive operations loaded on separate factors in samples of children from various environments in Norway and Hungary. In comparisons of village children with isolated farm children who experienced little social interaction, Hollos found that the farm children in both countries were better than the other children on the measures of cognitive operations, but much worse on the measures of perspective taking. It thus appears that environmental differences differentially affect the growth of social and nonsocial cognition.

Moral Judgment

Like the study of social cognition, research on moral development has been shaped by Piaget's early work. On the basis of their responses to stories raising questions of morality and justice, Piaget (1932) categorized children into developmental stages roughly corresponding to the stages of cognitive development that formed the framework for his findings in many other areas. Although Piaget thereafter concentrated on the more purely cognitive aspects of development, Kohlberg (1976) has elaborated Piaget's general scheme into a sequence of six stages of moral judgment which he assesses by scoring people's responses to moral dilemmas presented in story form. According to Kohlberg, the moral stages are partially dependent on cognitive development, because each level of moral reasoning requires a particular type of logical operation. However, because amount of social experience is also hypothesized to determine whether a logical operation will be applied to moral issues, Kohlberg and Gilligan (1971) have maintained that, of individuals matched for cognitive level, the older ones should be more advanced in moral judgment.

A variety of questions have been raised about Kohlberg's approach to moral development. One is whether subjects' verbal responses to the hypothetical moral dilemmas reflect anything more than cognitive ability. To test the Kohlberg–Gilligan hypothesis that, among individuals matched for general cognitive level, the older ones would be at the highest moral stages, Taylor and Achenbach (1975) administered Kohlberg's moral dilemmas to normal and cultural–familial retarded children who were matched for mental age (MA). The level of moral judgments was correlated significantly with MA in both groups and no significant differences were found between the moral judgments of the normal and retarded children, despite the fact that the retarded children averaged four years older than the normals. Furthermore, no differences in moral scores were found between subjects who were matched for MA but who differed in whether they passed or failed measures of specific cognitive operations hypothesized by Kohlberg to be required for particular moral stages. Thus, general cognitive developmental level appears to account for more of the variation in moral judgment than do length of experience or attainment of particular cognitive operations.

Kohlberg has also been criticized for his failure to demonstrate either the reliability of his measures of moral development or their validity in terms of correlations with moral behavior (Kurtines and Greif, 1974). While reliability and validity are important to the evaluation of any psychological measure, Kuhn (1976) has argued that high stability should not be expected in a developing individual's moral judgment scores and that overt behavior is not an appropriate validity criterion because different levels of moral reasoning may lead to the same behavior in certain circumstances. As an alternative to traditional criteria for reliability and validity, Kuhn proposes that the reliability and validity of Kohlberg's measures be judged by whether subjects tested longitudinally show a progression through the sequence of stages hypothesized by Kohlberg. If they do, this would indicate that the measures reflect moral development with at least some degree of accuracy. If they do not, however, it would not be known whether their failure to do so results from lack of reliability and validity in the measures or from inaccuracy in the theory. Because only positive results can be interpreted in a clearcut way, attempting to establish the reliability and validity of the measures while testing the theory is an imprecise approach to research. Nevertheless, the lack of well-established independent measures of complex constructs often necessitates this sort of "bootstrapping" approach in behavioral research.

When she employed this approach by readministering moral dilemmas to children after six months and one year, Kuhn found only nonsignificant increases in moral level during the six-month interval, but highly significant increases over the one-year interval. Whether the lack of consistent increases during the six-month interval was due to the low sensitivity of the measures, to the lack of developmental advances, or to the fact that moral levels fluctuate up and down over short periods could not be determined. However, the one-year increases support the hypothesized sequence in moral judgments. Furthermore, employing his standardized Defining Issues Test of Moral Judgment, Rest (1975) has obtained test–retest correlations as high as .81 for moral scores over two weeks. Significant increases in scores were also found over a two-year period, but it has not been demonstrated that these reflect anything beside cognitive development. No matter how psychometrically sound their instruments become for measuring moral judgments, the biggest challenge facing researchers on moral development is to demonstrate relationships between moral judgments and overt behavior (Burton, 1976).

Prosocial Behavior

The two major paradigms most concerned with motivation, the psychodynamic and S–R paradigms, both imply hedonic explanations for human behavior. According to the classical psychodynamic paradigm, all motives are initially derived from the instinctual drives of sex and aggression, while the S–R paradigm encompasses motivational theories ranging from the Hullian drive-reduction model to the Skinnerian model which, without invoking a biological mechanism for reinforcement, nevertheless portrays behavior as being hedonically motivated. Although the psychodynamic and S–R paradigms treat prosocial behavior as being ultimately traceable to selfish motives, current research is focused upon the nature of prosocial behavior in itself, unfettered by the assumption that such behavior is inevitably reducible to baser motives. In fact, at one extreme, Hoffman (1975) has proposed that humans have evolved an innate altruistic motive that enhances the survival of the species by inducing its members to help one another. He hypothesizes that humans start life equipped with an empathic distress response that is triggered by signals of distress from other people. This response becomes more differentiated and mature as cognitive development brings the ability to discriminate the self from others, to think of others as having feelings, and to conceive of other people's feelings in the larger contexts of their life experiences. Although evidence for Hoffman's theory is indirect at best, an observational and experimental study of 3- to 7-year olds has revealed that they spontaneously engaged in a good deal of helping, sharing, and comforting, with no differences attributable to age or sex (Yarrow and Waxler, 1976). Sharing has also been well documented in 18-month olds (Rheingold, Hay, and West, 1976).

Another approach to prosocial behavior has been to study individual and cultural differences in it. Gottman, Gonso, and Rasmussen (1975), for example, found that children chosen as friends by many of their classmates were superior on role-playing tasks involving effective communication and the making of new friends, and that they also gave and received more positive reinforcements than unpopular children. Several studies employing the Madsen Cooperation Board, an experimental game in which four children can each earn more rewards by cooperating than competing, have shown children from nonindustrial societies to be more cooperative than those from urban industrialized environments (e.g., Thomas, 1975). This indicates that some aspects of prosocial development may be differentially shaped by general cultural factors.

Interactions between Child and Adult Behavior

To varying degrees, the major psychological paradigms stress that behavioral development results from an interaction between characteristics of the organism and the inputs it receives from the environment. However, most research has been directed at identifying either the consequences of specific environmental inputs or the characteristics of individuals categorized by age, sex, SES, etc., rather than at the ways in which characteristics of the individual and the environment interact to produce particular outcomes. An extensive review of research on socialization has revealed that most of the correlations reported between socialization practices and children's behavior can be as plausibly ascribed to the triggering of particular parent behaviors by particular child characteristics as to the shaping of child behavior by parental socialization practices (Bell, 1968). This finding has stimulated efforts to capture the process of behavioral interaction between children and adults.

One approach has been to analyze adult responses to various child behaviors. In a study originally designed to examine the effects of nurturant vs. nonnurturant adult behavior on nursery school children, Yarrow, Waxler, and Scott (1971) trained two women to be especially nurturant or nonnurturant. Each woman played the nurturant role and the nonnurturant role with different groups of children. Despite instructions to be consistently nurturant or nonnurturant, the women were noticed to behave very differently with different children. Reversing the intended analysis in order to treat child behavior as the independent variable and the observed behavior of the women as the dependent variable, Yarrow et al. obtained a correlation of .92 between the number of bids for attention by the children and the number of subsequent nurturant contacts by the women in their nurturant role. Thus, even though all children were to get nurturant inputs from a particular woman, the number of nurturant contacts actually received by a child depended almost entirely on how many times the child sought attention! Conversely, the children's bids for attention correlated .99 with the number of subsequent rejecting responses received from the women in their nonnurturant role. Thus, for children intended to receive nonnurturant inputs, the number of such inputs was determined by the child's own behavior. Clearly, a particular type of child behavior can elicit very different responses from adults having different orientations toward children, and different children can elicit very different responses from the same adult even when the adult is attempting to treat all children the same.

Another approach to assessing the interaction between child and adult behavior has been to examine adult responses to child behavior that was deliberately varied according to an experimental design. Osofsky and O'Connell (1972) did this by scoring the reactions of parents to the behavior of their 5-year-old daughters when the girls were given easy puzzles to complete and when they were given very difficult puzzles. As intended, the easy puzzles elicited independent behavior while the difficult puzzles elicited dependent behavior from the girls. Even though both parents interacted more with their child and displayed more controlling behaviors when she acted dependent, mothers were found to be significantly more controlling than fathers in response to dependency.

In a somewhat similar study designed to assess parents' reactions to children of both sexes, Marcus (1975) had parents tell what they would do or say in response to video tapes of boys and girls engaging in a set of prearranged dependent and independent behaviors. Consistent with the Osofsky and O'Connell (1972) finding, the parents responded more directively to children of both sexes when they behaved dependently, and mothers reinforced dependent behavior more than fathers. In addition, parents were significantly less directive in response to children of their own sex than children of the opposite sex, particularly when the children were behaving independently. Although our methods for tracing interchanges between children and adults are still primitive, there can be little doubt that much of development is best understood in terms of interactions between what the child does, how others respond to what he does, and how he in turn continues the behavioral dialogue.

Cognitive–Behavioral Approaches to Development

While the organismic–developmental and S–R paradigms in their purer forms continue to guide a significant portion of developmental research, these two paradigms are being increasingly combined in various cognitive–behavioral approaches to development. Cognitive–behavioral approaches have also become popular in the study of psychopathology (Mahoney, 1977). This amalgamation of paradigms resembles in some respects the information-processing paradigm of adult cognitive psychology, which employs a computer-like model for representing behavior. The organism is portrayed as a complex information processing system that encodes, transforms, stores, and relates inputs to other data it possesses. Like the S–R paradigm, the information-processing paradigm stresses rigorous operational definitions of stimuli and responses, as well as experimental manipulation of input conditions. However, like the Piagetian version of the organismic–developmental paradigm, the information-processing paradigm deals with cognitive processes and structures inferred from behavior.

The information-processing paradigm differs from the S–R and Piagetian approaches mainly in being geared more to representing an attained and stable level of functioning than to explaining behavioral change. This is not to say that the information-processing paradigm is inapplicable to developmental research, as various versions of it have been employed to represent the behavior of subjects at various levels of development (e.g., Klahr and Wallace, 1976). However, the information-processing paradigm has not yielded explanations for developmental change to rival the power and generality of S–R and Piagetian explanations. It is its failure to account for developmental change that seems so far to have prevented the information-processing paradigm from making more than a methodological contribution to developmental research.

One of the most ambitious attempts to integrate cognitive–developmental and S–R approaches has taken the form of what Mischel (1973) calls a "cognitive social learning reconceptualization of personality." Mischel argues that complex human behavior cannot be adequately accounted for either by trait theories that focus only on persisting individual differences in personality or by S–R theories that focus only on the effects of external determinants. Instead, behavior should be conceptualized in terms of the way in which people's cognitive characteristics lead them to construe and react to particular inputs. Mischel enumerates five cognitive social learning variables that may produce individual differences in behavior: The *ability* to construct particular cognitions and behaviors, as roughly indexed by measures of cognitive and social maturity; individual *encoding strategies* for categorizing events and for construing oneself and others; *expectancies* associated with particular stimuli and responses in particular situations; the subjective *values* placed on the outcomes expected; and *self-regulatory systems*, including plans, rules, and self-imposed standards for perfomance. Although individual differences in these variables may be shaped by experience, these variables can influence the subsequent course of learning over and above the more external determinants emphasized by S–R approaches.

Mischel's proposal is an attempt to integrate existing theories and findings into a new hybrid paradigm. The paradigm itself has not yet gelled sufficiently to generate much developmental research, but cognitive and behavioral approaches are being increasingly integrated in the study of specific aspects of development (Mischel and Mischel, 1976). One thrust of these efforts is to relate reinforcement contingencies to the cognitive factors involved in what Mischel calls self-regulatory systems. The ways in which children set standards for their own behavior and reward or fail to reward themselves have been found to be influenced by reinforcement, modeling, verbal cues, and attention (Masters and Mokros, 1974). In a related area, Parke (1974) has studied age changes in the effectiveness with which various kinds of punishment and prohibition inhibit behavior. For example, the effects of a concrete, object-oriented rationale for not handling a toy ("it might break") was compared with the effects of a more abstract rationale stressing the property rights of the owner ("you don't handle other people's property without their permission"). As shown in Figure 9-2, the object-oriented and property rationales were about equally effective in inhibiting 5-year olds from handling the toy, but the property rationale was far less effective than the object rationale with 3-year olds. This was consistent with other evidence that there were significant developmental changes in the interaction between the cognitive level of prohibitions and subsequent transgressions.

Another tack taken in the integration of cognitive and behavioral approaches is to analyze reinforcement in terms of its informational value for telling the subject whether he is behaving appropriately. Certain predictions from these analyses contradict those yielded by the S–R theory of a reinforcer as owing its effectiveness to a deprivation state of the organism. One of the clearest contradictions between an informational interpretation of reinforcement and an interpretation in terms of deprivation has arisen in research on the effectiveness of social reinforcement. Gewirtz (1969) has argued the S–R view that social approval functions like reinforcers such as food and water in that deprivation of them is followed by an increase in their effectiveness as reinforcers. To demonstrate that the influence of adult approval on children's behavior depends upon deprivation of such approval, Gewirtz had an exper-

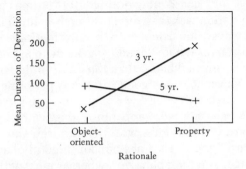

Figure 9-2. Duration of prohibited behavior by 3- and 5-year-old children receiving different prohibitory rationales. (From Parke, 1972.)

imenter say "good" as a reinforcer in a discrimination learning task performed by children who had previously heard the experimenter noncontingently say "good" either twice or 16 times during a pretest period. Because children who had heard the experimenter say "good" only twice subsequently made many more correct discrimination responses than the children who had heard "good" 16 times, Gewirtz concluded that the latter group had become satiated for social approval, thereby reducing the effectiveness of social approval as a reinforcer.

Countering Gewirtz's interpretation with one based on the informational value of "good" to the subjects, Perry and Garrow (1975) hypothesized that the subjects who had heard "good" 16 times had concluded that it was in no way contingent on their behavior. They therefore did not interpret the experimenter's use of "good" during the discrimination task as signaling the correctness of their responses. To test their hypothesis, Perry and Garrow first exposed children to conditions under which "good" was made to appear contingent on the subject's own behavior, on the experimenter's behavior, or not contingent on anything. One group receiving each condition heard "good" twice, while a second group heard it 16 times. All the children were then tested on a discrimination learning task in which the experimenter reinforced correct responses by saying "good." According to Gewirtz's satiation–deprivation hypothesis, all the groups hearing "good" 16 times should perform worse than the groups hearing it only twice. By contrast, according to the informational hypothesis, the two groups for whom "good" appeared contingent on their own behavior should perform the best, whereas the groups for whom "good" appeared noncontingent should perform the worst. The relative performance of the groups for whom "good" was contingent on the experimenter's behavior would depend on how the subjects interpreted this contingency.

As Figure 9-3 shows, Gewirtz's (1969) finding was replicated —children hearing "good" noncontingently 16 times performed worse on the discrimination task than did children hearing it noncontingently only twice. However, consistent with the informational hypothesis, both groups of children for whom "good" was made to appear contingent on their behavior performed better than the children hearing "good" noncontingently. Those hearing "good" 16 times performed the best of all. The subjects for whom "good" was made to appear contingent on the experimenter's behavior were apparently unaffected by the number of times they heard it. Interviews with the children showed that most of those who heard "good" 16 times noncontingently had noticed that it was not contingent on their behavior, whereas most of those in the other conditions believed it to be contingent on their behavior. The children's beliefs about the informational value of "good" appeared to be decisive in determining whether it served as a reinforcer of their learning performance.

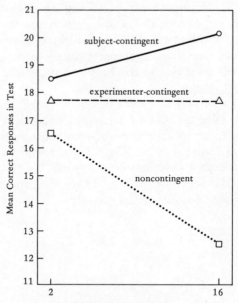

Figure 9-3. Correct responses on discrimination learning test by children previously exposed to low frequency or high frequency approval on subject-contingent, experimenter-contingent, or noncontingent basis. (From Perry and Garrow, 1975, p. 685.)

Summary

Among the directions in which developmental research has expanded, *life-span developmental psychology* stresses the application of developmental strategies to the entire life-span and the need for complex designs to disentangle the effects of aging, characteristics of particular cohorts, and the environment existing at a particular time.

Developmental psycholinguistics, developmental psychobiology, and *developmental psychopathology* have all originated with the application of developmental strategies to areas that were not generally studied from the developmental point of view. Developmental psycholinguistics has moved from a preoccupation with the development of syntax to a more broadly gauged approach to language that includes the semantic aspects of language and the relationships of language to cognitive and social development. Developmental psychobiology encompasses the study of relations between behavioral and biological development, including research on higher cognitive processes in nonhuman species, genetic influences on behavioral development, and biologically based infant capabilities. Developmental psychopathology has brought the developmental perspective to research on psychopathology in children and to the longitudinal study of the origins of adult psychopathology.

Interest in *social development* has been greatly influenced by cognitive viewpoints, as manifested in current research on social cognition, moral judgment, prosocial behavior, and the mutual interaction between child and adult behavior. The influence of cognitive viewpoints is also evident in *cognitive–behavioral* approaches to development that have yielded a hybridization of the S–R paradigm and cognitive versions of the organismic–developmental paradigm.

10 Ethical Issues

ONE OF the most fundamental questions in planning behavioral research is whether it presents risks to the subjects or anyone to whom the findings might be applied. New attitudes, laws, and regulations concerning privacy and the use of human subjects have greatly complicated the ethical context of research. A few years ago, it might have seemed sufficient to begin a book like this with a general statement of ethical principles that could presumably be honored in all research. Today, however, it seems more appropriate to discuss ethical issues after the reader has been exposed to a broad array of research concepts, strategies, and methods. This is because neither past practices nor a set of general principles can provide adequate guidelines for research today. The greater intricacy has resulted largely from an expansion of efforts to protect the rights of the individual on a broad front. This has affected behavioral research in two general ways. One effect has been to stimulate intensive questioning of the social risks and values of research. A second effect has been a mandate that each research project be subjected to ethical review.

Although both the questioning of research and the mandate for ethical review reduce the researcher's autonomy, there is no doubt that they represent justified trends in the protection of the rights and freedoms of people affected by research. While requiring extra effort on the part of researchers, the increasing constraints on behavioral research need not threaten the existence of such research. Indeed, as Haywood (1977) has argued, our ignorance about how to remedy severe problems of behavioral adaptation makes it unethical to refrain from attempting to increase our knowledge through research. However, evidence of occasional failures to safeguard subjects of research, public ambivalence about research of all kinds, and the vociferousness of diverse pressure groups when they disagree with research findings have made research support and regulation a political hot potato.

255

One result has been the appointment of the Presidential Panel on Biomedical Research to make recommendations for national policy on research support. In its final report, the Panel endorsed the basic structure of biomedical and behavioral research support through the Public Health Service and recommended increases in support for mental health research, which had been cut drastically during the Nixon–Ford Administration (President's Biomedical Research Panel, 1976). A second result was the appointment of the National Commission on Protection of Human Subjects to make recommendations for safeguarding participants in research. Testimony before the Commission included proposals to ban research on institutionalized populations, and certain states reacted by banning research with prisoners. However, prisoners' groups have argued that this infringes on their rights to serve as research subjects if they so choose.

In the absence of comprehensive consensual standards for the use of human subjects, we will attempt to lay out issues that are particularly pertinent to developmental research and to distinguish among those for which consensual solutions already exist and those for which the lack of consensus requires a careful weighing of pros and cons in each case. Thereafter, we will discuss the ethical implications of drawing socially significant conclusions from behavioral research.

Protecting the Subjects of Research

Independent Review of Research Proposals

Probably the most basic innovation growing out of recent concern for human subjects is the requirement that research be approved by reviewers who are not involved in the research. Creation of review boards in institutions doing research with humans was required by a 1969 regulation of the Public Health Service (PHS), which funds most of the biomedical and behavioral research in this country. Before being submitted to the PHS, each application for funds must be certified by the applicant's institutional review board as demonstrating that human subjects will be properly protected. Furthermore, if PHS funds are granted, the review board must approve each specific use of human subjects before the research is undertaken and must periodically review the research. This applies not only to research funded directly by the PHS but to research carried out by holders of PHS fellowships. In addition to identifying potential hazards in proposed research, the institutional review boards are to insure that informed consent is obtained from subjects or their guardians, that no coercion is implied in obtaining consent, that potential benefits to subjects be carefully weighed against potential risks, and that subjects be free to withdraw from the research even after giving initial consent. Since the requirement of review boards by the PHS, there has been an increasing effort to guarantee the boards' independence by including nonscientists and people representing elements of the community not affiliated with the institution whose researchers are reviewed. Whether review boards should pass on the scientific as well as the ethical aspects of research is a largely unsettled issue.

Even for research not subject to scrutiny under PHS or other regulations, independent review by people who hold no vested interest in the research is one of the best ways to safeguard subjects. It is too easy for any researcher, caught up in his own quest for knowledge and facing diverse pressures in the conduct of research, to overlook possible risks to subjects and to omit safeguards that may complicate the research. Consequently, anyone considering research on human subjects who is not otherwise obliged to obtain approval from a review body should take the initiative in seeking review from people experienced in relevant areas and should be willing to abide by their judgment. Just as questions of scientific objectivity cannot be resolved by the potentially biased observations of a single observer, ethical questions arising in the course of research cannot be left entirely to the individual researcher who has a vested interest in carrying out his work. Whether or not laws are enacted to require it, the independent review of all research involving human subjects is a safeguard likely to command broad consensus.

Informed Consent

In addition to independent review of research proposals, the informed consent of the subjects of research is another important ethical safeguard. Ideally, every potential subject of research should be presented a nontechnical description of the research and its purpose; the risks, discomforts, and benefits to him if he participates; a guarantee of confidentiality of data obtained about him; a statement of his right to withdraw from participation whenever he chooses; and an assurance that, if he declines to participate, he will not be denied anything to which he would otherwise be entitled. However, obtaining informed consent raises some of the most difficult dilemmas for reconciling research methodology with ethical requirements, and institutional review boards are requiring ever more complex and legalistic consent forms to spell out the rights and obligations of all parties to a research project. Among the most difficult issues are those raised by deception and incomplete disclosure of all details of a study, the use of subjects who cannot give informed consent, and naturalistic research. These will each be discussed in turn.

Deception and incomplete disclosure.   Deliberately deceiving subjects to induce their participation in research involving risks or discomforts that would otherwise deter participation is unquestionably incompatible with informed consent and is ethically indefensible. However, short of this extreme, there may be situations in which conflicts arise between the principle of informed consent and legitimate methodological principles that argue for disguise or incomplete disclosure of research procedures. Consider placebo control conditions, for example. Although few behavioral researchers are qualified to prescribe medical treatments, placebo effects are of interest because behavioral researchers are often involved in medical research and because similar issues arise in the evaluation of many nonmedical treatments, such as behavior therapy and educational curricula. If subjects know they are receiving a placebo, their subsequent responses will not provide an appropriate baseline with which to compare the effects of a drug, because the subjects' expectations of the placebo and drug differ. It would thus be impossible to determine whether the apparent effects of a new drug were due only to the more favorable expectations aroused in those receiving it than in those who knew they were receiving a placebo.

However, the principle of informed consent would not be compromised if the need for a placebo-controlled study were explained and all subjects were told that they would receive either a placebo or the drug, but that neither they nor the person evaluating their reactions would be informed which until the end of the study. Where feasible, another approach is to employ a cross-over design in which subjects are told that a placebo will be alternated with medication, but are not told when they will be getting each one.

If the subjects were patients in need of immediate treatment, or, say, school children on whom a new curriculum was to be tested, a placebo or Hawthorne control condition might not be defensible if an existing treatment or curriculum was demonstrably effective. In this case, research on a new treatment or curriculum would have to be structured as a comparison between it and the established procedure. Because it is unethical to deny effective treatment to people merely because they decline to participate in research, the validity of treatment comparisons depends upon the willingness of a large percentage of potential subjects to participate. Otherwise, attrition due to refusals may sharply bias the selection of subjects. Findings by Park and Covi (1965) have suggested that, at least for psychiatric outpatients, being asked to participate in a placebo condition may not meet with many refusals, even when patients are explicitly informed that they are being given a placebo and no true medication is promised. Each of 15 patients was told the following (p. 337):

> Mr. Doe, at the intake conference we discussed your problems and your condition and it was decided to consider further the possibility and the need of treatment for you before we make a final recommendation next week. Meanwhile, we have a week between now and your next appointment, and we would like to do something to give you some relief from your symptoms. Many different kinds of tranquilizers and similar pills have been used for conditions such as yours, and many of them have helped. Many people with your kind of condition have also been helped by what are sometimes called "sugar pills," and we feel that a so-called sugar pill may help you, too. Do you know what a sugar pill is? A sugar pill is a pill with no medicine in it at all. I think this pill will help you as it has helped many others. Are you willing to try this pill?

Fourteen of the 15 patients took the placebo for a week as requested. As a group, they showed greater improvement on a symptom checklist than did patients in double-blind drug studies by the same researchers! While neither the high rate of cooperation for a brief period nor the apparent benefits of the placebo can be generalized to other situations—especially since the placebo was urged on the patients by their therapists—the findings do indicate that informed consent need not entirely negate the value of procedures designed to control for subjects' expectations.

Beside placebo and Hawthorne control conditions, deception has often been used to induce particular emotional and motivational states in subjects. Experimental manipulations have ranged from creation of success and failure experiences by having children do tasks on which success was either certain or impossible, to creation of intense anxiety by giving college students false feedback from personality measures purported to reveal homosexual tendencies. The usual practice after such deception has been either to provide experiences intended to counteract any negative feelings (*desensitization*)—such as success experiences to counteract feelings of failure—or to debrief the subjects by explaining the deception (*dehoaxing*). The few studies of the effectiveness of postexperimental desensitization and dehoaxing have generally showed them to be successful in eliminating negative reactions by subjects (Holmes, 1976). However, there is very little evidence on their effectiveness with children, and deception designed to induce intense negative feelings is always difficult to reconcile with the principle of informed consent. By today's standards, some studies that have induced such feelings would clearly be unacceptable.

Excluding those that induce intense negative feelings, there may be manipulations designed to influence subjects' feelings and beliefs that can be reconciled with informed consent because they present no risks to the subjects, do not engender negative feelings, and do not create conditions that would deter participation if subjects knew about them in advance. However, when it appears that deception is absolutely necessary to the study of an important issue, the researcher assumes a burden to weigh the value of the deception for increasing knowledge against the compromise of informed consent, the increase in potential risks or negative feelings experienced by the subjects, and the threats to the credibility of other researchers when the deception is revealed. One rule of thumb for judging the acceptability of deception or incomplete disclosure is whether it results in effects on the subject any more severe than he is accustomed to in his normal environment. The more the effects deviate in severity from what he is accustomed to, the more difficult the deception is to justify. In the case of induced failure experiences with child subjects, for example, simply asking a child to attempt a task which he finds to be too difficult for him would not deviate so much from his everyday experience that it presents undue risks. However, pointedly criticizing a young child for failing such a task would not be acceptable even if later success experiences and debriefing were provided. In fact, debriefing may do more harm than good with subjects unable to comprehend the nature and purposes of research. The question of informed consent becomes especially intricate with such subjects, as discussed next.

Children and other dependent groups. Before children are employed as research subjects, written consent should be obtained from their parents or guardians. However, even if consent from a parent is obtained, children should not be used if they are resistant to participation. Furthermore, researchers working with children must be especially alert to anxiety and misunderstandings that would not be likely to occur with adult subjects. As an example, in a study where galvanic skin responses were being recorded from electrodes placed on the hand, an 8-year-old subject inexplicably became upset, left the room, and went home (American Psychological Association, 1973). The researcher later learned that the red plastic wires from the electrodes and the red ink from the recording pens made the child think blood was being drawn from his hand! The researcher may have been unable to anticipate this particular misconception on the part of the child, but informing the subject better, offering him the opportunity to ask questions, and probing to see if he was comfortable with the situation would have greatly reduced the risk of such misconceptions.

There is currently considerable debate about whether researchers should obtain written consent from child subjects as well as from their parents. Some institutional review boards insist that written consent be obtained from subjects as young as age 7. Since it is unlikely that children this young can truly understand the nature of research or make valid judgments on which to base consent, and since the written consent of persons below the age of majority (18 in most states) has no legal standing, the rationale for requiring written consent from children may be questionable. In any event, even if written consent is obtained from a child, the researcher is still obligated to monitor his participation closely and terminate it if any adverse effects are evident.

The use of institutionalized subjects, be they children or adults institutionalized because of mental retardation, mental illness, or criminal conviction, raises additional problems of consent. The parents of institutionalized children are often unavailable to give consent, while retarded and mentally ill adults may not be capable of giving informed consent. In such cases, review boards in the institutions responsible for the subjects must act in place of parents to protect the rights of their charges and to grant permission for participation when it seems warranted. As with young children, however, reluctance by retarded and mentally ill people to participate must be respected no matter how well they are protected and how clear the legal right of institutional authorities to give consent. Because much research on normal children is conducted in schools, developmental researchers must often obtain the consent of school officials before parents are approached. At one time, it was not uncommon for schools to permit research without informed consent from each child's parent, but this has become increasingly rare. Selective loss of potential subjects because some parents either refuse permission or simply fail to return signed consent forms can result in biased samples. Consequently, pilot testing of consent forms and of methods for approaching parents may be necessary to determine in advance how such biases can be minimized.

Other institutionalized subjects, those incarcerated for crimes, have been used for many types of biomedical research, although most behavioral research with them is designed to develop alternative methods of rehabilitation. Civil libertarians have argued that prisoners cannot give consent of their own free will because they are in an inherently coercive situation. Incentives such as money, special privileges, and sentence reductions are also said to make prisoners unduly willing to accept risks. The prohibitions against research spawned by these arguments have been protested by prisoners' groups, but it is clear that biomedical research on prisoners is in sharp decline.

Because most behavioral research with juvenile delinquents and prisoners is designed to study and perhaps alter the prison system itself, it presents a different set of problems for informed consent. During the late 1960s and early 1970s behavior modifiers were especially active in attempting to develop and evaluate new programs for delinquents and prisoners. However, the term "behavior modification" came to be indiscriminately associated with practices that had nothing to do with the systematic application of S–R principles, such as psychosurgery for violent offenders and extreme deprivation for infractions of institutional rules. It therefore became a target of civil libertarians, and the term has now become anathema in many penal systems. Efforts are still being made to conduct behavioral research designed to promote more appropriate treatment of offenders and better matching of treatment to the individual, but the need for individual informed consent to participate in research can make it difficult to try out new approaches with recalcitrant offenders, even when the research conditions offer substantial improvements over standard penal conditions.

Research under naturalistic conditions.   As discussed in chapter 7, efforts are sometimes made to study behavior without altering the subjects' natural environment in ways that might distort their behavior. Because obtaining consent or otherwise informing subjects that they are to be observed is likely to influence their behavior, much naturalistic observation has in the past been done without the subjects' knowledge. If the subjects are infants or young children, unobtrusive observation certainly seems justified as long as the informed consent of the parents has been obtained. The question grows thornier, however, when parental consent cannot be readily obtained for all the subjects in a group being observed, when the children are old enough to be concerned about being observed, and when the observation is to include parents.

When a group of young children is to be observed, as in nursery school, and the data are to be recorded in an anonymous fashion, must the parents of all the children in the group give informed consent before any can be observed? If no children are to be singled out or identified in the research, no other data are to be collected about them except what is observed to occur in the group setting, the research will not directly affect the children in any way, and the caregivers have informed the parents that such observation may occur, then the consent of each parent may not be necessary. However, the more specifically children are singled out, the greater the presumption in favor of obtaining parental consent. If a parent refuses consent, then no data should be recorded about his child despite the child's presence in the group being observed. With observation of older children in restricted settings such as school classrooms, an exclusive focus on group behavior may make it unnecessary to obtain individual parental consent, but the children themselves should be told that observations are to be made. Observation of people in more open settings, such as playgrounds and city streets where the subjects are not identified or affected in any way, does not typically require consent unless the subjects are made easily identifiable through the data collected, as when videotaping is employed. In rare cases, it may be permissible to collect the data first under naturalistic conditions and then ask permission to employ it for research purposes. If the subject refuses, the data should be destroyed.

Related to the issues raised by observations in naturalistic settings are issues raised by employing data that were not originally collected for research purposes but are later of value to researchers. As an example, in the Early Training Project for Disadvantaged Children (cf. chapter 1), Klaus and Gray analyzed achievement test scores obtained by non-Project children in previous years to determine whether one school had typically produced lower scores than another. Should the informed consent of the parents of these children have been obtained before the scores were analyzed? If the scores were compiled by the teachers and given to the researchers without personal identifying data, then informed consent would certainly seem unnecessary. However, the case for informed consent would grow stronger as the degree of individual identification, the personal nature of the data, and the chances of any child being affected by the research increased.

Longitudinal research in which data are obtained repeatedly on the same children obviously requires the informed consent of parents and explanations to the subjects as soon as they become old enough. Broad-gauged longitudinal studies like the Fels study described in chapter 1 typically entail naturalistic observations as well as the recording of behavior in situations structured by the researchers. Because new procedures and hypotheses are often developed during a longitudinal study, the complete course of the study can rarely be described in advance. It is therefore important to apprise potential participants of this and to enlist only those who are not likely to withdraw because of new procedures, as long as the new procedures do not increase the risk or inconvenience of participation. The close personal relationships that often develop between researchers and the subjects of longitudinal research may help to insure continued participation despite unanticipated changes in procedures.

Longitudinal studies of children at high risk for psychopathology, such as the Mednick et al. (1975) study described in chapter 9, raise greater problems of informed consent. It would certainly seem unethical to inform children of schizophrenics that they were at high risk for developing schizophrenia. Whether parents should be informed of this when being asked to permit their children to be studied is a more difficult question. In Denmark, where Mednick's study is being carried out, it was possible to locate schizophrenic parents through central data banks maintained on the whole population, but, in this country, it is usually necessary to locate parents through mental health agencies where they have been patients. While it may be unnecessary to tell the parent specifically that his children are at high risk for a psychiatric disorder, even indicating that the research is to focus on the relationship between child and adult psychopathology may arouse anxiety and may affect the parent's behavior toward his children. One possible approach is to have therapists raise the possibility of participation with their patients if they feel that it will not harm the patient or his relationship with his children. Another is to have the mental health agency send out inquiries to patients, asking them to return a signed form to the researchers if they would be willing to consider participating. Those who return the form are contacted for a fuller presentation of the study and asked for their consent to participation. Although the description of what the subjects will be asked to do must be as complete as for any other study, it may be deemed more harmful to detail the specific hypotheses than to describe the purpose in terms of research on child development in general. The importance of determining the developmental course of psychiatric disorders and of creating preventive interventions argues mightily for longitudinal high risk studies despite the difficulties raised for informed consent. However, in addition to informed consent, maintaining the confidentiality of personal data is essential in studies of children at risk, as discussed in the following section.

Confidentiality

Allowing teachers and others to know that children are at risk for psychopathology may create additional risks for the children, and revealing that members of a child's family are mentally ill could be a severe breach of confidence. When information about high-risk children must be obtained from teachers and others outside the family, elaborate precautions must be taken to prevent them from knowing why the children are being studied. As an example, in the Stony Brook High Risk Study of children having either a schizophrenic or depressed parent, the investigators first obtained parental consent and the consent of school boards to permit the gathering of information on high-risk children through their schools (Neale and Weintraub, 1975). However, in order to obtain teacher ratings on the target children, the teachers were asked to rate a number of "randomly selected" children, including the target child, and were not told the specific purpose of the research nor that one child was of special interest.

Clearly, any research in which data about particular subjects may stigmatize them must include stringent safeguards on confidentiality. However, almost any data about people, no matter how trivial it may seem, can prove harmful or embarrassing, or may unduly expose their private affairs. Consequently, care must be taken to keep data from being identified with the individuals on whom it was collected. One of the best safeguards is anonymity in the initial collection of data. When there is no need to know the names of subjects or to have data linked to names in any way, subjects should be identified only by a coding system and their names and other information that might identify them should not be recorded at all. Many studies in which data are collected only once on each subject do not require identifying individuals with particular responses. The signed consent forms obtained from subjects in such studies can be kept separate from the research data and there need be no way of linking the consent forms with the data.

Where subjects must be identified in order to follow them up for further study, care must be taken to separate the research data from the personal identification. When subjects' names are left on data sheets as they are processed, it is surprising how often the person sitting at the neighboring key punch, or walking by in the computer center, or working at the next desk in the office happens to know subjects whose names he notices. Moreover, innocent conversation about subjects can too often be overheard by people who know the subjects. A standard safeguard against having data identified with individual subjects is to label the data only by code and to keep in a separate location a master list or key which shows the code for each subject. In some cases, it may be desirable to have a double-key system whereby the code on the list of identifiable subjects is an intermediate code which is translated into a second code by means of another key kept in a separate location. The data are then labeled with the second code. This means that anybody who has only the list of subjects and the initial code on that list cannot match the data with individually identified subjects. Needless to say, any data on which individuals are identified by name should be kept under lock and key and the identifying information should be destroyed as soon as it is no longer needed. Furthermore, write-ups of research reports should not make it possible to recognize individual subjects, even if their identities are not explicitly revealed. For example, if there were but one 5-year-old boy in a research nursery school, the boy might be too easily identifiable to single out for detailed description, even anonymously. Reports of case histories must be written with special care to prevent the subjects from being identified and permission for publication of such reports should be obtained from the subjects if there is any chance they will be recognized.

The question of what happens to confidential data after it has been obtained raises other issues as well. Because research records—unlike lawyer–client records—are not protected from court subpoena, it may be impossible to guarantee confidentiality against court orders. While most data collected by developmental researchers are unlikely to be subpoenaed, there are certainly cases in which developmental researchers study behavior—such as delinquency and drug abuse—which may make them aware of law violations. The best safeguard of confidentiality for such data would, of course, be anonymity. There are also situations in which researchers may inadvertently learn of danger to subjects or other people. Here dilemmas arise not because of demands for data obtained in confidence, but because the researcher may have to decide whether to violate confidentiality in the service of other ethical imperatives. Discovery of evidence that a child subject was being abused by his parents, for example, could place a researcher in the position of having to decide whether he should report the parents to the police. Even if it seemed that the child was in danger and the researcher was convinced that he had to violate confidentiality, how best to protect the child might present further dilemmas. Despite the increasing severity of laws against child abuse, the legal options typically offer little real protection. Reporting parents to the police may make them still more dangerous to the child or may cause the child to be passed from one foster home to another. A direct approach to the parents might be a possibility, as at least some abusive parents welcome help with what they recognize to be a serious problem. Before any action is taken, however, it is helpful to consult professionals who have direct experience with such cases to determine what remedies are available in the community.

A somewhat different dilemma can be posed when a researcher discovers that a subject needs treatment or help not involving legal questions. Because most research procedures do not yield individual diagnoses, research data suggestive of psychopathology should rarely be used to draw conclusions about individual subjects. However, a researcher may unexpectedly obtain data that he strongly believes will benefit a subject. If using the data for the subject's benefit violates the terms of the original consent, then the subject or parent who gave consent should be consulted before anything is done. The longitudinal studies of high-risk children are especially likely to place researchers in the position of detecting psychopathology in the subjects. In the Stony Brook Study, this is handled by routinely sending parents an assessment of results on their children and offering help in getting treatment if any problems seem severe enough (Neale and Weintraub, 1975). Because current methods for diagnosing and treating psychopathology in children are of unproven worth, it must be asked whether the risks of stigmatizing the child and alarming the parents are not greater than the potential benefits of this practice. However, considering that the stigma and anxiety are probably present already, sharing relevant information with the parents may be the most defensible option.

Ethical Implications of Particular Types of Research

It should be clear by now that the principles of independent review, informed consent, and confidentiality provide general guidelines to the ethical conduct of research, but no definitive formulas for all situations. We now turn to issues beyond independent review, informed consent, and confidentiality.

Risks and discomforts.   The first issue concerns risk and discomfort to subjects. Independent review and informed consent are safeguards against excessive foreseeable risks and discomforts. Yet, if no risks or discomforts were ever permissible, the risks and discomforts involved in most medical treatment would make medical research nearly impossible. The discomfort that some children feel when asked to do school work would also preclude much research on educational curricula and cognitive development. Where prevailing practices in such areas as medical treatment and education already involve some risk or discomfort, research procedures must be assessed in terms of whether they significantly increase the risks or discomforts and whether such increases are offset by potential benefits to the subjects. Because the efficacy of many traditional therapeutic and educational practices has not been truly demonstrated, research on new approaches that do not significantly increase risk or discomfort is at least as justifiable as continued use of accepted but unproven approaches.

On the other hand, research procedures may carry unforeseen risks. This can be especially true with child subjects who are liable to misinterpret situations in unanticipated ways. The previously cited example of the child who thought the GSR electrodes were draining blood from his hands argues strongly for explaining the research situation as fully as possible and letting the subject ask questions about it. Care should also be taken to screen out potential subjects who are unduly anxious or who may be at additional risk for other reasons. However, even when this has been done, a debriefing should be provided wherein the researcher explains anything that may have given rise to anxiety or misinterpretation and the subject is free to ask further questions. The main emphasis in debriefing child subjects should be less on trying to convey all the details of the research—which may confuse them—than on insuring that they are not left with any negative feelings about themselves or the situation.

Inducement of unethical behavior by subjects.   Behavioral researchers have sometimes created situations which invited unethical behavior on the part of subjects so that such behavior could be studied. In one of the best known of these studies, Milgram (1963) led subjects to believe that they were administering electric shocks to another person. Contrary to the predictions of psychiatrists Milgram consulted prior to the research, many normal adults willingly administered intense shocks when told to do so, despite cries of anguish from the purported victim.

Milgram's findings on people's willingness to hurt others at the urging of the experimenter have gained wide publicity. However, the use of deception to induce unethical behavior and the possible effects of embarrassment and guilt on the subjects have also proven highly controversial. Baumrind (1964), for example, argued that it "is potentially harmful to a subject to commit, in the course of an experiment, acts which he himself considers unworthy, particularly when he has been entrapped into committing such acts by an individual he has reason to trust" (pp. 422–423). Although Milgram provided a debriefing in which the purported victim of the shock—actually a confederate— demonstrated that he had not been shocked, Baumrind maintained that sensitive subjects would remain anxious, whereas cynical subjects would become even more alienated and distrustful.

Milgram (1964) countered with data from follow-up questionnaires showing that 84 percent of the subjects said they were glad to have participated, 15 percent had neutral feelings, and only 1.3 percent had negative feelings. A psychiatrist who independently interviewed a sample of Milgram's subjects a year after the original study found no evidence of harm (Errera, 1972). Most claimed to have enjoyed participating, although some reported extreme distress during the experiment. This distress had been completely dispelled by a letter from Milgram describing the purpose of the study and its findings. A few of the subjects accepted personal responsibility for their willingness to inflict pain and felt that the experiment had taught them something valuable about themselves.

Further research inspired by the Milgram controversy has shown that dehoaxing greatly affects subjects' subsequent anxiety and anger about having been induced to behave unethically. Using a Milgram-type situation, Ring, Wallston, and Corey (1970) found that college-student subjects to whom the deception was not revealed remained angrier at both themselves and the experimenter than did subjects to whom the deception was revealed in a debriefing. Those to whom the deception was revealed indicated no resentment about having been deceived and said they would be willing to participate again in similar studies. However, Baumrind's contention that such experiments might instill distrust of authority figures was borne out to some extent, as many of the subjects reported an increase in such distrust. Since the authority figure in the experiment had induced the subjects to behave unethically, increasing resistance to this type of obedience may not necessarily be an undesirable outcome. The social implications of the development of obedience to authority are certainly important enough to warrant further research, although increasingly stringent constraints on deception may require new methods of study.

Several factors preclude the use of Milgram-type situations with young children. One is that pressure by an adult to hurt another person may have longer lasting effects in either encouraging antisocial behavior or in creating guilt. A second is that children are far less likely to comprehend the rationale for deception in the name of research. A third is that they are unlikely to benefit from self-knowledge or knowledge of the overall research results. However, other forms of deception have been used to study antisocial behavior and moral development in children. Recall the Liebert and Baron (1972) study of the effects of violent television, described in chapter 8. After having watched either violent or nonviolent television, children were led to believe that they could either help or hurt another (fictitious) child by pushing certain buttons. Although the experimenter neither encouraged nor discouraged pushing the "hurt" button, exposure to violent television increased children's use of the hurt button. Was it unethical to place children in this situation? Parents brought their children to the study in response to advertisements. The procedure was fully explained and the parents' written consent was obtained. The fact that no parents refused consent indicates that they did not expect the situation to subject their children to significant risks or discomforts. Should the deception have been explained to the children in a dehoaxing? Since the children were not pressured to push the hurt button and they did not hear any signs of pain from the purported victim, they were not placed in a conflict situation like Milgram's subjects. Considering the lack of stress and the lack of ability of 5- to 9-year olds to comprehend the rationale for the deception, a dehoaxing to reveal it would not seem necessary.

Another approach to studying the development of antisocial behavior has been to create a situation in which a child can cheat to give himself extra points on a game, ostensibly without being detected. The game is designed so that only one score can legitimately be attained. Children who report higher scores for themselves are assumed to have cheated and cheating is then assessed in relation to other variables (e.g., Nelson, Grinder, and Mutterer, 1969). Situations such as this are likely to place little stress on subjects, especially if the incentives to cheat are not large and the cheating is never exposed. However, the deception involved is a serious one and difficult to reconcile with ethical principles of research. Dehoaxing is not likely to be beneficial, as it would set an example of adult deceit, as well as revealing to the subjects that their cheating was detected. The importance of understanding the development of antisocial behavior may in rare cases justify deceptions to study such behavior, but the researcher bears a heavy burden to demonstrate that socially valuable knowledge can be obtained only in this way. Even if the research can be justified, failure to obtain fully informed consent from the subjects' parents would be a serious ethical breach.

Intervention research. Apart from issues raised by particular methodologies, a larger ethical issue has been raised in recent years by research intended to enhance the development of disadvantaged children. Such research has been criticized for its ethnocentric implication that poor children and their environments are defective because they lack certain middle-class characteristics. Even if a researcher does not hold a bias of this sort, a commitment to developing new intervention programs does imply a judgment that the child's current environment needs improvement and that manipulation of his environment is justified. Despite the recent rise of ethnic pride among many disadvantaged groups, it is apparent that failure to master basic academic skills severely limits the options available to the developing child in our society, no matter how the values of his subculture differ from those of the dominant culture.

As most parents of disadvantaged children want them to succeed in school, there is typically no conflict between parents' desires and the ultimate goal of intervention programs. However, questions can arise around the degree to which the minimally educated parents of disadvantaged children can understand the technical and theoretical aspects of intervention research and around the degree of control they should exercise over such programs. The control of Follow Through by local parents and school officials made it virtually impossible to validly compare the various models in the Planned Variation Study described in chapter 8. As the scope of intervention has been expanded to include efforts at changing mothers' behavior, the question of informed consent has become still more intricate. Susan Gray (1971), one of the pioneers of intervention research, has argued that intervention researchers should inform the mother as well as they can and then work with her to increase her understanding of how to achieve her own goals for her child, without raising false hopes. Gray thus regards informed consent as involving a collaborative approach with parents. Such an approach, of course, requires great skill and tact to avoid alienating or manipulating the parents. The importance of systematic comparison of various approaches also requires that researchers be able to communicate to parents the need for such procedures as random assignment.

Another major question raised in recent years is whether efforts to help disadvantaged children should be directed instead at reforming the entire social system that permits poverty to exist. There is no doubt that most intervention researchers would favor immediate abolition of poverty, but their research efforts are based on the assumption that the poverty cycle can best be broken in the long run by helping disadvantaged children develop better skills for helping themselves. Furthermore, when done with appropriate sensitivity, individual testing in the course of research may be directly beneficial to disadvantaged children, as it provides opportunities for one-to-one interaction with an adult who encourages the child to use his abilities. Probably because they receive little individual adult attention, young disadvantaged children are often eager to be tested and this may help to prepare them for the testing they will inevitably face in school.

Drawing Socially Significant Conclusions from Research

Research on behavioral development can never be done in a social vacuum. The involvement of people with diverse viewpoints in the funding, ethical review, and implementation of research, plus the communication of findings, place all research in a social context. Furthermore, the efforts of developmentalists to make their work more socially relevant and their increasing involvement in mission-oriented research oblige them to be sensitive to the effects of their research. Researchers may have no intention of causing harm, but they must consider the ways in which the results of their work can be harmful and how the risks of harm can be reduced.

Insofar as knowledge represents power, it can be used for harmful ends. Research on nuclear fission for peaceful purposes can yield knowledge that will be used to build destructive weapons. Recombinant DNA research may play a crucial role in the fight against cancer, but the artificial creation of genetic material may engender new strains of disease against which no defenses exist. Should such research be carried on? The risk of harm from behavioral findings stems primarily from the attitudes and policies that conclusions from research may support. Consequently, the behavioral researcher must be cautious in the conclusions he draws from data, the way in which he presents them, and the claims he makes for his evidence.

The ethical constraints on interpretations of behavioral data are largely congruent with the guidelines for scientific inference outlined in chapter 4. In particular, a clear distinction must be maintained between *ideas* generated in the context of discovery and *findings* obtained in the context of confirmation. Too often, there is a blurring of the distinction between a researcher's *belief* and the *evidence* with which he supports the belief. As discussed in chapters 2 and 3, empirical evidence is inextricably intertwined with the conceptual and methodological paradigms of those who gather it, but, when socially significant conclusions can be drawn from a researcher's work, he must be extremely careful to distinguish between the evidence and the implications of such evidence. The more harmful the possible implications, the more carefully must the researcher weigh the evidence supporting them, the desirability of gathering more evidence before drawing conclusions, and the ways of communicating the conclusions so as to minimize the potential harm. He should also be prepared to correct distortions of his conclusions by others, both inadvertent and deliberate.

The controversy over genetic bases for racial differences in IQ will be used to illustrate the ethical issues raised in drawing socially significant conclusions from developmental research. The focus here will be on the ethical implications of the stands taken, rather than on definitively answering the substantive questions about IQ and race. However, we will also consider an example of research that represents an empirical alternative to protracted argument on this difficult issue.

Arthur Jensen's Manifesto

It was on the assumption that a brief intervention could greatly enhance intellectual development that Project Head Start was launched as a summer program in 1965. When it was found that brief interventions had little lasting effect, Head Start was expanded to a full-year program and Project Follow Through was initiated to extend the intervention effort through third grade. However, in a paper that was to rekindle the nature–nurture controversy, Arthur Jensen (1969a) suggested that genetic limitations on the ability of the disadvantaged, primarily blacks, had doomed compensatory education to failure. Needless to say, Jensen's article provoked a storm of reaction. The *Harvard Educational Review*, which had invited Jensen's original paper, subsequently published critiques together with Jensen's (1969b) response. Thereafter, a great many reviews, critiques, rebuttals, counter rebuttals, and news stories appeared elsewhere, including two books by Jensen (1972, 1973) and a book by Leon Kamin (1974) aimed at discrediting Jensen's position. Nonbehavioral scientists, such as physicist William Shockley, have also joined the fray on one side or the other, but we will focus primarily on the issues raised for developmental researchers by the opposing stands of Jensen and Kamin.

Ethical implications of Jensen's approach.   Jensen's (1969a) paper begins, "Compensatory education has been tried and it apparently has failed" (p. 2). Certainly not an inflammatory statement by itself, this nevertheless forms one basis for Jensen's argument that genetic rather than environmental determinants are responsible for differences between blacks and whites in IQ and scholastic achievement. Suppose that, prior to the invention of the Salk vaccine, the following statement was made: "Prevention of polio has been tried and it apparently has failed." Would this be taken seriously as an argument that polio is inherently unpreventible? Compared to the length of time, the amount of coordinated effort, and the level of basic research and theory that preceded such scientific accomplishments as the Salk vaccine, there was virtually no basis for judging the potential success of compensatory education as of 1968, when Jensen wrote his conclusions. It should have been clear to any expert in the field that, despite the great fanfare accorded antipoverty programs, there was little well-supported theory to build on, almost no experience in translating developmental theory and methods into action programs, few people with the skills or commitment to implement intervention programs, political obstacles to careful objective research, and insufficient time for longitudinal comparisons of programs. While anyone is entitled to express his opinion, the researcher speaking as an expert must be as judicious in dismissing a particular hypothesis for want of positive evidence as he is in arguing for acceptance of a hypothesis, especially when the conclusions stigmatize particular groups. For an expert whose credentials give his opinion weight with nonexperts to have dismissed compensatory education as an apparent failure on the basis of the evidence available in 1968 and to build on this dismissal an argument for genetically determined racial differences in intelligence certainly strains the standard of judiciousness.

In addition to the question of whether compensatory education had been given a fair enough trial to be declared a failure, a question might also be raised about what it had failed to do. If the goal of compensatory education is to eliminate poverty, then it will be decades before its effects can be judged in terms of the economic success of its recipients. Because IQ scores have been found to predict scholastic achievement which, in turn, is assumed to be necessary for economic achievement, the IQ was the most widely used measure of the short-term effectiveness of the first compensatory education programs, and it was the absence of large or lasting gains in IQ that Jensen stressed as evidence for the failure of compensatory education.

Having selected IQ as the operational measure of general ability, Jensen went on to review the evidence for genetic influences on this measure. Here, years of research provided a far better basis for judgment about genetic effects than did research on compensatory education. Numerous studies had shown higher correlations between the IQs of identical twins than fraternal twins. Furthermore, the few existing studies of the IQs of adopted children and their biological parents showed correlations suggestive of genetic influences, despite differences in environments. From his survey of the correlations between the IQs of people differing in genetic relationship, Jensen concluded that approximately 80 percent of the variance in IQ is due to genetic differences among individuals, while 20 percent is due to environmental differences.

Without going into the details of how the proportion of genetic variance (*heritability*) in a trait is computed, it should be pointed out that this figure depends not merely on the biochemical mechanisms by which genes affect behavior, but on the range of variation of both genotypes and environments in the population for which the figure is computed. In concluding that the heritability of IQ is about .80, Jensen (1969a) states "This represents probably the best single overall estimate of the heritability of measured intelligence that we can make. But... this is an average value of (heritability) about which there is some dispersion of values, depending on such variables as the particular tests used, the population sampled, and sampling error" (p. 51). Despite Jensen's care in pointing out the relative nature of heritability estimates, his use of .80 as the "best estimate" for the heritability of measured intelligence implies that intelligence per se has a specific heritability. Because any figure for heritability depends not just on the genetic and environmental influences on a trait but on the range of variation in genetic and environmental influences within the group studied, it is simply not correct to speak of the heritability of intelligence. The various figures obtained for the heritability of intelligence in different studies cannot be regarded as random variations around a "true" heritability, unless all the studies were done on random samples from a single population with a specific dispersion of genotypes and environments. If such were the case, the heritability estimates for each sample would represent estimates of the heritability of intelligence in the population sampled. However, because the studies of heritability of intelligence test scores have been carried out in various countries, at various times, using different tests, and with subjects obtained in different ways, their heritability estimates cannot be regarded as random variations around some true figure for a single common population. Instead, they are better regarded as representing the different heritabilities of different test scores in the different groups studied.

When viewed in this way, the *range* of heritabilities is broad, being from .41 to .93 in 17 studies comparing identical and fraternal twins alone (cf. Achenbach, 1974, p. 234). Nearly all the relevant studies have yielded positive and significant estimates for the heritability of IQ scores, but there is no way to glean from them a single "best estimate" for the heritability of IQ. If instead of a "best estimate," one seeks a figure that summarizes the distribution of findings, then figures from about .60 to Jensen's figure of .80 can be justified on various grounds. The difference between inferring a best estimate for the heritability of IQ and choosing a representative figure to summarize the distribution of findings may seem slight, but it takes on great significance for Jensen's argument.

The significance of employing .80 as an estimate for the heritability of IQ grows as Jensen builds his case for genetic determination of racial differences in IQ. Because all the data on heritability of IQ were collected on northern European and American whites, Jensen acknowledges that it is not necessarily valid for groups having different genetic and environmental characteristics. However, upon reviewing findings that the mean IQ of blacks is lower than that of whites, he concludes (p. 82):

> There is an increasing realization among students of the psychology of the disadvantaged that the discrepancy in their average performance cannot be completely or directly attributed to discrimination or inequalities in education. It seems not unreasonable, in view of the fact that intelligence variation has a large genetic component, to hypothesize that genetic factors may play a part in this picture. But such an hypothesis is anathema to many social scientists. The idea that the lower average intelligence and scholastic performances of Negroes could involve, not only environmental, but also genetic, factors has indeed been strongly denounced (e.g., Pettigrew, 1964). But it has been neither contradicted nor discredited by evidence.
>
> The fact that a reasonable hypothesis has not been rigorously proved does not mean that it should be summarily dismissed. It only means that we need more appropriate research for putting it to the test. I believe such definitive research is entirely possible but has not yet been done. So all we are left with are various lines of evidence, no one of which is definitive alone, but which, viewed all together, make it a not unreasonable hypothesis that genetic factors are strongly implicated in the average Negro–white intelligence difference. The preponderance of the evidence is, in my opinion, less consistent with a strictly environmental hypothesis than with a genetic hypothesis, which, of course, does not exclude the influence of environment or its interaction with genetic factors.

Certainly a cautiously worded conclusion, although Jensen then goes on to strengthen it by criticizing environmental explanations and citing further evidence for the inferior performance of blacks on measures of ability. He also reviews evidence from his own studies that lower SES children (not necessarily black) are more inferior on tests of abstract reasoning than associative learning and proposes that intervention programs should focus on training specific skills by instructional techniques that do not require abstract abilities.

Cautious though it sounds, Jensen's ". . . not unreasonable hypothesis that genetic factors are strongly implicated in the average Negro–white intelligence difference" had immediate repercussions. In "A letter from the South" reprinted in the spring, 1969, *Harvard Educational Review* (pp. 440–41), William Brazziel reported that:

> a scant five days after Arthur Jensen made headlines in Virginia papers regarding inferiority of black people as measured by IQ tests, defense attor-

neys and their expert witnesses fought a suit in Federal District Court to integrate Greensville and Caroline County schools. Their main argument was that "white teachers could not understand the Nigra mind" and that the Nigra children should be admitted to the white schools on the basis of standardized tests. Those who failed to make a certain score would be assigned to all black remedial schools where "teachers who understood them could work with them." The defense in this case quoted heavily from the theories of white intellectual supremacy as expounded by Arthur Jensen.

It will help not one bit for Jensen or the HER editorial board to protest that they did not intend for Jensen's article to be used in this way. For in addition to superiority in performing conceptual cluster tricks on test sheets, the hard line segregationist is also vastly superior in his ability to bury qualifying phrases and demurrers and in his ability to distort and slant facts and batter his undereducated clientele into a complete state of hysteria where race is concerned.

As Scarr-Salapatek (1971) later commented, Jensen's cautious wording may have been like screaming "FIRE! . . . I think" in a crowded theater. Any damage the message may have done was unlikely to be mitigated by the qualifications accompanying it. But should a researcher withhold a hypothesis until it is either confirmed with certainty or until it no longer offends anyone? Where can the line be drawn between censorship—self-imposed or otherwise—and ethical constraints on publishing potentially harmful conclusions based on inadequate data? The case may become clearer as we consider Jensen's later statements. Although agreeing that heritability estimates for the IQ of whites say nothing about the genetic basis for differences between the mean IQs of whites and blacks, Jensen (1969b) refers without qualification to "the high heritability of intelligence" (p. 460) and poses the following as an abstract problem in quantitative genetics:

> Given two populations (1 and 2) whose means on a particular characteristic differ significantly by x amount, and given the heritability (H_1 and H_2) of the characteristic in each of the two populations, the *probability* that the two populations differ from one another genotypically as well as phenotypically is some monotonically increasing function of the magnitudes of H_1 and H_2. Such probabilistic statements are commonplace in all branches of science. It seems that only when we approach the question of genetic race differences do some geneticists talk as though only one or two probability values is possible, either 0 or 1. Scientific advancement in any field would be in a sorry state if this restriction were a universal rule. Would [a geneticist] argue, for example, that there is no difference in the *probability* that two groups differ genetically where H for the trait in question is .90 in each group as against the case where H is .10? In the absence of absolute certainty, are not probabilistic answers still preferable to complete ignorance?

Stated thusly, Jensen's argument implies that (a) IQ has high heritability in both whites and blacks, and (b) concluding that genetic differences probably account for racial differences in IQ is "preferable to
complete ignorance." Unfortunately, as Jensen had previously acknowledged, there was no evidence for high heritability of IQ among any
blacks, let alone disadvantaged blacks. Even if there were such evidence,
it would say nothing about the basis for differences in mean scores for
two groups differing environmentally. Environmental differences between groups can greatly affect the mean value of traits that have high
heritability within each group, and environmental changes can change
that mean value. Is it thus defensible to pose the options so that the
alternative to agreeing with Jensen's "probabilistic statement" (based on
heritability of IQ in whites alone) is to remain in complete ignorance?
Jensen himself repeatedly calls for more research on the topic and this
may indeed be a more appropriate solution than either of the alternatives
he poses.

Reactions to Jensen

In addition to the published attacks on Jensen's views, attempts were
made to have him fired from his Berkeley professorship and to prevent
him from voicing his views in lectures and debates (cf. Jensen, 1972,
1973). Others who expressed similar views, such as William Shockley
and Richard Herrnstein, were also subjected to harassment and threats
on campuses where they were invited to speak. The attempts to suppress
Jensen's views by force not only violated the principle of free speech, but
won him additional publicity and sympathy. However, it is important to
consider the more subtle ethical issues raised by the attacks of researchers who do not question Jensen's right to express his views. Since
Leon Kamin (1974) has devoted an entire book to criticizing Jensen's
position and himself adopts perhaps the most radically opposed position, we shall consider the ethical implications of his approach.

Ethical implications of Kamin's approach. Like Jensen, Kamin
begins his manifesto with a conclusion: "There exist no data which
should lead a prudent man to accept the hypothesis that IQ test scores
are in any degree heritable" (p. 1). He further concludes that IQ tests
have "served as an instrument of oppression against the poor—dressed
in the trappings of science, rather than politics" (p. 2). He supports the
second conclusion by quoting early mental testers to the effect that
standardized tests showed large proportions of nonNordic immigrants
to the United States to be retarded. Because the racist statements of some
of the early test developers were used to support the 1924 limitations on
immigration, and because disproportionate numbers of the poor con-

tinue to obtain low test scores, Kamin maintains that IQ tests have served as instruments of oppression. Not mentioned are efforts of early mental testers to identify and encourage exceptional ability in all social strata. In a longitudinal study of high IQ children begun in 1921, for example, Lewis Terman included children of a wide socioeconomic range and his findings on the life success of these children helped dispel the myth that bright children are social misfits (Terman and Oden, 1959).

After documenting the racist views of some of the early mental testers, Kamin devotes most of his book to assailing the evidence for the heritability of IQ in the northern European and American whites on whom nearly all the heritability research had been done. In checking the primary sources employed by Jensen, Kamin found much to criticize. Probably the severest criticism—and by other accounts the most deserved (Loehlin, Lindzey, and Spuhler, 1975)—is directed at the work of Sir Cyril Burt. For over five decades, Burt argued for the heritability of intelligence and supported his arguments with reports of correlations on ever increasing numbers of subjects having various degrees of genetic relationship. Unfortunately, Burt's descriptions of his methods are so careless as to raise suspicions about his results. It appears that the scores he employed were not always the actual scores obtained by the subjects on standardized tests, but estimates of subjects' intelligence based on interviewers' impressions or on test scores "adjusted" in light of other information about the subjects. His studies cannot, therefore, be given much weight in the heritability debate.

Beside Burt's, there have been three other studies of identical twins reared apart, all of which described their procedures in detail and reported significant correlations between intelligence test scores of co-twins reared apart (Juel-Nielsen, 1965; Newman, Freeman, and Holzinger, 1937; Shields, 1962). Here Kamin criticizes the evidence for heritability on the grounds that the twins' environments may not have been entirely dissimilar. However, even if the environments of twins reared apart were correlated to some degree because the twins were raised by relatives or were placed with families of similar SES, it is difficult to see how an exclusively environmental explanation could account for correlations between the separated twins' scores ranging from .67 to .77 in three studies. By comparison, the correlations between scores for *fraternal* twins reared *together* ranged from .42 to .72 in 14 studies, with a median of .62 (cf. Achenbach, 1974, p. 234). If there is no genetic variance in the test scores for the white populations sampled, why should the correlations for identical twins raised in *different* homes be larger than most of the correlations for fraternal twins raised in the *same* homes?

Another criticism Kamin levels at all three studies is that there may have been correlations between the age of the subjects and their test scores, because inadequate standardization could have permitted IQ means to differ with age. Since co-twins are of the same age, the high correlation between their scores may be due to their age similarities rather than their genetic similarities. As evidence for this possibility, Kamin reports correlations between age and score in various subgroups within the studies. Most of the correlations he cites are large, although they vary in direction according to the age and sex of the subgroups. However, the subsamples of twin pairs on which Kamin computed correlations were very small, and he fails to report the much smaller correlations in the other age and sex groups within the studies (cf. Loehlin, et al. 1975, pp. 294–5). Furthermore, the similarity of co-twins in age and IQ makes it likely that a correlation between age and IQ will be found when both members of twin pairs are included in the computations, as Kamin did. But this could be because the similarity in IQs of identical twins is due to their genetic similarity rather than their similarity in age. Basing the correlation between age and IQ on just one member of each pair would have been more appropriate, but then it would be obvious that the numbers within each group selected by Kamin would be too small for any meaningful conclusions.

Kamin has also made much of errors in Jensen's paper, although the errors appear to have little bearing on the case for heritability of IQ among the white groups studied and no bearing on Jensen's conclusions about racial differences, since none of the data were on heritability in nonwhites or on between-groups differences in heritability. Any inaccuracies in the reporting and interpretation of research are deplorable, but opinions as to whether Jensen's were any more serious or deliberately misleading than Kamin's are likely to depend on one's position on the heritability issue as a whole. While it is clear that Jensen's argument for the genetic inferiority of blacks is not supported by data and carries more obvious potential for harm than Kamin's argument, it also appears that Kamin makes misleading use of data to show that they are consistent only with an environmental interpretation of IQ differences, even among whites. In restating the conclusion with which he began his book, Kamin says (p. 176):

> The burden of proof falls upon those who wish to assert the implausible proposition that the way in which a child answers questions devised by a mental tester is determined by an unseen genotype. That burden is not lessened by the repeated assertions of the testers over the past 70 years. Where the data are at best ambiguous, and where environment is clearly shown to have effect, the assumption of genetic determination of I.Q. variation in any degree is unwarranted. The prudent conclusion seems clear. There are no data sufficient for us to reject the hypothesis that differences in the way in which people answer the questions asked by testers are determined by their palpably different life experiences.

Why should the proposition that IQ test performance is determined by an "unseen genotype" be any more implausible than the proposition that differences in test performance "are determined by palpably different life experiences?" A great many characteristics are believed to be at least partially determined by unseen genotypes. The fact that these characteristics are also affected by the environment does not make the assumptions of genetic differences any less tenable. Like Jensen, Kamin insists on a choice between genetic and environmental determination, but he holds that failure to prove genetic determination forces acceptance of the null hypothesis that IQ is determined exclusively by the environment.

Kamin ends with a lengthy quote from John B. Watson to restore "to us a psychological tradition [of behaviorism] richer and truer for our time and place than the strait-jacketed ideology of the mental testers" (p.178). Whether Watson's ideology is any less strait-jacketed than that of the mental testers is open to question. However, it is no less an *ideology*, with its own theoretical and methodological paradigm, and the "palpable experience" to which it appeals for explanation is no less an inferential abstraction than the "unseen genotype" to which geneticists appeal. Nor is the hypothesis of exclusively environmental determination a "null hypothesis" which must be accepted merely because doubt is cast on the hypothesis of exclusively genetic determination.

Subsequent Evidence on Race and IQ

It is unfortunate that the nature–nurture debate shed so much heat and so little light on the issue that really aroused interest outside the research community—the question of innate differences in ability. However, the debate did inspire new research to answer this question much more directly than any of the fiercely debated previous work. One of the most significant contributions has been made through research on black children adopted by upper-middle-class whites. As with most research, not all possible outcomes would be equally unambiguous. If the IQs of the adopted black children were close to those of the white mean, this would clearly argue that, given environments like those of whites, black children are not genetically handicapped in IQ test performance. On the other hand, if the IQs of the adopted black children were significantly below those of the white mean, this would not unambiguously argue for genetic inferiority, because environmental handicaps, such as arise from being black in a white family or from possibly poorer intrauterine and perinatal conditions, could be responsible.

Through agencies specializing in interracial adoptions, Scarr and Weinberg (1976) located 130 children who had one or two black biological parents but were adopted by white families. Only children who were at least 4 years old were included because IQs obtained prior to that age have low correlations with later IQ. All the children and their adoptive parents took individual IQ tests, and achievement test data were obtained from the schools of the older children. The mean IQ of the adopted children was found to be 106.3, which is above the mean of the national norms on the IQ tests and well above the means typically reported for disadvantaged black children. Despite the fact that the mean age of placement with the adoptive parents was about 18 months and the average age of the children was only 6 years, 2 months, this length of exposure to the upper-middle-class environment produced IQs well within the average range. Furthermore, the children's performance on school achievement tests was commensurate with their IQs, ranging from the 55th to the 57th percentile of national achievement norms for reading, mathematics, and vocabulary.

The findings certainly argue against Jensen's thesis that black–white differences are determined mainly by genetic factors. But does this evidence for a strong environmental effect negate the possibility of genetic influences? To assess the possible influence of genetic factors, Scarr and Weinberg compared the correlations of the children's IQs with characteristics of their adoptive parents and with characteristics of their biological parents. The correlation of the children's IQs with those of their adoptive mothers was .17 and with those of their adoptive fathers .18; the correlation with adoptive mothers' education was .22 and with adoptive fathers' education .34; the correlation with fathers' occupational status was .01 and with family income .00. On the other hand, the correlation between the children's IQs and the education of their biological mothers was .31 and of their biological fathers, .45. The finding of higher correlations between the adopted children's IQs and the abilities (as indexed by education, since IQs were not available) of their biological parents than of their adoptive parents argues for genetic influences on the rank ordering of IQs within the upper-middle-class environments to which the children were exposed.

The Scarr and Weinberg study will not by itself end the heritability debate. Several of the findings leave plenty of room for controversy. The 25 white adopted children among the families who adopted the black children had a mean IQ of 111.5 compared to that of 106.3 for the black children. The 21 adopted children of other races, mainly oriental and American Indian, had a mean IQ of 99.9. The adopted children who had two black parents obtained a lower mean IQ than those who had one white parent (usually the mother). Differences among the various subgroups in age of testing, age of adoption, and educational status of the biological and adoptive parents make it difficult to draw conclusions about the interactions among all these variables. Yet the findings cast immeasurably more light on a difficult and controversial issue than did all the preceding debate.

Summary

Although increasing concern for privacy and the protection of individual rights makes past practice an inadequate guide for the future, several basic principles have evolved for protecting the subjects of behavioral research. These include *independent review* of research proposals by people who have no vested interest in the research; *informed consent* by the subjects or their guardians; and *confidentiality* of all data identifiable with individual subjects. These principles provide general guidelines for most research, but they do not provide precise formulas for resolving all the ethical dilemmas that arise. Consequently, the researcher must weigh the potential advantages and disadvantages to his subjects in deciding on a particular course of action. Especially with children and other dependent groups, the researcher's responsibility for protecting subjects goes far beyond the requirements of independent review, informed consent, and confidentiality. The use of deception, the inducement of negative emotional states and unethical behavior, observations under naturalistic conditions, studies of high-risk groups, the discovery of criminal or dangerous situations, and intervention research all create special dilemmas for developmental researchers.

In addition to protection of subjects, developmental researchers must also be sensitive to the ethical issues raised by drawing socially significant conclusions from research. Scientific guidelines for objectively distinguishing between evidence and its theoretical implications, for appraising the internal and external validity of findings, and for drawing conclusions from data become all the more important when the conclusions may have harmful effects. The more harmful the possible implications of the conclusions, the more carefully must the researcher weigh the evidence, the desirability of gathering more evidence before drawing conclusions, and the ways of communicating conclusions so as to minimize harm. The debate over genetic bases for racial differences in IQ has raised ethical problems of particular intensity. Jensen's argument for genetic determination of differences between blacks and whites in mean IQ was based on little relevant evidence and had the harmful effect of stigmatizing blacks. On the other hand, some of the rebuttals of Jensen were also based on questionable use of research data. Defenders of both extreme hereditarian and environmentalist positions have presented the alternatives in either–or fashion inconsistent with the current state of knowledge and with a scientific approach to acquiring further knowledge. Subsequent empirical research has, in fact, demonstrated the fallaciousness of dogmatically posing the alternatives in either–or terms.

Appendix

A-1: Partial Correlation

THE PURPOSE of partial correlation is to remove from the correlation between two variables the effects of one or more other variables that may be contributing to this correlation. For example, suppose we find that scores on a test of impulsive vs. reflective cognitive style correlate .60 with reading achievement in elementary school children, such that reflective children tend to have higher reading scores than impulsive children. Suppose we also find that scores on the test of impulsivity–reflectivity correlate .70 with chronological age (CA) and that reading achievement correlates .80 with CA. Because impulsivity–reflectivity and reading performance both correlate substantially with CA, it is possible that the correlation between impulsivity–reflectivity and reading performance is merely due to the fact that older children happen to be more reflective *and* read better, rather than to any causal relationship between impulsivity–reflectivity and reading performance. In order to determine whether their joint correlations with CA indeed account for the correlation between impulsivity–reflectivity and reading, the effect of CA can be "partialled out" of the correlation between the two variables of interest. If their correlation remains significant after CA is partialled out, this means that their joint correlations with CA do not account for their correlation with each other—i.e., if all the subjects in the sample were of the same CA, impulsivity–reflectivity would still correlate significantly with reading performance.

To compute the partial correlation of two variables with the effects of a third variable removed, let r_{12} = the correlation between the two variables of interest; r_{13} = the correlation of one of the variables with the variable to be partialled out; and r_{23} = the correlation of the second variable with the variable to be partialled out. With the partial correlation designated as $r_{12.3}$, substitute the correlations between each pair of variables in the following formula:

$$r_{12.3} = \frac{r_{12} - r_{13}\, r_{23}}{\sqrt{1 - r_{13}^2}\,\sqrt{1 - r_{23}^2}}.$$

If the correlation between impulsivity–reflectivity and reading $=.60$, that between impulsivity–reflectivity and CA$=.70$, and that between reading and CA$=.80$, the substitutions would be:

$$r_{12.3} = \frac{.60 - (.70)(.80)}{\sqrt{1 - .70^2}\,\sqrt{1 - .80^2}} = \frac{.04}{.428} = .09.$$

The partial correlation of .09 is far lower than the correlation of .60, indicating that most of the correlation between impulsivity–reflectivity and reading was due to their joint correlations with CA. The significance of the partial correlation can be tested with the following formula, employing the t table with $N - 3$ degrees of freedom:

$$t = \frac{r_{12.3}}{\sqrt{\dfrac{1 - r_{12.3}^2}{N - 3}}}$$

Two variables can be partialled out of a correlation by using the formula:

$$r_{12.34} = \frac{r_{12.3} - r_{14.3}\, r_{24.3}}{\sqrt{1 - r_{14.3}^2}\,\sqrt{1 - r_{24.3}^2}}.$$

The t test for the significance of a correlation with two variables partialled out would have $N - 4$ degrees of freedom. In order for partial correlation to be valid, both variables in the partial correlation must have a linear regression on the variable(s) partialled out. (See chapter 5 for a discussion of regression and Appendix A-2 for the statistic *eta* for assessing nonlinear regression.)

A-2: The Correlation Ratio

The correlation ratio, designated as η (Greek letter eta), reflects the accuracy with which one variable, Y, can be predicted from a second variable, X. It is the ratio of the variance in Y predictable from scores on X to the total variance in Y. If each subject has a score on X and a score on Y, then $\eta_{yx} = \sigma_y'/\sigma_y$ where: $Y' =$ the mean of Y scores obtained by all subjects who obtain a particular value of X; σ_y' is the standard deviation of these means; $\bar{Y}$ is the mean of all the Y scores; and σ_y is the standard deviation of all the Y scores.

To compute σ_y', the Y' is first computed for all subjects having the lowest value of X, then for the next value of X, and so on, until a Y' is obtained for the subjects having each value of X. If there are twelve values of X (about the smallest number for which η is useful), there will be a Y' for each of these twelve values. Next, the variance of Y' is computed by obtaining the difference between each Y' and $\bar{Y}$ and then squaring each of these differences, i.e., there will be one $(Y' - \bar{Y})^2$ for each of the twelve values of X. In order to weight each $(Y' - \bar{Y})^2$ according to the number of subjects on which Y' is based, each $(Y' - \bar{Y})^2$ is multiplied by n_g, the number of subjects in the group on which Y' was computed. Adding up the $n_g(Y' - \bar{Y})^2$ for each of twelve groups of subjects and dividing by the total number of subjects—i.e., taking $\Sigma \, n_g(Y' - \bar{Y})^2/N$—yields $\sigma^2_{y'}$, which is then divided by σ^2_y. The square root is taken to produce $\sigma_y'/\sigma_y = \eta_{YX}$. To compute the η for the prediction of X from Y, simply employ the same procedure to find $\sigma_x'/\sigma_x = \eta_{XY}$.

Statistical Significance of η

The statistical significance of a particular η is computed with the formula:

$$F = \frac{\eta^2/(G-1)}{(1-\eta^2)/(N-G)}$$

where G is the number of groups of subjects having different scores on the predictor variable, e.g., the twelve values of X in the example above, and N is the total number of subjects. The significance of the F is obtained from the ANOVA table for $(G-1)/(N-G)$ degrees of freedom.

Curvilinearity of Regression

Since the chief value of η is to reflect the strength of regression of one variable on another when this relationship is not linear, it is important to determine whether a particular η is significantly higher than r computed on the same data. This is done with the formula:

$$F = \frac{(\eta^2-r^2)/(G-2)}{(1-\eta^2)/(N-G)}$$

where G is the number of groups of subjects having different scores on the predictor variable and N is the total number of subjects. If F is significant with $(G-2)/(N-G)$ degrees of freedom, it can be concluded that the regression deviates significantly from linearity. If so, η, rather than r or a linear regression coefficient should be employed to represent the relationship between the variables.

A-3: Fisher's Exact Test

When a 2 × 2 contingency table is to be analyzed, but the number of subjects is too small for the chi square test, the p value for various outcomes can be obtained with Fisher's exact test. Let the cells of a 2 × 2 table be represented thusly:

	pass	fail
Group I	A	B
Group II	C	D

Groups I and II are independent groups of subjects who have been tested on a particular item. In order to determine whether the groups differ in the proportion who pass and fail the item, the number of Group I who pass is entered in Cell A and the number who fail in Cell B. The number of Group II who pass is entered in Cell C and the number who fail in Cell D. The exact chance probability of any particular combination of proportions for the two groups is obtained with the formula:

$$p = \frac{(A+B)!\ (C+D)!\ (A+C)!\ (B+D)!}{N!\ A!\ B!\ C!\ D!}$$

This probability, plus the probability of all combinations of proportions that differ more than the obtained proportions, are summed. In this way, the p obtained represents the chance probability of the obtained outcome plus more extreme outcomes.

Because the computational procedure is so laborious, tables are presented here for the sample sizes for which Fisher's test is most useful, i.e., those ranging up to 13 subjects in each group. With larger samples, the chi square using Yates' correction is generally satisfactory, although Fisher's tables have also been published for sample sizes up to 20 in each group (Pearson and Hartley, 1966).

To use Table A-3, follow these steps: (1). Locate in the two lefthand columns the combination of numbers corresponding to the numbers of subjects in Groups I and II of your data. For example, if one of your groups has 6 subjects and the other has 5, use the eighth row of the table. (2). If the number of subjects in the A cell of your data is listed in the column headed "A (or B)," look in the two columns headed "C (or D)" to

TABLE A-3. Two-tailed Significance Levels for 2 X 2 Contingency Tables.[a]

Group I	Group II	A (or B)	C (or D) $p=.05$	C (or D) $p=.01$	Group I	Group II	A (or B)	C (or D) $p=.05$	C (or D) $p=.01$
4	4	4	0	–	9	9	9	4	3
5	5	5	1	0			8	3	1
		4	0	–			7	1	0
	4	5	0	–			6	1	–
	3	5	0	–			5	0	–
6	6	6	1	0		8	9	3	2
		5	0	–			8	2	1
	5	6	0	0			7	1	0
		5	0	–			6	0	–
	4	6	0	0			5	0	–
		5	0	–		7	9	3	2
	3	6	0	–			8	2	0
7	7	7	2	1			7	1	0
		6	1	0			6	0	–
		5	0	–		6	9	2	1
	6	7	2	1			8	1	0
		6	2	1			7	0	–
		5	0	–			6	0	–
	5	7	1	0		5	9	1	1
		6	0	–			8	1	0
	4	7	1	0			7	0	–
		6	0	–		4	9	1	0
	3	7	0	–			8	0	–
8	8	8	3	2			7	0	–
		7	2	1		3	9	0	0
		6	1	0			8	0	–
		5	0	–		2	9	0	–
	7	8	2	1	10	10	10	5	4
		7	1	0			9	3	2
		6	0	–			8	2	1
		5	0	–			7	1	0
	6	8	2	1			6	0	0
		7	1	0			5	0	–
		6	0	–		9	10	4	3
	5	8	1	0			9	3	2
		7	0	0			8	2	1
		6	0	–			7	1	0
	4	8	1	0			6	0	–
		7	0	–			5	0	–
	3	8	0	–		8	10	4	2

TABLE A-3. Continued.

Group I	Group II	A (or B)	C (or D) p = .05	p = .01	Group I	Group II	A (or B)	C (or D) p = .05	p = .01
10	8	9	2	1	11	9	7	1	0
		8	1	0			6	0	-
		7	1	0		8	11	4	3
		6	0	-			10	3	1
	7	10	3	2			9	2	1
		9	2	1			8	1	0
		8	1	0			7	0	-
		7	0	-			6	0	-
		6	0	-		7	11	3	2
	6	10	2	1			10	2	1
		9	1	0			9	1	0
		8	1	0			8	1	0
		7	0	-			7	0	-
	5	10	2	1			6	0	-
		9	1	0		6	11	2	1
		8	0	-			10	1	1
		7	0	-			9	1	0
	4	10	1	0			8	0	-
		9	0	0			7	0	-
		8	0	-		5	11	2	1
	3	10	0	0			10	1	0
		9	0	-			9	0	0
	2	10	0	-			8	0	-
11	11	11	6	4		4	11	1	0
		10	4	3			10	0	0
		9	3	2			9	0	-
		8	2	1		3	11	0	0
		7	1	0			10	0	-
		6	0	-		2	11	0	-
		5	0	-	12	12	12	7	5
	10	11	5	4			11	5	4
		10	4	2			10	4	2
		9	3	1			9	3	1
		8	2	0			8	2	1
		7	1	0			7	1	0
		6	0	-			6	0	-
	9	11	4	3			5	0	-
		10	3	2		11	12	6	5
		9	2	1			11	5	3
		8	1	0			10	3	2

TABLE A-3. Continued.

Group I	Group II	A (or B)	C (or D) p = .05	C (or D) p = .01	Group I	Group II	A (or B)	C (or D) p = .05	C (or D) p = .01
12	11	9	2	1	12	5	10	0	0
		8	1	0			9	0	-
		7	1	0			8	0	-
		6	0	-		4	12	1	0
		5	0	-			11	0	0
	10	12	5	4			10	0	-
		11	4	3			9	0	-
		10	3	2		3	12	0	0
	10	9	2	1			11	0	-
		8	1	0			10	0	-
		7	0	0		2	12	0	-
		6	0	-	13	13	13	8	6
	9	12	5	3			12	6	4
		11	3	2			11	5	3
		10	2	1			10	4	2
		9	2	0			9	3	1
		8	1	0			8	2	0
		7	0	-			7	1	0
		6	0	-			6	0	-
	8	12	4	3			5	0	-
		11	3	2		12	13	7	6
		10	2	1			12	5	4
		9	1	0			11	4	3
		8	1	0			10	3	2
		7	0	-			9	2	1
		6	0	-			8	1	0
	7	12	3	2			7	1	0
		11	2	1			6	0	-
		10	1	0			5	0	-
		9	1	0		11	13	6	5
		8	0	-			12	5	3
		7	0	-			11	4	2
	6	12	3	2			10	3	1
		11	2	1			9	2	1
		10	1	0			8	1	0
		9	0	0			7	0	0
		8	0	-			6	0	-
		7	0	-		10	13	6	4
	5	12	2	1			12	4	3
		11	1	0			11	3	2

TABLE A-3. Continued.

Group I	Group II	A (or B)	C (or D) p = .05	p = .01	Group I	Group II	A (or B)	C (or D) p = .05	p = .01
13	10	10	2	1	13	7	10	1	0
		9	1	0			9	0	0
		8	1	0			8	0	–
		7	0	–			7	0	–
		6	0	–		6	13	3	2
	9	13	5	4			12	2	1
		12	4	2			11	1	0
		11	3	1			10	1	0
		10	2	1			9	0	–
		9	1	0			8	0	–
		8	1	0		5	13	2	1
		7	0	–			12	1	0
		6	0	–			11	1	0
	8	13	4	3			10	0	–
		12	3	2			9	0	–
		11	2	1		4	13	1	0
		10	1	0			12	1	0
		9	1	0			11	0	–
		8	0	–			10	0	–
		7	0	–		3	13	1	0
	7	13	3	2			12	0	–
		12	2	1			11	0	–
		11	2	1		2	13	0	–

Adapted from Pearson and Hartley (1966)

[a]For more extensive tabulations of the p values for C in sample sizes up to 20, see Pearson and Hartley (1966).

see if the number of subjects in the C cell of your data is listed. If so, look above it to obtain the significance level. If the number for your C cell or a larger number is not listed, then the p value is not significant. For example, if your group sizes were 6 and 5, your A were 5, and your C were 1, the p value would not be indicated because it is > .05. However, if the C were 0, the p value would be ≤ .05. (3). If the number in your A cell is not listed in the "A (or B)" column, but the number in your B cell is listed, then look in the columns headed "C (or D)" for the number in your D cell. If it or a larger number is there, look above for the significance level.

A-4: The Binomial Test

The purpose of the binomial test is to provide the chance probability for an obtained distribution of two outcomes occurring in a particular number of independent observations, when each outcome is assumed to have a particular probability in the population sampled. For example, if it is assumed that boys should be as likely as girls to become high-school valedictorians, a sample of 50 high-school graduating classes could be checked to determine whether the proportions of boy and girl valedictorians deviate significantly from the expected proportions of $\frac{1}{2}$ for each sex. Suppose we found that girls were valedictorians of 40 classes and boys of only 10. The formula for computing the chance probability of the obtained proportion is:

$$p(x) = \binom{N}{x} P^x Q^{N-x}$$

where x is the number of outcomes in the less frequent category (the 10 valedictorians found to be boys) and $N-x$ is the number of outcomes in the opposite category (the 40 valedictorians found to be girls); P = the proportion of x (boy) outcomes expected by chance; $Q = 1 - P$, the proportion of non-x (girl) outcomes expected by chance; and

$$\binom{N}{x} = \frac{N!}{x! \, (N-x)!}$$

In this case, because the assumption was that boys and girls are equally likely to be valedictorians, P and Q are both $\frac{1}{2}$. Substituting the obtained numbers in the formula $\binom{N}{x} P^x Q^{N-x}$ gives $\frac{50!}{10!40!} (\frac{1}{2})^{10}(\frac{1}{2})^{40}$. In other cases, P and Q could have values other than $\frac{1}{2}$. In determining the p value for obtaining four 2s in ten throws of a fair die, for example, P would be 1/6 and Q would be 5/6, because, of the six possible outcomes of the throw of a die, 5/6 are numbers other than 2 and only 1/6 is 2.

Like Fisher's exact test, the binomial test employs not just the probability of the specific obtained outcome, but of the obtained outcome plus all the more extreme outcomes. Thus, the appropriate p value for the obtained outcome of 10 boy valedictorians in 50 high school classes is the sum of the p values for 10/40, 9/41, 8/42, and so on to 0/50. Where the expected proportions are both $\frac{1}{2}$, these computations may be avoided by using Table A-4, which provides the .01, .05, and .10 p values for outcomes in sample sizes up to 90. To use Table A-4, locate your total number of observations in one of the columns headed N. If x—the less frequent of your two outcomes—or a larger number is listed in one of the

TABLE A-4. Two-tailed p Values of x for the Binomial Test where $P = Q = .5$.[a]

N	.01	.05	.10	N	.01	.05	.10
1				46	13	15	16
2				47	14	16	17
3				48	14	16	17
4				49	15	17	18
5			0	50	15	17	18
6		0	0	51	15	18	19
7		0	0	52	16	18	19
8	0	0	1	53	16	18	20
9	0	1	1	54	17	19	20
10	0	1	1	55	17	19	20
11	0	1	2	56	17	20	21
12	1	2	2	57	18	20	21
13	1	2	3	58	18	21	22
14	1	2	3	59	19	21	22
15	2	3	3	60	19	21	23
16	2	3	4	61	20	22	23
17	2	4	4	62	20	22	24
18	3	4	5	63	20	23	24
19	3	4	5	64	21	23	24
20	3	5	5	65	21	24	25
21	4	5	6	66	22	24	25
22	4	5	6	67	22	25	26
23	4	6	7	68	22	25	26
24	5	6	7	69	23	25	27
25	5	7	7	70	23	26	27
26	6	7	8	71	24	26	28
27	6	7	8	72	24	27	28
28	6	8	9	73	25	27	28
29	7	8	9	74	25	28	29
30	7	9	10	75	25	28	29
31	7	9	10	76	26	28	30
32	8	9	10	77	26	29	30
33	8	10	11	78	27	29	31
34	9	10	11	79	27	30	31
35	9	11	12	80	28	30	32
36	9	11	12	81	28	31	32
37	10	12	13	82	28	31	33
38	10	12	13	83	29	32	33
39	11	12	13	84	29	32	33
40	11	13	14	85	30	32	34
41	11	13	14	86	30	33	34
42	12	14	15	87	31	33	35
43	12	14	15	88	31	34	35
44	13	15	16	89	31	34	36
45	13	15	16	90	32	35	36

Adapted from Dixon and Massey (1957).
[a]For more extensive tabulations of the p value for x, see Dixon and Massey (1957).

columns to the right of your N, look above the column for the p value. For our survey of valedictorians, for example, we find 50 in the fifth row from the top of the second column headed N. Since 10 is smaller than 15, the smallest number in the columns to the right of 50, and 15 is significant at $p = .01$, the p for our outcome of 10/50, plus all the more extreme outcomes, is $< .01$.

If NPQ equals at least 9, no matter what the values of P and Q, a test based on the normal distribution can be employed by computing

$$z = \frac{(x \pm .5) - NP}{\sqrt{NPQ}}$$

The p value for the z thus obtained can be found in table of z scores. In this formula, the term $\pm .5$ is used to reduce the difference between x and NP as a correction for continuity like Yates' correction for the 2×2 chi square.

A-5: The Cochran Q Test

The purpose of the Cochran Q test is to determine whether three or more matched samples of dichotomous scores differ significantly among themselves. The samples of scores may be considered matched because they are obtained on the same subjects or because individual subjects in one sample are systematically matched with individual subjects in each other sample.

To employ the Cochran test, first convert the scores to 0s and 1s. Next arrange them in a table in which each row consists of the scores obtained on the same subject or block of matched subjects, and each column consists of one sample of scores. Then compute Q from the formula:

$$Q = \frac{c(c-1) \sum_{j=1}^{c} C_j^2 - (c-1)N^2}{cN - \sum_{i=1}^{r} R_i^2}$$

where c = the number of columns (samples) of scores; C_j = the number of 1s in column j; N = the number of 1s in the entire table; r = the number of rows (subjects or blocks of matched subjects); and R_i = the number of 1s in row i. Because the sampling distribution of Q is approximated by the chi square distribution, Q has the same level of significance as chi square of the same size, with $c - 1$ degrees of freedom.

A-6: The Mann–Whitney Test

The purpose of the Mann–Whitney test is to determine the chance probability that two independent samples of scores are drawn from the same population. Its function is like that of the t test for independent samples, but it is more powerful than the t test if the samples are of unequal size and if they are markedly skewed and/or the standard deviation of one sample is two or more times greater than that of the other sample.

To perform the Mann–Whitney test, first combine the scores from both groups and rank these in order of increasing size. If some of the scores are negative, the largest negative numbers receive the numerically smallest ranks. If there are ties, assign each of the scores in a tie the average of the ranks they would have if no ties had occurred. Thus, if three scores are tied, assign all of them the rank the middle one would have received if they were successive instead of tied scores.

Next, sum the ranks of one of the two groups (call it n), using the smaller of the groups if they are unequal in size. If the sample sizes are ≤ 8, simply look in Table A-6 for the p level for the sum of the ranks of group n—abbreviated as $\sum_{i=1}^{n} r_i$. If the sum of the ranks is either as small as the lefthand figure or as large as the righthand figure in the columns to the right of the appropriate sample sizes, the difference between the samples is significant at the p level indicated above the column. For example, suppose the sample sizes were 3 and 6, and the sum of the ranks for group n (the group with three subjects) totalled 6. The second row of Table A-6 shows 7, 23. Since 6, the obtained sum of ranks for group n is less than 7, the groups differ significantly at $p < .05$ by a two-tailed test.

If the samples are larger than eight, first compute

$$U = nm + \frac{n(n+1)}{2} - \sum_{i=1}^{n} r_i$$

where n = the number of subjects in one group; m = the number in the second group; and $\sum_{i=1}^{n} r_i$ = the sum of the ranks of the subjects in group n. Then find the p value for z computed from the formula:

$$z = \frac{U - nm/2}{\sqrt{\dfrac{nm(n+m+1)}{12}}}$$

TABLE A-6.   Two-tailed Significance Levels for $\sum_{i=1}^{n} r_i$ in the Mann–Whitney Test.[a]

Sample sizes	p levels		Sample sizes	p levels	
	.05	.01		.05	.01
$n = 3, m = 5$	6,21	–	$n = 5, m = 5$	17,38	15,40
6	7,23	–	6	18,42	16,44
7	7,26	–	7	20,45	16,49
8	8,28	–	8	21,49	17,53
$n = 4, m = 4$	10,26	–	$n = 6, m = 6$	26,52	23,55
5	11,29	–	7	27,57	24,60
6	12,32	10,34	8	29,61	25,65
7	13,35	10,38	$n = 7, m = 7$	36,69	32,73
8	14,38	11,41	8	38,74	34,78
			$n = 8, m = 8$	49,87	43,93

Adapted from Mosteller and Rourke (1973).

[a]For more extensive tabulations of the p value for $\sum_{i=1}^{n} r_i$, see Mosteller and Rourke (1973) Table A-9

A-7: The Wilcoxon Matched-pairs Signed-ranks Test

The Wilcoxon test, like the dependent t test (t test for matched samples), is designed to compare two samples in which each score in one sample is paired with a particular score in the other sample, as when scores are obtained on the same subjects on two different occasions. The primary value of the Wilcoxon test is that it is nearly as powerful as the dependent t test under conditions appropriate for the t test and can be considerably more powerful than the t test with distributions deviating greatly from normality (Conover, 1971).

To perform the Wilcoxon test, first find the difference, d, between the scores in each matched pair of scores. Then rank all these ds, giving the rank 1 to the smallest d, 2 to the next smallest d, and so on, no matter what the signs of the ds. That is, a d of −1 should be ranked in the same way as a d of +1, and both would be ranked lower than ds of −2 or +2. If there is no difference between a pair of scores, drop them from the ranking. However, if the ds for two or more pairs are equal in size, give them the mean of the ranks they would have received if they were of successive sizes rather than tied.

After ranking the ds, place the appropriate sign with each rank. Thus, if for the d ranked 1, the second score of the matched pair is greater than the first, place a minus sign before the 1. If the first score of the pair is greater than the second, place a plus before the 1. Next, sum all the ranks given minus signs and all the ranks given plus signs. The smaller of

TABLE A-7. Two-tailed Significance Levels for W_s in the Wilcoxon Matched-pairs Signed-ranks Test.[a]

N	p levels		N	p levels	
	.05	.01		.05	.01
6	0	–	14	21	12
7	2	–	15	25	15
8	3	0	16	29	19
9	5	1	17	34	23
10	8	3	18	40	27
11	10	5	19	46	32
12	13	7	20	52	37
13	17	9			

Adapted from Dixon and Massey (1957), Table A-19.
[a]For more extensive tabulation of W_s, see McCornack (1965).

these two sums is designated as W_s. For sample sizes up to 20, W_s is significant if it is no greater than the figure shown for the appropriate sized sample in Table A-7. For larger samples, find the p value for z computed with the formula:

$$z = \frac{W_s - N(N+1)/4}{\sqrt{\dfrac{N(N+1)(2N+1)}{24}}}$$

where W_s is the sum of the smaller group of ranks and N = the total number of pairs ranked, excluding those where $d = 0$.

A-8: The Kolmogorov–Smirnov Test

To compare the shapes of the distributions of two samples of scores, first determine the cumulative proportion of subjects obtaining each score in each sample. This can be done either by graphing a cumulative frequency distribution for each sample or by listing the cumulative proportion of subjects at each score in each sample side-by-side. For example, if the possible scores are 1, 2, 3, 4, and 5, and the smaller sample, n, has six subjects while the larger sample, m, has 18 subjects, find the proportion of subjects in sample n who have a score of 1; the proportion who have scores ≤ 2 (i.e., scores of 1 or 2); the proportion who have scores ≤ 3; and the proportion who have scores ≤ 4. (The proportion who have scores ≤ 5 will, of course, be 1.0). Next find the cumulative proportion of subjects obtaining each score in sample m.

Then find the point at which the cumulative proportion for sample n differs most from the cumulative proportion for sample m. This largest difference between proportions for the two distributions is designated as D. Lastly, consult Table A-8 to determine whether the difference, D, between the two proportions is large enough to reach statistical significance.

In the example with five scores and sample sizes of 6 and 18, suppose that the largest difference, D, occurred at a score of ≤ 3, with one of the six subjects (i.e., a proportion of .167) in sample n having a score ≤ 3 but with 15 of the 18 subjects (i.e., .833) in sample m having scores ≤ 3. Since the difference between the proportions .167 and .833 is .666, look beside sample sizes $n = 6$ and $m = 18$ in Table A-8 to determine whether a D of .666 reaches statistical significance. Although .666 does not appear in the table for $n = 6$, $m = 18$, a D of .61 is significant at the .05 level and a D of .72 is significant at the .01 level for these sample sizes. The p value for a D of .666 is therefore $< .05$ but $> .01$.

For sample sizes not presented in Table A-8 the D needed to reach significance at the .05 level (two-tailed) can be found with the formula $D = 1.36\sqrt{m + n/mn}$. The D needed for the .01 level is computed using $D = 1.63\sqrt{m + n/mn}$.

A-9: The Kruskal–Wallis One-way Analysis of Variance

The Kruskal–Wallis test, like the one-way ANOVA, is designed to determine whether several independent samples of scores differ significantly among themselves. However, it can be used with smaller samples than the ANOVA. Furthermore, when sample sizes differ considerably and the variances and/or shapes of their distributions also differ considerably, the Kruskal–Wallis test may be more powerful than the ANOVA.

To perform the Kruskal–Wallis test, rank the scores from all the samples in one continuous series, giving tied scores the mean of the ranks they would receive if they were successive rather than tied. Then place the ranks obtained by each sample in a separate column and sum the ranks for each column. Next, compute H in the formula:

$$H = \frac{12}{N(N + 1)} \sum_{i=1}^{c} \frac{R_i^2}{n_i} - 3(N+1)$$

where N = the number of subjects in all samples combined; C = the number of columns (samples); R_i = the sum of ranks in column i; and n_i = the number of cases in column i. If there are more than three samples

TABLE A-8. Two-tailed Significance Levels for D in the Kolmogorov–Smirnov Test.[a]

Sample sizes	p levels .05	p levels .01	Sample sizes	p levels .05	p levels .01
$n = 2, m = 8$	.875	–	$n = 6, m = 10$	.633	.733
9	.889	–	12	.583	.750
10	.900	–	18	.611	.722
$n = 3, m = 5$	.800	–	24	.583	.667
6	.833	–	$n = 7, m = 7$	.714	.714
7	.857	–	8	.625	.750
8	.750	–	9	.635	.746
9	.778	.889	10	.614	.714
10	.800	.900	14	.571	.714
$n = 4, m = 4$	.750	–	28	.536	.643
5	.800	–	$n = 8, m = 8$	.625	.750
6	.750	.833	9	.625	.750
7	.750	.857	10	.575	.700
8	.750	.875	12	.583	.667
9	.750	.889	16	.563	.625
10	.700	.800	32	.500	.594
12	.667	.833	$n = 9, m = 9$	.556	.667
16	.688	.813	10	.578	.689
$n = 5, m = 5$	.800	.800	12	.556	.667
6	.667	.833	15	.533	.644
7	.714	.857	18	.500	.611
8	.675	.800	36	.472	.556
9	.689	.800	$n = 12, m = 12$	.500	.583
10	.700	.800	15	.500	.583
15	.667	.733	16	.479	.583
20	.600	.750	18	.472	.556
$n = 6, m = 6$	.667	.833	20	.467	.567
7	.690	.833	$n = 15, m = 15$	.467	.533
8	.667	.750	20	.433	.517
9	.667	.778	$n = 16, m = 16$	.438	.563
			20	.425	.513

Adapted from Massey (1952).
[a]For more extensive tabulations of p values for D, see Conover (1971), Tables 16 and 17.

or more than five subjects in each sample, the p value for H is approximately the same as for chi square with $C - 1$ degrees of freedom. If there are only three samples, with five or fewer subjects in each, consult Table A-9 for the significance level of the obtained H.

TABLE A–9. Significance Levels for H in the Kruskal-Wallis One-way Analysis of Variance.[a]

Sample sizes n_1	n_2	n_3	p levels .05	.01	Sample sizes n_1	n_2	n_3	p levels .05	.01
3	2	2	4.7143	–	5	2	2	5.1600	6.5333
3	3	1	5.1429	–	5	3	1	4.9600	–
3	3	2	5.3611	–	5	3	2	5.2509	6.8218
3	3	3	5.6000	7.2000	5	3	3	5.6485	7.0788
4	2	2	5.3333	–	5	4	1	4.9855	6.9545
4	3	1	5.2083	–	5	4	2	5.2682	7.1182
4	3	2	5.4444	6.4444	5	4	3	5.6308	7.4449
4	3	3	5.7273	6.7455	5	4	4	5.6176	7.7604
4	4	1	4.9667	6.6667	5	5	1	5.1273	7.3091
4	4	2	5.4545	7.0364	5	5	2	5.3385	7.2692
4	4	3	5.5985	7.1439	5	5	3	5.7055	7.5429
4	4	4	5.6923	7.6538	5	5	4	5.6429	7.7914
5	2	1	5.0000	–	5	5	5	5.7800	7.9800

Adapted from Kruskal and Wallis (1952).

[a]For more extensive tabulations of p values for H, see Mosteller and Rourke (1973), Table A-14.

A-10: Wilson's Nonparametric Analysis of Variance

Wilson (1956) has provided a method for analyzing the effects of two orthogonal factors and their interaction analogous to the two-way ANOVA but where the data are inappropriate for the ordinary parametric ANOVA because of extreme skewness or differences in the size of samples which also differ markedly in the variance or shapes of their distributions.

To perform Wilson's ANOVA, first find the median for the entire set of scores. Next construct an $r \times c$ contingency table where r is the number of rows corresponding to the levels of one factor and c is the number of columns corresponding to the levels of the other factor. Then divide each cell of the $r \times c$ table in half. In one half of each cell, enter the number of scores from that cell that are at or above the overall median. In the other half of the cell, enter the number of scores from that cell that are below the overall median. The result is an $r \times c \times 2$ table in which the two levels of the third factor consist of scores at or above the median vs. scores below the median.

The total chi square for the table is computed with the formula:

$$\chi^2_T = \sum_{i=1}^{r} \sum_{j=1}^{c} \left[\frac{({}_af_{ij} - n_{ij}n_a/n)^2}{n_{ij}n_a/n} + \frac{({}_bf_{ij} - n_{ij}n_b/n)^2}{n_{ij}n_b/n} \right]$$

where ${}_af_{ij}$ = the number of scores at or above the overall median in cell ij; n_{ij} = the total number of scores in cell ij; n_a = the number of scores at or above the median in the entire table; n = the number of scores in the entire table; ${}_bf_{ij}$ = the number of scores below the overall median in cell ij; and n_b = the number of scores below the median in the entire table. If the total chi square is significant with $rc - 1$ degrees of freedom, then compute the chi squares for row effects using the formula:

$$\chi^2_R = \sum_{i=1}^{r} \left[\frac{({}_af_{i.} - n_{i.}n_a/n)^2}{n_{i.}n_a/n} + \frac{({}_bf_{i.} - n_{i.}n_b/n)^2}{n_{i.}n_b/n} \right]$$

where $n_{i.}$ = the sum of n_{ij}s for row i and the degrees of freedom = $r - 1$.

And compute the chi square for column effects using the formula:

$$\chi^2_C = \sum_{j=1}^{c} \left[\frac{({}_af_{.j} - n_{.j}n_a/n)^2}{n_{.j}n_a/n} + \frac{({}_bf_{.j} - n_{.j}n_b/n)^2}{n_{.j}n_b/n} \right]$$

where $n_{.j}$ = the sum of n_{ij}s for column j, and the degrees of freedom = $c - 1$. The chi square for the interaction between the rows factor and the columns factor is found by subtracting the chi squares for row and column effects from the total chi square: $\chi^2_I = \chi^2_T - \chi^2_R - \chi^2_C$. The p value is found in the chi square table with $(r-1)(c-1)$ degrees of freedom. Wilson (1956) also presents extensions of his ANOVA to three or more independent factors.

A-11: The Friedman Analysis of Variance for Matched Samples

The Friedman test makes it possible to test the significance of the differences among three or more samples of scores when the samples are related because they consist of repeated measures on the same subjects or measures on matched subjects, as in the randomized blocks design. With three or more samples, the power of the Friedman test is generally close to that of the parametric ANOVA and may be greater with samples that deviate markedly from normality (Conover, 1971).

First arrange the scores in a table in which each row contains the scores obtained on a single subject or on matched subjects, and each column contains the scores obtained under a particular condition. Then rank the scores in each row. Thus, if there are four columns (conditions), the scores in Row 1 are ranked from 1 to 4, as are the scores in Row 2, and so on. If two or more scores are tied within a row, give the scores the average of the ranks they would have received if they had been successive instead of tied. Next, sum the ranks in each column separately and compute:

$$\chi_r^2 = \frac{12}{NC(C+1)} \Sigma R_j^2 - 3N(C+1)$$

where N = the number of rows; C = the number of columns; and R_j = the sum of ranks in column j. The p value of χ_r^2 is approximately the same as for chi square with $C - 1$ degrees of freedom, unless there are only three columns and less than ten rows, or four columns and less than five rows. In these cases, find the significance level for the obtained χ_r^2 in Table A-11.

TABLE A-11. Significance Levels for χ_r^2 in the Friedman Analysis of Variance for Matched Samples.[a]

Sample sizes	p levels		Sample sizes	p levels	
	.05	.01		.05	.01
N = 3, *C* = 3	6.00	–	*N* = 4, *C* = 2	6.00	–
4	6.50	8.00	3	7.40	9.00
5	6.40	8.40	4	7.80	9.60
6	7.00	9.00			
7	7.14	8.86			
8	6.25	9.00			
9	6.22	8.67			

Adapted from Friedman (1937).
[a]For more extensive tabulations of p values for χ_r^2, see Mosteller and Rourke (1973), Table A-15.

A-12: The Spearman Rank Correlation Coefficient

The purpose of the Spearman rank correlation coefficient, designated as r_s or ρ (rho), is to provide a measure of correlation between two sets of paired ranks or of paired scores that are transformed into ranks because the extreme nonnormality of their distributions makes them inappropriate for the Pearson r. Each set of scores (call them Xs and Ys) is first ranked separately. Tied scores are assigned the average of the ranks they would have received if they had been successive. Then compute the difference, d, between the rank of the X and Y score in each pair. Lastly, square each d, sum all the d²s, and compute:

$$r_s = \frac{6\Sigma d^2}{N^3 - N}$$

where N = the number of pairs of scores. If N > 30, the p value for r_s is approximately the same as for the z score found by computing $z = r_s \sqrt{N-1}$. Where N ≤ 30, find the significance level for r_s in Table A-12.

TABLE A-12. Two-tailed Significance Levels for the Spearman Rank Correlation Coefficient.

Sample Size	p levels .05	.01	Sample Size	p levels .05	.01
5	.90	—	18	.47	.60
6	.83	.94	19	.46	.58
7	.75	.89	20	.45	.57
8	.69	.86	21	.44	.55
9	.68	.82	22	.42	.54
10	.64	.78	23	.42	.53
11	.61	.75	24	.41	.52
12	.58	.73	25	.40	.51
13	.55	.70	26	.39	.50
14	.53	.67	27	.38	.49
15	.52	.65	28	.37	.48
16	.50	.63	29	.37	.47
17	.49	.62	30	.36	.47

Adapted from Glasser and Winter (1961).

A-13: Kendall's Coefficient of Concordance

If several scores are obtained on the same subjects, as when several raters independently rate or rank them on some characteristic, Kendall's coefficient of concordance, W, can be used to determine the average degree of agreement among all the sets of scores. The scores are first arranged in a table with each row consisting of the scores obtained by one subject and each column consisting of the scores assigned by one rater to all the subjects. If the scores are not already in the form of rankings assigned by each rater, rank the scores within a column. Give ties the average of the ranks they would otherwise have obtained. Thus, if seven subjects had each been scored by four raters, Column 1 would contain ranks from 1 through 7 assigned by Rater 1, Column 2 would contain ranks from 1 through 7 assigned by Rater 2, and so on for Raters 3 and 4.

To compute W, sum the ranks, R_j, in Row j and likewise for each successive row of the table. Then employ the formula:

$$W = \frac{s}{1/12 C^2 (N^3 - N)}$$

where:

$$s = \sum \left(R_j - \frac{\Sigma R_j}{N} \right)^2 ;$$

TABLE A-13. Significance Levels for s in the Kendall Coefficient of Concordance.

Sample sizes	p levels .05	p levels .01	Sample sizes	p levels .05	p levels .01
$N = 3, C =$ 8	48.1	66.8	$N = 5, C =$ 8	183.7	242.7
9	54.0	75.9	10	231.2	309.1
10	60.0	85.1	15	349.8	475.2
12	71.9	103.5	20	468.5	641.2
14	83.8	121.9	$N = 6, C =$ 3	103.9	122.8
15	89.8	131.0	4	143.3	176.2
16	95.8	140.2	5	182.4	229.4
18	107.7	158.6	6	221.4	282.4
20	119.7	177.0	8	299.0	388.3
$N = 4, C =$ 4	49.5	61.4	10	376.7	494.0
5	62.6	80.5	15	570.5	758.2
6	75.7	99.5	20	764.4	1022.2
8	101.7	137.4	$N = 7, C =$ 3	157.3	185.6
10	127.8	175.3	4	217.0	265.0
15	192.9	269.8	5	276.2	343.8
20	258.0	364.2	6	335.2	422.6
$N = 5, C =$ 3	64.4	75.6	8	453.1	579.9
4	88.4	109.3	10	571.0	737.0
5	112.3	142.8	15	864.9	1129.5
6	136.1	176.1	20	1158.7	1521.9

Adapted from Friedman (1960).

R_j = the sum of the ranks in Row j; ΣR_j = the sum of the ranks across all the rows; C = the number of columns (e.g., raters); and N = the number of rows (subjects). For $N > 7$, the significance of W approximates that for χ^2 with $N-1$ degrees of freedom, where $\chi^2_w = C(N-1)$ W. For $N \leqslant 7$, the significance level of s is found directly in Table A-13. The significance of s for the omitted sample sizes up to seven can be found by interpolation in the Table.

A-14: Scalogram Analysis

Green's Method for Computing and Evaluating Rep

Green's (1956) method is designed to simplify computation of the reproducibility (Rep) of a scaled ordering of dichotomous items and to evaluate Rep in comparison with the minimal reproducibility that can occur with the obtained overall frequencies of positive and negative responses. The items are first ranked according to how many positive responses each one received. The item that received the most positive responses is given rank 1 and constitutes one end of the Guttman scale, whereas the item that received the fewest positive responses is given rank k and constitutes the other end of the scale. Tied items should be ranked in arbitrary order.

The Rep of the resulting scale is computed as follows: (1). For items 1 through $k - 1$, tabulate $n_{g+1, \bar{g}}$. This is the number of subjects who gave a positive response to item $g + 1$ while giving a negative response to item g, the item one rank higher in total positive responses than item $g + 1$. (2). For items 1 through $k - 1$, tabulate $n_{g+2, g+1, \bar{g}, \overline{g-1}}$. This is the number of times a subject gave positive responses to items $g + 2$ and $g + 1$, and negative responses to items g and $g - 1$. For example, if a subject responded positively to items 3 and 4 but negatively to items 1 and 2, he would contribute one point to the overall tabulation of $n_{g+2, g+1, \bar{g}, \overline{g-1}}$. (3). Compute Rep with the formula:

$$Rep = 1 - \frac{1}{Nk} \sum_{g=1}^{k-1} n_{g+1, \bar{g}} - \frac{1}{Nk} \sum_{g=2}^{k-2} n_{g+2, g+1, \bar{g}, \overline{g-1}}$$

where N = the total number of subjects; k = the total number of items; and the other terms are as defined in (1) and (2) above.

Once the Rep has been computed for the obtained scale, compute Rep_{Ind}, the Rep that would occur if the items had their obtained frequencies but were mutually independent:

$$Rep_{Ind} = 1 - \frac{1}{N^2 k} \sum_{g=1}^{k-1} n_{g+1} n_{\bar{g}} - \frac{1}{N^4 k} \sum_{g=2}^{k-2} n_{g+2} n_{g+1} n_{\bar{g}} n_{\overline{g-1}}.$$

The Index of Consistency for the obtained Rep is given by:

$$I = \frac{Rep - Rep_{Ind}}{1 - Rep_{Ind}}.$$

If $I=0$, the obtained Rep is no higher than the minimum possible by chance, while if $I=1.00$ the obtained Rep indicates perfect scalability. An I of well above .60 is indicative of a substantially unidimensional scale (Nie et al. 1975).

Leik and Matthews' Method for Developmental Scale Analysis

Because developmental sequences often involve the disappearance of early behaviors as more advanced ones are acquired, Leik and Matthews (1968) have proposed a modification of the scalogram approach that allows for scale types in which series of negative responses precede series of positive responses. In such scale types, the lowest level patterns may involve positive responses to primitive items (e.g., counting on one's fingers, talking aloud to oneself) accompanied by negative responses to more advanced items (e.g., mental arithmetic and subvocal verbal mediation), whereas the higher-level patterns involve negative responses to the primitive items, accompanied by positive responses to the advanced items.

Unlike the Guttman and Green procedures, the Leik and Matthews procedure does not rank items according to the number of positive responses they elicit. Instead, the items are ordered according to the joint frequency of positive responses to each $pair$ of items. To order items according to their joint frequencies, first display the various response patterns and their frequencies in a format like that illustrated in Table A-14a for 24 subjects and five items (a, b, c, d, and e). Then count the number of subjects who gave positive responses to each pair of items and enter these joint frequencies in an item-by-item matrix like that shown in Table A-14(b).

Next, rearrange the items so that the smallest joint frequency is placed in the upper right hand cell and the other items are arranged so that the cell frequencies increase from right to left across the top row. If there is a tie, break the tie by determining which of the items has a higher joint frequency with the item defining the second row and place it to the left of the item with which it is tied in the first row. As shown in row 1 of Table A-14(c), both item d and item e occur six times with item c. However, because item d occurs twelve times with item a, whereas item e occurs only six times with item a (see row 2), item d is placed to the left of item e. To display the response patterns according to the order obtained in Table A-14(c), arrange them in a format like that shown in Table A-14(d), where n = the frequency of each pattern and Errors = the

TABLE A-14. Illustration of Leik and Matthews's Developmental Scale Analysis

(a) Response Patterns

Items

a	b	c	d	e	n
+	−	+	+	+	6
+	−	+	−	−	7
+	−	−	+	−	3
+	+	−	+	−	3
−	+	−	−	+	5

(c) Items Rearranged According to Joint Frequencies

Items

	c	a	d	e	b
c	13	13	6	6	0
a		19	12	6	3
d			12	6	3
e				11	5
b					8

(b) Joint Frequency Matrix

Items

	a	b	c	d	e
a	19	3	13	12	6
b		8	0	3	5
c			13	6	6
d				12	6
e					11

(d) Developmental Scale

Items

c	a	d	e	b	n	Errors
+	+	−	−	−	7	0
−	+	+	−	−	3	0
+	+	+	+	−	6	0
−	+	+	−	+	3	1 X 3 = 3
−	−	−	+	+	5	0

number of times negative responses occur between the positive responses of a pattern.

Because there is no criterion for ordering individual items—such as number of positive responses, as used to order items in Guttman scaling—the order chosen depends on decisions of the researcher. For example, if a positive response to item c is assumed to represent the developmentally most primitive level of functioning, and item a the next most primitive, then scale types including positive responses to these two items would be placed first.

Leik and Matthews have provided a Coefficient of Scalability for comparing the obtained scale with that expected from a random ordering of responses. This is analogous to Green's Index of Consistency (I) for Guttman-type scales, but it compares the obtained average number of scale errors with the average expected by chance, rather than with the minimal reproducibility possible with the obtained frequencies of positive and negative responses. Letting $\bar{Y}$ signify the average number of violations per scale pattern occurring in a sample of responses, the value of $\bar{Y}$ expected by chance is:

$$E(\tilde{Y}) = \frac{1}{n} \sum_i n_i E(Y_i)$$

where n = the number of subjects and $E(Y_i)$ is the number of violations occurring in a pattern having i positive responses. Each $E(Y_i)$ is found with the formula:

$$E(Y_i) = \frac{(i-1)(m-i)}{i+1}$$

where m = the number of items. Thus, for example, patterns containing two positive responses were produced by a total of 15 subjects in Table A-14(d). Therefore, n = 15; the number of items (m) = 5; and the number of positive responses in a pattern (i) = 2. Substituting these numbers in the formula for $E(Y_i)$ and multiplying by $n_i = 15 \times (2 - 1)(5 - 2)/(2 + 1) = 15$. Likewise, because three subjects produced patterns containing three positive responses, $n_i E(Y_i)$ where i = 3 is: $3 \times (3 - 1)(5 - 3)/(3 + 1) = 3$. And because six subjects produced patterns containing four positive responses, $n_i E(Y_i)$ where i = 4 is: $6 \times (4 - 1)(5 - 4)/(4 + 1) = 3.6$. Thus, $E(\tilde{Y})$, the value of $\tilde{Y}$ expected by chance is: $1/24 (15 + 3 + 3.6) = 21.6/24 = .90$. The Coefficient of Scalability = $[E(\tilde{Y}) - \tilde{Y}]/E(\tilde{Y})$. Because the obtained number of scale violations in the example was 3, the obtained $\tilde{Y} = 3/24 = .125$, and the Coefficient of Scalability = $(.90 - .125)/90 = .775/.90 = .861$. Since 1.00 would represent perfect scalability and .00 would represent no improvement over random ordering, .861 indicates a high degree of scalability.

Leik and Matthews have also provided a test for the statistical significance of the obtained patterns, although the test is too cumbersome to present here and is probably of less value than a comparison between the size of the Coefficient of Scalability and Green's Index of Consistency for deciding whether a set of items is more appropriately scaled using their procedure or the Guttman approach. However, those interested in the use of scalogram analysis as an inferential statistic should refer to Leik and Matthews' test as well as to Proctor's (1970) method for testing the statistical significance of Guttman type scales.

Lingoes' Multiple Scalogram Analysis

Lingoes' (1963) method involves repeatedly applying scalogram analysis to a set of data in order to identify subsets of items, each of which may qualify as a Guttman scale. It begins with arranging the positive and negative responses in a matrix where each row represents the response of one subject to all items and each column represents the responses of all subjects to one item. The number of positive responses to each item is then summed and all items that received unanimous positive or negative responses are eliminated. If the sum of positive responses to any of the remaining items is less than $N/2$ (where N = the number of subjects), the scoring of the item is reversed ("reflected") by substituting pluses for the negative responses and minuses for the positive responses.

To begin forming the first Guttman scale, find the item with the largest sum of positive responses, breaking ties between items arbitrarily. Then form 2×2 tables of the first item, designated as i, with each other item, e.g., item j, thusly:

These tables are used to find the item that is most like item i in eliciting positive and negative responses. The item that is most like i is the one that is found to have the smallest sum of $-+$ and $+-$ patterns in a table with i, i.e., the smallest sum of cells B and D. Ties are broken by selecting the item with the smallest sum in the D cell. When the item most similar to item i has been found, it is placed in 2×2 tables with each of the remaining items until the remaining item most like it is found. The procedure of chaining items in this way is repeated until one of the following cut-off points is reached: (1). If cell $D > .1(2A + B + D)(2C + B + D)/N$ for a candidate item and all of its predecessors in a chain, then do not add the candidate item. (2). If condition (1) is not met, but if the χ^2 for the 2×2 table between a candidate item and its immediate predecessor is < 10.83 ($p = .001$), then do not add the candidate item. (3). If $AC < BD$, reverse ("reflect") the scoring of the candidate item and resume the chaining process. When chaining cannot continue because all candidate items meet conditions (1) or (2), then begin a new chain with the remaining item having the largest number of positive responses. Each of the resulting chains can be tested for scalability using Green's procedure.

References

Achenbach, T. M. (1969). Conservation of illusion-distorted identity: Its relation to MA and CA in normals and retardates. *Child Development* 40, 663–679.

———— (1973). Surprise and memory as indices of concrete operational development. *Psychological Reports 33*, 47–57.

———— (1974). *Developmental psychopathology*. New York: Ronald Press.

———— (1978). The Child Behavior Profile: I. Boys aged 6 through 11. *Journal of Consulting and Clinical Psychology 46*, 478–488.

Achenbach, T. M., and Edelbrock, C. S. (1977). Stability and change in the Child Behavior Profile following child guidance clinic contacts. Paper presented at the meeting of the American Association of Psychiatric Services for Children, Washington, D. C. November.

———— (1978). The classification of child psychopathology: A review and analysis of empirical efforts. *Psychological Bulletin 85*.

Achenbach, T. M., and Weisz, J. R. (1975a). A longitudinal study of relations between outer-directedness and IQ changes in preschoolers. *Child Development 46*, 650–657.

———— (1975b). Impulsivity–reflectivity and cognitive development in preschoolers: A longitudinal analysis of developmental and trait variance. *Developmental Psychology 11*, 413–414.

American Psychological Association (1973). *Ethical principles in the conduct of research with human subjects*. Washington, D. C.: American Psychological Association.

Ames, L. B.; Learned, J.; Metraux, R.; and Walker, R. (1952). *Child Rorschach responses*. New York: Harper.

Anderberg, M. R. (1973). *Cluster analysis for applications*. New York: Academic Press.

Anderson, S.; Messick, S.; and Hartshorne, N. (1972). *Priorities and directions for research and development related to measurement of young children.* Princeton, N.J.: Educational Testing Service.

Appleton, T.; Clifton, R.; and Goldberg, S. (1975). The development of behavioral competence in infancy. In *Review of child development research. Volume 4.* Edited by F. D. Horowitz. Chicago: University of Chicago Press.

Asher, S. R., and Markell, R. A. (1974). Sex differences in comprehension of high- and low-interest reading material. *Journal of Educational Psychology 66*, 680–687.

Baer, D. M. (1970). An age-irrelevant concept of development. *Merrill—Palmer Quarterly 16*, 238–245.

——— (1973). The control of developmental processes: Why wait? In *Life-span developmental psychology: Methodological issues.* Edited by J. R. Nesselroade and H. W. Reese. New York: Academic Press.

Baldwin, T. F., and Lewis, C. (1971). Violence in television: The industry looks at itself. In *Television and social behavior, reports and papers. Volume 1: Media content and control.* Washington D. C.: U. S. Government Printing Office.

Baltes, P. B. (1968). Longitudinal and cross-sectional sequences in the study of age and generation effects. *Human Development 11*, 145–171.

Bandura, A. (1972). Modeling theory: Some traditions, trends, and disputes. In *Recent trends in social learning theory.* Edited by R. D. Parke. New York: Academic Press.

——— (1974). The case of the mistaken dependent variable. *Journal of Abnormal Psychology 83*, 301–303.

Baratz, J. C. (1969). A bi-dilectal task for determining language proficiency in economically disadvantaged Negro children. *Child Development 40*, 889–901.

Barber, T. X.; Forgione, A.; Chaves, J. F.; Calverly, D. S.; McPeake, J. D.; and Bowen, B. (1969). Five attempts to replicate the experimenter bias effect. *Journal of Consulting and Clinical Psychology 33*, 1–6.

Barker, R. G., and Wright, H. F. (1951). *One boy's day.* New York: Harper.

——— (1955). *Midwest and its children: The psychological ecology of an American town.* New York: Row, Peterson.

Bart, W. M., and Airasian, P. W. (1974). Determination of the ordering among seven Piagetian tasks by an ordering-theoretic method. *Journal of Educational Psychology 66*, 277–284.

Baumrind, D. (1964). Some thoughts on ethics of research—after reading Milgram's "Behavioral study of obedience." *American Psychologist 19*, 421–423.

Bell, R. Q. (1968). A reinterpretation of the direction of effects in studies of socialization. *Psychological Review 75*, 81–95.

Bell, S. M. (1970). The development of the concept of object as related to infant–mother attachment. *Child Development 41*, 291–311.

Bell, S. M., and Ainsworth, M. D. S. (1972). Infant crying and maternal responsiveness. *Child Development 43*, 1171–1190.

Beloff, H. (1957). The structure and origin of the anal character. *Genetic Psychology Monographs 55*, 141–172.

Bentler, P. M. (1971). Monotonicity analysis: An alternative to linear factor and test analysis. In *Measurement and Piaget*. Edited by D. R. Green, M. P. Ford, and G. B. Flamer. New York: McGraw-Hill.

Bereiter, C., and Engelmann, S. (1966). *Teaching disadvantaged children in the preschool*. Englewood Cliffs, N. J.: Prentice-Hall.

Berlyne, D. E. (1965). *Structure and direction in thinking*. New York: Wiley.

Bernstein, B. (1970). A sociolinguistic approach to socialization: With some reference to educability. In *Language and poverty: Perspectives on a theme*. Edited by F. Williams. Chicago: Markham.

Binet, A., and Simon, T. (1905). New methods for the diagnosis of the intellectual level of subnormals. *L'Anneé Psychologique*. Translated and reprinted in A. Binet and T. Simon (1916), *The development of intelligence in children*. Baltimore: Williams & Wilkins.

Bissell, J. S. (1973). Planned variation in Head Start and Follow Through. In *Compensatory education for children ages two to eight*. Edited by J. C. Stanley. Baltimore: Johns Hopkins University Press.

Blank, M. (1975). Eliciting verbalization from young children in experimental tasks: A methodological note. *Child Development 46*, 254–257.

Block, J. (1971). *Lives through time*. Berkeley, Ca.: Bancroft.

Bloom, L. (1970). *Language development: Form and function in emerging grammars*. Cambridge, Ma.: MIT Press.

————— (1973). *One word at a time*. The Hague: Mouton.

Bloom, L.; Lightbown, P.; and Hood, L. (1975). Structure and variation in child language. *Monographs of the Society for Research in Child Development 40*, 2 (Serial No. 160).

Boneau, C. A. (1960). The effects of violations of assumptions underlying the *t* test. *Psychological Bulletin 57*, 49–64.

Borke, H. (1975). Piaget's mountains revisited: Changes in the egocentric landscape. *Developmental Psychology 11*, 240–243.

Bornstein, M. H.; Kessen, W.; and Weiskopf, S. (1976). The categories of hue in infancy. *Science 191*, 201–202.

Bowerman, M. (1973). Structural relationships in children's utterances: Syntactic or semantic? In *Cognitive development and the acquisition of language*. Edited by T. E. Moore. New York: Academic Press.

————— (1975). Commentary. In Structure and variation in child language, by L. Bloom, P. Lightbown, and L. Hood. *Monographs of the Society for Research in Child Development* 40, 2 (Serial No. 160).

Bowlby, J. (1969). *Attachment and loss*, Vol. 1. New York:Basic Books.

——— (1973). *Attachment and loss*, Vol. 2. New York: Basic Books.

Box, G. E. P. (1954). Some theorems on quadratic forms applied in the study of analysis of variance problems. *Annals of Mathematical Statistics* 25, 290–302, 484–498.

Bracht, G. H., and Glass, G. V. (1968) The external validity of experiments. *American Educational Research Journal* 5, 437–474.

Braine, M. D. S. (1963). The ontogeny of English phrase structure: The first phase. *Language* 39, 1–13.

Braun, P. H. (1973). Finding optimal age groups for investigating age-related variables. *Human Development* 16, 293–303.

Brazziel, W. (1969). A letter from the South. *Harvard Educational Review* 39, 440–448.

Brown, R. (1973). *A first language: The early stages.* Cambridge, Ma.: Harvard University Press.

Brown, R., and Fraser, C. (1964). The acquisition of syntax. In the acquisition of language. Edited by U. Bellugi and R. Brown. *Monographs of the Society for Research in Child Development* 29, 1 (Serial No. 92).

Burton, R. V. (1976). Assessment of moral training programs: Where are we going? Paper presented at meetings of the American Psychological Association, Washington, D.C., September.

Buss, A. R. (1973). An extension of developmental models that separate ontogenetic changes and cohort differences. *Psychological Bulletin* 80, 466–479.

Campbell, D. T., and Boruch, R. F. (1976). Making the case for randomized assignment to treatments by considering the alternatives: Six ways in which quasi-experimental evaluations in compensatory education tend to underestimate effects. In *Central issues in social program evaluation.* Edited by C. A. Bennett and A. Lumsdaine. New York: Academic Press.

Campbell, D. T., and Stanley, J. C. (1963). *Experimental and quasi-experimental designs for research.* Chicago: Rand-McNally.

Castaneda, A.; McCandless, B. R.; and Palermo, D. S. (1956). The children's form of the Manifest Anxiety Scale. *Child Development* 27, 317–326.

Cater, D., and Strickland, S. (1975). *TV violence and the child: The evolution and fate of the Surgeon General's Report.* New York: Russell Sage Foundation.

Chandler, M. J. (1973). Egocentrism and antisocial behavior: The assessment and training of social perspective-taking skills. *Developmental Psychology* 9, 326–332.

Chandler, M. J.; Greenspan, S.; and Barenboim, C. (1974). Assessment and training of role-taking and referential communication skills in institutionalized emotionally disturbed children. *Developmental Psychology* 10, 546–553.

Chomsky, N. (1957). *Syntactic structures*. The Hague: Mouton.

———(1959). Review of *Verbal behavior* by B. F. Skinner. *Language* 35, 26–58.

——— (1965). *Aspects of the theory of syntax*. Cambridge, Ma.: MIT Press.

Ciaccio, N. V. (1971). A test of Erikson's theory of ego epigenesis. *Developmental Psychology* 4, 306–311.

Clarke-Stewart, K. A. (1973). Interactions between mothers and their young children: Characteristics and consequences. *Monographs of the Society for Research in Child Development* 38, 6–7 (Serial No. 153).

Cline, M. G. (1975). *Education as experimentation: Evaluation of the Follow Through planned variation model*. Cambridge, Ma.: Abt Associates.

Cochran, W. G. and Cox, G. M. (1957). *Experimental designs*, 2nd ed. New York: Wiley.

Columbia Broadcasting System, (1976). Statement quoted in "Violence dispute," *Washington Post*, April 2, p. B1.

Committee on the Judiciary, U.S. Senate. (1956). *Television and juvenile delinquency*. Washington D.C.: U.S. Government Printing Office.

Comrey, A. L. (1973). *A first course in factor analysis*. New York: Academic Press.

Conover, W. J. (1971). *Practical nonparametric statistics*. New York: Wiley.

Constantinople, A. (1969). An Eriksonian measure of personality development in college students. *Developmental Psychology* 1, 357–372.

Cooley, W. W. and Lohnes, P. R. (1971). *Multivariate data analysis*. New York: Wiley.

——— (1976). *Evaluating research in education*. New York: Wiley.

Cronbach, L. J., and Furby, L. (1970). How should we measure "change"–or should we? *Psychological Bulletin* 74, 68–80.

Darwin, C. R. (1872). *The expression of the emotions in man and animals*. London: Murray.

——— (1877). A biographical sketch of an infant. *Mind* 2, 286–294.

Décarie, T. G. (1965). *Intelligence and affectivity in early childhood*. New York: International Universities Press.

Dixon, W. J. (1975). *BMDP: Biomedical computer programs.* Berkeley, Ca.: University of California Press.

Dixon, W. J., and Massey, F. J. (1957). *Introduction to statistical analysis.* New York: McGraw-Hill.

Donaldson, T. S. (1968). Robustness of the F-test to errors of both kinds and the correlation between the numerator and denominator of the F-ratio. *Journal of the American Statistical Association 63*, 660–676.

Dworkin, R. H.; Burke, B. W.; Maher, B. A.; and Gottesman, I. I. (1977). Genetic influences on the organization and development of personality. *Developmental Psychology 13*, 164–165.

Economic Opportunity Act, (1967). P.L. 90–92. Section 22a.

Edelbrock, C. S. (1978). Comparing the accuracy of hierarchical clustering algorithms using the mixture model: The problem of classifying everybody. *Psychological Bulletin*, submitted.

Efron, E. (1972). A million-dollar misunderstanding. Part III. *TV Guide*, November 25.

Eimas, P. D. (1975). Speech perception in early infancy. In *Infant perception: From sensation to cognition. Vol. 2. Perception of space, speech, and sound.* Edited by L. B. Cohen and P. Salapatek. New York: Academic Press.

Eimas, P. D.; Siqueland, E. R.; Jusczyk, P.; and Vigorito, J. (1971). Speech perception in infants. *Science 171*, 303–306.

Elkind, D. (1961). Children's discovery of the conservation of mass, weight, and volume: Piaget replication study II. *Journal of Genetic Psychology 98*, 219–227.

Engel, G. L. (1971). Attachment behavior, object relations and the dynamic-economic points of view. *International Journal of Psychoanalysis 52*, 183–196.

Erikson, E. H. (1963). *Childhood and society.* 2nd ed. New York: Norton.

Erlenmyer-Kimling, L. (1974). A program of studies on children at high risk for schizophrenia. Paper presented at the Congress of the International Association for Child Psychiatry and Allied Professions. Philadelphia, August.

Eron, L. D.; Huesmann, L. R.; Lefkowitz, M. M.; and Walder, L. O. (1972). Does television violence cause aggression? *American Psychologist 27*, 253–263.

Errera, P. (1972). Statement based on interviews with forty "worst cases" in the Milgram experiments. In *Experimentation with human beings.* Edited by J. Katz. New York: Russell Sage Foundation.

Everitt, B. (1974). *Cluster analysis.* New York: Wiley.

Fairbairn, W. R. D. (1952). *Psycho-analytic studies of the personality.* London: Tavistock.

Freud, A. (1946). *The ego and the mechanisms of defense.* New York: International Universities Press.

――― (1965). *Normality and pathology in childhood.* New York: International Universities Press.

Freud, S. (1905). Three essays on the theory of sexuality. (Original publication). In (1955) *Standard edition of the complete psychological works of Sigmund Freud,* Vol. 10. London: Hogarth Press.

――― (1908). Character and anal eroticism. (Original publication). In (1954) *Standard Edition of the Complete Psychological Works of Sigmund Freud,* Vol. 9. London: Hogarth Press.

――― (1914). On narcissism: An introduction. (Original publication). In (1957) *Standard edition of the complete psychological works of Sigmund Freud,* Vol. 14. London: Hogarth Press.

――― (1940). *An outline of psychoanalysis.* (Original publication). Republished 1949, New York: Norton.

Friedman, M. (1937). The use of ranks to avoid the assumption of normality implicit in the analysis of variance. *Journal of the American Statistical Association 32,* 688–689.

――― (1940). A comparison of alternative tests of significance for the problem of m rankings. *Annals of Mathematical Statistics 11,* 86–92.

Friedrich, L. K., and Stein, A. S. (1973). Aggressive and prosocial television programs and the natural behavior of preschool children. *Monographs of the Society for Research in Child Development 38,* 4 (Serial No. 151).

Fromm, E. (1947). *Man for himself.* New York: Holt.

Fulweiler, R. L., and Fouts, R. S. (1976). Acquisition of American Sign Language by a noncommunicating autistic child. *Journal of Autism and Childhood Schizophrenia 6,* 43–51.

Furth, H. G. (1974). Two aspects of experience in ontogeny: Development and learning. *Advances in child development and behavior,* Vol. 9. Edited by H. W. Reese. New York: Academic Press.

Gagné, R. M. (1968). Contributions of learning to human development. *Psychological Review 75,* 177–191.

――― (1970). *The conditions of learning.* New York: Holt.

Galton, F. (1885). Regression towards mediocrity in hereditary stature. *Journal of the Anthropological Institute 15,* 246–263.

Gardner, B. T. and Gardner, R. A. (1974). Comparing the early utterances of child and chimpanzee. In *Minnesota Symposia on Child Psychology,* Vol. 8. Edited by A. D. Pick. Minneapolis, Mn.: University of Minnesota Press.

Garrity, L. I. (1975). An electromyographical study of subvocal speech and recall in school children. *Developmental Psychology 11,* 274-281.

Gelman, R. S. (1967). Conservation, attention, and discrimination. Ph. D.

dissertation, University of California at Los Angeles. Ann Arbor, Mi.: University Microfilms, No. 67–16,013.

————— (1969). Conservation acquisition: A problem of learning to attend to relevant attributes. *Journal of Experimental Child Psychology 7*, 167–187.

Gerbner, G. (1976). Statement quoted in "Violence dispute," *Washington Post*, April 2, pp. B1, B10.

————— (1977). Statement quoted in *ADAMHA News*, March 15, 1977, p. 4.

Gesell, A. (1954). The ontogenesis of behavior. In *Manual of child psychology*. Edited by L. Carmichael. New York: Wiley.

Gewirtz, J. L. (1969). Potency of a social reinforcer as a function of satiation and recovery. *Developmental Psychology 1*, 2–13.

Girgus, J. S.; Coren, S.; and Fraenkel, R. (1975). Levels of perceptual processing in the development of visual illusions. *Developmental Psychology 11*, 268–273.

Glasser, G. J., and Winter R. F. (1961). Critical values of the coefficient of rank correlation for testing the hypothesis of independence. *Biometrika 48*, 444–448.

Goodman, L. A. (1970). The multivariate analysis of qualitative data: Interactions among multiple classifications. *Journal of the American Statistical Association 65*, 226–256.

Gorsuch, R. L. (1974). *Factor analysis*. Philadelphia: Saunders.

Gottesman, I. I. (1974). Developmental genetics and ontogenetic psychology: Overdue détente and propositions from a matchmaker. In *Minnesota Symposia on Child Psychology*, Vol. 8. Edited by A. D. Pick. Minneapolis, Mn.: University of Minnesota Press.

Gottlieb, G., ed. (1973). *Behavioral embryology: Studies on the development of behavior and the nervous system*, Vol. 1. New York: Academic Press.

Gottman, J.; Gonso, J.; and Rasmussen, B. (1975). Social interaction, social competence, and friendship in children. *Child Development 46*, 709–718.

Graham, P., and Rutter, M. (1968). The reliability and validity of the psychiatric assessment of the child. II. Interview with the parent. *British Journal of Psychiatry 114*, 581–592.

Gray, S. W. (1971). Ethical issues in research in early childhood intervention. *Children 18*, 83–89.

Gray, S. W., and Klaus, R. A. (1970). The Early Training Project: A seventh-year report. *Child Development 41*, 909–924.

Green, B. F. (1956). A method of scalogram analysis using summary statistics. *Psychometrika 21*, 79–88.

Gruber, H. E.; Girgus, J. S.; and Banuazizi, A. (1971). The development of object permanence in the cat. *Developmental Psychology 4*, 9–15.

Guttman, L. (1950). The basis for scalogram analysis. In *Measurement and prediction*. Edited by S. A. Stouffer, L. Guttman, E. A. Suchman, P. F. Lazersfeld, S. A. Star, and J. A. Clausen. Princeton, N.J.: Princeton University Press.

Hamel, B. R., and Riksen, B. O. M. (1973). Identity, reversibility, verbal rule instruction, and conservation. *Developmental Psychology 9*, 66–72.

Harlow, H. F. (1961). The development of affectional patterns in infant monkeys. *Determinants of infant behavior*, Vol. 1. Edited by B. M. Foss. New York: Wiley.

Harman, H. H. (1967). *Modern factor analysis*. Chicago: University of Chicago Press.

Harris, C. W., ed. (1963). *Problems in measuring change*. Madison, Wi.: University of Wisconsin Press.

Harris, R. J. (1975). *A primer of multivariate statistics*. New York: Academic Press.

Hartmann, H. (1939). *Ego psychology and the problem of adaptation*. New York: International Universities Press.

Hartmann, H.; Kris, E.; and Loewenstein, R. M. (1946). Comments on the formation of psychic structure. *Psychoanalytic Study of the Child 2*, 11–38.

———— (1949). Notes on the theory of aggression. *Psychoanalytic Study of the Child 3/4*, 9–36.

Haywood, H. C. (1977). The ethics of doing research . . . and of not doing it. *American Journal of Mental Deficiency 81*, 311–317.

Hess, E. H. (1970). Ethology and developmental psychology. In *Carmichael's manual of child psychology*. Vol. 1. (3rd ed). Edited by P. H. Mussen. New York: Wiley.

Hetherington, E. M., and Brackbill, Y. (1963). Etiology and covariation of obstinacy, orderliness, and parsimony in young children. *Child Development 34*, 919–943.

Hoffman, M. L. (1975). Developmental synthesis of affect and cognition and its implications for altruistic motivation. *Developmental Psychology 11*, 607–622.

Hollander, M., and Wolfe, D. A. (1973). *Nonparametric statistical methods*. New York: Wiley.

Hollos, M. (1975). Logical operations and role-taking abilities in two cultures: Norway and Hungary. *Child Development 46*, 638–649.

Holmes, D. S. (1976). Debriefing after psychological experiments. *American Psychologist 31*, 858–875.

Homans, G. C. (1958). Group factors in worker productivity. In *Readings in social psychology*. Edited by E. E. Maccoby, T. M. Newcomb, and E. L. Hartley. New York: Holt, Rinehart, & Winston.

Honzik, M. P., and Macfarlane, J. W. (1970). Personality development and intellectual functioning from 21 months to 40 years. Paper presented at the meeting of the American Psychological Association, Miami, September.

Hornblum, J. N., and Overton, W. F. (1976). Area and volume conservation among the elderly: Assessment and training. *Developmental Psychology 12*, 68–74.

Huck, S. W., and McLean, R. A. (1975). Using a repeated measures ANOVA to analyze the data from a pretest–posttest design: A potentially confusing task. *Psychological Bulletin 82*, 511–518.

Hull, C. L. (1952). *A behavior system: An introduction to behavior theory concerning the individual organism*. New Haven, Ct.: Yale University Press.

Hutt, S. J., and Hutt, C. (1970). *Direct observation and measurement of behavior*. Springfield, Il.: Thomas.

Inhelder, B.; Sinclair, H.; and Bovet, M. (1974). *Learning and the development of cognition*. Cambridge, Ma.: Harvard University Press.

Jarvik, L. F.; Blum, J. E.; and Varma, A. O. (1972). Genetic components and intellectual functioning during senescence: A 20-year study of aging twins. *Behavior Genetics 2*, 159–171.

Jarvik, L. F., and Cohen, D. (1973). A biobehavioral approach to intellectual changes with aging. In *The psychology of adult development and aging*. Edited by C. Eisdorfer and M. P. Lawton. Washington D.C.: American Psychological Association.

Jensen, A. R. (1969a). How can we boost IQ and scholastic achievement? *Harvard Educational Review 39*, 1–123.

——— (1969b). Reducing the heredity–environment uncertainty. *Harvard Educational Review 39*, 449–473.

——— (1972). *Genetics and education*. New York: Harper & Row.

——— (1973). *Educability and group differences*. New York: Harper & Row.

Joint Commission on Mental Health of Children, (1969). *Crisis in child mental health: Challenge for the 1970s*. New York: Harper & Row.

Jolly, A. (1974). The study of primate infancy. In *The growth of competence*. Edited by K. Connolly and J. Bruner. New York: Academic Press.

Juel-Nielsen, N. (1965). Individual and environment: A psychiatric–psychological investigation of monozygotic twins reared apart. *Acta Psychiatrica et Neurologica Scandinavica 40*, 158–292. (Monograph Supplement 183).

Kagan, J.; Rosman, B.; Day, D.; Albert, J.; and Phillips, W. (1964). Information processing in the child: Significance of analytic and reflective attitudes. *Psychological Monographs 78* (whole No. 578).

Kamin, L. J. (1974). *The science and politics of IQ*. Potomac, Md.: Erlbaum.

Kangas, J., and Bradway, K. (1971). Intelligence at middle age: A thirty-eight year follow-up. *Developmental Psychology 5*, 333–337.

Katz, P., and Zigler, E. (1967). Self-image disparity: A developmental approach. *Journal of Personality and Social Psychology 5*, 186–195.

Kendler, T. S., and Kendler, H. H. (1970). An ontogeny of optional shift behavior. *Child Development 41*, 1–27.

Kennedy, W. A. (1969). A follow-up normative study of Negro intelligence and achievement. *Monographs of the Society for Research in Child Development 34*, 2 (Serial No. 126).

Kennedy, W. A.; Van De Riet, V.; and White, J. C. (1963). A normative sample of intelligence and achievement of Negro elementary school children in the southeastern United States. *Monographs of the Society for Research in Child Development 28*, 6 (Serial No. 90).

Kenny, D. A. (1975). Cross-lagged panel correlation: A test for spuriousness. *Psychological Bulletin 82*, 887–903.

Kerlinger, F. N., and Pedhazur, E. J. (1973). *Multiple regression in behavioral research*. New York: Holt, Rinehart, & Winston.

Kessen, W. (1965). *The child*. New York: Wiley.

Klahr, D., and Wallace, J. G. (1976). *Cognitive development: An information processing view*. New York: Wiley.

Klaus, R. A., and Gray, S. W. (1968). The Early Training Project for Disadvantaged Children: A report after five years. *Monographs of the Society for Research in Child Development 33*, 4 (Serial No. 120).

Kohlberg, L. (1976). Moral stages and moralization. The cognitive developmental approach. In *Moral development and moral behavior*. Edited by T. Lickona. New York: Holt, Rinehart, & Winston.

Kohlberg, L., and Gilligan, C. (1971). The adolescent as moral philosopher. *Daedalus*. Fall issue, 1051–1086.

Kruskal, W. H., and Wallis, W. A. (1952). Use of ranks in one-criterion variance analysis. *Journal of the American Statistical Association 47*, 614–617.

Kuenne, M. R. (1946). Experimental investigation of the relation of language to transposition behavior in young children. *Journal of Experimental Psychology 36*, 471–490.

Kuhn, D. (1976). Short-term longitudinal evidence for the sequentiality of Kohlberg's early stages of moral judgment. *Developmental Psychology 12*, 162–166.

Kuhn, T. S. (1970). *The structure of scientific revolutions*, 2nd ed. Chicago: University of Chicago Press.

Kurdek, L. A. (1977). Convergent validation of perspective-taking: A one-year follow-up. *Developmental Psychology 13*, 172–173.

Kurtines, W., and Greif, E. B. (1974). The development of moral thought: Review and evaluation of Kohlberg's approach. *Psychological Bulletin 81*, 453–470.

Labov, W. (1970). The logic of nonstandard English. In *Language and poverty. Perspectives on a theme*. Edited by F. Williams. Chicago: Markham.

LeCompte, G. K., and Gratch, G. (1972). Violation of a rule as a method of diagnosing infants' level of object concept. *Child Development 43*, 385–396.

Leik, R. K., and Matthews, M. (1968). A scale for developmental processes. *American Sociological Review 33*, 62–75.

Lenneberg, E. H., ed. (1964). *New directions in the study of language*. Cambridge, Ma.: MIT Press.

——— (1967). *Biological foundations of language*. New York: Wiley.

Lessac, M. S., and Solomon, R. L. (1969). Effects of early isolation on the later adaptive behavior of beagles. *Developmental Psychology 1*, 14–25.

Levitt, E. E. (1971). Research in psychotherapy with children. In *Handbook of psychotherapy and behavior change: An empirical analysis*. Edited by A. E. Bergin and S. L. Garfield. New York: Wiley.

Liben, L. S. (1975). Evidence for developmental differences in spontaneous seriation and its implications for past research on long-term memory improvement. *Developmental Psychology 11*, 121–125.

Liebert, R. M., and Baron, R. A. (1972). Some immediate effects of televised violence on children's behavior. *Developmental Psychology 6*, 469–475.

Lingoes, J. C. (1963). Multiple scalogram analysis: A set theoretic model for analyzing dichotomous items. *Educational and Psychological Measurement 23*, 501–524.

Loehlin, J. C.; Lindzey, G.; and Spuhler, J. N. (1975). *Race differences in intelligence*. San Francisco: Freeman.

Lorenz, K. Z. (1965). *Evolution and modification of behavior*. Chicago: University of Chicago Press.

Love, L. R., and Kaswan, J. W. (1974). *Troubled children: Their families, schools, and treatments*. New York: Wiley.

Maccoby, E. E., and Jacklin, C. N. (1974). *The psychology of sex differences*. Stanford Ca.: Stanford University Press.

Maccoby, E. E., and Masters, J. C. (1970). Attachment and dependency. In *Carmichael's manual of child psychology*, 3rd ed, Vol. 2. Edited by P. H. Mussen. New York: Wiley.

Mahoney, M. J. (1977). reflections on the cognitive-learning trend in psychotherapy. *American Psychologist 32*, 5–13.

Marcus, R. F. (1975). The child as elicitor of parental sanctions for independent and dependent behavior: A simulation of parent–child interaction. *Developmental Psychology 11*, 443–452.

Marwit, S. J., and Neumann, G. (1974). Black and white children's comprehension of standard and nonstandard English passages. *Journal of Educational Psychology 66*, 329–332.

Massey, F. J. (1952). Distribution table for the deviation between two sample cumulations. *Annals of Mathematical Statistics 23*, 435–441.

Masters, J. C., and Mokros, J. R. (1974). Self-reinforcement processes in children. In *Advances in child development and behavior*, Vol. 9. Edited by A. W. Reese. New York: Academic Press.

Mather, K. (1971). On biometrical genetics. *Heredity 26*, 349–364.

McCall, R. B., and Appelbaum, M. I. (1973). Bias in the analysis of repeated measures designs: Some alternative approaches. *Child Development 44*, 401–415.

McCall, R. B.; Appelbaum, M. I.; and Hogarty, P. S. (1973). Developmental changes in mental performance. *Monographs of the Society for Research in Child Development 38*, 3 (Serial No. 150).

McClelland, D. C.; Atkinson, J. W.; Clark, R. A.; and Lowell, E. L. (1953). *The achievement motive*. New York: Appleton-Century-Crofts.

McCornack, R. L. (1965). Extended tables of the Wilcoxon matched pair signed rank statistic. *Journal of the American Statistical Association 60*, 867–871.

McGrew, W. C. (1972). *An ethological study of children's behavior*. New York: Academic Press.

McNeill, D. (1966). Developmental psycholinguistics. In *The genesis of language: A psycholinguistic approach*. Edited by F. Smith and G. A. Miller. Cambridge, Ma.: MIT Press.

McNemar, Q. (1969). *Psychological statistics*, 4th ed. New York: Wiley.

Mednick, S. A.; Schulsinger, F.; and Garfinkel, R. (1975). Children at high risk for schizophrenia: Predisposing factors and intervention. In *Experimental approaches to psychopathology*. Edited by M. L. Kietzman, S. Sutton, and J. Zubin. New York: Academic Press.

Meltzoff, A. N., and Moore, M. K. (1977). Imitation of facial and manual gestures by human neonates. *Science 198*, 75–78.

Milgram, S. (1963). Behavioral study of obedience. *Journal of Abnormal and Social Psychology 67*, 371–378.

———— (1964). Issues in the study of obedience: A reply to Baumrind. *American Psychologist 19*, 848–852.

Miller, W., and Ervin, S. (1964). The development of grammar in child language. In The acquisition of language. Edited by U. Bellugi and R. Brown. *Monographs of the Society for Research in Child Development 29*, 1 (Serial No. 92).

Mischel, W. (1973). Toward a cognitive social learning reconceptualization of personality. *Psychological Review 80*, 252–283.

Mischel, W., and Mischel, H. N. (1976). A cognitive social-learning approach to morality and self-regulation. In *Moral development and behavior*. Edited by T. Likona. New York: Holt, Rinehart, & Winston.

Mischel, W.; Zeiss, R.; and Zeiss, A. (1974). Internal–external control and persistence: Validation and implications of the Stanford Preschool Internal–External Scale. *Journal of Personality and Social Psychology 29*, 265–278.

Money, J., and Ehrhardt, A. A. (1972). *Man and woman. Boy and girl. The differentiation and dimorphism of gender identity from conception to maturity.* Baltimore: John Hopkins University Press.

Montemayor, R. (1974). Children's performance in a game and their attraction to it as a function of sex-typed labels. *Child Development 45*, 152–156.

Morris, D. (1967). *The naked ape.* London: Jonathan Cape.

Mossler, D. G.; Marvin, R. S.; and Greenberg, M. T. (1976). Conceptual perspective taking in 2- to 6-year-old children. *Developmental Psychology 12*, 85–86.

Mosteller, F., and Rourke, R. E. K. (1973). *Sturdy statistics: Nonparametric and order statistics.* Reading, Ma.: Addison-Wesley.

Mulaik, S. A. (1972). *The foundations of factor analysis.* New York: McGraw-Hill.

Neale, J. M., and Weintraub, S. (1975). Children vulnerable to psychopathology: The Stony Brook High-Risk Project. *Journal of Abnormal Child Psychology 3*, 95–113.

Nelson, E. A.; Grinder, R. E.; and Mutterer, M. L. (1969). Sources of variance in behavioral measures of honesty in temptation situations: Methodological analyses. *Developmental Psychology 1*, 265–279.

Nelson, K. (1973). Structure and strategy in learning to talk. *Monographs of the Society for Research in Child Development 38*, 1–2 (Serial No. 149).

Nesselroade, J. R., and Baltes, P. B. (1974). Adolescent personality development and historical change: 1970–1972. *Monographs of the Society for Research in Child Development 39*, 1 (Serial No. 154).

New York Times (1972a). TV violence held unharmful to youth. January 11, p. 1.

———— (1972b). The violent strain. Editorial, January 15.

Newman, H. H.; Freeman, F. N.; and Holzinger, K. J. (1937). *Twins: A study of heredity and environment.* Chicago: University of Chicago Press.

Nie, N. H.; Hull, C. H.; Jenkins, J. G.; Steinbrenner, K.; and Bent, D. H. (1975). *Statistical package for the social sciences,* 2nd ed. New York: McGraw-Hill.

Noblin, C. D.; Timmons, E. O.; and Kael, H. C. (1966). Differential effects of positive and negative verbal reinforcement on psychoanalytic character types. *Journal of Personality and Social Psychology 4,* 224–228.

Norris, R. C., and Hjelm, H. F. (1961). Nonnormality and product moment correlation. *Experimental Education 29,* 261–270.

Orne, M. T. (1969). Demand characteristics and the concept of quasi-controls. In *Artifact in behavioral research.* Edited by R. Rosenthal and R. L. Rosnow. New York: Academic Press.

Osofsky, J. D., and O'Connell, E. J. (1972). Parent–child interaction: Daughters' effects upon mothers' and fathers' behaviors. *Developmental Psychology 7,* 157–168.

Page, E. B. (1958). Teacher comments and student performance: A seventy-four classroom experiment in school motivation. *Journal of Educational Psychology 49,* 173–181.

Park, L. C., and Covi, L. (1965). Nonblind placebo trial: An exploration of neurotic patients' responses to placebo when its inert content is disclosed. *Archives of General Psychiatry 12,* 336–345.

Parke, R. D. (1972). Rationale effectiveness as a function of age of the child. Fels Research Institute, Yellow Springs, Oh.

———— (1974). Rules, roles, and resistance to deviation: Recent advances in punishment, discipline, and self-control. In *Minnesota Symposia on Child Psychology,* Vol. 8. Edited by A. D. Pick, Minneapolis, Mn.: University of Minnesota Press.

Pearson, E. S., and Hartley, H. O. (1966). *Biometrika tables for statisticians,* Vol. 1, 3rd ed. Cambridge, Eng.: Cambridge University Press.

Perry, D. G., and Garrow, H. (1975). The "social deprivation–satiation effect": An outcome of frequency or perceived contingency? *Developmental Psychology 11,* 681–688.

Piaget, J. (1928). *Judgment and reasoning in the child.* New York: Harcourt, Brace.

———— (1932). *The moral judgment of the child.* London: Kegan Paul.

———— (1951). *Play, dreams, and imitation in childhood.* New York: Norton.

———— (1954). *The construction of reality in the child.* New York: Basic Books.

———— (1964). Development and learning. In *Piaget rediscovered.*

Edited by R. E. Ripple and V. N. Rockcastle. Ithaca, N.Y.: Cornell University Press.

———— (1968). *On the development of memory and identity.* Worcester, Ma.: Clark University Press.

———— (1969). *The mechanisms of perception.* New York: Basic Books.

———— (1970). Piaget's theory. In *Carmichael's manual of child psychology,* 3rd ed, Vol. 1. Edited by P. H. Mussen. New York: Wiley.

———— (1974). Foreword. In *Learning and the development of cognition.* Edited by B. Inhelder, H. Sinclair, and M. Bovet. Cambridge, Ma.: Harvard University Press.

———— (1977). The role of action in the development of thinking. In *Knowledge and development,* Vol. 1. *Advances in research and theory.* Edited by W. F. Overton and J. M. Gallagher. New York: Plenum.

Piaget, J., and Inhelder, B. (1956). *The child's conception of space.* London: Routledge and Kegan Paul.

————, and Inhelder, B. (1973). *Memory and intelligence.* New York: Basic Books.

Pollack, R. H. (1969). Some implications of ontogenetic changes in perception. In *Studies in cognitive development.* Edited by D. Elkind and J. Flavell. New York: Oxford University Press.

President's Biomedical Research Panel, (1976). *Final report.* Washington, D.C.: U.S. Government Printing Office.

Proctor, C. H. (1970). A probabilistic formulation and statistical analysis of Guttman scaling. *Psychometrika 35,* 73–78.

Quay, L. C. (1971). Language, dialect, reinforcement, and the intelligence test performance of Negro children. *Child Development 42,* 5–15.

Reid, J. B. (1970). Reliability assessment of observation data: A possible methodological problem. *Child Development 41,* 1143–1150.

Rest, J. R. (1975). Longitudinal study of the Defining Issues Test of Moral Judgment: A strategy for analyzing developmental change. *Developmental Psychology 11,* 738–748.

Rheingold, H. L.; Hay, D. F.; and West M. J. (1976). Sharing in the second year of life. *Child Development 47,* 1148–1158.

Ricks, D. F.; Thomas, A.; and Roff, M., eds. (1974). *Life history research in psychopathology,* Vol. 3. Minneapolis, Mn.: University of Minnesota Press.

Ring, K.; Wallston, K.; and Corey, M. (1970). Mode of debriefing as a factor affecting subjective reaction to a Milgram-type obedience experiment–An ethical inquiry. *Representative Research in Social Psychology 1,* 68–85.

Rivlin, R. M., and Timpane, P. M. (1975). *Planned variation in edu-*

cation: Should we give up or try harder? Washington, D.C.: Brookings Institution.

Robins, L. N. (1970). The adult development of the antisocial child. *Seminars in Psychiatry 2*, 420–434.

Rose, S. A.; Blank, M.; and Spalter, I. (1975). Situational specificity of behavior in young children. *Child Development 46*, 464–469.

Rosenblum, L. A., and Harlow, H. F. (1963). Approach–avoidance conflict in the mother surrogate situation. *Psychological Reports 12*, 83–85.

Rosenthal, R. (1966). *Experimenter effects in behavioral research.* New York: Appleton-Century-Crofts.

Rosenthal, R., and Jacobson, L. (1968). *Pygmalion in the classroom: Teacher expectation and pupils' intellectual development.* New York: Holt, Rinehart, & Winston.

Rosenthal, R., and Rosnow, R. L. (1975). *The volunteer subject.* New York: Wiley.

Rozelle, R. M., and Campbell, D. T. (1969). More plausible rival hypotheses in the cross-lagged panel correlation technique. *Psychological Bulletin 71*, 74–80.

Rubin, K. H. (1976). Extinction of conservation: A life-span investigation. *Developmental Psychology 12*, 51–56.

Rutter, M., and Graham, P. (1968). The reliability and validity of the psychiatric assessment of the child. I. Interview with the child. *British Journal of Psychiatry 114*, 563–579.

Sameroff, A. J., and Chandler, M. J. (1975). Reproductive risk and the continuum of caretaking casualty. In *Review of child development research*, Vol. 4. Edited by F. D. Horowitz, Chicago: University of Chicago Press.

Sandell, R. G. (1971). Note on choosing between competing interpretations of cross-lagged panel correlations. *Psychological Bulletin 75*, 367–368.

Scarr, S. and Weinberg, R. A. (1976). IQ test performance of black children adopted by white families. *American Psychologist 31*, 726–739.

Scarr-Salapatek, S. (1971). Unknowns in the IQ equation. *Science 174*, 1223–1228.

Schachter, F. F.; Cooper, A.; and Gordet, R. (1968). A method for assessing personality development for follow-up evaluations of the preschool child. *Monographs of the Society for Research in Child Development 33*, 3 (Serial No. 119).

Schachter, F. F.; Kirshner, K.; Klips, B.; Friedricks, M.; and Sanders, K. (1974). Everyday preschool interpersonal speech usage: Methodological, developmental, and sociolinguistic studies. *Mono-*

graphs of the Society for Research in Child Development 39, 3 (Serial No. 156).

Schaefer, E. S. (1965). Does the sampling method produce the negative correlation of mean IQ with age reported by Kennedy, VanDeRiet, and White? *Child Development 36*, 257–259.

Schaffer, H. R., and Emerson, P. E. (1964). The development of social attachments in infancy. *Monographs of the Society for Research in Child Development 29*, 3 (Serial No. 94).

Schaie, K. W. (1965). A general model for the study of developmental problems. *Psychological Bulletin 64*, 92–107.

Schlesinger, I. M. (1971). Production of utterances and language acquisition. In *The ontogenesis of grammar. A theoretical symposium.* Edited by D. I. Slobin. New York: Academic Press.

Schwartz, M. M., and Scholnick, E. K. (1970). Scalogram analysis of logical and perceptual components of conservation of discontinuous quantity. *Child Development 41*, 695–705.

Seay, B.; Alexander, B. K.; and Harlow, H. F. (1964). Maternal behavior of socially deprived rhesus monkeys. *Journal of Abnormal and Social Psychology 69*, 345–354.

Shepherd, M.; Oppenheim, B.; and Mitchell, S. (1971). *Childhood behavior and mental health.* New York: Grune & Stratton.

Shields, J. (1962). *Monozygotic twins brought up apart and brought up together.* London: Oxford University Press.

Siegel, S. (1956). *Nonparametric statistics for the behavioral sciences.* New York: McGraw-Hill.

Skinner, B. F. (1957). *Verbal behavior.* New York: Appleton-Century-Crofts.

Solomon, R. L., and Lessac, M. S. (1968). A control group design for experimental studies of developmental processes. *Psychological Bulletin 70*, 145–150.

Sontag, L. W.; Baker, C. T.; and Nelson, V. L. (1958). Mental growth and personality development: A longitudinal study. *Monographs of the Society for Research in Child Development 23*, 2 (Serial No. 68).

Spence, K. W. (1937). The differential response in animals to stimuli varying within a single dimension. *Psychological Review 44*, 430–444.

Suinn, R. M., and Oskamp, S. (1969). *The predictive validity of projective measures.* Springfield, Il.: Thomas.

Surgeon General's Scientific Advisory Committee on Television and Social Behavior, (1972). *Television and growing up: The impact of televised violence.* Washington, D.C.: U.S. Government Printing Office.

Taylor, J. J., and Achenbach, T. M. (1975). Moral and cognitive development in retarded and nonretarded children. *American Journal of Mental Deficiency 80*, 43–50.

Terman, L. M., and Oden, M. H. (1959). *Genetic studies of genius, V.: The gifted group at mid-life*. Stanford, Ca.: Stanford University Press.

Thomas, A.; Chess, S.; and Birch, H. G. (1968). *Temperament and behavior disorders in children*. New York: New York University Press.

Thomas, D. R. (1975). Cooperation and competition among Polynesian and European children. *Child Development 46*, 948–953.

Thomas, R. K., and Peay, L. (1976). Length judgments by squirrel monkeys: Evidence for conservation? *Developmental Psychology 12*, 349–352.

Thorndike, E. L. (1913). *Educational psychology, Vol. 2: The psychology of learning*. New York: Teacher's College, Columbia University.

Tinbergen, N. (1951). *The study of instinct*. Oxford: Clarendon Press.

United States Children's Bureau, (1924). *Infant care*. Washington, D.C.: U.S. Government.

Vaughter, R. M.; Smotherman, W.; and Ordy, J. M. (1972). Development of object permanence in the infant squirrel monkey. *Developmental Psychology 7*, 34–38.

Waber, D. P. (1977). Sex differences in mental abilities, hemispheric lateralization, and rate of physical growth at adolescence. *Developmental Psychology 13*, 29–38.

Waldrop, M. F., and Halverson, C. F. (1975). Intensive and extensive peer behavior: Longitudinal and cross-sectional analyses. *Child Development 46*, 19–26.

Washington *Evening Star*. (1972). TV violence study called whitewash, January 18.

Waterman, A. S.; Geary, P. S.; and Waterman, C. K. (1974). Longitudinal study of changes in ego identity status from the freshman to the senior year at college. *Developmental Psychology 10*, 387–392.

Watson, J. B. (1913). Psychology as the behaviorist views it. *Psychological Review 20*, 158–177.

Watt, N. F. (1974). Childhood and adolescent routes to schizophrenia. In *Life history research in psychopathology*, Vol. 3. Edited by D. F. Ricks, A. Thomas, and M. Roff. Minneapolis, Mn.: University of Minnesota Press.

Webb, E. J.; Campbell, D. T.; Schwartz, R. D.; and Sechrest, L. B. (1966). *Unobtrusive measures: Nonreactive research in the social sciences*. Chicago: Rand-McNally.

Wechsler, D. (1955). *Manual for the Wechsler Adult Intelligence Scale.* New York: Psychological Corporation.

Weikart, D. P. (1972). Relationship of curriculum, teaching, and learning in preschool education. In *Preschool programs for the disadvantaged: Five experimental approaches to early childhood education.* Edited by J. C. Stanley. Baltimore: Johns Hopkins University Press.

Werner, H. (1957). The concept of development from a comparative and organismic point of view. In *The concept of development.* Edited by D. B. Harris. Minneapolis, Mn.: University of Minnesota Press.

Werner H., and Kaplan, B. (1963). *Symbol formation.* New York: Wiley.

Wilson, K. (1956). A distribution-free test of analysis of variance hypotheses. *Psychological Bulletin 53,* 96–101.

Wilson, R. S. (1972). Twins: Early mental development. *Science 175,* 914–917.

———— (1975). Analysis of developmental data: Comparison among alternative methods. *Developmental Psychology 11,* 676–680.

Wilton, K. M., and Boersma, F. J. (1974). *Eye movements, surprise reactions, and cognitive development.* Rotterdam, Holland: Rotterdam University Press.

Winer, B, (1971). *Statistical principles in experimental design,* 2nd ed. New York: McGraw-Hill.

Wirt, R. D., and Broen, W. E. (1956). The relation of the Children's Manifest Anxiety Scale to the concept of anxiety used in the clinic. *Journal of Consulting Psychology 20,* 482.

Witkin, H. A.; Dyk, R. B.; Faterson, H. F.; Goodenough, D. R.; and Karp, S. A. (1962). *Psychological differentiation.* New York: Wiley.

Wright, S. (1921). Correlation and causation. *Journal of Agricultural Research 20,* 557–585.

Yarrow, M. R. (1960). The measurement of children's attitudes and values. In *Handbook of research methods in child development.* Edited by P. H. Mussen. New York: Wiley.

Yarrow, M. R., and Waxler, C. Z. (1976). Dimensions and correlates of prosocial behavior in young children. *Child Development 47,* 118–125.

Yarrow, M. R.; Waxler, C. Z.; and Scott, P. M. (1971). Child effects on adult behavior. *Developmental Psychology 5,* 300–311.

Zubin, J.; Eron, L.; and Schumer, F. (1965). *An experimental approach to projective techniques.* New York: Wiley, 1965.

Indexes

Name Index

Subject Index